Spawn of Skull Island:

The Making of King Kong

Spawn of Skull Island: The Making of King Kong

by George E. Turner
with Dr. Orville Goldner

Revised and Expanded
by Michael H. Price
with Douglas Turner

MMP
Baltimore, Maryland

Also by George E. Turner & Michael H. Price:

Forgotten Horrors: The Definitive Edition (1929-1937)
Forgotten Horrors 2: Beyond the Horror Ban (1936-1942)
Forgotten Horrors 3: Dr. Turner's House of Horrors (1943-1946) (In Preparation)
The Ancient Great Plains and *The Palo Duro Story* (In Preparation)
Southern-Fried Homicide
Aw-Shucks Suspense Stories: Mo' Southern-Fried Homicide
Human Monsters: The Bizarre Psychology of Movie Villains
V.T. Hamlin's Collected Alley Oop, Vols. No. 2 & 3
The Cinema of Adventure, Romance & Terror
The Spider (With Timothy Truman & Quique Alcatena)
Roy Crane's Collected Wash Tubbs & Captain Easy, Vol. No. 10
Al Capp's Collected Li'l Abner, Vol. No. 6
Forgotten Horrors: Early Talkie Chillers from Poverty Row (Two Prior Editions)

The Wizard, Gorilla, Ingagi, The Monkey's Paw, Stark Mad, The Strange Case of Captain Ramper, and *The Lost World* (page 25), *The House of Mystery* courtesy Hollywood Movie Posters
Interior and Cover Design: Susan Svehla
Copyright © and ™ 2002 by Michael H. Price

King Kong and all related indicia and images are trademarks of Warner Bros. Studios, Inc. This book is a work of scholarship, unrelated to any trademark status, and represents no venture of Warner Bros. Studios, Inc. Referential usage of the name *King Kong* and related images is not to be construed as a challenge to any trademark status.

All pictorial material reproduced herein derives from memorabilia in the private collections of the authors and the artisans thus interviewed; and from selected archives and individual contributors. The inconsistent quality of illustrative reproduction is a consequence of the varying ages and conditions of rare source material. This material appears here for the sole purpose of illustrating and illuminating the creative processes involved in the making of the motion pictures thus discussed.

Lyric from "Up Jurassic Park," by Michael H. Price, is copyright © 1993 by Ray-Bruton-Price Publ. (ASCAP) and appears by permission.

Key portions of this book first appeared as *The Making of King Kong* (A.S. Barnes & Co./The Tantivy Press; 1975); these have been significantly revised, corrected, amended and expanded for the current edition. Scattered additional portions of the text have appeared, in markedly different form, in *The Cinema of Adventure, Romance & Terror* (A.S.C. Press; 1989); in *Forgotten Horrors: The Definitive Edition* and *Forgotten Horrors 2: Beyond the Horror Ban* (Midnight Marquee Press; 1999-2001); and in *V.T. Hamlin's Collected Alley Oop, Vol. No. 3* (Kitchen Sink Press; 1995); in the magazines *RetroVision, The American Cinematographer, Alley Oop: The Magazine* and *Wrapped in Plastic*; in the Fort Worth *Star-Telegram* and the New York *Times*; and as wire-service dispatches of the New York Times News Service.

Without limiting the rights reserved under the copyright above, no part of this publication may be reproduced, stored in or introduced into a retrieval system, or transmitted, in any form, or by any means (electronic, mechanical, photocopying, recording, or otherwise), without the prior written permission of the copyright owners or the publishers of this book.
ISBN 9781936168651
Library of Congress Catalogue Card Number 2002101689
Manufactured in the United States of America
Printed by Sheridan Books, Fredericksburg, VA
First Printing by Luminary Press an imprint of Midnight Marquee Press, Inc., April 2002
Second Printing by Liminary Press an imprint of Midnight Marquee Press, Inc., January 2005
Paperback Edition, June 2006

Dedication

The devoted interest, encouragement and help of family and friends over many years have made this book both inevitable and possible.

The book is dedicated in memory of four authentic pioneers of the cinema: **Willis H. O'Brien**, **Merian C. Cooper**, **Ernest B. Schoedsack** and **Ruth Rose Schoedsack**. These artists and adventurers had uniquely distinct personalities and talents. Together and separately, they made truly original and important contributions to the arts and sciences of the motion picture. Their influence has yet to be measured with full accuracy.

Spawn of Skull Island

Table of Contents

8	**Foreword by Ray Harryhausen & Ray Bradbury**
10	**Introduction by Michael H. Price**
16	**Introduction to the Original Edition**
22	**Author's Preface: Why Kong Is Still King**
34	**Acknowledgments**
35	**Preamble & Laundry List**
69	**The Launching of Cooper-Schoedsack Productions**
76	**An Adventure for Three**
82	**"There Is the Ultimate in Adventure"**
86	**The Genius of OBie O'Brien**
94	**Production 601 Gets the Green Light**
102	**The Eighth Wonder**
108	**Pathé, Its Perils & Pitfalls**
120	**"We Really Had a Happy Company, There"**
128	**When Inventions Become Necessary**
138	**The Expedition to Skull Island**
146	**Pipes, Pliers, Primroses & Other Problems**
152	**"It Wasn't Easy, Working for Coop"**
160	**The King in New York**
172	**The Finishing Touches**
180	**An Outbreak of Sequelitis**
187	**Remember Cavalcade—?**
192	**Preludes, Prologues & Progeny: Kong & Crucial Kin**
234	**George E. Turner's The Ancient Great Plains**
239	**The Lost She Comic Strip**
243	**Afterword by Sam Calvin**
245	**Index**

Words to the Fore from Ray Harryhausen and Ray Bradbury

In ancient times, the Alchemists were eternally searching for the means of creating a perfect Homunculus—a little creature, artificially produced, humanoid in form and made of mandrake root and potions, and brought to life with the help of the occult. Paraceleus, the great Swiss philosopher and forerunner of modern medicine, was an ardent supporter of these exciting experiments. After all these years, their successes can only be speculated upon in the form of legends and myths.

Because of the invention of the motion picture, what one might call a 20th-century homunculus appeared on screens all over the world: King Kong—the Eighth Wonder of the World. In the film, he appeared to be over 50 feet tall; in reality, he stood only 18 inches. Although Kong's life-force was not controlled by telekinesis or occult means, he was made to appear alive, moving about the screen with great agility, through the stop-motion process. When watching the film, the audience knew instinctively that he was not real. Yet he and his magnificent prehistoric companions looked amazingly lifelike—so lifelike that the suspension of disbelief took place even though the story was excessively fantastic. In that early period of filmmaking, there was a magic about their movements that defied definition.

Technically, *King Kong* was a milestone of achievement in its ability to create the Grand Illusion. But it was not only the technical qualities that were so fascinating, but the structure of the story itself. It masterfully succeeded in taking one by the hand and leading us from the mundane world of the Depression era into the most outrageous fantasy adventure ever to be put on the screen. It proves to be an enduring classic that should never be remade—a point proved by attempts at remakes that were soon forgotten.

The three men largely responsible for this inimitable production were Merian C. Cooper, Ernest B. Schoedsack and Willis O'Brien. Willis O'Brien's contribution to the story's qualities has many times been overlooked. Eastman Kodak, stop-motion animation, the imaginations of Cooper and O'Brien, the input of Schoedsack and the great audio contribution of composer Max Steiner—all reacted chemically in the laboratory of RKO-Radio Pictures' studios to produce a cinematic miracle that became *King Kong*. Paraceleus would have been more than pleased.

This reissue and revamp of the book, *The Making of King Kong*, is really a treasure chest of information of how this unique production came about and developed into a memorable piece of film history.

—Ray Harryhausen
London, 2001

When Kong fell off the Empire State Building, he landed on Ray Harryhausen and me. We haven't been the same since. We climbed out from under him and started a mad love affair with that 50-foot ape. In 1983, we attended the 50th anniversary of *Kong* at Grauman's Chinese. They had a giant replica of Kong outside the theatre, and Ray and I climbed up on it for photos. All of a sudden, Fay Wray rushed out of the crowd, climbed up in Kong's arms, and kissed both of us on the cheek. How perfect can you get?

I saw *Kong* in Tucson in the spring of '33, when I was 13 years old. I was working on radio. I hung around the radio station, and they finally put me to work. I read the comics to the kiddies every Saturday night. My pay was free tickets to see *The Mummy*, *King Kong* and *Mystery of the Wax Museum*. We were a very poor family and couldn't afford to go to the movies. But with those free tickets, I felt like I was overpaid. I've never been so rich since.

And about that legend-spawning giant-spider sequence: It's very short. It's only about four or five seconds, I suppose. It was in the film then—and it's disappeared since. Some people say it

never existed. Well, I don't think I could remember something like that, that vividly, had it not existed. When Bruce Cabot was in the little cave and Kong's trying to reach down to get him, reptiles were coming up the other way. The spider was down below, at the bottom of the pit where the other men fell in. I can't prove it exists—but I know I saw it. The memory is just too vivid. You can't make that up.
—Ray Bradbury
Los Angeles, 2001

[Lifelong friends Ray Bradbury and Ray Harryhausen, like George E. Turner, found their callings early on as a consequence of their discovery of *King Kong* and its wondrous immersion in the spirit of adventure. Mr. Bradbury proceeded to become the pre-eminent fantasist in American literature, with such enduring works as *Fahrenheit 451* and *Dark Carnival*. Mr. Harryhausen inherited the mantle of master dimensional animator Willis H. O'Brien on the *Kong*-family reunion film, *Mighty Joe Young*, during the late 1940s—and followed through with such classic special-effects movies as *The Beast from 20,000 Fathoms* (from a Bradbury story) and *The Seventh Voyage of Sinbad*. Our thanks to Terry Pace for his help in securing Mr. Bradbury's remarks.]

In 1983, Baltimore's historic Senator Theatre showcased *King Kong* for local classic film fans.

The Making of King Kong

Introduction
by Michael H. Price

George E. Turner had just begun settling into his new digs at Film Effects of Hollywood during the late 1970s when he cabled back home to Texas with a tantalizing exclamation: "Youse guys won't believe whose old drawing board they've assigned me!" George raved in a Telex wire. Now, George was prone to excitability over just about any developments or revelations having to do with the filmmaking arts; paleontology, anthropology and archeology; Southwestern cowboy lore; literature, from Shakespeare to the pulps; the fine and/or commercial realms of painting, sculpture, illustration and cartooning; music, from Eurocentric pyrotechnical classicism to Duke Ellington and Fats Waller; and the dining experience as a class, whether cheeseburgers at Fritz's Beanery or chateaubriand at Yamashiro. But his tone here bespoke a greater astonishment than usual.

"Sounds important," I said when finally we caught up by telephone. "So whose old drawing board *is* it, anyhow?"

"Willis O'Brien's!" replied George in a tone of reverence. "Willis H. O'Brien's drawing board!"

"Not *the* Willis H. O'Brien?" asked I.

"Nobody *else*," returned George. "It's been locked away in dead storage since, prob'ly, *The Black Scorpion* and *The Giant Behemoth* [aka *Behemoth the Sea Monster*] in the late '50s. Nobody had any idea who had last used the thing, but there were papers and sketches stapled and tacked and glued onto it—ideas ol' Obie had kept kickin' around in his head ever since the '30s, stuff that he kept goin' back to, time and again, like that *Frankenstein vs. King Kong* project that never came *near* gettin' realized."

If ever a piece of professional equipment had a destiny, it was the utterly fitting fate of this battered and pockmarked drafting table to wind up under the control of George E. Turner. Far more than merely an admirer of Willis O'Brien's work, George was the one party in the history of film scholarship who had determined to give O'Brien his due as a Master-with-a-capital-*M* at a time when the industry O'Brien had helped to invent had all but abandoned the artist to death-in-obscurity.

In short, George had written *The Making of King Kong*, a seminal book over which the shade of OBie towers like an oilfield derrick over the wild Texas back-country where George was born, or even like Kong over the popular culture at large. And once in fated possession of the O'Brien drawing table, George—never a superstitious sort, but nevertheless in awe of ancestral resonances—put himself to work on projects that would honor the curious karmic legacy.

The inspiration prevailed even as George toiled at other effects houses: He delivered main-title designs and glass-matte paintings for *Dead Men Don't Wear Plaid* and *One from the Heart*, and he conceived the futuristic cityscapes and ominously barren outlying terrain of a little-seen Canadian-made takeoff on H.G. Wells' *Things To Come*. He designed his own makeup and costuming for a European-backed 70-millimeter featurette, *Dangling Death*, in which he starred as a mad puppeteer done in by his ungodly creations. He sketched out the particulars of an electrocution scene for *Titan Find* (finally issued as *Creature*), an *Alien* knockoff that required a burst of Turner-made voltage-plus-Rotoscoping to mask an amateur stuntman's pathetically faked collapse. After the O'Brien drawing board followed George home in the wake of a savvy career move to the American Society of Cinematographers, he used the table for a mounting burden of freelance sidelines, storyboarding feature films and sitcoms and *Star Trek* spin-offs and Saturday-morning cartoon shows, for which he concocted monsters and villains that Willis O'Brien could only have loved. (Some of George's *SHAZAM!* menaces were deemed too scary by the arbiters of institutional taste—a distinction that amused George, even as he grumbled about having to tone them down for mass consumption.) George returned at this table to a long-dormant ambition to become a practicing comic-strip artist, resurrecting three of his original *Tarzan* yarns from the early 1960s and completing a jewel of a true-crime yarn called *Blues Passover*, which he and I included in our 1998 anthology, *Southern-Fried Homicide*.

When George cashed in—unexpectedly, during a seeming recovery from a patch of questionable health—at age 73 in June 1999, I set out to make secure our works-in-progress, which we had continued at a daunting pace during the 21 years since George had quit Texas for Southern California.

The centerpiece of those projects is the revision and expansion of *The Making of King Kong*—rechristened *Spawn of Skull Island*, in view of a broadened agenda. I feel honored to have Douglas Turner aboard as an enthusiastic and well-informed collaborator, ably representing the family legacy.

Doug, the next-to-youngest of George's four sons, has long since forged his own Hollywood career in the field of visual effects. Doug also has preserved a formidable archive of memorabilia, information and *Kong*-related photographic negatives, while I have proceeded to work George's and my continuing research on *Kong*, spanning 1975-1999, into the update that we had begun planning in 1990. Though fundamentally revision-proof as a superior product of its time and place, the original book can only benefit from the knowledge that has come to hand during the generation-plus since its début.

That added knowledge often has as much to do with What Is Not as with What *Is*. A perpetual popular interest in *King Kong* keeps the devotees talking and Internet-chatting about *Kong* as fervently as if the film were a fresh arrival, with perpetually excited speculation about revelations yet in store.

The hot-button topic at the start of this new century would be a recurring rumor that excised giant-spider footage from *King Kong* has survived against formidable odds to surface in an elusive video edition. I tested the mail-order-only purveyor of this trumpeted "uncensored French version" and found my order filled, in the expected bait-and-switch manner, with a factory-fresh copy of the same blessedly familiar *King Kong* that one finds at 'most any neighborhood Schlockbuster Video Emporium. This Warners-label version is the sparkling restoration on which George Turner served as a consultant during the 1980s for the Ted (no kin to George) Turner interests, and of course it is substantially complete as first relished by the masses in 1933.

Still and all, the rumor persists, even to the extent of one fan's diehard remembrance of having viewed a French-release print, complete with the legendary crawling denizens of Skull Island's abyss, at a Denver art-film theatre in 1974. ("Goofy-looking, with big eyes," is this particular enthusiast's description of the elusive monsters.) Indeed, a foreign-film house in Denver did herald a showing that year of a French edition of *Kong*. At the Boulder, Colorado, *Daily Camera*, a newspaper colleague of George's and mine called

A production design by Mario Larrinaga for the infamous spider scene deleted because, Cooper said, "It stopped the show."

us in Texas to mention the showing—after the fact—and George wondered aloud for years how that foreign-market cut might have differed from the U.S. release. It was in 1974, of course, that George was polishing the manuscript for the first edition of *The Making of King Kong*.

When George finally caught up with a French cut of *Kong*, years later in Hollywood, he found that it differed little from the domestic version, though with an abbreviated beginning and scattered internal alterations. His notes from that screening contain this marginal exclamation: "*Drat!* No BUGS!"

If we may hammer the issue a bit further, Douglas Turner adds: "I've always been skeptical of any reports on the spider footage's coming to light, simply because no other excised *Kong* footage has been found. When [co-creator] Merian Cooper cut something out, he made sure it was out. On *Chang*, he and [Ernest] Schoedsack went so far as to *burn* all of the leftover footage, so the studio couldn't put it back in."

(On the other hand, Ray Bradbury, in his Foreword to this volume, recalls seeing such footage back in the day when *Kong* was a brand-new picture. Some mysteries are more to be appreciated than solved.)

"As the *legend* has it," writes Doug, "there was an advance screening in January 1933, possibly in San Bernardino, and after that the bugs were removed. This is suspect, inasmuch as Cooper was still shooting material in January—the elevated-train sequence, the last scene at the bottom of the Empire State Building, *et cetera*. That doesn't leave much time for a re-shooting of the people falling into the chasm with floppy dummies instead of stop motion, or for re-doing sound and music for the New York release in early March. I think a screening for studio folks of a rough edit was a more likely timing. Which is so much speculation, of course."

It seems the spider-pit issue has supplanted the actor-in-ape-suit fantasy and the Freudian-hogwash reinterpretations that plagued the popular understanding of *Kong* during the 1960s

George Turner spent years debunking the man-in-ape-suit fantasy surrounding *King Kong*.

and '70s. George Turner spent as much time and energy debunking such balderdash as he spent unearthing the film's hidden truths, and he'd no doubt be amused to find us doing likewise in this enlightened present day. Is it just us, or does this bold New Millennium feel a whole lot like the old worn-out one?

The spider-pit scuttlebutt aside, there are still many "new things to learn about old things," as one of our savvier editors of times gone by, Dave Schreiner, has described that Rediscovery Imperative. While preparing an expanded edition of another Turner & Price book, a survey of villainy called *Human Monsters*, I recently screened one of RKO's Kay Kyser comedies, *You'll Find Out* (1940), and was surprised to notice one of the *Kong* dinosaurs, a Triceratops, standing stock-still among the incidental props.

My role in *The Making of King Kong* originally was that of errand boy—transcribing information from Depression-era show-business publications and newspaper microfilm, reading manuscript pages and galley proofs and matching captions with illustrations, and finally helping with the tedious compilation of an index, in those pre-Microsoft Wizard days, once the book had been paginated for publication.

Today, the primary concern rests with reconciling the book-as-published with George's several reams and innumerable scraps of subsequent notes; and with original typescript pages that were altered arbitrarily, either well-meaningly by co-author Orville Goldner or recklessly by the first publisher. George periodically would backtrack to re-word certain passages (often, merely to re-Americanize the peculiarly British spellings that the London-based original publisher, Tantivy Press/Barnes & Co., had imposed upon George's Royal newsroom-typewriter manuscript), and to sketch in a halt-and-go pageant of fresh revelations. Many of the attribu-

A sculptural confrontation

tions were first given in the present tense—"as Ernest Schoedsack recalls," and so forth—as if in hopes of keeping the surviving principals of *Kong* among the living for a while longer; the raw fact of mortality has dictated a resort to the past tense. I also have eliminated some peculiarities of *The Associated Press Stylebook*, under whose numbing influence we both labored as journalists, and replaced that with a more workable admixture of the *Chicago Manual of Style* and the Luminary Press style-sheet.

George and I originally worked together as newshound colleagues at the *Daily News & Globe-Times* in Amarillo, Texas, and although I graduated from cub reporter to city editor during the years, 1968-75, that *The Making of King Kong* was in preparation, I counted myself throughout an apprentice to George's shirtsleeves scholarship and effortless air of cultural authority. George gave top billing in the byline to his co-author of record, Dr. Orville Goldner (1906-1985). Dr. Goldner—who had been a key effects technician on *Kong*, known among his colleagues as

The Stegosaurus in the jungles of Skull Island—the trees and foliage are miniatures combined with artwork on glass panels.

"Goldy"—was quick to acknowledge, however, that "George really did all the work on this book. I'm more of a glorified source and fact-checker than any kind of 'author.'"

George, however, never kept score as to which party was contributing the greater effort at any given moment. It was the finished result that mattered, and he realized that Dr. Goldner's good name had put him in touch with sources deeper than might otherwise have proved attainable. In the main, George simply relished the opportunity to reveal the backstage lowdown on a film that had in practical fact changed his life for the good, better and best: George was an impressionable 7-year-old when his father treated him to a first-run matinee of *King Kong* in 1933 at Santa Monica, and the experience set George on a course that never wavered. He sought out a career in the arts and sciences, inspired by the unbridled imagination and paleontological relevance of *King Kong*. He "growed where he was planted," as the locals say, for many years in a Southwestern cultural backwater, because West Texas is a wellhead of prehistoric rediscoveries and because the local newspaper afforded him a means of reaching an admiring, however provincial, readership with his stories and illustrations. He split for Hollywood after a shabbier new management at that same newspaper had demonstrated its contempt for the arts, for regional historical lore, and for damned near everything else that George held dear. And once situated in Hollywood, George demonstrated that a near-lifelong appreciation of the cinema; a background as a working artist and writer; and a measure of Texas-bred resourcefulness would be all the background required to forge a new career in the movie industry. We all should experience such productive mid-life crises.

In the final resolve, all that really matters here is that George got to develop his *magnum opus* of film research, *The Making of King Kong*, and that his tireless work in follow-through has enabled the expansion he had envisioned. I'd selfishly prefer to have kept George around for another generation's span of the association that he generously called "this epic collaboration of ours," but which I still regard as my apprenticeship.

—Michael H. Price
Fort Worth, Texas
www.fortworthfilmfest.com

Introduction to the Original Edition

Regarding the "surfeit of technical talk which hardly touched on the sexual and racial mythology," it should be noted that the title [of the book] was *The Making of King Kong*, not *Fanciful Interpretations of King Kong*.
—George E. Turner, 1976; from his letter of rebuttal to a high-hat review in the Los Angeles *Times*

"It's weird, wild, wonderful—the stuff for which movies were made!"

So proclaimed a Hollywood ballyhoo man in 1933. Need we add that the film he was publicizing was *King Kong*?

Nobody has ever accused a publicity man of being married to the truth, but this flack would have given Diogenes cause for hope. *King Kong* truly *was* "the stuff for which movies were made," a logical extension of the works of Meliés, Porter, Griffith and every other filmmaker who

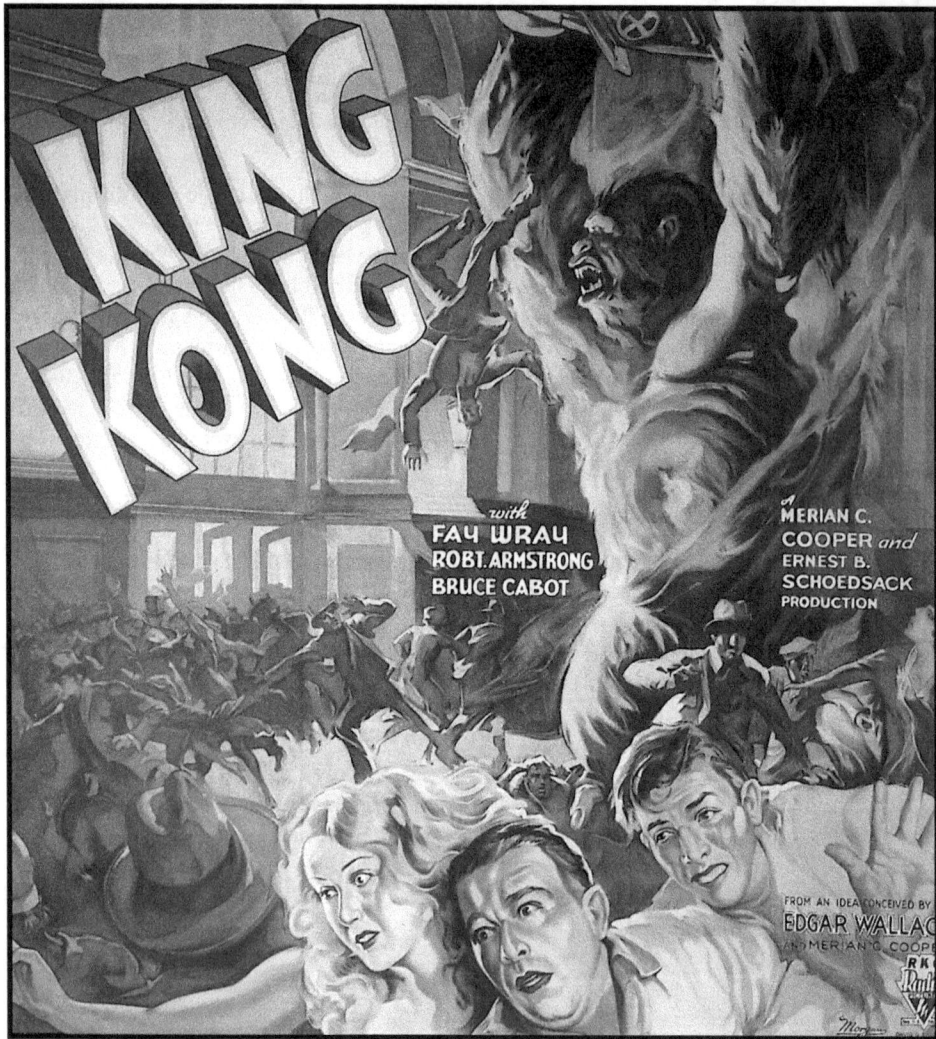

sought to record on film ideas beyond the scope of any other medium. Here, for once, was a movie that justified the most immodest claims put forth in its behalf. It *was* "a show sired by the spirit of P.T. Barnum," the "strangest adventure drama this thrill-mad world has ever seen," a "mastodonic miracle of the movies" and "the picture that out-thrills your maddest dreams."

King Kong was released to massed acclaim on April 10, 1933, and has gained in popularity throughout the years. It is probable that as a folk hero the titular character is known to more individuals of all ages than is Paul Bunyan. Tourists

The model kit for King Kong

visiting the Empire State Building buy postcards showing Kong perched atop the mooring mast. Youngsters wear lapel buttons declaring that "King Kong Died for Our Sins" or "King Kong Wears a Toupee" or "King Kong Has an Edifice Complex." Entertainers from yodeling hillbillies and blues moaners to techno-funksters and hip-hop braggarts invoke the name of Kong as a metaphor for their own fancied strength. Comedians such as Bob Newhart, Jonathan Winters and Don Adams [and, since this book's original publication, Robin Williams and Rogn Mitchell and Steve Martin and Eddie Murphy and Chris Rock, to name only several] have *Kong* routines in their repertoires. Innumerable wrestlers, football players and weight-lifters have adopted the film's title as their sobriquets. There are *King Kong* model kits, comic books, mechanical toys and dolls. And the music-copyright logs of Broadcast Music, Inc., and the American Society of Composers, Authors & Publishers list hundreds of compositions—quite apart from *Kong*-specific film scores—referring to the ape regent.

Theatrical showings of this venerable film still break attendance records, even though living-room video has long since become the new repertory house. *Time* magazine named *King Kong* its "Movie of the Year" in 1952, when a reissue brought home two-and-a-half times the gross of a new prefabricated-hit release. A New York City television station [in those prehistoric days before the home-video boom] ran *Kong* 17 times during a single week and each time trounced every other channel in the city.

Imitations abound. There are valid reasons why none of these dozens of imitations has succeeded in duplicating *Kong*'s grasp upon the massed popular imagination. One is that, however fantastic and implausible the film may be, it resonates with conviction because it is built upon solid biographical fact. It is as personal a statement of its guiding geniuses—Willis H. O'Brien, Merian C. Cooper, Ernest B. Schoedsack and Ruth Rose—as is anything by Chaplin or Stroheim. The viewer senses the underlying truths.

The Making of King Kong

This crucial early scene in *King Kong* was inspired by a real world encounter.

The technical virtuosity for which *King Kong* is celebrated is due in great measure to a career of experimentation and innovation by the remarkable Willis O'Brien, who compensated for a life overburdened with tragedy and disappointment by pouring into his work an unsurpassed level of imagination, dedication and exuberance. Those who knew him say that O'Brien *was* Kong, recognizable on the screen in every gesture and response.

Carl Denham, the daredevil producer who seeks and finds Kong, is a personality composite of Cooper and Schoedsack. Denham possesses the same courage and constancy of purpose that had made possible the filming of *Grass*, *Chang* and *Rango* under incredibly difficult conditions. Denham accepts hardship and danger willingly as the price of the game. He knows he must avoid the monsoon because he ran afoul of it in Thailand; cranks his own camera because his cinematographer in Sumatra was rendered helpless by a fear of wild animals; and conscripts a beautiful leading lady for his new epic because Real World exhibitors had complained that if *Chang* only possessed a spark of love interest it would have made twice as much money. It is said that if Denham wants a picture of a lion he just walks up and tells it to look pleasant—an approach no more brazen than Schoedsack's foolproof use of the bilabial fricative to provoke tigers to a rampant state.

It probably would never have occurred to Denham to visit the Bowery in search of a pretty girl desperate enough to accept a dangerous job—had not Steve Clemente, the Yaqui Indian knife marksman who is among the cast of the film, done that same thing when he was unable to hire an actress for his Vaudeville act through conventional channels. Denham's friend, the tough and reluctantly romantic Jack Driscoll, clearly resembles Schoedsack.

Ann Darrow, the heroine immortalized by Fay Wray, springs as surely from the life of Ruth Rose, co-author of the shooting script. Like Ann, the writer was an unemployed actress who had found adventure and romance in faraway, primitive lands. Had she not met her future husband,

Freudians point with priapical glee to the supposed irony of Kong's retreat to the top of "the most elaborate phallic symbol in the world"—the Empire State Building, which is so much bologna.

Schoedsack himself, aboard the expedition ship *Arcturus*, it is likely that the love scenes aboard the *Venture* in *King Kong* would have been played in the Philip Barry style of stilted dialogue that typified films of the period, instead of the clumsily sincere tough-guy style that is so touching because it seems real. The crusty Capt. Englehorn and his roughneck crew seem lifelike because the writer and the producers knew well the living counterparts of these characters.

King Kong also bears the hallmarks of other creative individuals—the artists, craftsmen, technicians, actors and musicians who contributed the breath of life to the most intemperate imaginings of the principal creators.

Many ringside authorities have attempted to justify the public's fascination with a gigantic, temperamental ape by reading into the film a great deal more mock-significance than was intended by the artists in charge. European Communists insist that Kong's assault upon the native village symbolizes Karl Marx. A French critic, apparently confusing Ruth Rose with Rose La Rose or Gypsy Rose Lee, attributed the picture's erotic tensions to the "fact" that the tale was written in part by "a former strip-tease *artiste*." Others insist that the (true-to-nature) coloration of Kong represents the plight of the Negro, who also was brought to these shores in chains and faced exploitation by the white man. Freudians point with priapical glee to the supposed irony of Kong's retreat to the top of "the most elaborate phallic symbol in the world"—the Empire State Building, which is so much bologna. Strictly for the Freudians, too, are the "mock-crucifixion" of Kong; the "proxy gratification" of Depression-angered audiences via Kong's destructive rampage in New York; a Brontosaurus that reminds them of Leda's swan, and so on, *ad infinitum, ad nauseam*. Such crackpot notions were all steadfastly rejected by the people behind the film, who regarded the theorists variously with disgust, pity and amusement. (And yes, *all* art, irrespective of time or place, represents a struggle to comprehend the mysteries of creation. So what else is new?)

We earnestly suggest that simple explanations are best: Kong is no darker of hue than any other gorilla; he smashes the gates simply to recapture Fay Wray; his atrocious behavior in New York has nothing to do with politics or economic conditions; and he climbs the Empire State Building because it is the highest point in the city, corresponding to his mountaintop lair in his homeland: Any wild beast, in retreat or repose, seeks the high ground. *King Kong* is nothing more nor less than what it was meant to be: a highly entertaining, shrewdly conceived work of pure cinema.

To understand the factors that made *King Kong* the classic it has become, it is necessary to know something about the people involved in its making. It is essential, as well, to have a modicum of familiarity with several related films, ranging

Kong misbehaves on a New York rooftop; Fay Wray is in miniature rear projection.

from the early works of O'Brien, Cooper and the Schoedsacks to the De Mille Biblical epic, *The King of Kings*; the unfinished *Creation*; the often combative tandem production of *The Most Dangerous Game*; the sequel, *The Son of Kong*; the innumerable films, most of them inferior, that are derivative of *Kong* and its kindred pioneering productions; and even the one film of Old Hollywood which possibly exceeds *Kong* in popularity: *Gone with the Wind*.

All these considerations are essential components of this book, which should at least dispel some of the controversy regarding the means used to bring to the screen a story that many experts insisted could not be filmed. Little of this has been told until now, despite the large body of material (we balk at distinguishing hyperbole and rumor by calling them "information") that has been published over the long haul. *King Kong* was made on closed sets to protect the methods used in its production. Most of the published stories were based upon surmise and deliberately false information disseminated by press agents to measure the gullibility of the gee-whiz journalistic racket.

Although commercial success is anathema to many lovers of the arts—and don't we all cherish lost causes and thwarted geniuses?—it should be noted that one of the more important aspects of *King Kong* is that it made a great deal of money. It didn't come along quite soon enough to rescue RKO-Radio Pictures from a bad patch with bankruptcy, but the film *did* pull the studio out of a state of equity receivership, which is rather a greater feat than just preventing a bankruptcy. Thus did *Kong* prove directly responsible for the hundreds of films made by that long-lamented company during the last 20-odd years of its existence. This is quite an important function when one considers the number of outstanding films that are, in a very real sense, the offspring of *King Kong*. Among the many are the Fred Astaire-Ginger Rogers musicals; *The Informer*; *The Lost Patrol*; *Little Women*; *The Last Days of Pompeii*; *Gunga Din*; the Val Lewton thrillers including *Cat People* and *The Leopard Man*; *All That Money Can Buy*; *Citizen Kane*; *Mighty Joe Young*—and the list goes on and on.
—George E. Turner
Amarillo, Texas, and Hollywood, 1968-1999

[Transcribed from the Barnes/Tantivy edition of *The Making of King Kong* and reconciled with handwritten notes and annotated typescripts found in Mr. Turner's working files.]

George E. Turner's Preface to the Revised Edition: Why Kong Is Still King

> That DeLaurentiis version of *Kong*—? It was crap! Unadulterated crap! Worse crap, even, than those Japanese imitation-*Kongs*! The Japanese, at least, had their own tradition of crap to honor. Now, this version that Bob Zemeckis and I've cast an eye toward making, one of these days—it might turn out to suit, and then again it might not. But no matter how good, or how ill, any version I might have a hand in should turn out, one thing is certain: It'd be naught more than a remake of one of the greatest motion pictures ever made.
>
> —Peter Jackson; from an interview with Michael H. Price, 1996

Great Men are involved in every Great Undertaking, whether the exploration of unknown lands, the invasion of the unplumbed depths, the conquest of space, or the creation of a lasting work of literature or artistry.

King Kong—that wildly imaginative motion picture that has enthralled many a generation of armchair adventurers—was the product of as remarkable a group of daredevils, artists and craftsmen as ever worked together toward a goal. Imagination merged with skill to give a Depression-crushed world an entertainment that Russell Swanson, a publicist for RKO-Radio Pictures, called "the stuff for which movies were made!" Exclamation point, indeed.

The Hollywood cynics snickered in their cocktails at another of Swanson's claims: "If ever there was a show sired by the spirit of P.T. Barnum, it's this Hippodrome of thrills staged in the arena of Earth's creation! It's the mastodonic miracle of the movies!" Even within an industry that spoke in exclamations, the hyperbole seemed extravagant.

The snickering soon took on a timbre of envy, however, for these and other comparably extravagant bits of flackery preceded the release of a picture that—to everyone's surprise—justified every last superlative. The publicity department was, after all, only speaking the language of the explorer-turned-filmmaker hero, Carl Denham, when he embarked upon the expedition to Kong's fabled Skull Island: "They'll have to think up a lot of new adjectives when I come back!" Exclamation point.

The notion of Kong originated in the mind of a stocky, broad-shouldered young man who had been not only a sensation-hounding newspaper reporter but also a midshipman who went "over the hill," as the saying goes, for the love of a dame—a daredevil World War I flying ace who refused to accept the Distinguished Service Cross because he didn't care to be singled out from among his buddies—a flight commander of the Polish Air Force during the Russo-Polish War—an explorer of jungles and deserts—chief of staff of the Flying Tigers—co-founder of two airlines—and through much of this pageant of adventures, a writer and movie producer. His escape from a Russian prison and its trigger-happy guardsmen made international headlines. He was Merian Coldwell Cooper, of Jacksonville, Florida.

Cooper's visions were brought to reality with the help of a similarly remarkable man of action, Ernest Beaumont "Monte"[1] Schoedsack. A lanky, six-foot-six adventurer from Council Bluffs, Iowa, Schoedsack was a cinematographer for the Mack Sennett Studio before he became a combat cameraman during World War I, the Russo-Polish War and the Græco-Turkish War. He and Cooper met in 1919 in war-shattered Vienna and—several separate escapades later—met again as members of the Southwestern Museum's expedition to Africa and the islands of the Indian Ocean and the South Pacific. Cooper joined the exploring ship *Wisdom II* in Singapore and sailed with it through the Indian Ocean and up the coast of Africa; Schoedsack joined there, at the port of Djibouti. The men formed a movie production partnership with this slogan: "Make It Distant, Difficult and Dangerous." Their exploits took them on harrowing expeditions that

Ernest B. Schoedsack and Merian C. Cooper

yielded the classic Natural Dramas, as they called them, of *Grass* (1925), filmed in the mountains of Persia; *Chang* (1927), a trek through the jungles of Siam, climaxing with a stampede of elephants; and *The Four Feathers* (1929), a magnificent African adventure. On his own, Schoedsack made *Rango* (1931) in the wilds of Sumatra; shot the Indian expeditionary scenes for *Lives of a Bengal Lancer* (1931-35); and led an Arabian excursion for RKO-Radio. Many genuine Cooper & Schoedsack adventures would be depicted in *King Kong*, beefed up with all the exaggerations appropriate to a fantasy-adventure yarn.

But for their artistry, their daredevilry and their sense of meta-drama, the men were as unalike as their contrasting appearances. "That's why we made such a good team," Schoedsack said. "Each of us made up what the other lacked." Cooper was a flamboyant, consummate showman, brimming with enthusiasm and perseverance. Schoedsack was a quiet intellectual who could bring Cooper down to earth when the brainstorms became impractically heady.

Following their expeditionary work on *The Four Feathers*, Cooper found himself forced by business interests to remain in New York. So while Schoedsack was filming tigers in Sumatra, Cooper swapped tall tales at a Mecca for explorers, the Boone & Crockett Club. He was especially fascinated with the adventures of a young friend, W. Douglas Burden, of the American Museum of Natural History and the New York Zoological Society.

Burden in 1926 had explored the Island of Komodo in the Lesser Sundras, Dutch East Indies, where Dutch naturalists had finally confirmed what the natives had sworn for centuries: There *were* living dragons. Burden encountered there a gigantic species of Varanian lizard, counted extinct since the Pleistocene epoch. He published his findings in *The Dragon Lizards of Komodo*, an account that covered the discovery as far as Burden's importing of two such creatures to a New York City zoo—where they languished and died. That these 10-foot, 250-pound flesh-eaters, now known as Komodo Dragons (*Varanus Komodoensis*), should have survived the ages on a small island and nowhere else is a miracle that still baffles science. (The fascination continues apace; as late as the dawning of the 21st century, carefully imported and nurtured Komodo Dragons have thrived as a mainstay of the Fort Worth [Texas] Zoological Gardens.)

The Burden influence proved of inestimable bearing upon *King Kong*: Cooper, whose fascination with gorillas dated from childhood, could to his last days quote at length from a favorite book, the 1861 edition of *Explorations & Adventures in Equatorial Africa*, in which the expeditioner Paul du Chiallu described "the fierce, untamable gorilla... [whose] ferocity has made it the terror of the bravest native hunters." Considering Burden's abduction of the Komodo Dragons to their doom in America, Cooper imagined the enslavement, with disastrous consequences, of a massive ape. Burden had taken along his beautiful young bride on the dangerous expedition—a fact that Cooper found an inspiration to the storytelling urge.

While working with Schoedsack in Siam and Africa, Cooper had become fascinated with the humanoid antics of apes and monkeys. Ever the dreamer, he conjured up a fantastic fable in which a gigantic gorilla with a calculating intelligence would be pitted against prehistoric reptiles on a lost island in the Indian Ocean. As he pondered this idea, he began inventorying the tallest of man-made peaks in Manhattan—first, the New York Life Building; then the rise of the Chrysler Building; and finally, the construction-in-progress of the 102-story Empire State Building. He envisioned an ape, impossibly immense, brought in chains to the United States, escaping, and making a last stand against warplanes from atop the world's then-tallest building.

Cooper made futile attempts to obtain financing for expeditions to Africa and Komodo. The movie executives deemed the scheme unfeasible, and they were probably correct. The unique talents of yet another moviemaker were needed.

Willis O'Brien

That man was Willis Harold O'Brien, a former boxer and cowboy from Oakland, California, who had brought to near-perfection a picturemaking technique he called dimensional animation, or animation-in-depth. Since the middle 1910s, O'Brien had devoted his energies to making dinosaurs and other fanciful beasts appear to traverse the screen. His methods were painstaking: He constructed articulated figures and, by photographing them in barely perceptible changes of position one frame at a time, made them act, as it were, for the camera. Sixteen such sequential photos were required to give the illusion of one second of lifelike movement—16 frames per second being the customary cranking speed for silent-era movies.

O'Brien made a series of caveman-vs.-dinosaur comedies

for Thomas A. Edison, then in 1919 co-produced a more earnestly exciting dinosaur adventure, "The Ghost of Slumber Mountain." This successful novelty short led to the production of First National's silent epic of 1925, *The Lost World*, which picturized in 10 reels Sir Arthur Conan Doyle's novel about dinosaurs surviving into modern times on a plateau in Brazil. Among the technicians assisting O'Brien in this monumental task was a young Mexican sculptor, Marcel Delgado, who constructed 49 dinosaurs with rubber muscles and skins over tooled dural skeletons.

In 1930, O'Brien and Harry O. Hoyt, who had directed *The Lost World*, began work on another dinosaur epic, *Creation*, at RKO-Radio Pictures in Hollywood. Delgado again created the animals, and the great cinematographer/director/author Karl Brown contributed his expertise. More sophisticated methods had been developed by O'Brien and others, permitting a finer integration of the actors with the model dinosaurs. A unit task force of artists and technicians was enlisted from the studio personnel and assigned to Hoyt and O'Brien.

About a year later, Cooper came to RKO as executive assistant to the new vice president in charge of production, David O. Selznick. Cooper and Pandro S. Berman were given the job of assessing story properties under way at the studio. Cooper decided that *Creation*, with its enormous budget, had scant commercial possibilities—"just big beasts running around"—but declared that the addition of a quality of "ferocious menace," to say nothing of "a prehistoric Giant Gorilla," would give the studio a property with which to reckon.

Wallace Beery announces his plan to discover a land forgotten by time in *The Lost World* (1925).

Most of the studio brass felt the idea a sure loser, but Selznick secured permission and $10,000 to shoot a reel of test footage. Delgado was assigned to create a model gorilla with some human characteristics—a daunting chore, for Cooper kept having him re-design the creature. The final version was almost a pure gorilla with a trimmed-down torso. Enlisting writer James Ashmore Creelman, Cooper and O'Brien filmed a semi-improvised sequence in which Robert Armstrong, Bruce Cabot and a handful of extras were chased by an enraged Brontosaurus through a dense jungle. They were further harassed by a Triceratops and an Arsinoitherium (actually, scenes lifted from *Creation*), which chased them onto a log bridging a chasm. Kong, a gorilla standing 18 feet tall, left his captive, the luscious Fay Wray, in the crotch of a tree while he went back to deal with his human pursuers. He shook the men off the log into a pit filled with huge and voracious spiders and other creatures, then returned to fight a flesh-eating dinosaur—Cooper insisted upon calling it an Allosaurus, although the physiognomy and dimensions are more those of the Tyrannosaurus Rex—that had taken a culinary interest in Miss Wray.

The scenes with stars were shot at night.

The scenes with the actors were shot at night on a jungle set at the RKO-Pathé Studio in Culver City, where Schoedsack was directing that classic chase movie, *The Most Dangerous Game*. There were many heated confrontations between Cooper and Schoedsack, their long-standing partnership notwithstanding, when the hard-nosed directors kept getting in one another's way. O'Brien's miniature scenes of Kong and the dinosaurs were made at RKO-Radio on Sound Stage No. 3. Kong was an 18-inch-tall Delgado creation with a jointed skeleton of dural, muscles of latex and sponge rubber and a skin of pruned rabbit fur. The players were combined with animated beasts (retrieved from *Creation*) via special processes involving full-scale background projection (to enlarge the previously filmed animals behind the actors), O'Brien's invention of miniature projection (to place previously photographed actors into the miniature settings), and matted composites.

Test shot depicting relative scale.

The test reel was screened for the studio executives, along with illustrations made by Mario Larrinaga and Byron L. Crabbe depicting other highlights envisioned for the final picture. The test was a rousing success. Schoedsack, having completed *The Most Dangerous Game*, joined in as co-producer and co-director. He directed the scenes involving the actors, and Cooper hovered over the animation and special-effects crew.

The famous British author, Edgar Wallace, was brought over to write the shooting script. Wallace, whose extravagant tales of crime and high adventure had earned him the rank of the world's most fashionable novelist, wrote a first-draft screenplay in a few days along with several other ideas for the studio. The Wallace version had a woman and a boatload of escapees from a penal colony landing on the uncharted island. Cooper nixed the idea. Then, he and Wallace, a diabetic, were stricken with pneumonia. "I went to the hospital and lived," Cooper said. "Edgar refused to go, and he died."

Several other writers worked on the screenplay, as well. It was Creelman who completed the official shooting script early in 1932. The studio approved it, but Cooper and Schoedsack were not satisfied. They felt the piece required almost a Victorian romantic tone to bolster the fantasy. The Creelman version differs greatly from the actual movie, which was rewritten—day-by-day, all during its 55 weeks of real-time production—by Ruth Rose, wife of Schoedsack.

The story has Carl Denham (Robert Armstrong), producer of authentic jungle films, leading an expedition to the uncharted Skull Island, somewhere "'way west of Sumatra," which is said to be dominated by a god known as Kong. The natives of the island are fascinated by the blonde beauty of the company's actress, Ann Darrow (Fay Wray), and offer to trade six of their women for her to be "the bride of Kong." At night, they kidnap Ann from the ship and, in a spectacular ceremony, place her on a jungle altar beyond an ancient great wall and call forth Kong to receive his sacrifice. Kong is as amazed as Ann, and he carries her into the jungle as more a prize than a victim. Denham and 13 sailors, including Ann's lover, Jack Driscoll (Bruce Cabot), follow.

Byron Crabbe created this key drawing of the appealing mother Triceratops and her young.

They kill a pugnacious Stegosaurus. A Brontosaurus kills several of the sailors, and Kong kills all the survivors except Denham and Driscoll. Driscoll rescues Ann from Kong's mountaintop eyrie while Kong is battling a Pteranodon that had tried to carry her away. Kong follows them to the native village, breaks open the massive gates and almost destroys the settlement before Denham fells him with a gas bomb. Kong is taken to New York and exhibited in a theatre, but breaks free and recaptures Ann. After wreaking havoc in the city, he climbs to the summit of the Empire State Building, where at last he is killed by Navy pursuit planes. As Denham sadly surveys the crushed body of the ape god, a policeman comments, "Well, Mr. Denham, those airplanes really got 'im." Denham replies, "Oh, no. It wasn't the airplanes. It was *Beauty* killed the Beast."

A more outrageously fantastic shaggy-dog yarn could hardly be imagined, but the lightning pace of the picture and the underlying reality of the fantasy—it is, after all, shot through with multiple autobiography—makes any but the most scornful viewer forego the tendency to

The Terror (England, 1938) starring Richard Bird and Alastair Sim, was an Edgar Wallace adaptation.

The Making of King Kong 27

Audiences feel a tremendous identification with Kong even though they see innocent people killed, as in this native village with the Kong-trampled mannequin.

scoff. Kong's battles with the dinosaurs and the atmosphere of a prehistoric jungle are realized in telling detail. Strangest of all is the affecting performance of Kong himself, which can only be a case of Willis O'Brien channeling his own scrappy, indignant personality into the animated creature: Audiences feel a tremendous identification with a horrendous beast that, before their eyes, kills scores of innocent human beings and even wrecks an elevated train. To this day, an audience will cheer when Kong sends a U.S. Navy aircraft crashing in flames.

Ruth Rose Schoedsack, daughter of the famed Broadway dramatist Edward E. Rose, shared her husband's love of adventure. They had met as members of William Beebe's *Arcturus* expedition to the Galapagos Islands. Ruth knew her way around the jungles of Kartabao and Tierra del

An early test for the battle between Kong and the U.S. Navy

Ruth Rose on Broadway in *Cheating Cheaters*. Interestingly, Fay Wray would appear in the 1934 film version of the show.

Fuego; had been with the Cooper-Schoedsack African expedition; and assisted her husband on his shoots in Sumatra and India. The petite young woman had been a successful leading lady on Broadway until, idled by an Equity strike, she chose a new career in scientific exploration. She had written factual material for monographs and magazines dealing with the natural history of South America and the West indies—but only one piece of fiction, for the November 1927 issue of *The Ladies' Home Journal*.

Just as the producers had known she would, Ruth put a great deal of herself into the personality of the feminine lead. The fictional Ann Darrow, as played by Ruth's good friend Fay Wray, is also an out-of-work actress who sets off on a bold adventure and meets her husband on an expedition ship. The idea of having the producer discover his leading lady while she tries to steal an apple from a vendor's stand had come from a Schoedsack family friend, Steve Clemente, who found his stage partner while rescuing her from starvation on the street. (Clemente plays the Witch King in the movie.) Ruth imbued the leading men, a daredevil producer and a tough sailor, with essential traits of Cooper and Schoedsack. The dialogue is realistically peppered with slang—of the Broadway and shipboard varieties—with no concession to the broad-stroke theatricalism that permeated most early talking pictures. (Even MGM's *Tarzan, the Ape Man* has a certain boudoir quality, with its dialogue provided by the European matinee idol, Ivor Novello.)

Twin 18-inch models of Kong, on an inch-equals-foot scale, were used for animation in the jungle sets. The Tyrannosaurus, Brontosaurus, Stegosauri, Styracosaurus, Desmatosuchus and Pteranodon were built to the same scale. Each animal appeared to breathe by a means of animating air in and out of a football bladder concealed within its rib cage. There were two Stegosauri, one for walking and the other for thrashing in the throes of death. A cantaloupe-sized Brontosaurus head and long neck were animated for projection close-ups when the animal snatches a man out of a tree. A mechanical swimming (on wheels) version of the Bronto was made in an inch-and-a-half scale for scenes where it kills some men in the water. A noticeably larger, 24-inch Kong was used in the Manhattan scenes, risking a violation of continuity but in fact giving the ape a dramatically varying immensity that works to intensify the terrors. Schoedsack said the producers' rationale

Willis O'Brien in his own native habitat.

here was simple: "You can't get much drama out of a fly crawling up the Empire State Building." Wooden carvings of the animation models were made by the Italian sculptor John Cerisoli for use as stand-ins because the working models suffered under the intense studio lights.

O'Brien, whom Delgado called "the Master," manipulated Kong and most of the other models during much of the production. He was assisted in some of this tedious work by a husky grip, E.B. "Buz" Gibson. Because sound film is projected at a higher rate of speed than the silent pictures, it proved necessary to photograph 24 increments of movement of each model to produce one second of action. Only 15 to 20 feet of animation footage could be completed in a 10-hour day. Each scene was planned out in detailed illustrations and intermediate sketches by Mario Larrinaga and Byron Crabbe, the team that also contributed the scenic art seen in the finished picture. The oppressive textures of the jungle were derived from the demoniacal woodcuts of the French illustrator, Gustave Doré.

Another artist and camera technician, Carroll Shepphird, prepared charts to demonstrate camera placements, lenses to be used, necessary special processes and other critical details. Orville Goldner created many of the weird jungle settings in miniature; helped to match up the various combinations of settings, art painted on glass and animation models; grew many of the tiny plants used in the miniature jungles; designed special piano-wire riggings; and animated the birds and airplanes. It was Goldner who sculpted the twisted trees of Skull Island out of Plasticene over wooden forms, detailed their bark, covered them over with tissue paper, applied shellac and painted in still finer details. Some of the leaves and small branches are genuine foliage, made from the roots of grapevines and desert plants, and much of the undergrowth was cut from thin sheets of copper. The organic is indistinguishable from the synthetic. The metal shrubbery stayed in place during the long hours of animation; paper or cloth would have been disturbed by air currents and even the wisps of breath from the artisans.

O'Brien animates the fight at the great cave.

The miniature airplanes, built to four scales with wingspans ranging from four to 16 inches to create a sense of perspective, were intercut with four actual U.S. Navy aircraft from Bennett Field—which Schoedsack filmed as they buzzed the Real World's Empire State Building. On screen, Cooper is the pilot and Schoedsack the gunner of the command plane.

Almost anything can happen, for good or ill, in dimensional animation. The producers were appalled when, upon viewing the rushes, they realized the rabbit fur on Kong's head and shoulders was rippling with each frame. This was caused by the fingerprints of the animators. Schoedsack recalled that his heart almost stopped when one of the visiting executives from New York shouted, "Hey! Look!"—and then added, enthusiastically: "Kong is mad! Look at him bristle!" B.B. Kahane, the toughest executive of them all and one of the most vocal of early-day nay-sayers against *Kong*, said, "I'm so anxious to see this picture, I can almost taste it!"

One animator worked for hours before he discovered he had left a pair of pliers lying within camera range. Another spent 10 hours staging a scene featuring a dinosaur. During the morning, a tiny primrose in the foreground blossomed unnoticed, and at the end of the day the blossom closed. When the footage was screened, the seemingly gigantic flower opened as the dinosaur entered and closed upon the creature's exit. Goldner and an assigned crew spent three days lining up and matching the various components of an unusually complicated miniature scene. After repeated adjustments and camera tests, the setup—which included several paintings on glass, a dinosaur, numerous props and a projection device—was judged camera-ready. The crew broke for lunch and, while they were enjoying their sandwiches, the ground trembled for a moment: A small earthquake had occurred. When they returned, they found their miniature was no longer camera-ready.

A huge mechanical bust of Kong, for use in close-ups, was created of wood, rubber, glass and pruned bearskin. Three men huddled within to operate levers and air compressors to move the eyes, brows, nostrils and mouth. The big head was able to assume expressions ranging from tenderness to rage, and even the biting motions necessary for chomping down on incidental characters. Two full-scale right hands and arms were made. One was a simple affair that can be seen reaching for Cabot when he hides in a cave; the other was an intricately structured piece, built over a steel bar for raising and lowering, that can be seen holding Fay Wray and, elsewhere, dropping a screaming woman earthward. (That victim is Sandra Shaw, a.k.a. Victoria Balfe, who shortly thereafter became Mrs. Gary Cooper.) Each finger could be articulated via levers. For the Pteranodon, a full-scale lower body and legs were built to pick up Miss Wray in close-ups.

Montage of preparatory shots and artwork

Edwin Linden was director of photography in charge of both live action and animation. "Eddie kept from two to 10 camera set-ups available at all times," recalled Linwood Dunn, of the camera-effects department. Much of the intricate composite work, merging miniature and full-scale elements, was accomplished by Dunn and his crew of optical technicians.

"O'Brien was a genius at creating visual effects," Dunn said in 1976, providing the first bits of additional information beyond the scope of the first edition of *The Making of King Kong*. "[But O'Brien was] so much a loner that he worked in techniques of his own design and wasn't too aware of our work."

O'Brien was doing his composites *in the camera*, Dunn explained: "This often entailed retakes of complex shots that took a long while to set up, with much time out for making tests to check the balances. In these composites, there was a consistent problem of mismatched quality between the foreground and the background elements. At some point, partway through production, I was able to convince OBie that I could save him a whole lot of trouble by working out on the optical printer such compositing problems, where there was much greater control and much lower cost."

Over the years, rumors have persisted that a man in an ape-suit impersonated Kong in certain scenes. Seemingly knowledgable how-it-was-done stories in popular magazines have amplified the myth, but these are only cases of half-baked guesswork. On the basis of the producers' and key artisans' insistence that such was never the case, we will go to the mat to debunk this notion. The rumor is fueled, of course, by the extraordinarily smooth scenes of a distant Kong climbing the Empire State Building. The only reason for this lack of animation jitters is that the image is so remote that such details cannot be ascertained. The noted gorilla impersonator Charlie Gemora—of films as diversified as the 1930 talkie version of *The Unholy Three*, not to mention the bogus documentary *Ingagi*—has been falsely identified as the climber. Actually, Gemora *did* once portray Kong, but only in a never-completed short-subject spoof of 1934 called "The Lost Island." One Ken Roady, alias Carmen Nigro, once claimed to have portrayed Kong throughout *King Kong*. Which is so much hogwash.

Max Steiner

Music became so much more than a finishing touch that Max Steiner's thundering compositions have gained acclaim as one of the handful of greater-than-great movie scores, as welcome in the concert hall as in its truer element. Steiner added dimension to

Spawn of Skull Island

the already dimension-ful animation. Cost-conscious executives had ordered Steiner to utilize music from other pictures. With Cooper's connivance, Steiner was able to spend eight weeks composing original themes. The Viennese maestro enlarged the 28-piece studio orchestra to 46 instruments, plus singers and drummers. The ingenious sound effects were added by another musician, Murray Spivack, who even altered the sonic contours of the great mass of roars and screams so that they would be consonant with the music. This unprecedented touch has spared millions of moviegoers from headaches.

Many others contributed their talents to the realization of *King Kong*. Most of them had long, illustrious careers afterward, but solving the unprecedented problems of "the mastodonic miracle of the movies" remained for most the great highlight of their lives. Of the key members of the Skull Island expedition, one would long outlive all the rest: That would be the petite yet magnificent Fay Wray, whose Beauty killed the Beast. After having fielded questions about *Kong* from thousands of fans for most of her life, Miss Wray would at length admit her greater preference for a picture she had made earlier, with Erich von Stroheim: *The Wedding March*.

It is often said that David O. Selznick thought up the final christening for the picture that had been a work-in-progress as *The Beast*, *The Eighth Wonder* and simply *Kong*. Both Cooper and Douglas Burden said otherwise. They agreed that the word *Kong* was derived from *Komodo*, and that the *King* bit was inspired by something an old-time hunter named Defosse told Burden as they surveyed the Island of Komodo by moonlight from a clifftop: "I would like to bring my whole family and settle here, and be King of Komodo."

Kong's actual cost, according to Cooper, was about $430,000. Studio overhead and the $177,633 that had been spent on *Creation* brought the official negative cost—literally, the cost of everything required to create the finished negative—to $672,254.75. The box-office returns were quite enough to boost RKO out of the receivership into which it had been placed by the Irving Trust Co.[2] The film is an amazing show, enjoyable on several levels and so packed with detail that people who have seen it many times say they always discover new delights to savor.

The one quality that defies rational explanation is the performance of Kong himself. Associate producer Archie Marshek told us that Kong could "in general, assume more expressions than many of our actors can. As we watched a certain personality develop in the ape, we could see something of OBie showing through." Cooper acted out some of Kong's moves for the animators to emulate, and many who knew him said they could see Cooper in Kong's every move. Friends of O'Brien said they could see *O'Brien* in Kong's every expression and gesture. Through some alchemy that has yet to be rediscovered, Kong's creators combined to give their bestial Galatea of metal, rubber, wood, fur and glass a personality to rival that of any flesh-and-blood movie star. It is futile to attempt an explanation, for Kong's unique charm is, now and always, beyond words.

—George E. Turner
Hollywood, 1998-99

1 Cooper spelled his partner's nickname as *Monty*, but Schoedsack and his wife, Ruth Rose Schoedsack, preferred Monte.

2 And just how much money did *King Kong* actually make as a first-run attraction? The question is of course unanswerable, but our filmmaker/historian colleague Ryan Brennan offers a persuasive perspective: "As with so many films made prior to the mania for accurate record-keeping, there never were any official box-office figures for *Kong*. However, in response to requests,... *Variety* finally listed both *Kong* and [D.W. Griffith's] *The Birth of a Nation* [1915] as having grossed $5 million apiece. For *Nation*, that figure represented only the money accruing to the production company which, in a states'-rights [or region-by-region] booking arrangement, contractually took only a paltry 10 percent of the box-office returns. Exhibitors usually under-reported the actual box office. (It was said that Louis B. Mayer, then an exhibitor only, made his fortune from the proceeds of *Nation*.) That means that *Nation*, in its original run, ran up a minimum gross of $50 million. Adjusted for inflation, I believe that makes *Nation* the biggest-grossing film ever, even surpassing James Cameron's *Titanic*. In the case of *Kong* [which had a massed national release, as opposed to a states'-rights distribution arrangement],... it was one of the biggest hits of all time, and I personally believe the *Variety* figure to be a low one."

Acknowledgments

To these vital sources of information, encouragement and assistance, our thanks:

Anthony Ambrogio; Robert Armstrong; Robert Bloch; Ray Bradbury; Ryan Brennan; Steve Brigati; Karl Brown; Larry Buchanan; Bruce Cabot; Sam Calvin; Woodfin Camp; Wah Ming Chang; Merian C. Cooper; Marcel Delgado; Linwood Dunn; Martin Grams, Jr.; John Hall; Vern Harben; Ray Harryhausen; Jan Alan Henderson; Peter Jackson; Ben Johnson; Mario Larrinaga; Bessie Love; Cecil Love; Greg Luce; Scott MacQueen; Jerry McDonough; Leonard Maltin; Archie S. Marshek; Bonnie Merriman; Brad Musick; Darlyne O'Brien; Willis H. O'Brien; Terry Pace; Bill Paxton; Kenneth Peach, *pére et fils*; Sam Peeples; Zöe Porter; Ernest B. and Ruth Rose Schoedsack; Peter Schoedsack; Jo Ann Schov; Carroll Shepphird; Allen Shifrin; Fred Shepphird; Dennis Spies; Murray Spivack; Frank Stack; Max Steiner; Clifford Stine; Susan & Gary Svehla; Ellis "Bud" Thackery; Mary Kate Tripp; Peter Von Sholly; Michael Weldon; John Wooley; Fay Wray; and Harold Wellman

And on the institutional and corporate fronts: (Ted) Turner Entertainment; the Motion Picture Academy; the American Society of Cinematographers; the Screen Actors Guild; the Screen Directors Guild; the Hoblitzelle Theatre Arts Library and its Selznick Collection, Austin, Texas; the Amarillo [Texas] *Globe-News*; the American Society of Composers, Authors & Publishers; the Academy of Motion Picture Arts & Sciences; Fort Worth Film Festival, Inc.; the Edgar Wallace Estate; Turner Classic Movies Network; Movie Wonderland of Goleta, California; Sinister Cinema; Janus Films; Panhandle-Plains Historical Museum, West Texas A&M University at Canyon; Southwest Film & Video Archive, Southern Methodist University at Dallas; and Warner Bros. Studios, Inc.

Preamble & Laundry List

> Well, now, Sylvester Stallone
> And even Meryl Streep,
> They're gonna have to clear a path
> For all these Mesozoic creeps.
> And when the craze runs its course
> And the box office droops,
> They're gonna bring in Arnold
> Schwarzenegger to play Alley Oop...
>
> —Michael H. Price; from "Up Jurassic Park," *The Dr. Demento Show*, 1993

The odd scrap of prophecy reproduced above has yet to come to pass in any lasting sense—and may never do so within the viable ticket-selling spans of the marquee names thus dropped. But when I penned that lyric, in anticipation of the opening of Steven Spielberg's first-of-a-series *Jurassic Park*, it seemed eminently reasonable that a stampede of special-effects monsters might steal the affections of a massed audience away from any number of flesh-and-blood movie stars.

I am frankly surprised that nobody *has* railroaded Arnold Schwarzenegger into playing Alley Oop, the long-popular comic-strip caveman hero created during the early Depression years by Vincent T. Hamlin. It was George Turner, in fact, who had predicted a Schwarzenegger-as-Oop movie, back during the mid-to-late 1980s when the Schwarzenegger name had become practically a synonym for barbaric high adventure with a hooligan's sense of humor.

Nevah hoppen, as the wise old Oriental saying goes. The closest we ever came to such a spectacle was John Goodman as Fred Flintstone, a bit of scrofulous grotesquerie that has continued to sequelize itself. The first and perhaps only rule in the brawling arena of film appreciation is that There's No Accounting for Taste, and I mean that in the nicest way possible. Myself, I always wanted to see Rodney Dangerfield as Fred Flintstone, cast opposite Jerry Falwell as Barney Rubble. Which would have been almost as astonishing as Schwarzenegger astride a ridgeback dinosaur—yes, and Alley Oop smokes cigars, too. (Ryan Brennan, one of our more helpful kibitzers, adds: "I'm really surprised that someone hasn't taken a close-up of the huge King Kong bust, added a white mustache, and made it a part of the *Got Milk?* campaign.")

What is most amazing about the close-of-a-century resurgence of dinosaur movies and ape-escape escapades as a class is that it happened at all. The insipid but well-meaning *Land before Time* cartoon features; the comparatively more daunting *Jurassic Park* franchise and the save-the-rainforest remake

Resurgence of a specialized genre—1998

of *Mighty Joe Young*; and the queasily skewed postmodern Darwinism of the Roger Corman company's *Carnosaur* productions—each, in its way, signifies a healthy willingness to reconnect with the bold imaginative qualities that were crucial to filmmaking in times past when the very act of filmmaking was still not far removed from a science-fictional concept.

For we as a people have grown increasingly difficult to shock or thrill in the decaying generations since *The Lost World* (1925) and the *King Kong/Son of Kong* combo of 1933. Such crucial artists as Vince Hamlin and master animator Ray Harryhausen had lamented for years—roughly speaking, the span between the Harryhausen *One Million Years B.C.* (1966) and the 1993 release of *Jurassic Park*—that the monsters of paleontological rediscovery and heroic imagination had become irrelevant to a society coarsened by the more pressing and inescapable horrors of Vietnam, Charles Manson and the Son of Sam and Jeffrey Dahmer, and even the confrontational quasi-escapism of such picture-show anti-personalities as *Friday the 13th*'s Jason Voorhees and the spectral pervert Freddy Kreuger of *A Nightmare on Elm Street*. Harryhausen, though wholly aware of his own influence upon James Cameron's two *Terminator* films, told us in 1992 that he had seen just enough to draw this conclusion: "Their pretensions to imagination are a veneer, and a thin one, at that... They are about cruelty, whose depiction requires little imagination."

Hamlin had said as much as early as 1969-70, when the artist was reluctantly considering retiring from *Alley Oop*: "Nobody's interested in prehistory or dinosaurs or imaginative science anymore. Few people even want a story that carries them away on its crest of wild adventure. They all want a quick gag or a sudden jolt that they can shrug off and forget about until the next one comes along.

"They're not interested in playing 'what-if?' the way they used to be. Everybody's more caught up in the 'what-it-*is*,' and my entire career has been built upon providing a daily refuge from reality," Hamlin complained. "That doesn't leave much room for those of us who can't spring a joke or a good shock without feeling compelled to build a story around it."

Hamlin was an inveterate movie buff whose very invention of *Alley Oop* was inspired in part by the 1925 dinosaur epic *The Lost World*. Hamlin lived on to the age of 93 in 1993, and in fact our last conversation with Hamlin had to do with the matter of *Jurassic Park*'s having helped to reawaken a popular fascination with dinosaurs. George and I contributed commentaries and art restorations to two hefty volumes of *Alley Oop* reprints at about this same time, but Hamlin seemed more astonished than outright pleased that the passage of time had vindicated his concern with such matters.

But the shared interests of Hamlin and Harryhausen were more often in than out of synch with popular tastes. Hamlin's prime years as the writer and principal illustrator of *Alley Oop* coincided with Harryhausen's emergence as a moviemaker with whom to reckon, during the early 1950s. And the massed readership that could hardly wait for the next day's newspaper episode of *Oop* was virtually as one with the picture-going masses who made a hit of Eugene Lourié and Ray Harryhausen's savvy Atom Age variant on *Kong*, 1953's *The Beast from 20,000 Fathoms*.

This book is more pointedly concerned with the making of the 1933 epic *King Kong*, and with the epic-calibre careers of the people who made *Kong* a movie for the ages. Prior editions (1975-76) of *The Making of King Kong* kept a forcibly narrow focus on *Kong* and its origins and immediate upshots; principal author George Turner declared flatly: "The less said, the better" about any and all other big-ape movies (beyond *The Son of Kong* and *Mighty Joe Young*, of course) and most other dinosaur thrillers.

This cold-shouldering of a vast genre is a luxurious conceit that we can ill afford today, for we maintain with all due respect that context and perspective are crucial. *King Kong*, when experienced without context beyond its close-kin productions, is a Great Film, and so what else is new? *King Kong*, when experienced in context with the dreadful likes of *King of Kong Island*, *A-P-E*, and even the Japanese-made abominations of *King Kong vs. Godzilla* and *King Kong Escapes*, is yet a Greater Film.

And so it happens that we offer herewith a broad but nevertheless selective array of pictures whose rediscovery can only enhance one's appreciation of the essential picture of its kind. Compulsive retentionalists are directed herewith to the category indexes of *Video Hound's Golden Movie Retriever*, if not the nearest Internet movie-chat site. If we paused to weigh in, thoughtfully or fatuously, on *every* movie that features an anthropoid ape, *every* prehistoric fantasy or dimensional-animation opus that has graced or befouled the screen (and why, indeed, bother with *Queen Kong*?), then we would be stranded here rather longer than good sense dictates. The opinions below belong in great measure to George Turner, as spontaneously registered during our conversations from the 1960s through the 1990s. If we may appropriate the title of one of the more annoying come-lately knock-offs: *King Kong Lives!*
—Michael H. Price

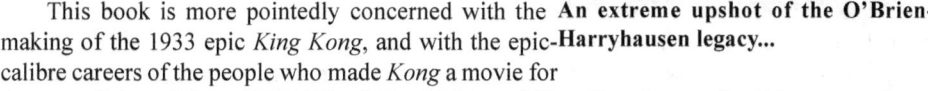

An extreme upshot of the O'Brien-Harryhausen legacy...

...and a betrayal of the legacy.

The Silent Age

Joe, the Educated Orangoutang and ***Joe, the Educated Orangoutang, Undressing*** **(1898)**—In the first of these comic novelties, Joe devours a meal of sliced bananas from a glass dish, using a spoon. In the latter, Joe stages an elaborate disrobing act. Joe was a well-known headliner of Vaudeville and the circus. The archaic spelling of *orangutan* is correct per copyright and Joe's Carney billing.

Human Apes from the Orient **(1906)**—Novelty short, photographed by the great G.W. "Billy" Bitzer, involving the docking of the expeditionary ship S.S. *Werderntels* at Brooklyn.

The Escape of the Ape **(1908)**—Presumably a title-tells-all entry; no print appears to have survived.

The Human Ape; or, Darwin's Triumph **(1909)**—Danish production, also variously known as *Menneskeaben: Darwins Triumf*; *The Ape*; and *Darwin's Triumph*.

Balaoo, the Demon Baboon **(1913)**—Victorin Jasset's French-made tragedy, based upon a 1912 tale by *The Phantom of the Opera*'s Gaston Leroux, centers on what the cultural historian Phil Hardy has called "an ancestor of King Kong's who also died for love." Surgical tampering produces a manlike ape that proves menacing but ultimately sets his wrongs right. See *The Wizard*, below.

Brute Force **(1913-14)**—D.W. Griffith's cavemen are menaced by a life-sized—although far from life*like*—mechanical Ceratosaurus. Its jaws snap, its eyes blink and its tail twitches, but its rigid body is hinged only at the hips. Still, the creature is more impressive than the dressed-up reptiles that masquerade as dinosaurs elsewhere in the picture. Also known as *In Prehistoric Days*, *War of the Primal Tribes* and *The Primitive Man*.

Gertie the Dinosaur **(1914)**—Winsor McCay's pioneering hand-wrought cartoon shows a playful brontosaurus cavorting along a beach and interacting with artist McCay, who appears on screen in surviving prints—but who made crowd-pleasing in-person appearances with the film's larger engagements in its day.

The Romance of Tarzan **(1918)**—And no, it's not for nothing that they call him Tarzan of the Apes. This condition applies to the jungle-lord's various incarnations right up into the present day, and an inventory here beyond one representative title would only amount to a case of Superfluous Redundant Overkill.

A Scream in the Night **(1919)**—Mad scientist John Webb Dillon kidnaps a politician's daughter and has her raised as a savage, significantly christening her Darwa. Played as a lovely young woman by Ruth Budd, Darwa escapes a carnivorous ape and finds a soul-mate in heroic Ralph Kellard.

Go and Get It (1920)—The popular fascination with the concept of ape-as-marauder found its way from popular literature into the movies well before *King Kong*, of course. And nobody said the menace must be a particularly *gigantic* ape, or even a genetically correct primate. This wild entry pivots on a serial-murder case involving a slain surgeon (Noah Beery), who proves to have transplanted the brain of a murderer into the body of a gorilla. The ape-man is interpreted with a snarling ferocity by Bull Montana, in a role prefiguring his menacing cliff-dweller of the 1925 *The Lost World*.[1] Agnes Ayres plays a newspaper heiress whose star reporter (Pat O'Malley) tracks down the cause of the mayhem.

From a tattered newspaper tearsheet that was preserved by George Turner.

The Original Movie (1922)—Tony Sarg—the master puppeteer who developed the crowd-pleasing gimmick of larger-than-life balloon characters for the Macy's Thanksgiving Day Parade—takes an eight-minute flight of fancy into prehistoric days with this satirical look at a caveman moviemaking project. The animation process is a bridge between drawn cartoons and sculpted miniatures, consisting of smoothly maneuvered figures in silhouette. The dinosaur element is minimal but strategic: A long-necked lizard creature serves as the camera crane. A presentation of Herbert M. Dawley, the charlatan who had claimed credit for Willis O'Brien's "The Ghost of Slumber Mountain" in 1919.

Three Ages (1923)—Caveman Buster Keaton (who also directs) makes his entrance atop the head of a Brontosaurus. Shots of Keaton astride a full-sized head are intercut with an extremely well-animated stop-motion miniature sporting a mannequin in the likeness of Keaton. Wallace Beery—only two years away from his star turn in *The Lost World*—appears as the villain.

Pathé Review, Vol. 40, No. 27: "Monsters Of The Past" (1923)—A clever and effective reverse-motion sequence shows a sculptor identified as Virginia May apparently forming a dinosaur from clay. In actuality, she systematically smashes the sculpture, but the film is printed in reverse. The creatures come rather absurdly to life via a lurching form of animation, which is leagues behind the sophistication that Willis O'Brien had achieved on "The Ghost of Slumber Mountain."[2]

Lorraine of the Lions (1925)—And yes, apes proliferate in the jungle-adventure features and serials over the long haul. Which scarcely means we should find ourselves compelled to catalog the things. This historic adventure-thriller stars Patsy Ruth Miller as jungle-dweller Lorraine, who is brought back to civilization with her pet gorilla (played by Fred Humes), with tragic results—for the ape, in any event.

The Unholy Three (1925 and 1930)—Filmed in both silent and talkie versions, each starring Lon Chaney and Harry Earles, the expressive dwarf leading man of 1932's *Freaks*. Charles Gemora plays the gorilla (in the remake) that ultimately kills off the unholiest of the unholies.

The Gorilla Hunt/Ben Burbidge's African Gorilla Hunt (1926)—Expeditionary thrills on a safari to capture six young gorillas for exhibition. The fording of a crocodile-infested stream is a highlight.

The Lost Whirl (1927)—This parody of *The Lost World* features stop-motion dinosaurs by Joseph L. Roop (given as Roupé in some sources), chasing a dapper man and a flapper girl. The animation is decent, if one accepts its comical intent, but the out-of-focus monitor lizard cut in for a Brontosaur's close-up is glaringly ill placed. Roop also worked for Willis O'Brien as an animator on *The Lost World*.

The Wizard (1927)—An ape-like creature (George Kotsonaros) is trained as an instrument of vengeance by a scientist (Gustav von Seyffertitz). Directed by Richard Rosson, from a scenario by Harry O. Hoyt and Andrew Bennison. Source: Gaston Leroux' 1912 serialized novel, *Balaoo*.

Flying Elephants (1927)—One of the last pre-MGM comedies of Hal Roach and Laurel & Hardy, held in escrow until after Roach had moved uptown to MGM, and then released as part of the official L&H program. In fact, the prehistoric fantasy *Flying Elephants* catches Stan Laurel and Oliver Hardy still performing as solo artists within the same picture, barely hinting at the teaming that would make them more genuinely famous. Shot on some of the same locations that Roach would use for 1940's *One Million B.C.*, this relic echoes D.W. Griffith's *Brute Force* and Charles Chaplin's "His Prehistoric Past" and anticipates the Fleischer Bros.' knockabout *Stone Age Cartoons* series of 1940.

The Gorilla **(1927)**—Ralph Spence's stage play *The Gorilla, a Mystery in Three Acts*, is the source. This pioneering adaptation, directed by Alfred Santell, recaptures the original's *Cat and the Canary*-like atmosphere—with a spooky mansion, a series of murders purportedly committed by an ape and, at length, the unveiling of a too-helpful friend-of-the-family type as the genuine culprit. With Charlie Murray, Fred Kelsey and Alice Day.

The Leopard Lady **(1928)**—Robert Armstrong co-stars in this gem about a heroic big-cat trainer (Jacqueline Logan), a villainous Russian (Alan Hale) and a man-killing ape. From Edward Childs Carpenter's New York production, *The Leopard Lady, a Play in Five Acts*.

Ramper der Tiermensch **(Germany; 1928)**—Max Reichman's wild-man epic, imported to America by First National Pictures, stars screenwriter Paul Wegener as a long-lost explorer, degenerated to savagery, who is captured and exploited as a freak-show attraction. In America: *The Strange Case of Captain Ramper*.

Stark Mad (1929)—The nightmarish image of a bull ape, chained in an ancient Central American temple, foreshadows *Kong* even as it dominates this powerful entry from director Lloyd Bacon. A jungle guide (André Beranger), apparently maddened by his long years away from civilization, seems responsible for the mayhem, although there is also a ruins-dwelling hermit (Lionel Belmore) with whom to deal.

The 1930s

The Gorilla (1930)—Talking-picture remake of the 1927 version, with original director Ralph Spence back in charge and an ensemble cast including Joe Frisco, Henry Gribbon, Walter Pidgeon and Lila Lee.

Ingagi (1930)—Notoriously controversial gorilla-hunt mockumentary, covered in abundant detail in the Turner & Price book *Forgotten Horrors: The Definitive Edition*, and in the Felicia Feaster-Bret Wood book, *Forbidden Fruit*. The cultural historian Steve Brigati has since determined that *Ingagi* was used, possibly into the latter half of the 20th Century, as an indoctrination tract by the Ku Klux Klan, which seized upon the film's suggestion of an interbreeding of apes and African women. So corrupt an appropriation cannot have been part of the strategy of *Ingagi*'s producers, who were more concerned with luring in a thrill-hungry mass audience than with advancing any crackpot political agendas. In its time, *Ingagi* inspired such imitations as *Angkor, or Forbidden Adventure (In Angkor)* and *Love Life of a Gorilla*. See also: Turner & Price's *Forgotten Horrors 2: Beyond the Horror Ban*.

Mystery Of Life: A Drama Of Life As Told By Clarence Darrow (1931)—Released by big-time Universal Pictures, this sensationalized educational documentary takes the form of a lecture by Clarence Darrow and Prof. H.M. Parshley of Smith College, advancing evolutionary arguments. The sequence of key interest here—demonstrating, like 1923's "Monsters of the Past," that filmmakers outside the Willis O'Brien camp were at least dabbling in dinosaurs—portrays fancifully sculpted, scientifically suspect replicas of such creatures in

Was *Murders in the Rue Morgue* more Lovecraft than Poe? One can only speculate.

a "prehistoric habitat" setting. One "bird as big as an elephant" suggests an effigy of Sebek, the crocodile-god of Ancient Egypt, more so than any Pterosaur known to science. No creature-effects artisans are identified. The *Variety* review identifies much of the nature footage as coming from productions of the German company UFA. *Mystery of Life* was issued just half a dozen years after Darrow had defended classroom teacher John Scopes against charges of lecturing on matters Darwinian in defiance of Tennessee state law.

Murders in the Rue Morgue (1932)—Edgar Allan Poe's lurid tale, writ yet more so by director Robert Florey. Bela Lugosi takes his second star turn of the talking-pictures era as Dr. Mirakle, a fully fledged mad scientist intent upon proving a kinship between man and ape. A rejected early scenario took its cue from 1930's *Ingagi* in the suggestion of a mating between gorilla and woman, but this element was reduced to a mingling of the species via bloodletting. Where Poe's original concerns itself more with predatory rampages, Florey deepens the concern with renegade science; the film may well have a greater affinity with H.P. Lovecraft, whose expeditionary horror story "Arthur Jermyn" (a.k.a. "The White Ape"), concerning the corruption of an aristocratic bloodline with simian genes, dates from 1920.

The Monster Walks (1932)—Ape-escape shenanigans, mingled with the essential plotting of *The Cat and the Canary*—and a gloomy-mansion atmosphere to match. Mischa Auer plays a malicious half-wit who keeps the title creature caged against need of its predatory skills. Turns out that the monster is an adult chimpanzee, a sufficiently scary and dangerous animal in fact but too thoroughly well stereotyped as "cute" to register the desired impact. The film closes on a cringe-inducing racial gag, delivered in an unconscionable betrayal-of-culture by the black comedian Willie "Sleep 'n' Eat" Best—who would fare somewhat better once he had dropped the "Sleep 'n' Eat" moniker. See *Forgotten Horrors: The Definitive Edition*.

Curtain at Eight **(1933)**—Another man-killing chimp, after the fashion of *The Monster Walks*. See *Forgotten Horrors 2: Beyond the Horror Ban*.

Beast of Borneo **(1934)**—Mad-doctor expeditionary fare, as accounted for in *Forgotten Horrors: The Definitive Edition*.

The House of Mystery **(1934)**—Murderous trained gorilla stalks inhabitants of an accursed mansion. It all has to do with the pillaging long ago of an ancient temple and the slaying of a sacred ape. Details in *Forgotten Horrors: The Definitive Edition*.

The Gorilla **(1939)**—Third filming of the famous Broadway mystery-farce. The Ritz Bros., a comedy team stylistically stranded somewhere between the Three Stooges and the Marx Bros., play detectives investigating a threat against the life of Lionel Atwill. Bela Lugosi crops up to little advantage as a skulking servant.

The 1940s

One Million B.C. **(1940)**—D.W. Griffith's late-in-life affiliation with producer Hal Roach has provoked fascinated speculation all along. The film stars Victor Mature, Lon Chaney, Jr., and the tragic Carole Landis as tribal adventurers in conflict with nature and one another. It holds up as a cracking good entertainment despite its outlandish contradictions of natural history. The lizard-as-dinosaur effects work better than an attempt at a dinosaur mock-up.

Conventional wisdom supposes that Griffith (1875-1948), whose monumental career had run aground in 1931, was meant to be the director of *One Million B.C.* but wound up supervising portions of the film without acknowledgment.

Roach told us in 1992: "The story got out that I had hired [Griffith] to direct and that he didn't work out... [T]hat story has persisted, with nobody ever bothering to ask me what really happened."

Roach had long admired Griffith's genesis-of-man film, *Brute Force* (1913-14), to which he had even paid a spoofing tribute with 1927's *Flying Elephants*.

The lizard-as-dinosaur effects work better than an attempt at a dinosaur mock-up in *One Million B.C.*

"I asked Griffith if he'd like to help out...," Roach said. "He was a consultant... I wanted a Griffith kind of a *look* to the picture. So where better to get a Griffith look than Griffith himself?... And when the job was done, we parted ways cordially."

Stock footage was lifted for numerous lesser productions—most offensively, in a grindhouse titillator of 1970 called *One Million A.C./D.C.* Other pictures to use outtakes and/or stock footage from *One Million B.C.* include, in no particular order, *Tarzan's Desert Mystery*, *Gigantis, the Fire Monster*, Sam Katzman's first *Superman* serial, *Valley of the Dragons*, *Robot Monster*, *Teenage Caveman*, *Terror Vision*, *King Dinosaur*, *Untamed Women*, *Two Lost Worlds*, *Island of the Dinosaurs*, *Journey to the Center of Time*, *Adventure to the Center of the Earth*, *Vampire Men of the Prehistoric Planet*, *Planet of the Dinosaurs*, *She Demons*, *Jungle Manhunt*, *Smoky Canyon*, *Spaceship Sappy*, *The Ghost Jesters*, *In the Prehistoric Planet* and *Lost Volcano*.

Mr. Washington Goes to Town (1940)—A Mantan Moreland extravaganza, with the splendidly google-eyed comedian coming into possession of a haunted hotel, complete with gorilla. See *Forgotten Horrors 2*.

The *Stone Age Cartoons* Series (1940)—Eight Fleischer Bros. spoofs, explicitly prefiguring the Hanna-Barbera teevee series *The Flintstones*, but with abundantly more style and grace than Hanna-Barbera could muster. The assigned titles are jewels in their own right: "'Way Back When the Triangle Had Its Points"; "'Way Back When a Nag Was Only a Horse"; "Granite

Hotel" (parodying the famous *Grand Hotel*, naturally); "'Way Back When a Nightclub Was a Stick"; "The Foul Ball Player"; "The Ugly Dino"; "Wedding Belts"; "'Way Back When a Razzberry Was a Fruit"; "The Fulla Bluff Man" (a jab at the door-to-door Fuller Brush Co.; Red Skelton was still eight years away from his starring picture *The Fuller Brush Man*); "Springtime in the Rockage" (a double-pronged pun, nailing both the Stone Age and the popular tune "Springtime in the Rockies," with the feature-film *Springtime in the Rockies* yet two years distant); "Pedagogical Institution (College to You)"; and "'Way Back When Women Had Their Weigh."

The Ape (1940)—In which frustrated scientist Boris Karloff kills an escaped gorilla (played by Ray "Crash" Corrigan) and flays it to fashion an ape-suit for himself—the better to obtain human spinal fluids in a quest to combat polio. Dr. Salk was nowhere near this fascinatingly obsessed. See *Forgotten Horrors 2*.

Son of Ingagi (1940)—Spencer Williams, Jr., wrote the screenplay and tackled the key role of a bumbling detective who prefigures Williams' early '50s TV portrayal of Andrew Brown on *Amos 'n' Andy*. The marauding ape-man, who may or may not be a descendant of the fabled Ingagi,

is played by lanky Zack Williams, who may or may not be related to Spencer. Anyhow, the monster is known as N'Gena, which sounds a whole lot like the way we pronounce *Ingagi*. Not that we go around pronouncing *Ingagi* all that often. See *Forgotten Horrors 2*.

Fantasia (1940)—Walt Disney's arrogant bid to popularize Euro-classical music is a delight here, a snoozer there.

A scene from Stravinsky's *Rite of Spring*, from Walt Disney's *Fantasia*

One of the better sequences matches animated dinosaurs—painted, not dimensionally modeled, of course—with Stravinsky's *Rite of Spring*.

***Never Give a Sucker an Even Break* (1941)**—W.C. Fields' epic surrealist farce even allows the Great Man an encounter with a gorilla, played by Emil Van Horn.

***The Monster and the Girl* (1941)**—Persuasively directed by Stuart Heisler (of that splendid psychological thriller, *Among the Living*), this sentimentally grim tale of moral corruption, seduction of an innocent and righteous vengeance plays its defining absurdity—the transplanting of a human brain into the body of an ape—with utter conviction. The renegade surgeon is George Zucco, whose deeds force a straightforward proto-noir crime yarn squarely onto the horror-movie track. One of the better early-day *Batman* comic-book stories, "The Gorilla Boss of Gotham City," was inspired by *The Monster and the Girl*, with a nod toward *King Kong* for good measure.

***The Strange Case of Dr. Rx.* (1942)**—Mantan Moreland again, playing a resourceful valet to hot-shot detective Patric Knowles, who comes perilously near brain-swap surgery with a captive gorilla.

***Superman* Series: "The Arctic Giant" and "Terror on the Midway" (1942)**—These key entries in the Fleischer

Superman and the Arctic Giant

The Making of King Kong

Whackingham Creeps (Arthur Ray) and his gorilla in *Professor Creeps*

Bros.' cartoon series boast a formidable dinosaur on the one hand and a rampant ape on the other. George Turner believed that the fanciful ridgeback Tyrannosaurus-like creature of "The Arctic Giant" probably provided the inspiration for the looks of Japan's Godzilla.

John Shepperd, Lynne Roberts, George Zucco and J. Carrol Naish as the ape-into-manservant in *Dr. Renault's Secret*

Professor Creeps **(1942)**—Mantan Moreland yet again, in a preposterous delight about a mad doctor who is named Whackingham Creeps (Arthur Ray). His gizmos can transmogrify men into gorillas—among other creatures. See *Forgotten Horrors 2*.

Dr. Renault's Secret **(1942)**—Ape-into-human fantasies hardly come any grimmer than this tragic tale combining the myth of the White Man's Burden with traditional mad-doctor trappings and the transformation of a noble jungle creature into a cringing manservant with a murder-

Emil Van Horn and Bela Lugosi in *The Ape Man*

ous streak. The title accounts for two characters: George Zucco is Dr. Renault, and the all-'round dependable J. Carrol Naish is the Secret, a hulking handyman named Noel.

The Ape Man **(1943)**—Bela Lugosi is the title character/creature, a scientist reverted to an ape–like state as a consequence of his own reckless experiments. Much of the fun—although the undignified muddle can scarcely have been much fun for Lugosi—involves moments of guttural "conversation" exchanged between Lugosi and a caged gorilla, played by Emil Van Horn of *Never Give a Sucker an Even Break*. Lugosi could have used an even break right about here, but the performance finds him in control of his dignity if not his circumstances. See *Forgotten Horrors 2*.

Captive Wild Woman **(1943)**—Ape-into-human transformations seldom come off so well as in this launcher of a lesser franchise, which stars John Carradine as the scientist responsible and the lovely Acquanetta as the temperamental result. Director Edward Dmytryk had already become a founding father of the film noir movement with 1941's *The Devil Commands*; his less guardedly acknowledged noir classic, *Murder, My Sweet* (1944), had yet to come along when he tackled *Captive Wild Woman* as a potboiler—but a potboiler with style and a certain class. Acquanetta (Burunu Acquanetta Davenport) was born in Wyoming to an Arapaho father and an African-American mother, but Universal promoted her as a descendant of South American tribal royalty: "The Venezuelan Volcano."

Though hardly a particularly expressive screen player, Acquanetta had registered strikingly as a New York fashion model. Dmytryk told us in 1977 that he found her "a delightfully game talent, whatever her lack of range, and blessed with a very droll sense of humor." Once during the shoot, Acquanetta showed Dmytryk a photograph of her mother. "I did a double-take, and I said, 'Why—you're a *Negro*!' She grinned and said, 'Yeah, well, don't spread it around, or there'll be hell to pay with the Publicity Department. The studio wants people to think I'm some south-of-the-border Sun Goddess or somethin'.' What a delight Miss Acquanetta was!" Acquanetta repeated the role in 1944's *Jungle Woman*, a case of diminishing returns, then relinquished it to Vicky Lane for 1945's *Jungle Captive*.

***Crazy Knights* (1944)**—Shemp Howard, Billy Gilbert and Slapsie Maxie Rosenbloom play a Stooges-like threesome in this old-dark-house spoofer. And yes, there's a gorilla at large, courtesy of a circus subplot.

***Return of the Ape Man* (1944)**—Scientists Bela Lugosi and John Carradine resurrect an icebound cave-dweller, which winds up harboring Carradine's brain.

***The Hairy Ape* (1944)**—Eugene O'Neill's philosophical stage play, dating from 1922, concerns

the mental deterioration of an antisocial sailor, who is likened to a gorilla. In the original, the character is crushed to death in a confrontation with a genuine ape. This version softens the character's rebellious nature, breaks him temporarily with a hitch in jail, then restores his brutish confidence with a visit to a zoo. William Bendix stars.

Nabonga Gorilla (1944)—Odd and precarious bridge between *Tarzan* and *Mighty Joe Young* is a breakthrough semi-starring vehicle for Julie London, who would prove her greater worth to show business as a sultry torch singer. It all boils down to romance for Buster Crabbe and Miss London; a fatal thrashing-and-trampling for a pair of troublemaking explorers, courtesy of a heroic gorilla named Sampson; and a hero's death for the ape. All of which make it only too convenient for Miss London to give up her beloved jungle and accompany Crabbe back to civilization.

The White Gorilla (1945)—Drawn largely from a 1927 silent film, *The Perils of the Jungle*—to the extent of raising the question of why the more impressive original picture was simply not reissued with dubbing and sound effects. New footage features Ray Corrigan as an explorer who'll tell the world of how he was attacked by the legendary title creature. Executive producer Louis Weiss also had been responsible for the source film.

White Pongo (1945)—Not to be confused with *The White Gorilla*, this original production from brothers Sig Neufeld and Sam Newfield stars Richard Fraser and Maris Wrixon in the tale of a quest to find an albino gorilla of near-human intelligence. Neufeld had originally planned to call the film *Congo Pongo*.

Unknown Island (1948)—Costumed stunt-players appear as the monsters (augmented by unsophisticated puppetry) in this *Lost World* variant, which climaxes absurdly with a jump-cut battle

A victim is attacked by costumed monsters in *Unknown Island*.

between a supposed sloth—actually a red-haired ape from stuntman Ray "Crash" Corrigan's wardrobe of gorilla suits—and a vacantly staring Tyrannosaurus. Virginia Grey, Richard Denning and Barton MacLane star. The *Variety* critic found the monsters remarkably scary. Go figure.

Zamba **(1949)**—Ray Corrigan contributes his specialty as the title gorilla, which protects a feisty little kid (Beau Bridges, in an early assignment) from the perils of an African jungle.

The Great Rupert **(1949)**—Nary a gorilla nor any dinosaurs to be found, but a nifty job of dimensional animation (juxtaposed with trained-animal footage) from producer George Pal, in his first feature-lengther after several years' worth of *Puppetoons* short subjects. The story concerns a spirited squirrel that invades the orbit of struggling family man Jimmy Durante.

Africa Screams **(1949)**—Here we have the closest Bud Abbott & Lou Costello ever came to making a picture in the manner of the Three Stooges. It helps that co-founding Stooge Samuel "Shemp" Howard is on hand, along with Stooge-in-waiting Joe Besser. A Kong-like ape crops up for the rather abrupt finale; it is the work of Edward Nassour, better known for *The Beast of Hollow Mountain*.

The 1950s

Congolaise **(1950)**—This museum-sponsored trek into Equatorial Africa peaks with a visit to the land of a gorilla-obsessed tribe, whose ablest warriors kill a 775-pound specimen in an attempt to ape-pease their fertility god.

***Mark of the Gorilla* (1950)**—Sam Katzman's *Jungle Jim* series, starring Johnny Weissmuller, had plenty to do with apes, including this encounter with badmen masquerading as gorillas. The next year's *Jungle Manhunt* incorporates stock mock-dinosaur footage from *One Million B.C.* A later *Jungle Jim* entry, 1953's *Killer Ape*, is the most effective of the series, what with its gigantic ape-man marauder.

***Prehistoric Women* (1950)**—Cheesecake actioner-romance, with Allan Nixon and the lovely Laurette Luez.

***Two Lost Worlds* (1950)**—Stock footage from *One Million B.C.* more-or-less distinguishes this castaway adventure starring James Arness and Laura Elliott.

***Bride of the Gorilla* (1951)**—In which tropical planter Raymond Burr is hoodwinked by superstition into believing himself a gorilla.

***The Lost Continent* (1951)**—Cesar Romero toplines this *Lost World* knock-off from the low-budget producer Robert Lippert. The dinosaur footage *may* represent a salvage job from an unrealized project called *The Lost Atlantis*.³

***Bela Lugosi Meets a Brooklyn Gorilla* (1952)**—Duke Mitchell and Sammy Petrillo, doing a why-bother? imitation of the Dean Martin-Jerry Lewis *shtick*, find themselves stranded on a jungle island where Bela Lugosi is conducting forbidden experiments on gorillas.

***Port Sinister* (1952)**—In which RKO-Radio Pictures subsidizes a low-rent variation upon another lost-island theme, concerning a sunken pirate stronghold that re-emerges in the here-and-now, laden with 18th Century treasures and crawling with gigantic crabs. The creature effects are primitive, but the photography keeps the monsters helpfully obscured. James Warren and Lynne Roberts star.

***The Beast from 20,000 Fathoms* (1953)**—Ray Harryhausen's breakthrough picture in follow-through to *Mighty Joe Young*,⁴ about a prehistoric monster revived by an atomic explosion in the frozen North. The devouring of a New York cop, early along, and the Coney Island finale are among the most haunting images of the animated cinema. Anything and everything by Harryhausen will serve to honor and advance the legacy of *Kong*'s Willis O'Brien.

***The Neanderthal Man* (1953)**—Directed by the lapsed silent-era German master, E.A. Dupont, this somber fantasia on *Jekyll & Hyde* hangs on Robert Shayne's driven portrayal of a reclusive

scientist who wakes the beast in himself. Production resources fail the generally well-played yarn, what with a particularly inexpressive headpiece for the title character in lieu of a nuanced make-up job. But the lingering impression is one of a lurking, festering madness and an implied erotic deviance—especially in a quietly nightmarish sequence involving the discovery of photographs documenting Shayne's forbidden experiments upon a servant.

***Robot Monster,* a.k.a. *Monster from the Moon* (1953)**—Gorilla-suited space invader, wearing a breathing helmet for the sake of an extraterrestrial appearance, plots to decimate the human race. George Turner has recalled seeing *Robot Monster* "in what they called a 3-D process" at the State Theatre in Amarillo, Texas: "They had the red-and-green goggles, all the right trappings, but the image was as two-dimensionally flat as the screen itself." There appears to have been a more limited release elsewhere in a truer 3-D, for that is the format of a Rhino Home Video edition of more recent years. The deployment of three-dimensional effects is, however, so limited and unimaginative as to wonder why the low-rent production company even bothered.

***Godzilla* and Its Kindred Films and Sequels (1954 *ad nauseam*)**—All due respect: *Gojira* (meaning *gorilla-whale*) is the correct name, and there are perfectly valid genre-fied authorities who take these pictures vastly more seriously than we have any inclination to do. What was that we said about "no accounting for taste"—? The launcher of the Toho Pictures series fares rather better if seen in its Japanese cut, which packs a more nearly Homeric sense of doom than the Americanized *Godzilla, King of the Monsters*. It helps to remember that Gojira is an imaginative literalization of the nuclear-holocaust spectre, which took on the aspect of an epic meta-mythology in Japan following the climax of World War II. In further fairness yet, the *Godzilla*s and their close kin are immeasurably finer than their many Far Eastern imitators, as to which we *will* invoke George Turner's "the less said, the better" rule.

***King Dinosaur** should have been called **King Iguana Monster**.*

***Phantom of the Rue Morgue** (1954)*—WarnerColor-and-3D remake of *Murders in the Rue Morgue*, starring Karl Malden and Patricia Medina. Nor would the remakes stop here.

***Gorilla at Large** (1954)*—Mayhem on the carnival midway, with Cameron Mitchell and Raymond Burr. Originally in 3-D.

***Half Human** (1955)*—Americanized version of a Japanese picture, *Jujin Yokiotato*, about an abominable-snowman type of creature. The Hollywood tampering features John Carradine and Morris Ankrum.

***The Animal World** (1955)*—Hokey sham-documentary overall, but distinguished by a dinosaur sequence designed by Willis O'Brien and animated by Ray Harryhausen.

***King Dinosaur** (1955)*—Bert I. Gordon might at least have exhibited the gumption to call it *King Iguana Monster* and get the truth up front. His interplanetary-prehistoric fantasy was a big hit in its day, provoking many other such larger-than-live-action extravaganzas, including Gordon's own *Kong* variants *The Cyclops*, *The Amazing Colossal Man* and *War of the Colossal Beast*.

***The Beast of Hollow Mountain** (1956)*—Composite borrowing of Willis O'Brien's thwarted ideas for a cowboys-vs.-dinosaurs movie, as childishly interpreted by the rival animation shop of Edward and William Nassour. Lacks the finesse O'Brien would have brought to the table, but the action has its gripping moments and the creature is quite terrifying in its surreal way. Historically noteworthy, as our colleague Ryan Brennan points out, for its being the first model-animation/dinosaur film to be shot in CinemaScope. Brennan also cites the animators as Jan Baylor and Henry Lyon, who toiled anonymously; screen credit for the FX goes to Jack Rabin and Louis De Witt.

The Abominable Snowman of the Himalayas **(England; 1957)**—The ape-like Yetis, with their soulful eyes and Kong-like intelligence, cinch a decided kinship between this Hammer Films entry and the overall Spawn of Skull Island. Peter Cushing's star turn here occurred just as that fine actor was gaining a greater momentum with Hammer's revisionist *Frankenstein* and *Dracula* pictures.

The Giant Claw **(1957)**—Massive bird menaces civilization. Star player Jeff Morrow had envisioned a sleek, hawk-like creature while enacting his heroic role, only to learn too late—at a Westwood, L.A., preview screening—that cheapskate producer Sam Katzman had commissioned a cartoonish puppet from a Mexican creature shop. Morrow has told us he assumed a low profile for the duration of the showing, "and then tried to sneak out after the lights came up."

Monster from Green Hell **(1957)**—Anyone who resents being cheated of the opportunity to see *King Kong*'s gorge-full of gigantic spiders and insects—casualties of the cutting room—might be drawn to this time-waster, which concerns the spawning by radiation of a variety of big bugs in a tropical jungle. Scattered stop-motion animation, though hardly in the league of Willis O'Brien, justifies the indulgence.

The Black Scorpion **(1957)**—Willis O'Brien (with Peter Peterson) executes his own big-arachnid thrills, even to the extent of resurrecting surviving miniature creatures from the excised spider-pit sequence of 1933's *King Kong*. Though rushed and afflicted with low-budgetitis, the effects are

The silly giant bugs in *Monster from Green Hell* are hardly in the same league as the work of Willis O'Brien.

It's hard to believe, but *The Land Unknown* can be most entertaining.

impressive. Richard Denning is a heroic scientist. The scorpions are wondrously terrifying, and likewise for a spider and a fanciful caterpillar-worm creature.

The Land Unknown **(1957)**—Stuntman-in-monster-suit dinosaurs are usually a keep-away signal, but these creature designs are worth the viewing despite the usual problems with limited mobility and inexpressiveness. Jock Mahoney heads a small team of castaways at large in an anomalous tropical valley in the Antarctic. Robustly written and enacted, and most entertaining if seen in its original widescreen dimensions.

Rymdinvasion I Lappland*, a.k.a. *Invasion of the Animal People **(U.S.-Sweden; 1958-62)**—Ape-like creature from space on rampage. Which is halted, in Jerry Warren's U.S. patchwork re-edit, by scientists John Carradine and Robert Burton.

Monster on the Campus **(1958)**—Blood from a coelacanth—a prehistoric Devonian fish, found alive in a Real World revelation of the 20th Century—infects scientist Arthur Franz, transforming him into an ape-man. Jack Arnold's grim thriller plays the preposterous notion with a straight face, much as E.A. Dupont had done with *The Neanderthal Man*, although Franz' nice-guy martyr-to-science portrayal lacks the mad ferocity of Robert Shayne's *Neanderthal* enactment. Paddy Chayefsky's big-deal *Altered States* (filmed in 1980) is a heedless and self-important derivative of both films.

Teenage Caveman **(1958)**—Roger Corman nods to *One Million B.C.*—while prefiguring the twist ending of *Planet of the Apes*. Robert Vaughn stars. Strategic use of footage from *One Million B.C.*

***The Bride and the Beast* (1958)**—Like American-International's *The She-Creature* (1956), this filming of an original scenario by Edward D. Wood, Jr., takes its cue from the celebrated Bridey Murphy case: a matter of reincarnation if not *pre*incarnation. Charlotte Austin plays a newlywed beauty whose honeymoon travels take her to Africa—where, in some past life, she seems to have been a gorilla. Perverse and absurd, but also as sterile and insipid as one expects from Ed Wood, whose extravagantly wasted existence is practically a textbook case of self-delusion.

***Behemoth, the Sea Monster/The Giant Behemoth* (1959)**—Eugene Lourié, director of *The Beast from 20,000 Fathoms*, commits self-plagiarism with this tale of a radiation-spawned dinosaur at large in England. The master, Willis H. O'Brien, handled the animation on a demeaningly low budget and a tight deadline, but he came through with some agreeable results. The American proxy title is a marvel of redundancy.

***The Giant Gila Monster* (1959)**—Only marginally of interest as a dinosaur-type picture, with a big lizard on a slow-moving rampage through the boondocks of North Texas. From Southwestern broadcasting tycoon Gordon McLendon, who also delivered *The Killer Shrews* and *My Dog Buddy* during this ill-advised span as a movie producer.

***Journey to the Center of the Earth* (1959)**—Pretentious knockoff of Jules Verne, starring James Mason, Pat Boone and the expected (not to say desired) complement of falsely enlarged lizards. The musical score is the anomalously excellent work of Bernard Herrmann. Verne's story would seem to have fared better in a Spanish production of 1909.

The 1960s

***The Lost World* (1960)**—Claude Rains heads a distinguished cast—Michael Rennie, Jill St. John, David (Al) Hedison—that is rendered all but irrelevant by the awkward lizard-as-dinosaur effects. Producer Irwin Allen later cobbled together an episode of the teleseries *Voyage to the Bottom of the Sea* with footage from this particular *Lost World*; Hedison also starred in the *Voyage* series.

***Dinosaurus!* (1960)**—Good-looking but only laboriously mobile, the creatures here later wound up as stock-footage elements of a television series, *It's about Time*. Gregg Martel steals the show (that is, as far as the target juvenile audience of the day was concerned) as a disoriented caveman, thawed out into the present day. A climactic cliffside duel between dinosaur and earth-moving machinery is clearly a knockoff of the never-completed original *Gwangi*.

Konga **(1961)**—Forgiveness is a mighty stretch for this English-made entry, which requires a tolerance of both its ape-suited King Kong *poseur* and the producer Herman Cohen, who entertained no higher ambitions here than pure knock-off. Star player Michael Gough is another matter, however. Gough's irascible Grand Manner dignity as a lust-driven mad scientist is a wonder to behold, however shabby the circumstances.

Gorgo **(1961)**—Director Eugene Lourié, of *The Beast from 20,000 Fathoms* and *Behemoth, the Sea Monster*, returns to the well yet another time too often to re-state the theme with man-in-a-monster-suit variations. The first creature seen, echoing the force-of-nature extravagances of the *Godzilla* pictures, towers past 50 feet. Its parent, which arrives as if summoned, is more in the 250-foot range.

Reptilicus **(1962)**—Sid Pink's Scandahoovian snake-o-saurus epic is as laughable in execution as it is apocalyptic in intentions. The set-up promises visceral thrills aplenty as a drilling rig turns up fragments of mangled flesh from a long-buried creature. Better the creature should not have regenerated itself from these morsels, for it proves entirely goofy—a scowling abomination that spews toxic mucous while flailing about like an unattended Wooster Booster fire-hose nozzle. Handily as silly as the tree-demon of 1956's *From Hell It Came* or the Mexican-made bird puppet that Sam Katzman imposed upon *The Giant Claw*. George Turner called this one "Rib-Tickle-Us," alluding to its essential ridiculosity.

Black Zoo **(1963)**—Producer Herman Cohen again wastes the snide artistry of Michael Gough as the chief of a Los Angeles zoological garden where big cats and a gorilla—the hirsute hair-suit from *Konga*, neatly cleaned and pressed but scaled back to conventional height—are dispatched to attack his enemies. Gough is excellent, as usual, and Sinatra *poseur* Rod Lauren registers memorably as an ill-treated keeper.

The Ape Woman **(1963)**—Trans-species erotica and embittered social satire from Carlo Ponti's French-Italian coalition. Ugo Tognazzi plays a corrupt entertainer who exploits, then marries, a befurred woman (Annie Girardot). She dies in childbirth, whereupon Tognazzi places the corpses of mother and infant on view for a price. The American edition faked a happy ending.

King Kong vs. Godzilla and ***King Kong Escapes*** **(1963-67)**—Japan's Toho Pictures embellished its *Gojira/Godzilla* mythology with *Kingu Kongu Tai Gojira* (*King Kong vs. Godzilla*) and *Kingu Kongu No Gyakushu* (*King Kong Escapes*). Though worthy enough within their cultural context, these monster-suited wrestling matches only demean the legacy of *Kong*'s Willis O'Brien, who struggled in vain for years to find a berth for his more artistically ambitious follow-throughs. Toho's appropriation of *other* O'Brien concepts, in the films that became (in America) *Frankenstein Conquers the World* and *War of the Gargantuas*, are unconscionably awful mis-representations of O'Brien's thwarted dream to pit King Kong against a gigantic Frankenstein Monster in a legitimately animated feature.

Sound of Horror **(1964)**—Mexican-made cheat only *tells* us there is a dinosaur on the loose—but also informs us that the dinosaur is invisible.

One Million Years B.C. **(1966)**—Ray Harryhausen's animation renders this remake the superior of Hal Roach's original, although the human casting of the original remains tops. Raquel Welch's star turn in this one is no distraction from the creature-shop work, although her image here yielded one of the most prevalent cheesecake pinups of the period. The direct sequel, 1970's *When Dinosaurs Ruled the Earth*, features stop-motion animation by Jim Danforth. Fragments of *One Million Years B.C.* show up in Stanley Kubrick's *A Clockwork Orange* (1971).

Journey to the Center of Time **(1967)**—Near-remake of the more nearly cerebral *The Time Travelers* (1964), with a screenwriter in common. This version's special effects, ranging from "alien" "attacks" to "dinosaur" "rampages" (we use the terms advisedly) are entirely covered by the stock-footage department.

La Horripilante Bestia Humana/Night of the Bloody Apes **(Mexico; 1968)**—Quease-inducer from Mexico mingles the gorilla-at-large motif with a *Frankenstein* conceit: A transplanted ape-heart transforms a young man into an agent of rape and murder.

Island of the Lost **(1968)**—*Swiss Family Robinson* meets *The Lost World* in John Florea's desultory contribution to a genre, with anthropologist Richard Greene and company stranded on an island of mock-prehistoric artifice.

It's Alive! **(1968)**—Texas filmmaker Larry Buchanan's minimalistic and nihilistic filming of a Richard Matheson story, which has to do with a dinosaur kept hidden away by a rustic eccentric. The film's conception of a dinosaur is more of the stuntman-in-a-wetsuit variety, conceptually very close to that of Buchanan's *Curse of the Swamp Creature*. So lacking in the basic niceties of production values as to seem as surreal as a case of the D.T.'s, but some of the acting is another matter: Bill Thurman, later of Peter Bogdanovich's *The Last Picture Show*, is a study in barely controlled rage as the creature's captor, and Annabelle Weenick (a.k.a. McAdams) registers poignantly as a human captive of the madman.

Mad Monster Party? **(1968)**—And yes, the question-mark is correctly a part of the title. A Rankin-Bass production for the big screen, from that studio's heyday of televised holiday specials (including the splendid *Rudolph, the Red-Nosed Reindeer*), boasts the same quality of model animation. Boris Karloff lends his voice to his own caricatured likeness, and a climactic pageant of creatures includes a representation of King Kong himself.

The Valley of Gwangi **(1969)**—We're generally taking it on faith, here, that the reader will have a working familiarity with Ray Harryhausen. Even so, certain films of the second-generation master bear singling out within the present context. This cowboys-and-dinosaurs epic, descended from an abortive project by Harryhausen's mentor Willis O'Brien, turned out quite well, with a nicely characterized title creature and the most dazzling show of airborne animation since the Pterodactyl scene in *King Kong*. The real show-stopper is a tiny horse, fully animated, that shows up as a tantalizing prelude to the monsters.

The Mighty Gorga **(1969)**—Pageant of nightmarishly awful amateurism finds a desperate showman (Anthony Eisley) on the trail of a gigantic ape. The creature's costuming is shabby, with a particularly immobile face, and the lack of even rudimentary miniature work begs the viewer to accept that the ape is as big as everybody seems to believe. Appeal denied.

The 1970s

The Private Life of Sherlock Holmes **(1970)**—George Turner loved this under-appreciated film from Billy Wilder, for it immerses itself in two of George's favorite areas of interest: Conan Doyle's infallible English detective, and a prospect of survival by at least one species of dinosaur. That latter would be the Loch Ness Monster, which George (like many other adherents of the legend) believed likely to be a Plesiosaur. Loch Ness figures significantly in the film's view of Holmes as a character of brooding complexity. Robert Stephens stars, with Colin Blakely, Genevieve Page and Christopher Lee.

***Trog* is better than it has any right to be.**

***Trog* (1970)**—Unearthed prehistoric ape-man advances, then complicates, the ambitions of anthropologist Joan Crawford. Better than it has any right to be, for Herman Cohen as a producer existed at the mercy of his own hired talents—if they showed any artistry, then he came off looking okay—and approached the cinema more as hucksterism than as art. And so what of it? Enough artistry-by-default shows through in the Cohens to justify their existence as more than ticket-selling come-ons. And blessings upon Cohen regular Michael Gough, who weighs in here with a pleasingly antagonistic supporting performance. Dinosaur footage from *The Animal World* is worked in as an anachronous flashback.

***The Creeping Flesh* (1972)**—Ape-like resurrection from a prehistoric age proves to be the very embodiment of the vicious colonialism with which the British Empire once enslaved much of the planet. Peter Cushing is a benevolent scientist, Christopher Lee an unscrupulous relative who precipitates the mayhem. A provocative mingling of sensationalism and contemplative intellectualism.

***Panico en el Transiberiano/Horror Express* (1972)**—Cushing and Lee again, as rival scientists who encounter a hostile, ancient intelligence with the ability to possess various beings. Starting with a prehistoric ape-man, in whose frozen carcass the being has been stranded for centuries, it leaps from passenger to passenger aboard a hurtling train.

***Frankenstein and the Monster from Hell* (1973)**—The *Kong*-like notion of a brutish body motivated by a finer intelligence distinguishes this late entry in Hammer Films' *Frankenstein* series. Peter Cushing reads a certain brutishness into his own recurring role of the renegade surgeon.

The 1976 *King Kong* remake will be remembered mainly because of Kong's fall from the World Trade Center.

The Land That Time Forgot **(1975)**—Poorly suited monster stand-ins upstage ostensible hero Doug McClure in this English-made kid-stuff adaptation of Edgar Rice Burroughs. Companion films are *At the Earth's Core* and *The People That Time Forgot* (1976-77)

King Kong **(1976)**—Dino DeLaurentiis' over-hyped remake is essentially as lousy as *The Mighty Gorga*, although it camouflages its shabbiness with mock-epic bombast and the emerging star-appeal of Jessica Lange and Jeff Bridges. An Oscar unaccountably was awarded to the special-effects unit, whose desultory work is vastly less convincing than the painstaking trickery of the 1933 original. Just like George Turner said: The less said, the better.

A-P-E **(1976)**—Designed to cash in on the well-publicized DeLaurentiis *Kong*, this Korean-made misfire is actually the more earnest film. Decent opening, with some ape-vs.-shark and ape-vs.-

ship business, but a prompt deterioration. Special-effects historian Ryan Brennan notes that "you can see the stuntman through the rips in the underarms of his costume." Originally in 3-D.

The Crater Lake Monster (1977)—Prehistoric embryo, provoked into a milennia-overdue hatching and understandably angry as a consequence. Difficult in the watching, to be charitable.

Where Time Began (1977)—Made in Spain as *Viaje al Centro de la Terra*, and just as cheesy as anything Hollywood's Poverty Row ever cranked out. Jules Verne travelogue menaces inexpressive human players with back-projected fauna and ineptly crafted monsters. Also shown as *Journey to the Center of the Earth*.

The Last Dinosaur (1977)—TV-movie anti-thrills, with Richard Boone as a wealthy huntsman looking for a Tyrannosaurus to bag. As if the phony T-Rex costume weren't baggy enough already.

Planet of Dinosaurs (1978)—Unaccountably well-done stop-motion piece, with a nicely designed array of dinosaurs and a fairly involving expedition-type yarn. Starring James Whitmore.

King of Kong Island (1978)—*Frankenstein*-styled experimentation on gorillas yields brain-altered specimens that run amok. The less said—and you know the rest.

The 1980s

Caveman (1981)—Ringo Starr has the title role in this well-done spoofer, along with Barbara Bach and the creature effects of David Allen.

Q (1982)—Larry Cohen's tale of a prehistoric reptile—the *Q* stands for the Aztec monster-deity *Quetzalcoatal*—at large over New York echoes *King Kong* with imaginative variations. The

William Katt and Sean Young in *Baby,* from Touchstone Films

creature chooses the pinnacle of the Chrysler Building, as opposed to the Empire State Building or the World Trade Center, as its lair, and it makes its final stand against an armed attack from within, rather than from assault planes. Michael Moriarty is pure film noir antihero as the Carl Denham of the piece, an opportunistic petty crook who exploits his unique knowledge of the beast's hiding place.

The Man with Two Brains **(1983)**—Carl Reiner's mad-scientist comedy, starring Steve Martin, features an intelligent ape character—a convincingly articulated costume fabricated by Kevin Brennan, a cousin of Ryan Brennan. George Turner worked with Reiner on the prior Martin starrer, 1982's *Dead Men Don't Wear Plaid*.

Baby... Secret of the Lost Legend **(1985)**—Middling good special-effects romp from Disney, about a death-defying save-the-Brontosaurus campaign in Africa. Surprisingly mature in tone and content, though visually disappointing.

Massacre in Dinosaur Valley **(1985)**—Low-budgeter of considerably less ferocity than its title, with Michael Sopkiw.

My Science Project **(1985)**—Confiscated alien machinery from a top-secret federal-government base rips open the very fabric of time, enabling schoolkids to commune with prehistory.

One Crazy Summer **(Paramount; 1986)**—Teen-age misfit comedy from director Savage Steve Holland, starring John Cusack and Demi Moore—well before their breakthroughs to stardom. Little in the way of story, but abundantly fine sight-gags including an epic slapstick set-piece that Hal Roach might have envied: Comedian Bobcat Goldthwait is attired in a Godzilla-like costume, lurking about a ritzy party involving the unveiling of an elaborate architect's miniature of an upscale construction project. A smoker discards a lighted cigar, which lands in the mouth of Goldthwait's costume. The ersatz Godzilla, spewing smoke, tramples blindly onto the scaled-down property mock-up.

King Kong Lives! **(1986)**—Dino DeLaurentiis could scarcely resist another stab at *Kong*, even if he had to wait 10 years to take it. Direct sequel finds Kong in recovery from the big fall, to be matched up with a lady ape of compatible proportions. Brian Kerwin and Linda Hamilton account for the human-interest element, minus any particular *interest*.

Link **(Cannon Group; 1986)**—Call it *Psycho*-gone-ape, and you won't be far off base. A calculatingly intelligent orang named Link, comprehending that his privileged life as a house-servant to scientist Terence Stamp is endangered, pulls a Bates-and-switch act. Directed by the Australian Richard Franklin, an Alfred Hitchcock disciple who had helmed *Psycho II*, and rather a more worthwhile film than the critical consensus has been predisposed to acknowledge.

Amazon Women on the Moon **(1987)**—John Landis' outlandish smorgasbord-spoof hints at a prehistoric survival in a segment sending up *Ripley's Believe It Or Not!*—with Jack Palance's conspicuously absurd speculation that Jack-the-Ripper was actually the Loch Ness Monster.

Gorillas in the Mist **(1988)**—The tragic case of animal-rights activist Dian Fossey, as played with a thoroughgoing immersion in character by Sigourney Weaver. First-rate creature effects bespeak a tremendous sympathy with the mountain gorillas of Africa.

The 1990s and Early 2000s

The Lost World **and** ***Return to the Lost World*** **(1992-93)**—These slight evocations of Conan Doyle attempt to do the story justice but fail all 'round in the visual-effects department. Burly John Rhys-Davies, however, is quite another matter in his robust and antagonistic portrayal of Prof. Challenger.

Behind the scenes on *Jurassic Park*

Dinosaur Island **(1993)**—The combined exploit-ationary genius of Jim Wynorsky and Fred Olen Ray makes this throwback more a cheesecake-verging-on-softcore oglers' delight than any kind of action-adventure piece.

Jurassic Park **(1993)**—Breakthrough use of digital-effects technology, combined with more traditional forms of animation and life-size mechanical effects. Steven Spielberg's spectacular adaptation

Jurassic Park II: The Lost World

of the Michael Crichton novel was hailed by Ray Harryhausen as "the closest we are likely ever to come to seeing these dinosaurs in the flesh." Harryhausen added: "But y'know, our pictures were so much more *personal*." Sequelized with *The Lost World: Jurassic Park* and *JPIII*.

Carnosaur (1993)—From the Harry Adam Knight novel—it predates Crichton's *Jurassic Park*—about the growing of new dinosaurs from retrieved DNA. Ryan Brennan points out that Knight is actually John Brosnan, himself an authority on special-effects moviemaking. This provocative, often shocking, entry from the Roger Corman low-budget machine stars Diane Ladd as a scientist who intends to overrun civilization with the flesh-eaters. Ladd's daughter, Laura Dern, is of course a leading player in *Jurassic Park*. Sequels: *Carnosaur 2* (1994) and *Carnosaur 3: Primal Species* (1996).

The Scout (1994)—Albert Brooks' tribute to *King Kong*: Brooks plays a big-league baseball scout who finds a magnificently gifted player (Brendan Fraser) performing for the sheer love of the game in a Third World backwater. The ill-advised importing of the player to civilization causes severe emotional repercussions. A rare homage/analogy that actually works—somewhat better than all those *Wizard of Oz* hammerings in David Lynch's *Wild at Heart*—although Brooks trowels on the *Kong* references just a bit much.

The Flintstones (1994)—Smash-hit box-office rubbish, with John Goodman and Rick Moranis galumphing through the Fred-and-Barney roles. Deliberately unrealistic dinosaur effects compound the film's fundamental sin of "cartooning the cartoon," as it were. A prequel, *The Flintstones in Viva Rock Vegas*, reared its ugly head in 2000 A.D.

Godzilla (1998)—Digitally generated effects, for the most part, offer a welcome alternative to the *Godzilla* tradition's costume-party mayhem. This American-made licensing of a Japanese property also finally exhibits the sense to scale down some lesser monsters for a more terrifying intimacy with the victimized humans. Matthew Broderick stars as a scientist hell-bent for a confrontation.

Mighty Joe Young (1998)—Finely wrought gorilla-effects work, with impressive human-being characterizations from Charlize Theron as giant ape Joe's protector and Bill Paxton as a helpful outsider. Remade from the 1949 original[5] with all due Environmental Sensitivity.

The Cider House Rules (1999)—This Oscar-bait gem has nothing and everything to do with *King Kong*. The story takes place largely in a New England orphanage, where physician-in-charge

Michael Caine occasionally entertains the troops with a faulty 16-millimeter print of *Kong*. The screening ritual takes on a significance greater than mere entertainment value in the lives of some of the children.

***Walking with Dinosaurs* (1999)**—The excellent BBC series approaches the subject with an eye for documentarian realism—just like any other top-shelf nature film, except with the need to re-imagine a prehistoric reality. Extremely lifelike computer-generated dinosaurs, augmented by mechanized and hand-operated puppetry, appear perfectly integrated with genuine locations, with interactive water, foliage and landscapes. A condensed version graced American cable television in 2000 A.D.

***Dinosaur* (2000)**—The Disney machine retools its shopworn *Bambi* apparatus for a pixel-perfect digital-realm yarn in which yet another young creature of the wild must struggle, by turns boldly and preciously, to find its place in the Grander Scheme. The picture actually looks pretty impressive on first blush—until the various prehistoric beasts open their yaps to spew forth an array of Hollywood celebrity voices. Even larger problems lie in the forcibly cute facial expressions and body language, and in the suggestion of trans-species social-support groups in what can only have been a kill-or-be-killed age. *Kong* artisan Marcel Delgado, who championed ferocity and despised forcible cuteness, would have been appalled.

1 See "Preludes, Prologues and Progeny."
2 Likewise.
3 Likewise.
4 Likewise.
5 Likewise.

Spawn of Skull Island

The Launching of Cooper-Schoedsack Productions

> Holy mackerel—you think I want to drag a woman along?
> —Carl Denham in *King Kong*

"The biggest money picture of the year will be *King Kong*," David O. Selznick told his fellow executives at RKO-Radio Pictures, Inc., at the beginning of 1933. Selznick had great faith in this picture, even though it had been in production for more than a year and consisted, at this point, of 238,000 feet of unedited negative from which a 10,000-foot feature film had yet to be extracted.

Selznick's faith was not universally shared: B.B. Kahane, president of RKO, felt certain that *Kong* would prove strictly a novelty, doomed to flop with the mass audience. Selznick had weathered plenty of heat for allowing more than $1,000,000 to be spent on King Vidor's *Bird of Paradise*, a sum the studio could scarcely hope to recoup in paid admissions. *King Kong* had not cost nearly so much, but it had been responsible for the abortion of one major production—and it was an open secret that some of its costs had been cribbed from the budgets of other films.

And then there were the producers, Merian C. Cooper and Ernest B. Schoedsack—a colorful pair of vagabonds more willing to take risks than to seek any understanding of the intricacies of big-studio dealings. Kahane also considered the film's story preposterous.

King Kong is a fantastic fable, all right, but it is only *slightly* more fanciful than the genuine stories behind it, a conglomerate of Epic Adventures that had their origins many years before the fact in the whims of Fate that brought together the curious assortment of talents necessary to *Kong*. The initial links were forged at the close of the First World War, when Capt. Ernest Beaumont Schoedsack, a six-foot-six movie cameraman from Iowa, was mustered out of the U.S. Army Signal Corps in France. He had run away from his parents' farm at 14 and pursued a variety of jobs around the country before becoming a cameraman with Mack Sennett's comedy-pictures studio. Schoedsack had been a sergeant in the National Guard Corps of Engineers at the start of the war, but he was required to shed his stripes to assume the rank of private in order to enter the newly formed and ill-organized Signal Corps.

Following a stint as an instructor, Schoedsack traveled to Paris, and after much complaining he received permission to journey to the front. He hitched a ride to the combat zone, only to be turned back by military police because his superiors had neglected to assign him a helmet and a gas mask. He salvaged a damaged helmet and a mask from roadside graves and continued toward Ground Zero—where of course his heavy camera equipment compromised his mobility and safety.[1]

The Armistice found Schoedsack unwilling to return home. He became

Ernest B. Schoedsack

The Making of King Kong

interested in the plight of war-torn Poland, which declared its independence on the day of the Armistice, November 11, 1918. A huge German force required evacuation from what had been the Western part of the old Russian Empire, the several provinces lying between Poland and the new Russia. As the Germans quit each strip of land, it was quickly reoccupied by the Red Army. The tense situation was welcomed both by Germany, which stood to benefit from a Russian-Polish conflict; and by Lenin, who was hell-bent upon toppling the barrier that separated the Soviet Union from revolutionary Germany.

Schoedsack cast his lot with the heroic underdog Poles. He joined a Red Cross relief mission and began helping Polish refugees escape Russian-occupied territory. The country was seething with ethnic and political hatreds and plagued with famine, disease, unemployment, unstable currency and a near-total loss of agricultural and industrial capabilities. The Czechs and the Germans were still making trouble. By the end of January, the Red Army had advanced to the Brodno-Brest-Kovel Line, and on February 9 the Polish counter-offensive began. Schoedsack, finding his charges endangered by Czech combatants while on his first mission, arranged for a Swiss military guard to escort the group out of the hostile areas.

In mid-February, Schoedsack arrived in Vienna, which was occupied by the Italian Army. It was a bitter winter, and most of the city's trees were being felled for firewood. Occupation troops roamed the streets, smashing and looting. At the railroad station, while preparing to return to Warsaw, Schoedsack encountered a short, emaciated and battle-scarred young American who carried a Naval Academy sword. He was clad in a filthy rag-tag uniform and wore mismatched French and German boots. The Americans struck up an acquaintance, and Schoedsack, for once in his life, was in the company of a man as remarkable as himself.

Capt. Merian Coldwell Cooper, from Jacksonville, Florida, had just been repatriated from a German prison. He had sold his sword when he left Annapolis in 1914 after one rambunctious escapade too many; now he had found the weapon and bought it back. After Annapolis, Cooper was a sailor; a newspaperman in Minneapolis, Des Moines, San Antonio and St. Louis; and a Georgia National Guardsman in the campaign against Pancho Villa. Later, he joined the Infantry and then transferred to the Aviation Corps, earning his symbolic wings at Mineola in September of 1917. He served on the Western Front as a special tactical observer with the 20th Aero Squadron on the First Day Bombardment, flying low over German lines to mark enemy placements for the Allied gun crews. Gen. Billy Mitchell took note of Cooper's heroism and put him in charge of tactical missions in the Battle of St. Mihiel—a veritable suicide mission, in which many of Cooper's comrades were killed. Cooper's plane was shot down, crashing within Allied lines.

Later, in the Argonne, Cooper was brought down in flames. Refusing to abandon his injured gunner by parachuting to safety, Cooper piloted the burning plane to a crash landing behind German lines. Both men survived but were captured and remained in a prison hospital—where a German surgeon restored Cooper's burned face—until a month after the Armistice. Cooper was reported dead; his reappearance led at length to an official attempt to award him the Distinguished Service Cross. He refused to accept the honor, which he considered a slight to his fellow fighting men: "We all took the same risks," said Cooper.

Like Schoedsack, Cooper saw in the Bolsheviks a potential enemy. When he arrived in Vienna, Cooper was on his way to Warsaw to join the American Relief Association, which had been organized by Herbert Hoover to aid the famine-stricken pockets of Europe.

Schoedsack remained in the thick of the war until its end, convoying supplies across a still-hostile Germany, driving ambulances, shooting movies for the Red Cross and making a dangerous journey to the Black Sea to bring back Polish refugees from the Russian oilfields.

Cooper, sensing a need for action more direct than the American Relief Association could provide, went to Paris in August to join with Maj. Cedric E. Fauntleroy—late of the Lafayette Escadrille and the American Air Service—in forming a group of American war pilots to be incorporated into the Polish Army. Their 10-man Kosciusko Aerial Squadron, named for the Polish national hero who had aided Washington during the American Revolution, reported for duty on

October 1 as a fighting unit of the Polish Air Force, with Fauntleroy in command. The Americans, after a cold and frustratingly idle winter, began flying patrols over the Bolshevist lines. The mission was far from glamorous: Pay ranged from $8 to $10 a month; disease was rampant; death was everywhere. Three American pilots were killed, another crippled beyond recovery and two others wounded.

Schoedsack was in the Ukraine when the Polish lines broke southwest of Kiev and the great retreat began. Kiev was occupied by Polish troops under Gen. Edward Smigly-Rydz, who resisted courageously until ordered to evacuate and retreat westward. On June 12, the withdrawal from Kiev began.

"I had a great time in Poland and the Ukraine during that Polish-Russian campaign," Schoedsack recalled with his characteristic flair for understate-

Merian C. Cooper

ment. "The high point of the Polish adventure was, for me, at Kiev, when the great retreat began. I was the last to get across the great Dnieper Bridge, and the excited Poles blew it up on my heels, but I did get the chance to turn around and get the thing coming down with a motion-picture camera. After that, we had quite a time getting through the Commie lines and back to Warsaw."

Unknown to Schoedsack, Cooper also was at Kiev, flying escort for bombers and machine-gunning Russian steamboats. Cooper's plane was the last to leave the makeshift airfield, taking off just over the heads of the advancing cavalry.

Upon Fauntleroy's promotion to Aviation Chief of the Second Army on July 3, Cooper succeeded him as Squadron Commander. Cooper flew more than 70 strafing missions against Gen. Budenny's advancing forces until, on July 13, his aircraft was disabled by ground fire in Galicia. Cooper made a forced landing 20 miles from Rovno and, pursued by Cossacks from Budenny's cavalry, fled into a clump of woods. Surrounded, he put up a losing fight. The Cossacks were about to kill him when one soldier who spoke English intervened.

Cooper identified himself as Cpl. Frank R. Mosher—the name was stenciled on the second-hand underwear the Red Cross had given him. He was taken to Bolshevik headquarters and questioned by Budenny, who asked him to join the Red Army as a flight instructor. When Cooper refused, he was held prisoner for five days before he could make good an escape. Two days later, with an injured leg becoming gangrenous, Cooper was recaptured and taken under guard to Moscow.

The scrappy Poles retreated but slowly. Capt. Arthur D. Kelly of the Kosciusko Squadron was killed on the day following Cooper's departure. Fauntleroy was wounded by machine-gun fire a short time later—but soon became airborne again.

The tides turned in August, when President Pilsudski led a counter-offensive that resulted in an amazing series of Polish victories. As tens of thousands of Russian soldiers fled across Lithuania and East Prussia, the Poles advanced rapidly and by October had regained most of the territory occupied during 1919. An armistice was signed at Riga on October 12.

Cooper remained in prison because the Russians considered him an American criminal rather than a Polish war hostage. He was moved from jail to jail from month to month, finally arriving at Wladykino Prison, a work camp near Moscow. He spent much of the winter shoveling snow from the railways. No word had been received of him other than reports from peasants who had witnessed his capture, and the Russians were unaware of his identity. Cooper felt sure that he would be executed should it become known that he was commander of the despised American flying squadron. As efforts to secure his release were intensified, it became clear that his masquerade would soon be found out.

With two Polish lieutenants named Zalewski and Sokolowski, Cooper escaped on the night of April 12, 1921. The fugitives moved afoot until morning, then hid in the woods and slept during the day. At nightfall, they followed the railroad tracks because they had no compass. When they met peasants, Cooper represented himself as a German prisoner on his way home. Sometimes, they hopped aboard freight trains, and on the third day they found themselves in a boxcar full of Russians. Cooper made choking sounds to feign muteness.

After five more days, they were forced to travel on foot again, through forests and swamps. The bridges were under guard and one of the Poles could not swim, and so long detours proved necessary. They had only enough money to buy two pounds of bread, and when this was gone they traded articles of clothing for enough crude, homemade black bread to keep them alive. Once, they were obliged to hide for 36 hours above a brick stove in a peasant's hut; on another occasion, they spent a night lying in a pool of water.

By the time they reached the Latvian frontier, they had barely enough clothing to cover their bodies. A professional smuggler agreed to guide them across the border in exchange for shoes and an overcoat. Cooper relinquished his shoes and cut off his shirttail to bind his feet. Sokolowski gave up his coat. As they neared the border, the smuggler threatened to turn them over to the Bolsheviks unless he received further compensation. They told him they would kill him if he betrayed them. After studying their grim faces, the crook gave them no more guff.

The group reached Latvia after a journey of 14 days and 500 miles. A few days later, at Belvedere Palace in Warsaw, President Pilsudski presented Cooper with the Virtuti Militari or Cross of the Brave, Poland's highest honor, and Gen. Haller awarded him the Polish Service Medal. A statue was raised in Cooper's honor.

On his way to the United States, Cooper again met Schoedsack—this time in London, where Schoedsack was working as a newsreel cameraman for a company owned by Lewis J. Selznick, father of David O. Selznick. Recognizing their shared appetite for danger, adventure and natural beauty, the men discussed creating together an epic film of some little-known part of the world, but their financial straits rendered the idea hardly feasible. Cooper settled down temporarily in New York City as a feature writer for the *Times*, meanwhile studying maps at the American Geographical Society.

Schoedsack soon joined the Near East Relief for what he described as "a very interesting involvement" in the Graeco-Turkish War of 1921-22. He was present when the Greeks were driven out of the seaport of Smyrna (later known as Izmir) on the Agaean Sea. This savage engagement destroyed more than three-fifths of a city of some 400,000 souls, and a large portion of the Greek population was massacred. Schoedsack's films of the embattled city were shown widely, but he did far more than crank a camera. Years later, a delegation captured Schoedsack as he was leaving New York on the *Arcturus* expedition—*captured* is the correct word, for Schoedsack tended to flee in the face of any sort of publicity or accolade. He had been the object of a long search, and now, cornered, he was presented the Distinguished Service Medal "for humanitarian work in Smyrna and the refugee camps of the Near East." It was declared that "he risked his life in the performance of duty and was responsible for saving many lives."

Cooper, meanwhile, encountered Capt. Edward A. Salisbury, owner of the 88-foot, 83-ton *Wisdom II*, a two-masted schooner used for ethnological expeditions. Salisbury had been touring the world for two years under the auspices of the Southwestern Museum of California, and now he had returned to seek additional financial support. He intended to produce motion pictures, a book and a series of magazine articles about little-known places.

Salisbury was a skillful promoter with vaguely respectable credentials, but as a writer and cameraman he was quite limited. In September 1922, he hired Cooper as First Officer—actually, his ghost-writer—for $25 a month. When a cameraman quit after an ordeal by typhoon, Cooper cabled Schoedsack, who journeyed from Turkey to Africa to join the cruise.

"We were both just hired hands on somebody else's expedition," Schoedsack explained, describing Capt. Salisbury as "bumptious, ignorant and boastful."

"Arrayed in his gold-braided uniform and enthroned in a large wicker chair on the afterdeck," Schoedsack said of Salisbury, "he liked to entertain the local authorities—and their wives—with tea or cocktail parties while he regaled them with tall tales of his exploits. The business of procuring literary materials and motion-picture films was secondary, and he would not allow enough time to do justice to whatever opportunities presented themselves, however golden. There was always that next port to be gotten to."

The balance of the ship's company included four Americans, a Danish youth, two Samoan deckhands and a comical Ceylonese cook known as Shamrock. Most of the original crew had jumped ship in the Pacific. The *Wisdom II* was a rusty old tub, though solidly constructed.

The expedition saw strange sights, indeed, including the Pygmies of Murderer's Island—where widows would wear the skulls of their husbands as necklace-like adornments—but the high point was a week in Addis-Ababa. There, Ras Tafari, Prince Regent of the Abyssinian Empire (later, Emperor Haile Selassie of Ethiopia), assembled his mounted knights for review before Schoedsack's camera. The future Lion of Judah was but ill impressed with the pretentious Capt. Salisbury, but he entertained Cooper and Schoedsack in barbaric splendor and decked them out in full military regalia. Salisbury was anxious to press onward, but Cooper and Schoedsack managed to get photos that would adorn a celebrated three-part series in *Asia* magazine. They also shot abundant movie footage, from which they planned to edit a feature film.

The *Wisdom II* left Dkibouti, French Somaliland, in February 1923, sailing up the Red Sea into a monsoon that left most of the crewmen dizzy and retching. An erratic, zigzag course carried the ship dangerously near the coast of Yemen. During the night, while the ship was moving at full sail on a landward tack, the navigator anxiously watched for the Mocha Lighthouse, which was supposed to be visible for 18 miles. Suddenly, the ship struck a submerged reef. Stuck fast, broadside to the wind, the *Wisdom II* was buffeted by heavy waves. All hands were required to haul down the sails. A huge comber swept the ship off the reef, ripping away the leaden keel. She was anchored before she could be driven ashore. Now trapped in a lagoon beyond the banks, the ship wallowed helplessly, striking bottom with jarring force with each new swell. Water poured into the bilge through the holes left by the sundered keel-bolts.

Morning revealed greater terrors yet: Arab pirates, who had destroyed the Mocha Light, were lurking on the beach. A fresh tide, however, made it possible to get the ship under way. The anchor line was cut and the auxiliary motor started. The ship scraped over the reef and then was free. The bilge was hand-pumped sufficiently to allow partial repair of the leaks, and the top-heavy craft headed Northward into the monsoon.

After the company had made port at Jedda, Schoedsack shot the first movies of pilgrims journeying to Mecca. The ship struggled on through the Suez. Unable to find a stopping place to make repairs, the crew crossed the Mediterranean to land in Savona, Italy, during April 1923. With all hands relocated to a villa, the *Wisdom II* went into the presumable safety of dry dock. Workmen accidentally cut into a gas pipe in the bilge, and when a watchman entered the hold that night his lantern triggered an explosion. The ship burned—and with her, much of the footage that had been intended to become the first Cooper-Schoedsack production. Enough of the film survived, however, that Salisbury eventually could cobble together such pictures as *Gow, the Head Hunter* and *The Lost Empire*[2] (1928-29).

Even before their Abyssinian footage was lost, Cooper and Schoedsack had begun planning another production. By the time they made their way to Paris, they had determined to make a film depicting a struggle against nature—using as protagonists some nomadic tribe that must migrate to survive. The partners had no intention of making a commonplace travelogue. Their plan was to tell a story of dramatic conflict, much as Robert Flaherty had done in *Nanook of the North*. At this early stage of a long and happy partnership, Cooper and Schoedsack already had cinched the methods that would characterize all their work together: Fundamental aspects of production would call for full collaboration, with specialized duties divided according to the preferences and abilities of each.

Among Cooper's assets was a knack for selling ideas to investors. He returned to the States to secure backing. In New York, Cooper met a friend, Mrs. Marguerite Harrison, who had published books and articles detailing her adventures in Russia and the Orient. Cooper had first met the courageous Baltimore widow at a Red Cross-sponsored dance in Warsaw during the early days of the Russo-Polish conflict. Mrs. Harrison, who came from a wealthy shipping family, had been a world traveler since girlhood, but when fortunes turned and her husband died following a long illness, she supported herself and her teenaged son by working as a journalist. Mrs. Harrison combined reporting with espionage on missions to postwar Germany and, later, Moscow. She smuggled food, tobacco, clothing and money to American and British prisoners including Cooper until she, too, was jailed. Cooper, grateful beyond all good sense, had organized a daring attempt to rescue her: Bribed guards and Polish agents were to deliver Mrs. Harrison to a field outside Moscow so that Cooper might fly in, pick her up and return to Warsaw. It proved fortunate for them both that Mrs. Harrison was deported to America before Cooper could launch his foolhardy plan. Mrs. Harrison parlayed the experience into a lecture-circuit career, but she soon grew weary of merely talking about her exploits. She wanted a new adventure.

Cooper returned to Paris with $10,000, which was supposed to finance an entire expedition including the purchase of 40,000 feet of 35-millimeter film stock. To Schoedsack's dismay, Cooper also brought along Mrs. Harrison, who had raised half of the money. Schoedsack was opposed to taking a woman along on a dangerous journey, but the die had been cast.

The trio went to Turkey, planning to cross Anatolia to Kurdistan and there film the migration of a mountain tribe. Their youthful enthusiasm was scarcely shared by the new Turkish government of Mustafa Kemal Ataturk. Having just fought a bloody war with the Greeks and the British-French Alliance, the Turks viewed all Westerners with suspicion. Secret agents spied on the Americans while the bureaucrats stalled for weeks without granting permission to continue Eastward beyond the capital of Angora (later, Ankara). While waiting, Schoedsack shot newsreel and travelogue footage to keep the money coming in.

The expeditioners dodged surveillance just long enough to flee to the Taurus Mountains, hiding in a village where they became snowbound. The peasants took them hunting for mountain goats and sheltered them from the police. When the snow broke, the party crossed over to French-occupied Syria and thence across the desert—in an ancient Model T Ford—to Baghdad. Schoedsack went on to Mosul in search of a Kurdish tribe for the film. But the Kurds were fighting the British, and it proved impossible to photograph their usual folkways.

Meanwhile, Cooper learned from Sir Arnold Wilson, High Commissioner of Iraq, about the Bakhtiari tribes, who lived under an ancient feudal system with little interference from the central government. Hastening to the tribal grounds, the film company arrived just as the migrations were about to start. Most of the money and about half the film stock had been depleted—but there was no turning back because there was not enough cash for a return trip.

With no supplies of their own, the party joined the Baba Ahmedi tribe and lived as the nomads did, Cooper and Schoedsack bunking on the ground (or snow) with only a blanket each while Mrs. Harrison carried a small tent. Their diet consisted of sheep's buttermilk and stone-hard bread. Mrs. Harrison cracked a tooth while savoring her first Bakhtiari meal. Cooper later told the *New York Times* that Schoedsack damaged his revolver while trying to crack a chunk of bread; this nugget of information appears to be hyperbole, for Cooper, Schoedsack and Mrs. Harrison reported elsewhere that they took no guns along on the migration—the Turkish authorities had confiscated their weapons. Their shoes were their only concession to luxury; the Bakhtiari traveled barefoot. The Americans won the respect of their 30,000 hosts by being just as tough as the most hard-boiled of the natives.

Early on during the march, because of the withering heat of the day, camp was broken after midnight and new campsites established before sunrise. Schoedsack puzzled over how best to photograph "many spectacular things that took place in almost complete darkness."

One solution, he told us, was that "we would ride out ahead... and wait for the tribes to come along just as the sun rose, and get our one shot... and that would probably be all for the day."

Merian C. Cooper, Mrs. Marguerite Harrison and Ernest B. Schoedsack on the *Grass* expedition.

The crossing of the mighty Karun River provided ample spectacle. The boatless fording required five days and saw hundreds of animals and at least two people swept away in the icy torrent. Cooper called it "the greatest piece of continuous action I have ever seen."[3]

As the trek proceeded into ever-higher altitudes, the weather became progressively colder until, at last, the caravan reached the 12,000-foot barrier of Zardeh Kuh. The crossing of this frozen wall became one of the most spectacular motion-picture sequences of all time. For three days, Cooper and Schoedsack photographed the massed parade, each day seeking a higher vantage. On May 29, 1924, Cooper entered these words in his diary:

> Schoedsack and I are camped halfway up Zardeh Kuh. It is blowing like the devil, and cold. We are out of grub... and we are going to sleep a bit chilly here tonight almost at the top of Persia... But both of us are at the peak of happiness. We have done it. We have seen as great a struggle for existence as there is. And we have it for the screen! Tomorrow, the summit![4]

Mrs. Harrison, Cooper and Schoedsack were the first foreigners ever to cross the Zardeh Kuh. Schoedsack reached the other side with 80 feet of film remaining, which he used to shoot an ending. From Isfahan, Cooper cabled several editors in New York and received enough advance money to bring the partners home.

"We'd never developed any film," Cooper told a Los Angeles Film Club audience in 1964, "but we didn't have enough money to hire the pros. So we took our year's work and developed it ourselves—didn't lose a foot of film, either." While Cooper and Schoedsack edited the footage, Marguerite Harrison wrote articles, returned to the lecture circuit and soon, to the relief of her co-producers, dropped out of the moving-picture business.

The editing complete, Cooper began lecturing with the film at colleges. Schoedsack, in order to bring money into the destitute company, signed on for six months as cinematographer with the New York Geological Society's oceanographic expedition to the Sargasso Sea and the Galapagos Islands, sailing February 10, 1925, aboard the S.S. *Arcturus*. Among those to whom Cooper showed the Persian epic was the pioneering picture-show mogul Jesse L. Lasky, who promptly recognized the adventurers' dedication and genius.

1 A Kevin Brownlow documentary piece, *The War, the West and the Wilderness*, also relates this account of Schoedsack's adventures.
2 See "Preludes, Prologues and Progeny."
3 Cooper, in his 1925 book, *Grass*.
4 Likewise.

An Adventure for Three

> If it's there, you *bet* we'll photograph it!
> —Carl Denham in *King Kong*

Jesse L. Lasky, vice president of the Paramount-Famous Players-Lasky Corp., premiered the Cooper-Schoedsack production of *Grass* on February 19, 1925, at the New York Plaza Hotel. The critics were delighted. When the film opened on March 30 at the Criterion Theatre, with symphonic accompaniment by Dr. Hugo Reisenfeld and Dr. Edward Kilenyi, it proved a sensation. A long New York run repaid the $10,000 investment and brought in a modest profit, but without box-office stars or romantic interest the film was hardly a smash in national release. Lasky was sufficiently pleased, nonetheless, that he offered to subsidize another Cooper-Schoedsack expedition.

Meanwhile, Schoedsack's involvement in the *Arcturus* venture also proved important to the future of Cooper-Schoedsack Productions, for it served to bring aboard a new teammate.

Ruth Rose, historian and research technician of the expedition, was raised in the theatre by her father, Edward Rose, a leading producer and dramatist. Ruth, who lost her mother while still a youngster, grew up in the company of the great stage personalities of the day. Her idol and mentor was William Gillette, the author and actor whom history counts as the stage's finest Sherlock Holmes. As a petite and beautiful young woman, Miss Rose appeared in numerous plays and acted in films at Fort Lee, New Jersey. She had been leading lady to Otis Skinner for three seasons when suddenly the Actors Equity strike of 1919 caused the shutdown of Broadway's show houses.

Ruth Rose's career changed directions abruptly when she heard about the New York Zoological Society's Tropical Research Station at Kartabo, British Guyana, and its director, Dr. William Beebe. Beebe was charismatic, suave, articulate and equally at home in the jungle, under the sea or in upper-crust Manhattan society.

"When I read about William Beebe's work at Kartabao, I said, 'That's the man I'm going to marry!'" Ruth Rose Schoedsack told us many years after the fact, adding: "And that's why I quit the stage to join an expedition." Beebe, of course, would prove more a mentor than a marriage prospect.

Although she had no scientific training, Ruth applied to Dr. Beebe, volunteering to do whatever unskilled tasks might be required. Impressed by her zeal, Beebe hired her. Soon, she was hard at work with six technicians at capturing, looking after and studying an astonishing variety of creatures from a vast and largely unexplored jungle whose only other human inhabitants were Akawi Indians and the inmates of a penal colony.

Displaying remarkable adaptability and gumption, Miss Rose soon became a valued member of the research team, working in a bat-infested laboratory at an abandoned mining camp. She overcame a fear of serpents by making a pet of a small whipsnake; a short time later, she helped to capture alive a gigantic boa constrictor. During her several years with Beebe, she survived earthquakes, army ants, tropical storms, eye-to-eye encounters with jaguars and meetings with innumerable exotic snakes. Her writing abilities were recognized early on, and she was made historian of the Beebe expeditions. Magazines

A page from the *Hollywood Reporter*'s *King Kong* layout featuring Ruth Rose

76 *Spawn of Skull Island*

published her reports, and she wrote portions of some of Beebe's popular books. A love of all living things, even those that inspire fear in humankind, is evident in her essays.

The *Arcturus* sailed 12,000 miles and crossed the Equator 18 times. Schoedsack, while not at all stimulated by his chores as a photographer of marine fauna, was charmed by the lovely Ruth Rose. By the time Schoedsack returned to New York, Cooper was straining at the leash. Paramount had okayed the idea for their second Natural Drama—a term coined by Cooper and Schoedsack.

The theme would be man's conflict with the jungle. In their search for the most untouched of jungles, the producers went to Bangkok, the capital of Siam (later rechristened Thailand). For weeks, they searched for a fitting locale—Schoedsack exploring Indo-China while Cooper investigated Lower Siam. Each encountered too

Cooper and Schoedsack on the *Grass* expedition.

many big-game hunters and automobiles to suit the project. Then, they heard tales of the Nan district of Northeastern Siam, said to be the most forbidding jungle on the planet. While Cooper remained in Bangkok to secure the king's permission, Schoedsack journeyed as far northward as the country's single-line railroad would carry him, then continued by horseback, on foot and by log canoe to the Laotian Province of Nan.

Here, separated from the rest of the country by mountains, jungles and 67 river crossings, Schoedsack found a tropical forest that no white hunter had penetrated. From the only white inhabitants, a Presbyterian missionary and his assistants, he learned that nearly 400 villagers had been killed by tigers and leopards during the preceding five years. In some settlements, the mortality rate laid to predatory cats was 20 percent. Lao houses were elevated onto posts as a precaution. Although native hunters occasionally killed leopards with primitive flintlock rifles, little effort was made to control the tigers. This was because of a religious belief that whoever killed a tiger would be changed into a God Horse (tiger, that is) as a mount for the slain animal's Demon Spirit. It was considered dangerous even to utter the word *suar* (tiger), for should the spirit overhear and take offense, a terrible vengeance would ensue.

Here, indeed, was an ideal setting for Natural Drama: a jungle whose gigantic tangle of undergrowth was popularly regarded as a living evil, dominating the very souls of its inhabitants.

Cooper arrived presently, and production began on the film that would be known as *Chang*, the title being a Lao word meaning *elephant*. The partners cast a central family of characters from among photogenic tribespeople; concocted a story sufficiently flexible to allow for actual situations that might arise; and began filming sequences with regard for dramatic development. The other players were the beasts of the jungle—cats, pythons, bears, monitor lizards, buffalo, elephants and monkeys. Comedy relief was the province of Bimbo, an affectionate white gibbon whose antics have the appearance of real acting ability. Bimbo became known among the filmmakers as "the Wally Beery of the jungle." It proved fairly simple to capture most of the animal actors—but not so the tigers, which eluded Cooper and Schoedsack through cunning and were made more elusive by the passive interference of superstitious native crewmen. Cooper and Schoedsack took care not to kill any animals, except when necessary for protection.

The most notorious man-killer in the region was a legendary tiger known as Mr. Crooked, whose tracks—rendered distinctive by an inward-turning paw—had been found at the scene of many a tragedy. The cat was reputed to be as big as a house, and many people feared to venture outdoors. Cooper, no stranger to gross exaggerations himself, enlisted local help by boasting that he would take the tiger's spirit upon his own shoulders. Inasmuch as the filmmakers had no experience with big cats and the Laotians preferred to kill tigers rather than imprison them,

Cooper (top) and Schoedsack (bottom) pose for publicity photos to promote *Chang*.

it was with a great deal of difficulty that the producers captured Mr. Crooked and several other known man-eaters. A significant drop in the local mortality rate became apparent. It was later reported by the governor that the work of Cooper and Schoedsack reduced by two-thirds the number of deaths caused by tigers in Nan.

Although some writers have suggested otherwise, there is no trick photography or studio footage used in *Chang*, nor were any tame animals used. Schoedsack's equipment consisted of two tripod-mounted French Debrie cameras—400-foot-capacity, hand-cranked models with no provisions for special effects. Cooper sometimes cranked the second camera when he wasn't needed to man a rifle. Photography in the dense jungles was extremely difficult and was done for the most part with the f4.5 lens wide-open. The slow-speed orthochromatic film was overexposed purposely so that a soft developer could be used to produce a negative of fine definition. The climate made it mandatory to keep the film in sealed, dehumidified containers until time to shoot.

No telephoto lenses were used. Schoedsack had long since decided that the obvious safety advantage was less important than the greater field of vision, definition and steadiness afforded by the normal two-inch lens. All the photography was done at perilously close range, primarily from camouflaged shelters and pits placed near animal trails and watering-holes. These stake-outs required days, even weeks, of waiting for the right animal to happen by.

During one sequence, a tiger chased two natives up a tree. Sensing a chance to get an unusual shot for intercutting, Schoedsack built a lightweight platform in the tree, 13 feet above ground; Cooper, armed with a rifle, was stationed in another tree. Native bearers chased a tiger into the vicinity. Schoedsack, lying on his perch alongside the camera, infuriated the tiger by proffering a loud razzberry. Angrily circling the tree, the beast leaped and fastened its claws in the trunk, reaching for the platform. Cooper took aim, but Schoedsack called to him to hold his fire. Tigers are not supposed to be climbers, but this one left claw-marks *11 feet above ground*—so close to Schoedsack that its face fills the frame. After dropping to the ground, the tiger had to be killed to halt its rampage.

More harrowing yet was Schoedsack's method of filming an elephant stampede. A pit was dug about five feet square by seven deep, and roofed with logs. A log turret in the center permitted the camera to peek out, with head-room for Schoedsack to view the action. The turret was necessarily weaker than the rest of the roof. Natives then drove a herd of elephants toward—and over—the covered pit. Schoedsack, showered in debris, wondered if the roof would hold. After the herd had passed over, several elephants turned around and started back. One of them stepped on the turret, sending a hail of splintered logs onto Schoedsack. The elephant pulled its foot free and continued along.

Pythons attacked three native crewmen. One night, a 20-foot constrictor invaded Schoedsack's room, which was built on 30-foot stilts. Cooper's expert marksmanship more than once saved Schoedsack and others of the company.

Other perils were more difficult. The coming of the monsoon forced the producers to move to a different patch of jungle. A cholera epidemic killed seven native helpers. Schoedsack fell victim to malarial fever, and during 11 of the 14 months he was in Siam he often worked while on the verge of delirium. Both men returned to New York so emaciated as to be almost unrecognizable, but they brought back the picture they would consider their best over the long haul.

"Coop and I made *Chang* with the raw materials we found there and no help whatever," Schoedsack told us in 1969. "There was hard work, sweat and malaria—but in dollars, it only cost what it takes to operate a [second-unit, or backup, shoot] for two days."

While editing *Chang* with Cooper in New York, Schoedsack broke the news that he was going to marry Ruth Rose. Cooper was appalled at the thought of having another woman on the team, after having herded Marguerite Harrison across the Zardeh Kuh. Nevertheless, the wedding took place. Cooper's fears were not lessened by Mrs. Schoedsack's declaration that her lanky husband would no longer be called "Shorty" and thereafter would be nicknamed "Monte." Nor was Cooper's morale improved when Jesse Lasky agreed to pay Mrs. Schoedsack's expenses on the next Cooper-Schoedsack expedition for Paramount.

Chang opened at New York's Rivoli Theatre on April 28, 1927, with intercut title cards (a silent-era device for putting words on the screen) written by the popular novelist Achmed Abdullah. Hugo Riesenfeld's score was performed by an augmented symphony orchestra with two six-foot thunder drums concealed behind the screen to emphasize the tumult of the elephants' stampede—Sensurround in prototype. The sequence was further dramatized by the use of Paramount's Magnascope gimmick, a process that opened the screen from its normal size to full proscenium width as the first elephant started to run over the camera. After 300 pachyderms had trampled the village, the Magnascope closed back down onto a scene of a monkey playing with a shard of pottery.

Chang was enormously successful, justifying Lasky's faith in the Cooper-Schoedsack company. The reviews were almost without exception enthusiastic, and the Motion Picture Academy nominated *Chang* in the category of Most Artistic Production; it lost, reportedly by a single vote, to F.W. Murnau's *Sunrise*. (Schoedsack, unaccountably, did not learn of the nomination until 1968.) Paramount's chiefs were ecstatic: A genuine epic that cost only $60,000 would be immensely profitable.

Lasky next invited the producers to turn some favorite story of theirs into a movie, using that distinctive style. Cooper and Schoedsack wanted to try something new, combining a Natural Drama with in-studio production capabilities to adapt A.E.W. Mason's novel of African warfare, *The Four Feathers*.

In the late spring of 1927, the partners set out for Africa. From Dar es Salaam, they went south to the mouth of the Rovuma River and thence upstream to shoot jungle footage. One of these scenes shows two white men being chased by Sudanese slavers into a parched jungle. The natives torch the woods, and the flames drive out a horde of terrified baboons. After crossing a river, the

Ernest Schoedsack and Merian Cooper pose with Jean Arthur using native swords and shields from Africa which were seen in *The Four Feathers*.

fugitives weaken a bamboo bridge, which collapses when the apes swarm onto it. Then a herd of hippopotami stampedes over a bank and submerge. When the pursuers try to ford the stream, the hippos drive them back.

Neither hippos nor baboons are as cooperative as humans, and as a consequence several months were required to film these scenes. The District Commissioner, trying to impress Cooper and Schoedsack with the dangers of working with hippos, showed the Americans a photograph of a woman bitten in two by one of the creatures. The artists were undeterred. Schoedsack later went strolling down a narrow trail and met a hippo, weirdly limned by moonlight. "It's a strange feeling," he would recall—with characteristic understatement.

A large number of the ponderous beasts were rounded up and herded into a corral of thick walls, five feet tall. By morning, all had climbed out and another round-up proved necessary. They were made to stampede over the embankment by crowding them against a log barricade that could be cut free on a signal, permitting the animals to slide into the river. Cooper was standing against these logs when Schoedsack called to him. The man who was assigned to release the logs misunderstood "Coop!" for "Cut!"—and severed the trigger rope. Logs and hippos plunged down the bank, and Cooper leaped to safety.

The Schoedsacks were filming once from a platform in the river when Ruth moved suddenly, jarring the camera. Schoedsack began bawling her out, then realized she had nearly been seized by a hippo. The stampede had to be staged 13 times before the desired result was obtained.

Cooper soon changed his mind about Ruth Rose Schoedsack. She proved an invaluably worthy member of the team, managing the commissary, keeping the payroll, acting as doctor for some 200 native employees and manning guns and cameras as necessary. Ruth fired only one shot in Africa, but it saved someone from becoming a crocodile's lunch. She never forgave herself for killing the croc.

In December, they sailed north along the coast on the Indian Ocean, through the Gulf of Aden and the Straits of Bab el Mandeb, then up the Red Sea to Port Sudan. Christmas was spent aboard a Mohammedan ship crowded with pilgrims bound for Mecca. Overland they trekked 700 miles southwest to the Nuba Mountains, thence north and east to the Atbara River and at last into the Red Sea Hills, home of the famed Fuzzy-Wuzzy fighting tribes.

They found that the old slave port of Suakin, which had been deserted during the Dervish uprisings, lay unaltered, preserved perfectly by the desert. The clothing of the Sudanese likewise had not changed in over a century.

It was in the Red Sea Desert that the battle scenes were staged, with hundreds of descendants of the fanatical Dervish warriors re-creating the warfare of Kipling's day in the actual locale. The running charge of the Fuzzy-Wuzzy army, photographed from many angles, is a terrifying spectacle rivaling in excitement the elephant stampede of *Chang*.

"When we were filming the native charge," explained Schoedsack, "we had certain ones picked out to fall as though they were shot. Well, their idea of a fall was to select a likely spot, brush away the chunks of lava, and lie down carefully. Coop was furious, so he decided to show them how to fall. He ran a ways, clutched his heart, spun and took a spectacular fall—and nearly cut his leg off on the lava. It was an amazing piece of luck that we had a visitor who'd just arrived, who turned out to be a doctor. They rushed Coop off to the hospital, and for the next several weeks I was working alone."

The war scenes were long in the making because most of them had to be shot during the early-morning hours. Soon after sunup, the temperature soared to around 110 degrees, making it impossible to deploy people, camels and horses.

August 1928 found Cooper and Schoedsack arriving in California to begin directing dramatic scenes at Paramount and in the desert between Indio and Palm Springs, where the company built a replica of the British fort seen in the African footage. The cast included Richard Arlen, Clive Brook, William Powell, Theodore von Eltz, Noah Beery and Noble Johnson. The feminine lead was an up-and-coming player from Canada, Fay Wray. Johnson and Miss Wray thus began long associations and lasting friendships with Cooper and the Schoedsacks.

Adolph Zukor rejected a pitch to make *The Four Feathers* as a talking film, in that day when Hollywood had yet to accept sound as more than a novelty. Zukor appointed as supervisor the young David O. Selznick, for whom Schoedsack had shot some documentary films. Through careful planning, Cooper and Schoedsack were able to cut together their African, California desert and studio scenes without resorting to composite photography. The intricate and continual intercutting is matched so expertly that many critics and historians have boneheadedly declared that only a few shots were made in Africa.

After the producers had edited *The Four Feathers* and left Hollywood, Selznick decided additional scenes were needed and assigned the chore to Lothar Mendes; these unimaginative hackwork inserts, compounded by over-obvious title cards, only damage the show. The dumbing-down of the culture is no new development, nor was the generally over-praised David O. Selznick the only studio chief to harbor such contempt for his audiences' intelligence. By the time *Feathers* was ready to screen, silent pictures were extinct except in smaller theatres that had not yet installed sound equipment. An excellent musical score by William Frederick Peters and a sound-effects track by Roy Pomeroy were added. The film had its gala launching at New York's Criterion on June 12, 1929. Paramount again used the Magnascope process to enhance the spectacle of the native charge.

"David Selznick made a great mistake in putting in all that titling and those phony scenes directed by Mendes," Cooper told us. "It was a much better picture when Monte and I left it, when I went to New York to go into aviation and Monte went off to make a picture [*Rango*] in Sumatra. However, I was confident that the stuff Monte and I had shot would be sufficient to make it a success—and it was, despite the fact that it was the only silent picture playing in New York when everything else was a talkie."

Cooper's venture into aviation was the outgrowth of investments he had begun making in 1927, using profits from *Grass* and *Chang*, in a mutual fund restricted to aviation stocks. Not even the Depression could halt the growth of the airlines, and Cooper soon found himself deeply involved in the future of the flight industry. These interests made it essential that he remain in New York, even though Lasky was eager to get another Cooper-Schoedsack picture under way.

Schoedsack, unable to adjust to the confines of civilization, accepted Paramount's offer. After conducting research at museums and geographical societies in New York, he wrote his own shooting script and set out with Ruth and a cameraman in May 1929 for the Dutch East Indies, where they would film *Rango*.

Cooper, despite his success, was painfully aware that life as a Big Business executive was a pallid anticlimax to a decade of high adventure. It would not be the end. There would be other movies, other expeditions to unexplored worlds. In his spare time, Cooper studied maps at the Explorer's Club and the National Geographic Society.

It was during this dormant period that Cooper's imagination caught fire with what was to become the most celebrated of his creations. It was here that Cooper began dreaming up *King Kong*.

"*There* Is the Ultimate in Adventure"

> This isn't your standard ape, sir. It's between 18 and 19
> stories, depending on whether there's a 13th floor or not.
> —From Bob Newhart's "Night Watchman" Routine

"To thrill myself," Cooper replied when asked why he had dreamed up *King Kong*. "To please the public, too, of course, but I also wanted to please myself. I wanted to produce something that I could view with pride and say, '*There* is the ultimate in adventure.'"

And so it happened that—while Schoedsack was shooting his latest Natural Drama in the wilds of Sumatra—Cooper turned to a wholly imaginary adventure that would magnify the spirit of the Cooper-Schoedsack expeditions. His first concept, which would become the very industry's *dernier cri* in high adventure, was of a gigantic ape, 40 or 50 feet tall, perched atop the tallest of buildings, battling a fleet of warplanes.

One of Cooper's friends in New York was W. Douglas Burden, the noted explorer and naturalist, whose experiences in Brazil, Nicaragua and the Far East were the essence of adventure. Cooper was particularly intrigued by Burden's account of an expedition for the American Museum of Natural History to the Lesser Sundra Islands of Malaysia, undertaken at the same time *Chang* was shooting. The highlight of the safari was a collecting trip to the island of Komodo, home of the fabled Komodo dragons, the world's largest lizards.

Komodo itself was something of a lost world, a weird, volcanic jungle inhabited by only a handful of Malay convicts exiled there by the Rajah of Sumbawa. The Komodo lizards were first remarked to civilization in 1912 by P.A. Ouwens. A Dutch scientist from Java, Ouwens had followed native legends of living dragons to their source. Douglas Burden was the first to bring the great reptiles to civilization, the beautiful habitat group at the American Museum comprising specimens bagged during the 1926 expedition. Two other dragons were brought back alive and exhibited at the Bronx Zoo, but they languished and died in short order.

"Komodo was relatively unexplored, only a few white men having landed there," wrote Burden in the August 1927 issue of *The National Geographic* magazine. "With its fantastic skyline, its sentinel palms, its volcanic chimneys bared to the stars, it was a fitting abode for the great saurians we had come to seek. Deer, wild boar, water buffalo and game birds were abundant...

"The lizards, which attain a length of 10 feet and a weight of 250 pounds, are known to science as *Varanus komodoensis*. They are vicious, carnivorous reptiles, which attack their food much as the great flesh-eating dinosaurs must have done, ripping off great chunks with their sharp, recurved saw-edged teeth and swallowing them whole, bones and all.

"The Varanus lizards first appear as a genus in the early Eocene, some 60 million years ago; so that we have here not only the largest, but also the oldest, of living lizards," Burden explained.

Burden's description of the nearby island of Wetar also suggests an ideal setting for mystery and the possible discovery of prehistoric survivals:

"As it arose out of the sea, the island appeared a vast mass of torn and splintered mountains. The central portion is unexplored, and small wonder, for the tumble of jagged peaks presents insurmountable barriers..." Burden noted that Bali and other islands of the region were inhabited by Malays, but that "Wetar, on the other hand, is inhabited by Papuans, who belong to a large group of peoples classified by anthropologists as Oceanic Negroids. The Malays, being a mixture of Mongoloid-Polynesian, have no Negroid blood."

It is hardly a stretch to imagine how great a lure these islands exerted upon Cooper while he was beached in New York, wishing he could be alongside his friends in Sumatra, giving the Bronx cheer to enraged tigers. His own jungle experiences; his agonizing need to explore unknown places; and—finally—his talks with Burden combined to form the genesis of *King Kong*. To his original idea of a gigantic gorilla pitted against modern man, he added other elements basic to the story: There would be the discovery of gigantic prehistoric reptiles, existing on a remote island "'way west of Sumatra"; an isolated society of blacks who worship strange gods; an expedition to capture an awesome monster to amaze the public; and finally the inability of such a creature to survive as a captive of man. Even the name, *Komodo*, possessed an exotic resonance that influenced the christening of his key player. In a 1933 press release, Cooper said:

> I got to thinking about the possibility of there having been one beast, more powerful than all the others and more intelligent—one beast giving a hint, a suggestion, a prefiguration of the dawn of man.
>
> Then, the thought struck me: What would happen to this highest representation of prehistoric animal life in our materialistic, mechanistic civilization? Why not place him at the pinnacle of the tallest building, the symbol in steel, stone and glass of modern man's achievement and aspiration, and pit him against modern man?
>
> As I mulled the story over in my mind, I saw that I had conceived the climax rather than the beginning. How would King Kong get there? I saw that man would have to go to Kong's world first. I conceived him as impregnable to gunfire and too huge and swift to be killed by sword at close quarters.
>
> How, then, to capture him? I had it! Schoedsack and I had gone to remote places to make wild-animal pictures. Kong would be found in such a remote place—a survival of the early world—and he would be captured through a fragile and beautiful girl. There is only one thing that may undo a brute, provided the brute approximates man, and that is beauty!
>
> It is beauty that kindles the spark of something the brute never has sensed before. He is amazed, he is subdued, by this thing of beauty. So I decided it would be Beauty, personified by a girl, that would lead to Kong's capture and, ultimately, to his death.

If this touch of the sensual appears foreign to the thinking of one whose earlier films had pointedly avoided such complications, it must be remembered that the picture-show operators had tempered their enthusiasm for *Chang* with the criticism that the film would have pulled bigger numbers had it contained a love story. There had been a leading lady in *The Four Feathers*, but the stiff-upper-lip tone of that he-man picture permitted no hint of brute passion. In postwar articles for the *New York Times*, written under the curious byline "A Fortunate Soldier," and in his 1927 book *Things Men Die For*, Cooper had much to say about the women he had known and their fierce loyalty to their men in times of danger and deprivation.

Schoedsack had taken a cameraman to Sumatra, so that he might concentrate his larger energies on story and direction. He began to feel unease at sailing time when the photographer failed to appear. His anxiety only increased when the man finally came aboard unconscious, borne by several inebriated friends and accompanied by a large sack of bottled goods.

Rango was made in the high mountain jungles at the northwestern end of Sumatra, among the fierce Atjehnese natives and an abundant concentration of wildlife. The Dutch colonial government, which had been having trouble with the tribes, reluctantly granted entrance to the region but refused to accept responsibility for the visitors' safety. The Schoedsacks quickly befriended the natives and for nine months worked at a location 3,000 feet above sea level, living in a bamboo hut alongside a mountain torrent. The area was free of the excessive heat, malaria and mosquitoes that had plagued the *Chang* expedition, the only climatic problem being an overabundance of rain peculiar to the monsoon belt.

Schoedsack's misgivings about his cameraman soon were confirmed: The first brush with a tiger so terrified the man as to intensify his drinking problem until he was useless. In the evenings, the man usually drank a spot of Dutch beer with the Schoedsacks, but afterwards he would slip away to the native huts to quaff the local brew. He nailed his windows shut and kept a sword beside his bed. Often he was heard to mutter, "Those tigers aren't gonna get *me*!"

"I couldn't even trust him to can the film," Schoedsack told us. "The only film I lost was because of him. He went into the darkroom and locked the door and wouldn't come out. He had puked in the film can!" Schoedsack eventually put the cameraman on a ship bound for Europe and photographed most of *Rango* himself.

Schoedsack returned in June 1930 and began cutting the negative at the Paramount Eastern Studio at Astoria, Long Island. He tried to remain in seclusion while occupied with this time-consuming chore, but Paramount—which had sent out numerous press releases about the dangers he had encountered with wild beasts and hostile savages—was insistent that the filmmaker meet the press. Until then, Schoedsack had managed to pawn this distasteful part of the business off on the flamboyant Cooper. When at last a massed interview was arranged, Schoedsack (to the dismay of the publicity department) took pains to minimize any suggestion of adventure. When a *Times* reporter asked about the studio's hair-raising press releases, Schoedsack "looked perplexed," according to the published article, and then replied:

"Dangers—? As dangerous as your poison liquor and your automobiles here in New York, I suppose. Wild animals? Why, yes, there are the tigers. Naturally, the big cats come down into the village now and then and kill a few goats or oxen. But your taxi drivers kill a few people from time to time, don't they? New Yorkers don't go around in perpetual fear because of that."

When asked if he had had any narrow escapes, Schoedsack said: "Certainly not. I went to Sumatra to make a picture, not to risk my neck. No natives were killed. Three tigers were shot—for the picture. Aside from that, I only killed tigers when necessary...

"Seriously," Schoedsack continued, "there were no thrills. The finished film may seem packed with excitement, but making it is a long, slow, tedious business stretched over eight or nine months. Remember, only eight percent of the stuff I shot appears in the picture shown to the public. And honestly, there weren't many difficulties... The weather was wonderful.

"The point is that I have my own ideas about making motion pictures. Everyone seems to think that stories, to be vital, must have a love interest. A picture can't be good unless it's built around a throbbing scene between a male and a female. That's a mistake, as Cooper and I tried to show with *Grass* and *Chang*. We focus our lenses not on silly close-ups of lovesick females, but on the elemental clashes between nations and their fundamental problems, between man and nature.

"Another thing to remember is that when I go off like that, I don't have to take orders from producers. I work out my picture in my own way."

Five days after the premiere of *Rango*, Cooper received news that shattered one of his fondest hopes. For five years, now, he had been planning an expedition into the largest unexplored patch of land in the world, the so-called Empty Quarter, or Abode of Loneliness, of Arabia. No expedition had ever penetrated this region containing more than 500,000 square miles of desert—nearly half of all Arabia—because there was no water to be had at any known entrance and the surrounding areas were peopled by hostiles. Now it was reported that Bertram Thomas, Wazir to the Sultan of Muscat, had just made the first crossing of the Empty Quarter. Hiding his personal disappointment, Cooper issued a statement to the press, calling Thomas' feat "The greatest individual accomplishment, and the bravest one, in our day." Exploration proved, as Cooper had believed it would, that tribes hitherto unknown existed deep within the region. Cooper called it "truly the No Man's Land of the world."

In less than a month, Cooper was off on a dangerous adventure of his own, but this time there was no joy in the undertaking. A young friend, Varick Frissell, who had been making sound movies of a sealing expedition in the North Atlantic, was reported missing after the ship's explosion off Newfoundland. Undertaking a rescue mission with the famed Bernt Balchen, first pilot to fly over Antarctica, Cooper left Boston in a twin-engine Sikorsky amphibian plane. Eventually, all but 20 of the 155 missing men were brought back; Frissell and his cameraman, Arthur Penrod, were among the lost. The tragic quest reached a climax of cruel absurdity when the searchers returned to Boston—and were fined $500 for failing to conform to U.S. Customs regulations.

When Paramount acquired rights to *The Lives of a Bengal Lancer*, Francis Yeats-Brown's popular book about British and native troops in strife-torn India, Jesse Lasky envisioned a production in the manner of *The Four Feathers*. He proposed to send Cooper and Schoedsack to India to make location footage, then have them complete the film with Hollywood players and studio settings. Cooper's airline interests forced him to decline.

Schoedsack undertook the Indian expedition on his own. He set out early in July 1931, accompanied by his wife, his cameraman brother Felix, backup cameraman Rex Wimpy and several assistants. After seven weeks at sea, the party arrived at Calcutta on August 27 and traveled by train into the interior. During the next 15 weeks, they lived and worked in two train cars—one for residential accommodations, the other as a combination darkroom-workshop-warehouse. They shot in the Northern mountain country; at Delhi and Simla; in the Khyber Pass; at Peshawar, Kohat and Risalpur; in the jungles around Jhansi and Jaipur; in the southern states of Madras and Mysire; and finally in Bombay. Much of the work was done among the warlike Afridis, Mahduhs and Wasiris. On occasion, they found it necessary to halt production so that their performers, as it were, could research their roles by fighting real battles.

David O. Selznick had quit Paramount on June 8 and with his brother, Myron, sought backing to start an independent movie company. Cooper approached Selznick with the latest of several treatments on the gorilla story. Although David found the idea interesting and believed that Cooper had the gumption to see it through, he was in no position to help.

Cooper spent the summer of 1931 trying to interest Metro-Goldwyn-Mayer and Paramount in his project—including expeditions to Africa and Komodo—but no one was willing to risk such an expensive and likely impractical scheme.

Cooper's aviation interests had snowballed. He was elected to the boards of directors of four airlines including the first chartered domestic carrier, Western Air Express. His finances were now secure, but his creative instincts were thwarted. Oftentimes, Cooper's thoughts returned to that half-formed adventure-film idea about a gigantic ape amok amid civilization.

The Genius of "OBie" O'Brien

> O'Brien was the best trick man there ever was. And a genius in the story department, too.—Merian C. Cooper

There was, in fact, a man who possessed the know-how to make practical the filming of Cooper's mad daydream. He was Willis Harold O'Brien, a two-fisted, hard-drinking Irishman from Oakland. O'Brien was the outstanding practitioner of an art he called animation-in-depth, a method by which inanimate objects are given the appearance of life and willful movement on film.

The basic idea, known as stop-motion, is a simple one that had been exploited before 1900 by the pioneering French filmmaker Georges Méliès. A subject is placed in position, and a single frame is shot of that placement. The subject then is moved slightly, and another frame is exposed. Further related positions are photographed in this manner, describing the increments-of-movement of whatever action is to be simulated on the film. This strip of sequential frames, each a still photograph in itself, is then projected in the usual way. (*All* cinema, in this sense, is animation.) The viewer's persistence of vision blends these rapid-fire still photographs into an illusion of motion. The speed at which the subject appears to move is determined by the distance between the positions photographed: Fast-moving objects require less footage, and therefore their placements are farther apart than is necessary for slow-moving effects. It was by this method that a bedstead was made to leap and dance in Winsor McCay and Edwin S. Porter's wonderful trick film of 1906, "The Dream of a Rarebit Fiend."

Willis O'Brien

Although O'Brien was far from the first filmmaker to utilize dimensional animation, his efforts were more ambitious than those of his predecessors or even his contemporaries. It was O'Brien who refined and developed the technique to near-perfection.

O'Brien had been a cowboy, a prize-fighter, a cartoonist for the *San Francisco Daily World* and a sculptor for the 1915 San Francisco World's Fair before he entered the film industry. While he was making malleable clay figurines of boxers for an exhibit, working well in advance of the event, his brother began manipulating the arms of one, saying, "My fighter can beat yours." This unwitting inspiration led O'Brien to experiment with stop-motion photography of pliable clay models. Manipulating the mannequins by hand in gradual steps and photographing them with a borrowed newsreel camera, O'Brien produced a film in which the miniatures appeared to move about on their own—albeit jerkily and too rapidly.

Late in 1914, O'Brien made a picture 75 feet in length, featuring a caveman and a comical brontosaurus. An interested spec-

Willis O'Brien's "Missing Link" from the comedy "The Dinosaur and the Missing Link"

tator at the screening of some of O'Brien's experiments was Watterson R. Rothacker, president of the Rothacker Film Co. of Chicago.

O'Brien later filmed "The Dinosaur and the Missing Link," a comedy involving cavemen, an ape-man and other prehistoric beasts. The protagonists were constructed as miniatures of a pliable material, with skins of rubber and cloth over jointed wooden skeletons, and photographed among settings made from rocks and tree limbs; these were set up for photographing in the basement of the Imperial Theatre in San Francisco. Two months were required to complete the film, which was ready to show in late 1915. The Thomas A. Edison Co. of the Bronx, New York, bought the reel for $525—a dollar per foot—for theatrical distribution. O'Brien quickly set to work in another makeshift studio on the roof of the Bank of Italy Building at Powell and Market Streets, where he made two trick pictures, "Morpheus Mike" and "Birth of a Flivver."

In 1916, O'Brien went to New York to make additional dinosaur comedies for Edison's Conquest Film Programs. For this purpose, Mannikin Films, Inc., was formed, with O'Brien as its president. Mannikin then delivered "R.F.D. 10,000 B.C.," "Prehistoric Poultry" (in two versions), "In the Villain's Power," "Curious Pets of Our Ancestors," "Mickey and His Goat," "Sam Loyd's Famous Puzzles—the Puzzling Billboard" and "Nippy's Nightmare." The last-named has the distinction of being the first film to combine living actors with the mannequins, the live action being intercut with the animated scenes rather than composited. O'Brien had become suddenly dissatisfied with his earlier efforts, convinced now that a movie must have human elements.

The prehistoric-creature models had been designed after popular conceptions of dinosaurs, with no particular attempts at authenticity. When Edison dropped its Conquest line, O'Brien was asked to edit a weekly series containing an educational segment about extinct animals. In order to make his reconstructions more nearly accurate, O'Brien consulted with Dr. Barnum Brown, the distinguished vertebrate paleontologist at the American Museum of Natural History.

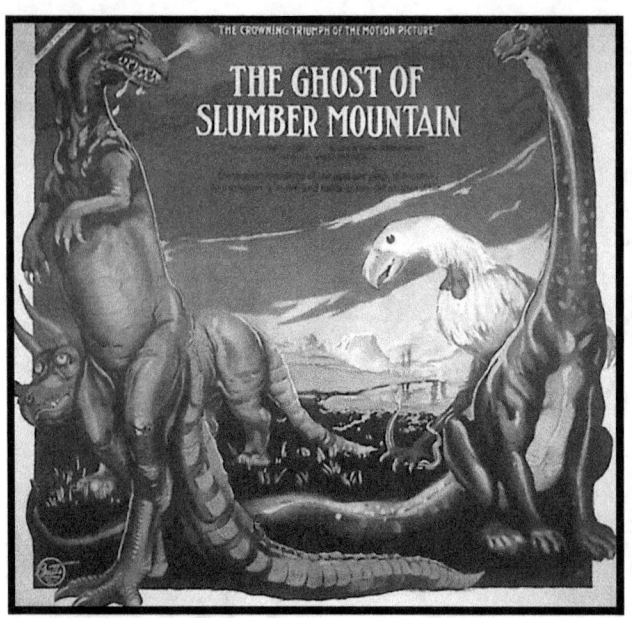

Edison sold out to Lincoln & Parker before the weekly series got under way, and the new owners decided to abandon the educational pieces. At this time, O'Brien met Maj. Herbert M. Dawley, a pioneering film technician and cameraman, who had been experimenting with a plastic dinosaur and had pasted a great number of exposures into a small book; when the pages were flipped, the image appeared to move. O'Brien and Dawley entered into an agreement to film "The Ghost of Slumber Mountain."

O'Brien set to work in the fashion of early-day D.W. Griffith, without a formal scenario, using only a sheet of titles as a guide. He constructed five prehistoric monsters under Dr. Brown's guidance, avoiding caricature and making the beasts as realistic as possible. Brown also suggested much of the action, which indulges in no slapstick. The original cut was approximately 3,000 feet in length, but it was trimmed to 520 feet before release. It is believed that Dawley used some of the excised footage in "Along the Moonbeam Trail" (1920), which is presumably a lost film.

When "The Ghost of Slumber Mountain" opened at the New York Strand, full credit was given O'Brien for its production. But O'Brien's name was removed for the general-release prints—replaced with a credit line reading, "Produced by Herbert M. Dawley." Dawley also assigned himself sole artistic credit. He exaggerated things to a preposterous length when interviewed by an easily bamboozled reporter named Charles W. Person for a popular magazine. The November 1919 issue of *Illustrated World* credulously informed its readers:

> Maj. Dawley... laid in a supply of lumber, cloth, paint, clay and other materials... He first prepared a rugged wooden skeleton,... with a covering of clay to express the muscles, tendons and bones... and over this placed a skin-like covering of cloth painted a dark brown color. After building several animals—one of the them was 17 feet high—he was ready to make them act for the camera... In addition to placing the legs in the proper posture each time an exposure was made, he had to change the position of the neck, the trunk and the tail each time a new step was taken...
>
> In one of Maj. Dawley's films, two animals are shown fighting... twice as much effort as a film showing but one monster in action. Yet this sculptor did not stop with two in the same picture; he put in three and even four, and the difficulty... was quadrupled.

A viewing of the film reveals that the monster "17 feet high" is—of course!—one of O'Brien's detailed miniatures, photographed in a miniature setting designed to match full-scale scenes of the human actors on location in the mountains. The one exception, a close-up of an Allosaurus, appears to have utilized a large-as-life head. Evident are trademarks of design and storytelling that will be familiar to anyone who has studied O'Brien's work: Despite an amusing shaggy-dog framing story, the body of the work is calculated to amaze and shock, and the dinosaurs are strikingly realistic. The story, which is sufficiently uncomplicated to cover about 15 minutes, carries a fair measure of suspense.

Close-ups are frustratingly lacking, with only two in the entire reel, and the lighting is merely that—illumination without dramatic purpose. But the animals are excellent. They seem properly heavy and ponderous, their actions are surprisingly smooth, and there are many bits of business peculiar to O'Brien's work, for example the mighty Diatryma that pauses to scratch itself just after it enters the setting. The very camera is animated on two occasions, panning across the landscape to reveal an approaching Triceratops and moving slowly up the towering body of the Allosaurus to a shot of the grinning head.

"The Ghost of Slumber Mountain" was released in 1919 by Paul M. Cromelin's World Cinema Distributing Co. of Fort Lee, New Jersey. The film cost only $3,000 to make and grossed more than $100,000. Dr. G. Clyde Fisher, of the American Museum of Natural History, remarked: "I was greatly pleased. It is astonishing how lifelike these [creatures] were. The whole thing was extremely well done."

Watterson Rothacker, the entrepreneur from Chicago, was favorably impressed with the film—but appalled at Dawley's crass attempt to discredit O'Brien. He placed O'Brien under contract and set him to making novelty reels. Both men lost interest in short films, however, when Rothacker bought the photoplay rights to Sir Arthur Conan Doyle's *The Lost World*, a fantastic novel about prehistoric monsters discovered on a Brazilian plateau.

It quickly became evident that the spectacular action envisioned for *The Lost World* would require technical work well beyond O'Brien's lone-wolf *modus operandi*. To this end, Rothacker agreed to co-produce the feature with First National Pictures, Inc., at the big company's Burbank lot. Here, O'Brien would have the collaboration of the head of the studio's special-effects department, Fred W. Jackman, whose genius embraced every facet of motion-picture technology. O'Brien realized, too, that dinosaurs made of wood, clay and cloth were inadequate for so ambitious an undertaking. He needed assistance of a highly specialized kind.

O'Brien was attending night classes at the Otis Art Institute. There, he met 20-year-old Marcel Delgado, a grocery clerk who was working as a teaching assistant to finance his studies. Some sixth sense told O'Brien that this wiry and pugnacious young sculptor possessed the determination and the talents needed to bring *The Lost World* to the screen.

In his native village of La Parrita, below the border near Laredo, Texas, Delgado had watched the labors of a bearded oldster known as the Patron Saint, who earned his bread by carving statues of the saints. By age 6, Delgado was making sculptures of his own, as well as developing mechanical skills by creating his own toys. During the Mexican Revolution, Delgado's large and impoverished family

Marcel Delgado used the paintings of Charles Knight to guide him in the creating of the dinosaurs for *The Lost World*.

moved to California, where they worked in the beanfields and walnut orchards around Saticoy. Marcel had little opportunity to attend school and did not speak English until age 17.

Delgado told us of his vividly remembered early meetings with O'Brien: "[O]ne night, he asked me, 'Would you like to work in motion pictures?' I told him I wouldn't because I wanted to be an artist and didn't want to lose any time. Every time he saw me, he asked again and offered me $75 a week... I always said no, and I don't really know why. I was only making $18 a week, but I guess I felt secure. One Friday, he asked me to lay off work and visit the motion-picture studio. OBie left a pass at the gate, and when I went in OBie met me and took me to his little shop. There was a phone, some cameras and pictures all around. 'How do you like your studio?' he asked. 'It's yours, if you want it.' It was a 20-year-old boy's dream! So I signed up and worked for the next couple of years, building dinosaurs for *The Lost World*. I made 49 or 50 of them, and it was all done under cover with no visitors allowed—although some of the studio big shots came in, anyhow."

Delgado used the paintings of Charles R. Knight to guide him in the appearance of the prehistoric animals. Knight's celebrated reconstructions at the Field Museum of Natural History and the American Museum of Natural History are the finest art of this highly specialized kind: They are not only as accurate as the day's scientific knowledge could make them—but they also are amazingly lifelike, and dramatically convincing. This same quality is evident in Delgado's creations: They have personality.

Delgado's dinosaurs averaged 18 inches in length, with the Stegosauri and Ceratopsians being somewhat smaller and the Brontosaurus being considerably larger. The skeletons were made of tempered dural with articulated backbones and ball-and-socket joints for all movable digits and appendages. Sponge-rubber muscles were applied and made to flex and stretch as real muscles do. The armature was then padded and shaped into the basic form of the animal. The skins were made of latex and rubber sheeting. All spines, plates, warty growths and other protuberances were made separately and applied to the realistically textured skins. Some of the reptiles were equipped with a breathing apparatus consisting of a bladder placed between skin and armature. By use of an air-compressor device, the amount of inflation could be controlled and animated along with the other movements.

By mid-1922, O'Brien had produced a reel of test footage in which the dinosaurs cavorted about very much as they must have done in real life. A print was given to Conan Doyle, who had come to America to give a series of lectures on spiritualism. Thus was provoked the author's epic prank on the Society of American Magicians, which attracted such widespread notice that Doyle found himself moved to explain the cinematic origins of his "psychic" film.[1]

Within days, O'Brien's crooked former producer, Maj. Dawley, brought suit against Rothacker and Doyle, issuing a public statement that Doyle's dinosaurs had been filmed via a process invented by Dawley and pirated by a former employee. Dawley threatened to sue Rothacker for $100,000 for patent infringement and to seek an injunction halting production of *The Lost World* and preventing use of existing footage. The case proved to be as big a load of hot air as Dawley's blowhard interview in *Illustrated World* magazine, however, and O'Brien carried on as usual.

In July 1924, First National announced that the full-scale work on *The Lost World* had commenced after "six-and-a-half years' preparation and research," and that more than $1 million would be spent on the production. Nor was this figure a press agent's boast. A set representing two streets in the heart of London ran an eighth of a mile in length and required the studio's maximum lighting capacity. The personnel ran to 2,000 players, 200 automobiles, 25 assistant directors and 18 cameramen. Equally impressive are interior and exterior views of the Royal Museum, which were re-created at the studio. Jungles, a trading post, caverns and a precipice were constructed on the lot along the Los Angeles River.

Direction of the live action was begun by Harry O. Hoyt, a graduate of Columbia and Yale who had practiced law before becoming a scriptwriter (initially, for D.W. Griffith) and an editor and director. Such was the scope of the production that supervisor Earl Hudson established a second unit when it became evident that a year would be needed to complete the film at the initial pace. William Dowling directed the second company, which eventually merged with Hoyt's main unit during the final few weeks. The leading players were Wallace Beery, Lewis Stone, Bessie Love, Lloyd Hughes and Bull Montana. Arthur Edeson was in charge of the corps of cameramen on the live action.

The dinosaur scenes were staged on a set measuring about 200 by 300 feet, with a vast jungle scaled to make Delgado's monsters feel properly at home. Miniature trees were constructed solidly to avoid unwanted jiggling, with many leaves and fronds being cut from sheet metal for greater stability. For scenes in which the animals seem to leap toward one another, special backgrounds were devised to permit the combatants to leave the ground. Animation was shot with seven cameras mounted on dollies that could be locked securely into position. The shutters were operated simultaneously from a single control.

The Lost World's greatest innovation was the depiction of live actors and animated dinosaurs in the same scenes. D.W. Griffith had moved a life-size Ceratosaurus through scenes with the players in *Brute Force* (1913), but the mock-up monster lacks the agility of O'Brien's animated beasts. Lubin's *On Moonshine Mountain* (1914) used living reptiles, which look vigorous enough but are never shown with the players. For *The Lost World*, O'Brien once again reinvented the realm of special effects to suit his mounting ambitions: He masked off portions of the negatives, then printed into the masked areas scenes of players photographed against matching backdrops. In her autobiography *Love from Hollywood*, Bessie Love has preserved a vivid memory of acting under such circumstances: "In place of yelling, 'Run!' when the prehistoric animals started chasing us, Mr. Hoyt explained in detail *why* we should run, namely, the Tyrannosaurus [*actually, Allosaurus*] was a carnivorous dinosaur. The animals were not actually on stage... it was double exposure. It didn't really matter if you called them Joe, Gus or Heimie as long as you looked terrified and scampered." When one sees husky Wallace Beery dwarfed by a monster convincingly 100 feet long, the effect is startling even today. The impact upon the moviegoer of 1925, when nothing of the like had been seen, can well be imagined.

Even more striking are the shots of the Brontosaurus running wild through London as hordes of extras scatter in terror. These scenes were accomplished through an early traveling-matte process. The dinosaur was animated against a stark white background, and the resulting film was made up in two ways: as a negative with the animal appearing against a black background, and as a high-contrast positive with the figure in silhouette against clear film. The high-contrast positive was used as a mask through which to print the street scene, producing a copy in which the contours of the animal were left unexposed. The negative then was employed to print the Brontosaurus into the masked areas. This process was rendered obsolete by the more dependable systems invented by C. Dodge Dunning and Frank Williams, and by the development of optical printing. It was effective, however, and suffered only from occasional matte-bleeds caused by variable shrinking of the different emulsions. The matching of miniature and full-scale perspectives was superbly managed. Several scenes used full-scale props: Here, a life-size Brontosaurus head crashes through a wall to invade a chess tournament, and there a gigantic tail tumbles a crowd of extras like ten-pins.

The real *tour de force* is a stampede of monsters during a volcanic eruption—the most spectacular piece of hand-wrought animation in *any* film, early or late. Dozens of dinosaurs are seen fleeing through the forest, sometimes in the same frames with the living actors, highlighted by an exploding volcano, flames and smoke. Even in this desperate situation, the Allosauri attack the other animals, which fight them off as they race along. One grim tableau finds a family of Allosauri feeding upon a fallen herbivore. The volcano sequence was printed on red stock for the initial release prints.

The Lost World was released in 1925—by all odds, *the* vintage year of the silent cinema—and received the deluxe roadshow treatment. The original version was in 10 reels, with a running time of about two hours. Audiences and the critics were so enthralled with the dinosaurs that they were willing to tolerate the long and unexciting portions dealing with a standard romantic situation. The players were popular favorites, particularly Wallace Berry, in a robust performance as the dogmatic and ill-tempered Prof. Challenger, the most uncharacteristic role of his long career, and vivacious Bessie Love.

Production chief Earl Hudson promptly announced that O'Brien and Hoyt were planning a sequel, which would be "entirely different" from the source film. Despite changes of ownership and policy, the studio kept plans for the sequel in motion as late as February 1928, when negotiations were made with Rothacker to begin production. With additional management changes,

Bessie Love and friends hide from the Brontosaurus in *The Lost World*.

however, O'Brien's follow-through was abandoned. His disappointment was compounded by the rejection of other proposals—including a version of *Frankenstein* in which the Monster would be portrayed by an O'Brien mannequin, and an adaptation of H.G. Wells' *The Food of the Gods*. O'Brien soon lapsed into the obscurity of First National's matte department while Delgado languished in the properties department.

"While *The Lost World* was in work, I got to be well known at the studio," Delgado told us. "Big stars like Milton Sills, Colleen Moore and Wally Beery were my friends. But after I was demoted to the prop shop, they treated me like I had the mange. A couple of years later, Warner Bros. had bought out First National, and I was laid off. But I was quickly hired to build miniatures and special props at the old William Fox Studio. I stayed there until OBie called again."

By 1930, however, the novelty appeal of talking pictures had waned just enough to set the studios searching for other means of enticing audiences. Most of the studios launched wide-screen productions, but these failed because Depression-stricken theatre owners, already forced to acquire sound equipment, were unwilling or unable to install the additional required equipment. Technicolor and other two-color processes enjoyed a sudden boom that proved transitory because added expense and other unresolved technical problems made color production a formidable undertaking. What the movies needed was virility—not gimmickry.

Outdoor adventure thrillers returned to the production schedules as audiences became increasingly apathetic to the visual dullness and excessive talkiness of the majority of new films. Numerous pictures appeared in answer to the massed outcry that the movies must *move* as well as yack: These robust breakthroughs included W.S. Van Dyke's *Trader Horn* and Howard Hughes' *Hell's Angels*, both of which had been conceived as silent epics; Wesley Ruggles' *Cimarron*; Roland West's *The Bat Whispers*; and Ernest B. Schoedsack's *Rango*.[2]

Here, at last, was an era in which O'Brien could function.

1 See the section on *The Lost World* in our "Preludes, Prologues & Progeny" chapter.
2 See *Rango* under "Preludes, Prologues & Progeny."

Production 601 Gets the Green Light

Kong was the product of many contributions.—Ernest B. Schoedsack

While Merian C. Cooper was working on his giant-gorilla yarn, Willis O'Brien was planning a rather similar project he called *Creation*. This collaboration with Harry O. Hoyt was envisioned as an epic production, combining elements of *The Lost World* with James Barrie's *The Admirable Crichton*, that classic tale of a shipwreck and its resourceful servant-turned-hero.

Late in April 1930, RKO slated *Creation* as Production 359. The brass had been persuaded thusly by Hoyt's 76-page "Detail for Cost Estimation" and a screening of *The Lost World*. Bertram Millhauser, assigned as supervisor, declared with gullible optimism that *Creation* could be "made on a 20-week preparation and shooting schedule" with a "budget of $652,242.52." That budget included "a liberal amount of protection," added Millhauser, who felt that 15 weeks and no more than $500,000 would do the trick.

Hoyt, having spent a year making *The Lost World*, should have known better, but then perhaps he was intentionally low-balling the time-and-money aspects in order to launch into production in the hope that additional resources would fall into place. This tactic is still alarmingly rampant in 21st Century Hollywood. Said Hoyt: "It would take O'Brien, Crabbe and their assistants about eight weeks to manufacture the animals (17 close-up and 20 or so background dinosaurs). However, within four weeks, a sufficient number should be completed to commence shooting."

Within eight weeks, Millhauser brought in his writing partner, Beulah Marie Dix, who had scripted some of Cecil B. DeMille's spectacles, to do a "wholly original adaptation, scenario and dialogue." Working throughout the summer, Miss Dix eliminated some of Hoyt's characters, combined others into single characters, transposed and telescoped incidents, and added what would have been a visually striking episode with a Tyrannosaurus at large in the ruins of a temple, before the obligatory volcanic eruption.

Matte drawing for *Creation* credited to O'Brien and Larrinaga

The Arsinoitherium traps the six-inch model Chilean sailors on a log in *Creation*.

Willis O'Brien, who was permitted to create his own production unit within the studio, started work on July 9 with key artists Byron Crabbe and Ernest Smythe. Crabbe had an outstanding reputation as a set designer and effects artist but died at the peak of his career during the middle 1930s. Smythe was an illustrator who had produced hundreds of posters and advertisements for Universal. Marcel Delgado, leaving his job at Fox, reported to the Gower Street studio to begin assembling a new menagerie. Others who assisted O'Brien were borrowed from the art, property and miniature departments. These grips, artists and technicians were trained in the extravagant intricacies of O'Brien's methods amid a great deal of trial and error.

By October 2, Millhauser's "20-week preparation and shooting schedule" had run its course—and nary a foot of film had been shot. But the company did have a shooting script; dozens of drawings; dinosaurs in various stages of completion; and a proposal to shoot a test sequence involving a Triceratops family and a hunter who shoots a baby and then is chased down and killed by the mother. For the test, four key drawings, 20 smaller sketches and a map detailing the action and camera angles were ready. Three weeks were scheduled to complete the animals and the sets (both miniature and full-size), with another three to shoot both live action and animation.

As the script went back to Beulah Marie Dix for rewrites, the tests finally began on November 15 and stretched on for 61 days. Animation now was more difficult than in the day of *The Lost World* because it had to be prepared for projection at 24 frames per second, the standard speed for sound film, where the earlier film had utilized the silent-screen rate of 16 f.p.s. O'Brien now had to provide animation with eight additional steps per second of screen time. This reduced by one-third the amount of footage that could be completed in an assigned period. Twenty-five feet of finished film, running less than 20 seconds, was a good day's work. (Hoyt had promised a daily average of 40 feet.)

Composite effects with animated monsters, trained animals and actors were achieved with a stunning realism undreamed of during the making of *The Lost World*. The most effective of these utilized the Dunning traveling matte system, which combines previously shot background animation with live action in a single operation without the telltale fringing that occurs with other systems. Other shots utilized an early version of miniature projection: Location footage of actor Ralf Harolde (as the hunter) was projected behind a stop-motion Triceratops (in an over-the-shoulder shot) and a mechanical head (in side view). A motor vibrated the screen to eliminate grain, but the projected scenes suffer from the washed-out look of most early-day rear-screen work, and the Verdugo Hills chaparral is jarringly less lush and atmospheric than the miniature settings.

The scope of the test was expanded to include a miniature storm sequence supervised by Karl Brown, who also photographed the live action and animation. Brown, a multi-talented artist who later became a popular screenwriter, had been trained by D.W. Griffith and G.W. "Billy" Bitzer before World War I; during the 1920s, Brown photographed *The Covered Wagon*, directed *Stark Love* and wrote *Mississippi Gambler*.

By the time the tests were completed, on January 24, 1931, the tab had run to $131,690. Although this sum was already inordinately high, the front office's attention was diverted elsewhere. William LeBaron, RKO's vice president for production, was so pleased with his first big-budget production, *Cimarron*, that he was not overly worried about *Creation*—not yet, at any rate.

Creation was one of the most intricately planned projects ever launched in Hollywood. Every aspect of lighting and action was decided upon before consideration was given to the mechanical techniques. O'Brien made numerous sketches depicting highlights of the tale. These were developed into large, comprehensive illustrations. Hundreds of continuity sketches linked the larger drawings so that each scene in the script was pictured. Lighting, camera angles, sets and props, planned action and the relative scale of all elements were illustrated. Precise diagrams showed camera positions, appropriate lenses and perspectives.

One of the temporarily assigned artists became so indispensable that he was made a permanent member of O'Brien's staff. Mario Larrinaga, born in Baja California of Basque parents, had started his art career without formal training at age 16. As an apprentice to his older brother, Juan, at a scenic studio in Los Angeles, Mario painted sets and curtains for dramatic and operatic productions and vaudeville. In 1916, he became a technical artist at the upstart Universal Studio, where he painted everything from miniatures to huge cycloramas. Eventually, he wound up in charge of the art-effects department at Warners. Larrinaga retired to Taos, New Mexico, in 1951 and gained new fame, both in the fine arts and as an architectural designer.

Work progressed but haltingly. Many elaborate full-scale sets were designed, but few were built. The studio chiefs despaired with each passing day: RKO, hit hard by the Depression, was on the verge of bankruptcy and in a state of organizational upheaval. Budget sheets after the initial tests show only a week and a half of Karl Brown's salary; no expenses for other cameramen; only nominal camera-and-film costs; and a notation that Brown's undersea sequence was "halted before its finish." This accumulation of evidence suggests that few, if any, animation sequences were filmed after the original tests.

A Larrinaga drawing for *Creation*

The tentative shooting schedule of April 23 had called for 60 days of live-action photography—principally on sets that had not been built. Production halted. A revised schedule from early June, calling for 41 shooting days plus 10 days on location in Florida with a reduced crew, also failed to pass muster. Bertram Millhauser, among other associate producers, was let go in a cost-cutting move.

Hoyt scaled down his epic from the spectacular to the minimalist, replacing the earth-in-upheaval scenario with a simple airplane crash and reducing the ranks of the dinosaurs. Ralf Harolde's character now became the only victim. A revised shooting schedule of July 24, based upon this simplified scenario, called for 36 days' shooting plus six days of pick-up shots on only two sets and nearby locations. Even this emasculated version would not fly.

William LeBaron found himself under intolerable pressure from the New York office. By late summer, he had escaped to a job at Paramount, and *Creation* had run up costs in excess of $175,000 (including 25 percent studio overhead). As minuscule as this sum may appear by modern-day inflationary standards, it represented a considerable outlay at a time when five profitable low-budgeters could be made for $100,000 and a respectable top-of-the-line feature could be brought in for $200,000. *Creation* could have cost millions.

LeBaron's successor, who arrived in September 1931, was Paramount's former boy wonder, David O. Selznick. The new boss was instructed to make whatever changes were necessary to put the company back on solid footing. Salaries were slashed. All productions were halted for evaluation, some to be aborted (a notable casualty was Luther Reed's elaborate *Babes in Toyland*), some to be revised and others to be remade entirely. Several directors were replaced amidships, and others were paired with directors from the New York stage as collaborators to perk up the dialogue. Script doctors arrived to rescue problematical scenarios. Budgets, which had been flexible, were now set in advance of all projects, with $200,000 established as a standard, if not a ceiling, for the most prestigious features.

Selznick soon realized that he needed a hard-nosed assistant to help appraise the welter of unfinished films, scripts and story properties. He made a wise choice: Merian C. Cooper arrived from New York in response to Selznick's summons, with the provision that he could develop his own projects, as well. Among the unfinished films screened by Cooper was O'Brien's *Creation* footage. Cooper was fascinated by the technical aspects but felt that the project, after nearly a year, was going nowhere. He did not, however, pull the plug immediately.

O'Brien saw the writing on the wall for *Creation* and, aware of rumors of Cooper's ape project, did an oil rendering in collaboration with Byron Crabbe. It depicted a large—though hardly gigantic—gorilla confronting a hunter, with a scantily clad jungle princess standing by. To generate interest in his techniques, O'Brien presented the painting to Cooper, who was already thinking along such lines. Although Cooper could see no commercial possibilities in *Creation*, he perceived in O'Brien's work a means of producing his giant-gorilla extravaganza without setting foot off the lot.

Cooper retained O'Brien's unit to illustrate key scenes and shoot a test of two dinosaurs fighting, combined with live actors. The dinosaur fight was to be made on a separate key or background plate from the men, so that the live-action element could be removed and the fight used in the finished picture. After consulting with O'Brien, Cooper assigned Delgado to design a gorilla that, on the screen, would appear as large as a dinosaur. After Cooper had left, O'Brien told Delgado to "make the ape almost human." Delgado designed a monstrosity combining the features of man and ape.

"That's the funniest-looking thing I've ever seen!" Cooper declared when he saw the completed job. "It looks like a cross between a monkey and a man with long hair. Damn it, I want to put a pure gorilla on that screen!" After a great deal more work, Delgado produced a second creature that was more lifelike but yet retained certain manlike characteristics. Cooper was no less dissatisfied.

"I want... the fiercest, most brutal, monstrous damned thing that has ever been seen," Cooper demanded. O'Brien argued that it would be impossible to win over an audience with a monstrous ape lacking in human qualities, but Cooper was adamant: "I'll have women crying over him before I'm through, and the more brutal he is the more they'll cry at the end." While O'Brien and Delgado retrenched in an attempt to comply, Cooper returned to his office and called the American Museum of Natural History in New York, requesting the exact dimensions of a bull gorilla. On the afternoon of December 22, 1931, he placed in O'Brien's hands a telegram from the Curator of Zoology:

> DIMENSIONS LARGE MALE GORILLAS HEIGHT HEEL TO CROWN SIXTY SEVEN INCHES SPAN OUTSTRETCHED ARMS HUNDRED TWO INCHES CHEST OVER NIPPLES SIXTY CIRCUMFERENCE AROUND BELLY SEVENTY TWO STOP PHOTOGRAPHY OF ADULT HUMAN AND GORILLA SKELETONS COMPARED SEE HAECKEL R NINETEEN THREE ANTHROPOGENIE VOLUME TWO PAGE SEVEN NINETY EIGHT FOR OTHER DATA YERKES NINETEEN TWENTY NINE THE GREAT APES AND DAICHALLU EIGHTEEN SIXTY TWO ADVENTURES IN EQUATORIAL AFRICA = HARRY C RAVEN

"Now, that's what I want," Cooper said, whereupon O'Brien announced his resignation and stalked out of the studio. After a few drinks at a neighborhood speakeasy, O'Brien returned to work. This scene would be repeated on several occasions during the year ahead.

A few days earlier, on December 19, Cooper had dealt the final blow to *Creation* in a memo to Selznick. The memo, along with four production drawings, the test scene and a budget for a more elaborate test, simultaneously destroyed *Creation* and pitched Cooper's gorilla yarn. *Creation* was struck from the schedule. Cooper received permission to shoot a test reel for consideration by the board of directors, and to retain O'Brien's unit until it could be ascertained whether this picture might be made successfully. The project that would become *King Kong* went onto the schedule as Production 601.

Now Cooper faced the problem of how to shoot—on an almost nonexistent budget of $10,000—a reel of film spectacular enough to impress a group of executives who could agree on nothing other than the pinching of pennies. His method of achieving the objective illustrates the genius for organization for which Cooper had become known.

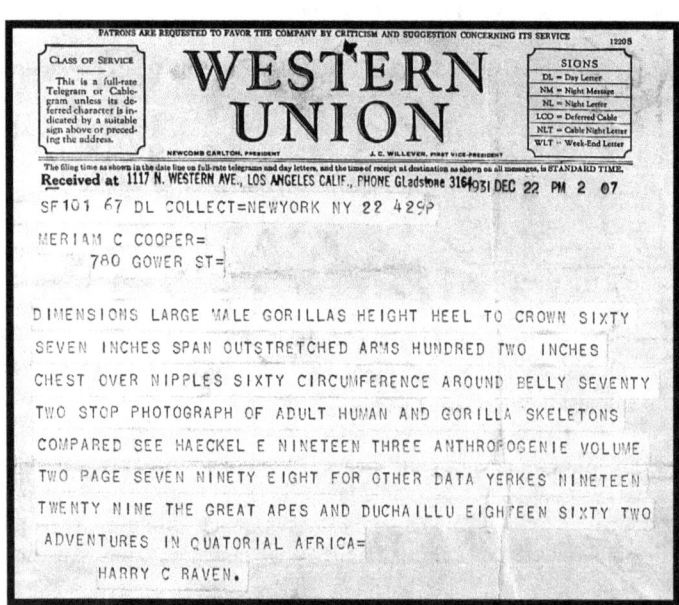

Edgar Wallace, the world-famous English author, had arrived from London on December 5, freshly contracted to write originals for RKO. Within days, Cooper had arranged for Wallace to be assigned to write *The Beast*, the studio's work-

The Triceratops chases Ralf Harolde in *Creation* in this side angle process shot.

ing title for Cooper's gorilla story, as soon as Wallace could complete *Death Watch*, a mystery later rechristened *Before Dawn*.

On December 12, Cooper had taken Wallace to meet O'Brien and watch the filming of a Dunning Process test shot of actors performing along with completed footage of two dinosaurs tangling. An entry in Wallace's diaries tells of his visit to a converted projection room that had become O'Brien's workshop. There, Wallace examined the emerging conceptions of what he called "the giant monkey [*sic*] which appears in this play." (To this day, there prevails a lunk-headed tendency to identify the great apes as monkeys.)

Wrote Wallace: "I saw a woodcarver fashioning the skull on which the actual figure will be built. In another place was a great scale model of an actual gorilla. One of the gorilla figures will be nearly 30 feet high. All 'round the walls are wooden models of prehistoric beasts. There are two miniature sets with real miniature trees, on which the prehistoric animals are made to gambol."

On Christmas Day, Wallace wrote: "Merian Cooper called, and we talked over the big animal play we are going to write, or rather, I am writing and he is directing." The next entry, dated December 29, adds: "An announcement has been made in the local press that I am doing a super-horror story with Merian Cooper, but the truth is it is much more his story than mine. I am rather enthusiastic about it, but the story has got to be more or less written to provide certain spectacular effects. I shall get much more credit out of the picture than I deserve if it is a success, but as I shall be blamed by the public if it's a failure, that seems fair."

Delgado this time made the gorilla to Cooper's specifications, cheating only as to the extent of paunch and rump.

"Kong was 18 inches high," Delgado told us. "The skeleton was made of high-tempered dural, and I gave him muscles that react, which is why Kong looks alive instead of stiff. I was given pruned rabbit fur to cover him with, and I never was satisfied with that because I knew it would show the fingerprints of the animators."

Ever prolific, Wallace dictated his first draft during the first few days of 1932. Cooper, Wallace and O'Brien went over the script page-by-page, and Wallace made significant changes a short time later. Although Wallace's 110-page script differs considerably in structure and tone from the finished film, it contains elements and events that would persist into the final release. This presence, however, cannot be accepted categorically as proof of Wallace's authorship: Many of the story points had already been established by Cooper. The Wallace script opens on Capt. Englehorn's ship. A monkey is seen plucking petals from a flower. Then:

Edgar Wallace

"You see," says Englehorn in an explicitly designated German accent. "It is der dawn of human intelligence, is it not? The admiration of the beautiful thing."

"Yeah! And he's pulling it to pieces—that's human," comments a cynical, far from heroic, Carl Denham. Show-business impresario Denham is returning from an expedition to collect wild animals. He complains that he has only lions, tigers, jaguars and baboons. He wants something no one has ever seen. Englehorn speaks of an island where he once saw a sea serpent. Denham is doubtful—but willing to investigate the claim.

Meanwhile, a vessel approaches an island that appears on no map. Aboard are a mob of escaped convicts and a female hostage. Laky, a black crewman, delivers the obligatory Bad Juju warning, which the others ignore as they cruise up a stream toward a landing. A Brontosaurus capsizes the craft.[1] As everyone scrambles for shore, the dinosaur devours two of the men.

A struggle follows over the possession of a gun, the leadership of the group, and the possession of the girl, to whom Wallace referred variously as Shirley and Zena. Two Americans, John and Tricks, emerge as leaders and Shirley's protectors. In a pile of human bones, the castaways discover a cache of spears and arm themselves. One of the men is plucked away by a Pterodactyl. Another is chased down and killed by a Triceratops.[2] Then, a carnivorous dinosaur attacks the Triceratops[3] while members of the group hide behind rocks. The distant sound of Kong pounding his chest adds tension at strategic intervals.

Salvaging supplies from the ship, John and Tricks build a tent for Shirley, and prepare fires for the night. A romantic attraction develops between John and Shirley. At dawn, mutineers seize John and Tricks. One, called Luis, crawls into Shirley's tent.

"There is death here, my little girl," says Luis, "but there is also love."

She protests: "Let me go, you beast!"

"Tomorrow I be dead—let me be a loving beast today!"

Kong enters, picks up the tent and grabs Luis. The scenario reads: "Here follows a sequence agreed and arranged by the director, ending in a fight between the convicts and Kong." The scene is depicted in one of the early production drawings: Kong—looking rather like a shaggy caveman, girl in one hand, tree in the other—fights a rag-tag group armed with spears. Kong carries Shirley away, and the survivors regroup in pursuit.

At the log bridge, John sends the others across, explaining that "Tricks and I will watch out for anything following." Kong deposits Shirley in the fork of a tree and turns back to the chasm.

The script explains: "Kong stoops, lifts the [log bridge], and throws it into the ravine with the men."

A flesh-eating dinosaur sees Shirley, whose screams draw Kong. The battle rages even as, at the bottom of the ravine, octopi, giant crabs and other creatures devour the convicts. John and Tricks cross the ravine on vines. Kong kills the dinosaur, retrieves Shirley and climbs a hill to a ledge before a cave. He proceeds to tear at her clothing but is interrupted by the noise of a dinosaur fight. Kong disables one offending creature with a boulder, then makes a nest of leaves for his new pet and goes to sleep.

In the morning, as Kong scavenges for food, a pterodactyl grabs Shirley—only to be caught and killed by Kong.

As Shirley and Kong engage in a playful bit of face-washing, John and Tricks plan a rescue. Meanwhile, Denham and Englehorn land on the beach. Tricks, in the jungle below, enrages Kong by yelling, "Hi, you Monk! Come down and meet your master!" Kong descends in pursuit of Tricks while John rescues Shirley. Just as Kong is about to kill Tricks, Shirley screams at sight of a snake. Kong drops Tricks and pursues John and Shirley. All concerned wind up on the beach just in time for Englehorn to subdue Kong with a gas bomb.

Dissolve to New York, where Kong is in a cage at Madison Square Garden amidst a circus-like atmosphere. As reporters snap photographs of Kong and Shirley, a jealous animal trainer lures Shirley into a tiger's cage. Kong breaks free and fights with the lions and tigers. John and Shirley take refuge in a hotel. Kong climbs a building. He pulls a woman out of a window and, seeing that she is not the one he seeks, tosses her away. He then recaptures Shirley.

Kong makes his way across the rooftops to the Empire State Building, where as a storm builds, he holds Shirley between his teeth and uses both hands to climb. At the top of the building, airplanes fly so close that Kong manages to crash one of them. When Kong puts Shirley down, police gain the rooftop and open fire with machine guns. Kong leans against the tower, which is struck by lightning. He beats his chest in a final gesture of defiance and topples off.

On the street below, Kong lies with his head against a wall. Kong opens his eyes and picks up Shirley. Holding her to his breast like a doll, Kong closes his eyes and lowers his head. Fade out.

In mid-January, RKO registered several prospective titles for Production 601. *The Beast* became the official title.

---

1 In Wallace's first draft, it is a lifeboat from a sinking prison ship that moves upstream; this would account for one known production drawing of a Brontosaurus capsizing a lifeboat containing a woman and a black sailor, among others.
2 This scene would refer to the *Creation* footage.
3 This bit presumably would correspond to the Dunning Process shot witnessed by Edgar Wallace.

The Eighth Wonder

"... badder than ol' King Kong—and there just ain't hardly *nobody* badder than ol' King Kong..."—Jim Croce; from an In-Person Performance of his song, "Bad, Bad Leroy Brown"

Early in February 1932, before Edgar Wallace could complete a final, approved shooting script and continuity or begin the novelization that he and Cooper envisioned, both men were sidelined by pneumonia. Cooper checked into a hospital and tried to persuade Wallace to do the same. The author remained in his apartment, which he kept overheated, and drank large quantities of heavily sweetened hot tea. On February 10, Wallace died of pneumonia complicated by diabetes.

David O. Selznick declared the bulk of Wallace's work on this project "either unusable or undeveloped." James Ashmore Creelman, a veteran writer with a knack for concocting imaginative adventure yarns, was recruited. Creelman also was attached to an adaptation of *The Most Dangerous Game*, another project that had been earmarked for Wallace.

Exactly how great a debt *King Kong* owes to Edgar Wallace is debate fodder that will remain volatile for as long as more than one person cares about it. Nothing that we report here about Wallace's participation can be taken as conclusive.

That said, it is certain that the premise, even the template of the story, was in place long before Wallace signed on. It is equally certain that key action and effects sequences had been developed by Merian C. Cooper and Willis O'Brien and translated into illustrations. Wallace is most likely to have contributed the wonderfully symbolic opening, the dialogue and events that bring the characters to the island and the narrative bridges that tie the action scenes together. The main characters, who have as many differences from as resemblances to characters in the finished film, are also likely Wallace's. His many novels, especially in the realms of citified crime and Third World adventure, contain many characterizing touches and philosophical attitudes in common with the discarded scenario for *Kong*.

The criminals at large in that script serve chiefly to provoke heroic deeds from Kong. Other attempts to render the ape sympathetic—making a nest for his captive woman, attempting to provide food for her—are sappy touches that conflict with Cooper's hard-boiled vision. Cooper had declared: "I'll have women crying over him... and the more brutal he is, the more they'll cry at the end." These themes are better ascribed to Wallace, likely with suggestions from O'Brien.

Whatever Wallace's contributions, the shooting script would evolve so drastically that, by the time principal photography began, Cooper could declare in a memorandum to Selznick: "The present script..., as far as I can tell, hasn't one single idea suggested by Edgar Wallace. If there are any, they are of the slightest."

"Actually," Cooper told us many years after the fact, "Edgar Wallace didn't write *any* of *Kong*, not one bloody word. I'd promised him credit, and so I gave it to him."

Even before Wallace's death, RKO fretted so over the story's similarity to *The Lost World* that Joseph Nolan of the New York office fired off a telegram to this effect:

> WOULD WE BE CLEAR AGAINST PLAGIARISM SUIT IF THE PART OF THE STORY CONCERNING ENGLEHORN AND DENHAM IS OMITTED AND WE ONLY HAVE SHIPWRECKED SAILORS AND GIRL STOP ALSO WOULD WE BE CLEAR FROM PLAGIARISM IF WE OMITTED THE PREHISTORIC ANIMALS AND ONLY HAVE THE APE AND OTHER NATURAL ANIMALS IN LARGE SIZES AS WELL AS LARGE INSECTS STOP

This concern was settled at length with the purchase of rights to *The Lost World* from the estate of Conan Doyle, with separate agreements with Warner Bros. and Rothacker Film Co.

Near the end of February, Cooper and O'Brien began shooting technical scenes for the test on Stage No. 3 at the RKO-Radio lot. The working title now was *The Eighth Wonder*. Visitors were barred as technicians and cameramen set to work in units separated by tall, black drapes designed to keep light from spilling onto neighboring sets. The only actors employed at this point were the 18-inch ape, several of the dural-and-rubber dinosaurs originally built for *Creation*, and a collection of six-inch sailor miniatures. Creelman collaborated with Cooper on the story while Larrinaga and Crabbe put the resulting ideas into illustrations.

Along with photographs of the story drawings, O'Brien issued to his artisans a collection of woodcut illustrations by the 19th Century French artist Gustave Doré. These were taken from the Old Testament, from *Paradise Lost*, from *The Divine Comedy* and other classic editions. "This is what I want," O'Brien explained, indicating the play of light over the tortured trees and menacing rock formations of Doré's hellish landscapes. A comparison of Doré's art with finished scenes from the film reveals a tremendous accuracy to the inspiration, as well as a marked shift from the softer, rosier environs of *Creation*. The settings were intricate combinations of miniature construction and paintings on flats and glass.

Glass painting had been used since the early days of filmmaking to add the upper portions of sets only partially built, such as the towers of a castle or the ceiling of a cathedral. The process enabled the creation of desired backgrounds that would otherwise have proved unavailable, adding clouds to bleak skies and mountain ranges to desolate flatlands. By the mid-1930s, the method was displaced by improved matte and optical processes; it found a brief resurgence during the waning 1980s—before digital matte painting came into fashion.

Glass paintings were rendered on sheets of plate glass that was flawless and free of iridescence, in tones of opaque gray (and later, as color cinematography gained acceptance, in hues). A high degree of precision was necessary in the matching of proportions, perspective, lighting and textures. Detail was critical, inasmuch as the product would be greatly enlarged on the screen. Painted areas were opaqued in black paint on the back while the remaining portions were left clear. The glass was placed between the camera and the set in such a position that, as seen through the lens, the lines of the set and the artwork would match.

Miniature trees, foliage and log with painted glass and backing used in *King Kong*.

O'Brien carefully aligned and blended the glass art and solid forms to produce a realistic atmosphere and a convincing illusion of depth.

O'Brien's adaptation of glass art was as distinctive as his modifications of basic animation technique: He ordered as many as three panes of painted glass for many of the jungle scenes, with constructed miniature set elements positioned *between* the panes. The art flats and the solid forms were carefully aligned and blended to produce a realistic atmosphere and a convincing illusion of depth. The settings were illuminated to match the light patterns of the original designs. Sometimes, the desired effect could not be achieved through actual lighting; here, the technicians would spray-paint the offending areas to conform to the original conception.

The nightmarish jungle trees were modeled in plasticine clay over wood-and-wire forms. These were covered with toilet tissue, then shellacked and painted. The tree foliage in some instances consisted of sprays from small shrubs, such as genista, which were wired onto the constructed branches. Palm fronds, ferns and other leafy forms were cut from copper sheeting thinner than writing paper. Mingled with man-made plants were tiny succulents, desert shrubs and other living plants. A crewman obtained grapevine roots from vineyards where old orchards were being replaced; these were used to make gnarled miniature trees and vines.

Animation is comparatively simple when applied to objects that operate from a fixed axis, but walking or running animals are much more difficult because their weight shifts with each step. For this reason, the sets were built upon tabletops of two-inch pine, through which numerous holes were drilled. The holes accommodated specially designed clamps that could be inserted from underneath into the metal feet of the beasts as they were manipulated in a walking motion. By this means, the feet were held securely in place each time the beasts touched down. The perforated tabletop was hidden from the camera's view by glass art, foliage and low angles. O'Brien's first assistant spent a great deal of time crawling about under the tables to set and tighten the clamps. Rods sometimes were concealed in the sides of the beasts and anchored into the sets to keep them in position.

The animators studied slow-motion films of elephants to aid them in developing the bodily movements of the dinosaurs. Eadweard Muybridge's sequential photos of animals and humans were consulted, as well. The human figures used in some scenes with the animals were six inches tall. These detailed characters were carved in wood and were firmly jointed so they would remain in any given position.

Tiny Archaeopteryxes and other birds were made to flit among the trees on invisible wires. The birds were about an inch-and-a-half in length, with bodies carved from wood and wings of pliable copper. They were advanced on the hair-thin piano wires in steps of a quarter-inch per exposure, and the wings were made to flap with minute cycles of animation. It was quickly learned that white birds are more difficult to animate than darker ones because they do not fade into the shadows among the foliage and branches.

Stand-ins for the dinosaurs were necessary because the latex skins of the working miniatures suffered under the heat of the studio lights. These wood-carved place-marking beasts were identical in size and color to the movable animals seen on screen.

The dinosaurs themselves represented a significant advancement in the synthesis of art with technology. The skeletal armatures were intricately planned by O'Brien and Delgado, then diagrammed by Carroll Shepphird and machined in the studio's mechanical department. Ball joints and small parts including fingers, hands and feet were made of machined steel while larger limbs were tooled in dural aluminum. Shoulder and hip blocks were cast in aluminum and machined to accept steel joints. Skulls—complete with teeth—were likewise cast in aluminum, then riddled with holes into which a series of wires could be installed. These wires were later imbedded in the rubber lips, brows, nostrils and other facial features to allow the animators to impart facial movement. Necks, backbones and tails were shaped as a series of alternating hinge-joints set with the axis of movement at right angles; thus, one hinge provided up-and-down motion, the next gave side-to-side action, and so forth. The Stegosaurs' tail, for example, was made up of more than 37 such joints.

Delgado bulked up the armatures to rough dimensions with cotton batting then refined the musculature with sponge-rubber in sheets that could be cut and shaped as needed. Sheets of dental rubber formed the basis of the skin itself, which then was detailed with warts, scales and textures that were made and applied one at a time. The tactic of firmly attaching the skin in some areas while leaving it loose in others allowed it to stretch, wrinkle and move realistically over the joints and muscles. Glass eyes were set in the aluminum sockets, and facial details were built up out of liquid latex and cotton. Horns, spikes, and the stegosaurs dorsal plates were carved in wood, attached to the armature with wire and screws, then blended into the skin with liquid latex and additional scales.

To breathe life into the creatures, a football inner-tube was padded with cotton, then encased in a rib cage of wire and screen mesh that was hinged from a rigid portion of the spine behind the shoulders. The inner-tube could be inflated by an especially designed pump attached to a tube running down the tail.

For *Creation*, two Stegosauri models had been built, each with a distinctive skin and facial detail to represent male and female. Both were used in *King*

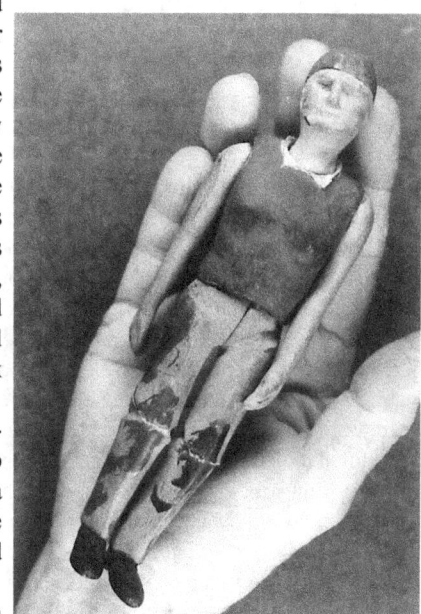

An articulated wooden figure used in many *King Kong* scenes.

The Making of King Kong

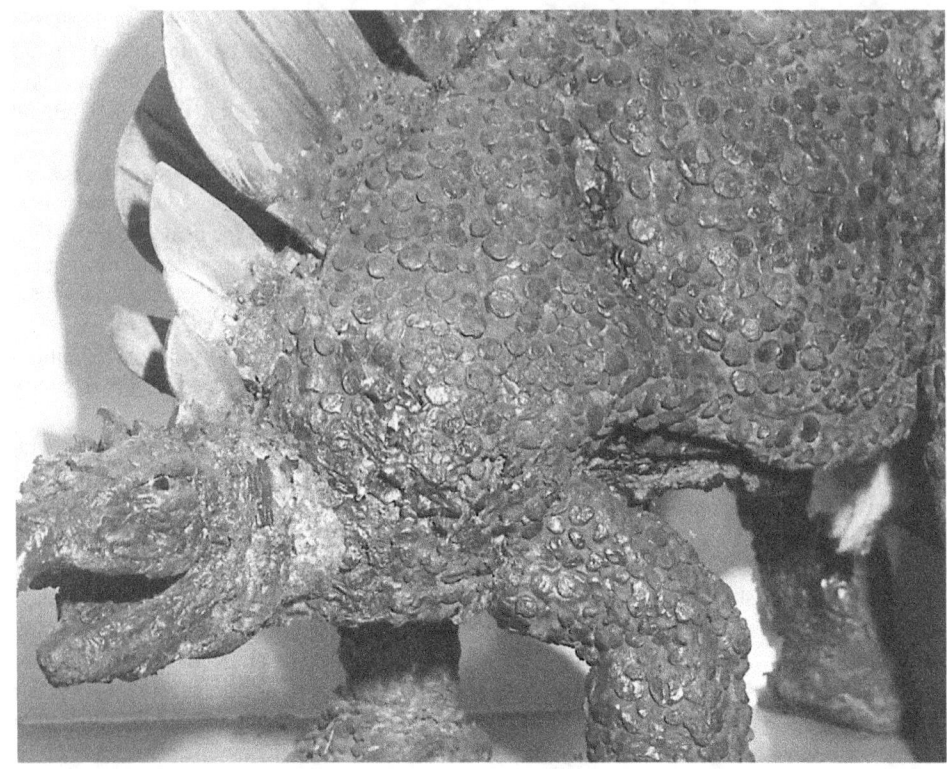

One of the Stegosaurus models used in *King Kong*

Kong, but here they represented the same animal. Although the charging stegosaurus is coarser, with large, densely packed scales, and the dying beast (seen as the actors file past) has a sparser, wartier texture, few viewers notice the differences. The use of both models enabled the technicians to work on both scenes simultaneously.

Three separate models were used for the Brontosaurus sequence. On land, the beast was a stop-motion miniature. But because water cannot be controlled from frame to frame, the water scenes employed a larger-scale head-neck-back apparatus that was operated mechanically and photographed at high speed to lend weight to the water and the flailing human dummies. The dinosaur's back was mounted on a wheeled cart that rode an elevated track in the studio tank. A series of loose hinge-joints ran up the neck to a universal joint at the base of the carved wooden skull. A coiled steel wire was spiraled around the armature to support the rubber skin and keep it from binding in the mechanism.

Tension springs at the base of the neck counterbalanced the head and provided lift to fling jointed dummies into the air. Bell cranks on both sides of the cart, through a series of gear and cable mechanisms, allowed the head to move independently of the neck and enabled the mouth to bite. Several similar mechanical Triceratopses had been built for *Creation* and later were scheduled to début in *The Son of Kong*—but never made it past the cutting room.

Finishing out the Brontosaurus sequence was a still larger-scale animation model of the head and neck; the head was about the size of a football. This piece was used for the scene where the creature menaces the man in the tree. It shows more detail and a finer expressive range than the smaller model could have provided.

Each scene was tested until its various elements were properly aligned and lighted. For this purpose, a portable darkroom measuring six by nine feet was kept on the stage. After a short length of film was exposed, the camera magazine was taken into the darkroom without disturbing the position of the camera, and the exposed strip of negative was developed. Frame enlargements, printed from these negatives, guided the technicians in adjusting artwork, props and lights until the desired effects and necessary alignments were achieved. Such precautions, though time-consuming, made it possible to avoid the errors in matching that compromise many a lesser film's trick scenes. It is fortunate that some of the crew members kept a few of these for souvenirs, for these faded prints—faded, because they were not *fixed* for permanency—are all that remain of many of the picture's scenes.

While designing, construction and tests proceeded at RKO, Schoedsack was experiencing hard times at Paramount. Returning from India in early January, he found the studio chiefs wrangling over the script and casting for *The Lives of a Bengal Lancer*, and in disagreement whether to complete the project at the studio or on location in the Sierras. A parade of noted writers tried reworking the script, and each version was rejected. Clive Brook, Phillips Holmes, Fredric March, Cary Grant and Richard Arlen were among the players whose names appeared on, then vanished from, the casting lists. Schoedsack, a devotee of direct action, became increasingly exasperated with the delays and was none too enthusiastic about time-marking assignments to shoot retakes for other directors.

"They called me in to direct a scene for a picture—I don't remember what it was," Schoedsack related. "I was to do a scene of Clive Brook on a ship, and all there was to it was that he walked over to the rail and looked out over the water. I told them they didn't need a director for that, just a cameraman, but they insisted." (The studio also insisted on having a parade of assistants, hairdressers, prop personnel and even a small orchestra.) "So I and a crew of about 35 went on the boat to Catalina and made the shot. A cameraman and the actor alone could have done it."

In March, John Cromwell was assigned to co-direct *Lives* with Schoedsack, but in the face of further delays Schoedsack secured a release from Paramount and joined Cooper at RKO, under contract as producer and director. Cromwell soon followed suit. Stephen Roberts next was named to direct *Lives*, which eventually was completed by Henry Hathaway—in 1935.

Creelman delivered his first reworking of *The Eighth Wonder* during the second week in March. The story still found the escaped convicts landing separately from Denham's expedition. "The chief criticisms on *Kong*," Cooper relayed in a memorandum, "seem to be that the dialogue is not consistent enough—the boy speaks in too bookish a fashion, and THAT THE HEAVY IS FAR TOO HEAVY." He also wanted the beauty-and-beast theme emphasized. He asked Creelman to make such changes in what time he had free from *The Most Dangerous Game*.

With the changes made, Selznick shipped this latest version to RKO's chief lawyer, Gordon "Tubby" Youngman, along with a note that the new version might be seen as an infringement upon—of all things!—a notoriously phony expeditionary film called *Ingagi*, issued two years earlier to immense box-office grosses and widespread condemnation from the scientific community. The next challenge over rights, however, came from Harold Kingsley, whose solicitors complained that the title *Kong* belonged to Kingsley's London play of the previous year. RKO paid Kingsley to go away.

In April 1932, Cooper and Schoedsack initiated pre-production on *The Most Dangerous Game*, for which James Creelman prepared an ingenious adaptation of Richard Connell's award-winning short-story from a 1930 issue of *Golden Book Magazine*. A large chunk of the film's $200,000 budget was allotted for the construction of an elaborate set on Stage No. 11 at the RKO-Pathé lot in Culver City. An eerie swamp, man-made cliffs, a waterfall and a ravine bridged by a fallen tree were dressed with authentic tropical trees and undergrowth. These elements were so designed by Carroll Clark, the art director, that they could be rearranged to create a variety of settings. With the addition of glass art by Larrinaga and Crabbe and atmospheric effects by Harry Redmond, Jr., the total set became—as far as the camera could discern—a vast jungle.

This accorded perfectly with Cooper's plans for *The Eighth Wonder*. Here was Kong's native heath, made to order—and already paid for.

Pathé, Its Perils & Pitfalls

> We didn't know what a good picture we had, there, until after it was done. Fay [Wray] still calls it "that awful thing we did."—Ernest B. Schoedsack on *The Most Dangerous Game*

Production 602, *The Most Dangerous Game*, was started early in mid-May under Ernest Schoedsack's direction, with Irving Pichel assigned to assist as dialogue director. "They hired Pichel because they were afraid I couldn't handle dialogue," Schoedsack told us. "He just stood behind me all the time and didn't do a damned thing." The cast included Joel McCrea, Fay Wray and Robert Armstrong.

Leslie Banks, a London and Broadway stage star who had never appeared in films, was imported for the pivotal role of Count Zaroff. Banks was witty and charming, a specialist in sophisticated comedy. Banks' features had been so marred in the World War I that his face presented two dramatically different profiles: The right side was classically handsome, while the left appeared rather brutish. This Jekyll-Hyde quality was useful in depicting the changing moods and warped longings of a man who displays Chesterfieldian manners and composes waltzes but is possessed by bestial desires.

Richard Connell's story depicts a battle of skills between two celebrated hunters when Rainsford is cast ashore on Zaroff's private island—where Zaroff lives for the stalking of human prey. Where Connell concentrated on the proto-survivalist concept of man against man, James Creelman twisted Zaroff's aberration a turn further by making the joy of the hunt a prerequisite to erotic indulgences. Zaroff says of a guest: "He talks of wine and women as a *prelude* to the hunt. We barbarians know that it is *after* the chase, and then only, that man revels... Kill, *then* love! When you have known that, then you have known ecstasy!"

This refinement hinged on the presence of a woman—the radiant Fay Wray. The addition of a romantic interest required the elimination of Connell's sardonic finale, where Rainsford becomes the proprietor of the death-trap island, but Creelman compensated with an attitude of rampant *virility* on either side of the struggle, and with a flamboyant exit for Zaroff.

Creelman spun wonderful yarns, but he had an impractical side that could cause production problems. He insisted, for example, that it would be more frightening if Zaroff used big cats rather than hounds to track his prey. Schoedsack, who knew the ways of the jungle felines, reluctantly borrowed a jaguar from the Selig Zoo. The animal was in the charge of a famous trainer, Olga Celeste.

Willis O'Brien had used a Celeste jaguar during *Creation*, with cringe-inducing results. Schoedsack's hired cat was equally uncooperative. Escaping into the fog-shrouded set, the creature caused a general panic before it could be recaptured. Schoedsack returned the jaguar and rented Harold Lloyd's magnificent pack of Great Danes and their trainer. The dogs' hair was darkened to make them appear more vicious, and they were sent in pursuit of Fay Wray and Joel McCrea, Banks following with a precision rifle.

Leslie Banks, Fay Wray and Joel McCrea in *The Most Dangerous Game*

In the course of the chase, Banks came bounding out of the fog, clutching his backside with his free hand.

"I *say*! One of those animals *bit* me!" the actor declared. The trainer protested that the pets absolutely would not bite. "Perhaps it was a cameraman, then," Banks replied, turning to reveal a lacerated *gluteus maximus*, "but *something* bit me on the arse!" Both the actor and his costume required patching before shooting could resume.

Another annoyance at Stage No. 11 was the nerve-wracking omnipresence of the affiliated company filming Production 601, by now retitled *Kong*. Merian Cooper hovered in the wings with his cast and crew, ready to barge onto the set between takes on Schoedsack's film. To make matters worse, Cooper insisted upon borrowing Armstrong and Miss Wray for hours at a time while Schoedsack fidgeted. A daily spectacle in the shared jungle of Kong and Zaroff was a Mutt-and-Jeff confrontation with the two producers gnawing their pipe stems and growling at one another.

The situation came to a head while Cooper was filming some difficult process scenes in which Miss Wray (who, at the time, was Mrs. John M. Saunders) lay pinned helplessly while Kong and a Tyrannosaurus fought over her. These shots required a great deal of intricate preparation because they combined full-scale properties, the actress, foreground glass art and previously filmed animation. Setting up and matching these various elements was a tedious business. Cooper was adjusting the actress's wig for the umpteenth time—she is a brunette in *Game* and a blonde in *Kong*—when Schoedsack rebelled.

"The camera is so far away, you could have a *prop boy* under that wig and nobody would know the difference!" Schoedsack insisted. Cooper felt otherwise but compromised by using photographer Eddie Linden, tech staffer E.B. "Buz" Gibson and a cut-out figure as stand-ins for

Bruce Cabot, Fay Wray and Robert Armstrong pose in a publicity shot for *King Kong*.

the actress between takes. In order that Schoedsack could meet the production schedule imposed by David O. Selznick, Cooper was obliged to do much of his filming at night.

Cooper had approached Fay Wray with the news that he had chosen her to be the leading lady in a film about "a discovery of gigantic proportions" and that she would play opposite "the tallest, darkest leading man in Hollywood." Her initial enthusiasm changed to panic as Cooper showed her Mario Larrinaga's official portrait of her assigned suitor, stalking through the jungle with Miss Wray clutched in one hairy paw. The role called for a blonde—for enhanced contrast—and Cooper had considered several blonde actresses, including Jean Harlow, Ginger Rogers and his wife-to-be, Dorothy Johran. But Cooper's high regard for Miss Wray prevailed. He decided, then, to cover Miss Wray's brown hair with a blonde wig and cast her as Kong's "golden woman."

Miss Wray's *other* romantic lead, Bruce Cabot, was a young contract player who had not yet appeared in a film. He came to Cooper's attention when he submitted some photos of himself made up as Zaroff, according to the description in the Connell story, with military mustache and white hair. Although he didn't come near landing the Zaroff role, Cabot found his tryout portrait used without his permission in an advertisement for *The Most Dangerous Game*! "Mighty upsetting, that was," Cabot told us, "and I let Mr. Cooper know I was plenty mad about it! I've always kind of thought *Kong* was somethin' of a consolation prize, if not a flat-out apology—but Mr. Cooper made me work plenty hard to get *Kong*, all the same." Indeed, Cabot's bid for the Jack Driscoll role in *King Kong* involved an extraordinary screen test: Cooper made him descend a rope suspended from the log bridge on Stage No. 11.

Armstrong, meanwhile, was hard at work on *The Most Dangerous Game*, handling a tragicomic role. Between scenes, Armstrong was instructed to swap his dress suit for a soiled and tattered safari get-up—the appropriate attire for his first day's work with Cooper on *Kong*. There was no script as yet, but Cooper and Creelman had decided there must be a chase through the jungle.

"... I *did* know that I was playing an adventurous motion-picture director who took a company to a mysterious island—and this was about all I knew," Armstrong recalled. "Mr. Cooper explained to me that this shot would be of myself and my crew, in single file, coming through the woods, and when I got to the log I was to hold up my hand and stop my followers. As I looked across the log, I was to see, across the chasm at the other end, a 50-foot ape.

"At this point, I said, 'Excuse me, Mr. Cooper, but if I understood you correctly, you said that I saw a 50-foot ape?' He said, 'Yes, that's right, Bob. Why?' I said, 'Well, am I supposed to take it big?' He said, 'Yes, Bob.' I said, 'Well, I've been in this business a great many years, but *you* tell *me* how to take a 50-foot ape *big*!'"

"Excuse me, Mr. Cooper, but if I understood you correctly, you said that I saw a 50-foot ape?" asked Robert Armstrong.

Script troubles continued. Creelman's fertile imagination produced good ideas, but he had difficulty keeping inside the bounds of financial and technical practicalities. Here, for example, is Creelman's description of Skull Island:

> FADE IN on a general view of Skull Island, at dawn, with the bridge of the ship in the foreground. Capt. Englehorn is leaning over the rail looking out at the grandeur of the spectacle. Sea and jungle are still in purple shadow. But high above, the east has drenched the mountains in the glory of its burning. One by one, the columnar peaks of snow are kindling downward, chasm by chasm, each in itself a new morning; white glaciers blaze their winding paths like fiery serpents; long avalanches cast down keen streams, brighter than lightning, each sending its tribute of driven snow, like altar smoke, to the heavens. The rose light of the silent domes flushes that heaven about them until the whole sky, one scarlet canopy, is interwoven with a roof of waving flame and tossing, vault beyond vault, as with the drifted wings of many companies of angels.

Although Schoedsack was not yet working on *Kong*, his renewed partnership with Cooper was already beginning to influence the film's storyline. *Kong* was taking on elements of *Grass* and *Chang* as well as aspects of its creators' adventures. The escaped convicts had been dropped, and Denham had become the daredevil chief of a motion-picture expedition that was ill-advisedly dragging a woman into danger—much as Cooper and Schoedsack had done with Marguerite

The biggest stumbling block was Cooper's insistence on having a native village with a human sacrifice.

Harrison on *Grass*. As the story found its truer streamlined shape, Kong made his appearance later along, like the elephants in *Chang*.

But knotty problems persisted, especially the need to bridge the action highlights so there would be no dull lapses. How to get the romantic leads from Kong's clutches and back to the native village; how to bring Kong to civilization without over-explanations; how to tell the purpose of Denham's expedition in as few words as possible—these were stumbling blocks that plagued Cooper and Creelman. Horace McCoy, a former journalist from Texas who had joined the writing staff at RKO after his acting career had fizzled, received his first scripting assignment with orders to help Creelman with *Kong*. McCoy became a well-known scenarist and author, his novels including *They Shoot Horses, Don't They?*

The biggest stumbling block was Cooper's insistence on having a native village with a human sacrifice. After weeks of drawing one blank after another, Creelman admitted defeat: "I can't seem to build to this and also to the prehistoric monsters at the same time," he confessed in a memorandum to Cooper. "The intrusion of the native village-human sacrifice angle, however, is a complication very considerably above that of the original setup, and that wasn't even mentioned until Horace McCoy first came on the story… I just can't imagine any way to do it."

By some alchemy of the minds, however, by the time shooting was winding down on *The Most Dangerous Game*, the native village was integrated into *Kong*, even allowing for an additional battle between the sailors and the villagers before the pursuit into the jungle after Kong.

Bruce Cabot's role—true to his try-out—required him to slide down a vine from the log bridge and swing into a cliffside cave. The ravine was built high above the floor of the stage, and the stunt extras had to fall from the log into a net. Bruised and fatigued after several days of this activity, the inexperienced Cabot became increasingly perplexed as to the nature of his assignment. He was relaxing one day with the stuntmen when one of them asked, "What part are you supposed to be playing in this crazy picture?"

"They tell me I'm the leading man," Cabot said.

"Then they lied to you," the stuntman told him. "You're just doing the rough stuff for Joel McCrea while he finishes that other picture." The other men agreed.

Cabot tried to convince himself that the story was just a rumor, but when he learned that the stuntmen were earning more than his modest contract salary, Cabot stormed up to Cooper and declared his resignation.

"But what about *Kong*?" Cooper demanded (unconsciously supplying a line for the film).

"You can shove *Kong*!" the actor shouted as he stormed off the set.

Cooper found Cabot before he could leave town and assured him that he definitely had the lead in *Kong*. It was true that McCrea—at the time, the studio's fair-haired boy— had been announced for the role, but RKO's insistence that McCrea be doubled in some strenuous scenes had led Cooper to seek out a less pampered actor.

"Don't go," Cooper urged. "You'll ruin us if you walk out now." Cabot agreed to return; it occurred to him only later that he should have demanded more money. As it turned out, his salary was *reduced* a short time later during a Selznick economy move.

There might have been more truth to the McCrea rumor if the actor had not proved so difficult on *The Most Dangerous Game*. Although lithe and athletic, McCrea was appalled by some of the derring-do Schoedsack expected of him. When McCrea balked at falling overboard during *Game*'s shipwreck sequence, a young Olympian swimming champ doubled for him. The stunt double was Larry "Buster" Crabbe, future Gold Medalist and star-to-be of the *Flash Gordon* and *Buck Rogers* serials. McCrea was equally unenthusiastic about a scene in which Steve Clemente was to throw a knife at him. "I don't care if he *is* the world's greatest knife thrower," McCrea

Joel McCrea and Fay Wray run for their lives in *The Most Dangerous Game*.

told Schoedsack. "He's not gonna throw a knife at me." The scene was simulated through adroit editing. Another stunt double was called in for some of McCrea's fight scenes. McCrea's performance turned out well overall.

Cooper, making full use of studio facilities and borrowed sets, had staged many scenes that he thought would be useful even though not needed for his test reel. Some of these scenes are in the final cut of *Kong*. Others were never seen outside the studio. By herding Denham and the sailors parallel to the edge of the gorge, Cooper was able to put the camera crane in the gorge and follow the action with remarkable freedom. The Fog Hollow set of *The Most Dangerous Game* provided the setting for the raft-building scene that leads into the Brontosaurus sequence, as well as the frantic chase that completes it.

Cooper staged a somewhat different version of the Stegosaurus charge: In one excised scene from the crevasse set, Denham and the others watch in horror as the Brontosaurus claims its final victim; in another, the characters react to a fight involving Kong and three Triceratopses. Additional shots, set up by the *Creation* footage, involve a sailor who becomes separated from the group and finds himself chased by a Triceratops.

Archie Marshek, the film editor assigned to *The Most Dangerous Game*, was one of the few men at the studio who believed that *Game* was potentially a classic. Even Schoedsack had his doubts; he said years after the fact: "I didn't think it would be very good, so I just decided to keep it moving so fast that nobody would notice. If a scene lasted 30 seconds, I'd say, 'I think it would play just as well in 20 seconds.' We didn't know what a good picture we had until it was finished." Marshek said that Schoedsack sometimes hid in the editing room when Cooper was on the set because each producer had his own ideas of how the chase should be filmed. By avoiding the issue, he was able to do it his own way. *The Most Dangerous Game* was brought in on schedule and within the budget.

The screening revealed that the Cooper-Schoedsack team had exceeded expectations. Their first all-talking picture provided ample proof that Schoedsack could no longer be typed as an outdoor-picture man, that his abilities embraced a far wider range than the documentary and the Natural Drama. His first studio film radiated atmosphere comparable with anything achieved by the great German stylists. Schoedsack insisted all along that he had no intention of making a horror movie, that he wanted only to tell an adventure yarn. Even so, as a spine-chiller *The Most Dangerous Game* holds its own with the best of James Whale or Tod Browning.

Especially notable is the characterization of Zaroff, a fantastic menace who is made to seem disconcertingly real via subtle touches seldom applied to melodrama. Early on, he is shown in evening attire—the perfect host, playing on the piano a lilting waltz of his own composition. Standing among

The familiar jungle set of *The Most Dangerous Game*

Especially notable in *The Most Dangerous Game* is the characterization of Zaroff (Leslie Banks).

the exaggerated shadows of his big-game trophies, Zaroff absently runs his fingers over the scar that symbolizes his madness. His eyes glisten with tears when he realizes that the only man in the world he dared hope would share his mania considers him insane, and he seems genuinely hurt when the woman he admires upbraids him for murdering her brother. In the jungle, garbed in black hunting togs, he becomes an unfettered savage as he races through the fog, gleefully sounding the horn to summon his hounds to the kill.

The mood is captured perfectly by cameraman Henry Gerard and heightened by Max Steiner's music. Steiner wrote Zaroff's piano material, which was performed for the soundtrack by Norma Boleslawski, and founded much of the overall score upon its theme. The score is among the most elaborate of the 1930s, containing 83 musical cues involving 14 compositions. The prolonged chase contains some of the most exciting original-for-film music extant.

Realism is evident even within the framework of fantasy. Schoedsack visited a medical morgue to learn how human heads are preserved. He already knew how to construct jungle traps because he had seen it done in Siam and Sumatra. The Malay deadfall was real, and the log shook the stage when it landed.

"I think of a film as though it were music," Schoedsack told us. "It must have a beginning, a middle and an end, and should build up to climaxes, then allow some rest, the build again. If necessary, I use a stopwatch on the actors." This credo is evident throughout *Chang*, which Schoedsack and Cooper considered their best work, and in *Rango*. It is fully crystallized in the thrilling pace of *The Most Dangerous Game*, which in this respect has yet to be surpassed.

The producers were convinced that most films of the period were too stagebound, with static photography and plodding scenes played more for the benefit of microphone than camera.

They had been upset when Selznick added stagey scenes to their otherwise cinematic *The Four Feathers*, and they had determined that none of their productions henceforth would be similarly crippled. To this end, they utilized in their initial talkie the best features of silent-screen technique—fluid camerawork, creative cutting and emphatic musical scoring—with dialogue calculated to complement, rather than dominate, the action.

The shipwreck sequence, for example, begins with an interruption of dialogue as the players are tumbled about by the impact of the ship's hitting the reef. A series of 20 flash-shots shows in only seconds the horror of the situation: the lurching ship; water rushing through the bulkheads; pandemonium on the bridge; pressure gauges swinging to the danger zone; the engine-room crew awash in scalding water; a superb miniature of the exploding ship; men and debris falling into the sea. Montages of this sort were not unusual in later films, but in 1932 it was a daring experiment—even though it had come about as a cost-cutting move.

Zaroff's aberrations are exposed early on so that no further explanations need intrude once the chase had begun. Suspense builds slowly at first, gathering momentum almost without interruption right to the end, with the few brief pauses artfully placed to allow the audience a chance to catch its breath. Each shot is of the exact duration needed to sustain the unrelenting tempo. The camera angles are superbly varied, with the hounds and hunters sometimes shown from below ground level, rushing over the camera like the elephants of *Chang* and taking on the aspect of gigantic beasts. Skillfully intercut are shots where the camera holds still to observe the action and, elsewhere, races along with the players.

The opening titles are superimposed over a door knocker depicting a wounded centaur bearing the body of a woman. This motif symbolizes the story itself, as adapted. Marcel Delgado made some of the special properties, including the desiccated human heads in Zaroff's trophy room.

By the time *The Most Dangerous Game* was in the can, *Kong*—despite the secrecy surrounding it—was the talk of the industry. The test reel, approximately 10 minutes of outrageous but

Early conception of the battle between monsters

Conceptual drawing of the clifftop encounter

enthralling action, was calculated to make its privileged studio brass want more. A dozen large, detailed drawings served to illustrate dramatically the highlights planned for the feature. Mario Larrinaga and Byron Crabbe rendered the scenes in carbon pencil after O'Brien's sketches.

Cooper unveiled the drawings to the studio's board of directors at the time the test reel was screened. Although they were drawn when only a hazy idea of the screen story existed, most of the action depicted in them appears in the final production. The scenes:

1. A Brontosaurus rises from the water, capsizing a lifeboat containing a girl and the male players.
2. Kong fights sailors.
3. Kong, carrying the girl, approaches the log bridge.
4. Kong shakes the log, tumbling men into the chasm.
5. Gigantic insects and a huge spider attack the sailors at the bottom of the gorge.
6. Kong fights the Tyrannosaurus.
7. Kong, seated on a ledge near the summit of Skull Mountain, tears at Ann's clothing.
8. Kong seizes a Pterodactyl as it tries to carry Ann away.
9. Kong, chained at centerfield in Yankee Stadium, breaks free.
10. Panic breaks out on a New York street as Kong holds an automobile above his head.
11. A girl in a hotel room awakes to see Kong reaching in through a window.
12. Kong, atop the Empire State Building, holds Ann in one paw and roars defiance at Navy pursuit planes.

The test reel contained some 138 scenes, the first being the shot from *Creation* in which a Triceratops pursues and kills a man. Then:

Perils attend either end of the log bridge.

The remaining nine men, including Denham and Driscoll, race madly through the jungle until they approach a gorge bridged by a fallen tree. They halt when they see Kong, who carries Ann, crossing the log. An Arsinoitherium charges the men, whom Driscoll leads to the log. Kong stops in a clearing and listens, then deposits Ann in the top of a dead tree and hastens back to the gorge. The men are across the log when they see Kong approaching. Driscoll descends a vine and swings into a cave about 10 feet below. Denham, at the other end of the log, ducks out of sight in the underbrush. The men on the bridge are trapped between Kong and the Arsinoitherium. Kong lifts the end of the log and shakes two men off. They land in deep mud. A third man falls, then two more and then another, until only one clings to the log. Kong angrily lifts the end of the tree and lets it drop into the gorge. Monstrous lizards and insects, a gigantic spider and an octopus-like creature swarm out to devour the men. The spider crawls up a liana toward Driscoll's cave. Driscoll cuts the vine and sends the spider tumbling just as Kong reaches into the cave. Eluding the paw, Driscoll slashes out. Kong withdraws his hand and licks it, then reaches again. Meanwhile, Ann stirs from her faint and looks down to see a monstrous snake at the foot of the tree. A Tyrannosaurus enters the glade. Ann screams; the dinosaur stops and scratches its ear. Kong almost has Driscoll in his grasp when he hears the scream. Hurrying back, Kong arrives just as the Tyrannosaur is about to seize the girl. The monsters engage in a titanic battle. Kong is flung against the tree, which falls, pinning Ann. Kong finally kills the dinosaur by tearing its jaws apart. Carefully, he lifts the tree from Ann, picks her up and carries her on into the jungle. Driscoll climbs to the bank and is hailed by Denham from the other side. Unable to cross the gorge, Denham heads back to get help while Driscoll continues to trail after Kong. The sequence ends as Driscoll steals past the still-breathing body of the Tyrannosaurus, frightening away a huge vulture.

The methods devised by O'Brien and his crew to film this remarkable phantasmagoria, while deriving from his earlier work, were more sophisticated by far. Cooper's imagination was even more vivid than O'Brien's, and the greatest ingenuity was required to put his ideas onto film. Several of Cooper's colleagues assured him that many of the scenes he envisioned could not possibly be produced.

"However," Cooper told us, "I knew that there was nothing a man could mentally conceive that the cameraman could not re-create or exceed by any number of processes available. "Frankly, I didn't know the details of how we were going to produce these strange prehistoric animals and mingle them with real persons in modern settings, but I was able to secure the services of two men eminently fitted for the work to be done. One was Mr. Schoedsack, who had made pictures with me before. The other was Willis O'Brien."

The reception of the test film was predominantly enthusiastic, although several highly placed executives were not sympathetic to the project and did their utmost to block it. Selznick offered his highest endorsement, and Cooper—with admonishments to keep the budget within realistic bounds—was given the green light to produce his feature in association with Schoedsack.

The producers dared not wait for a formalized script. Creelman was assigned to write the screenplay while Schoedsack began working with the actors. Cooper and O'Brien proceeded to plan and develop the animated sequences. The technicians continued to build settings and went to work constructing some larger props, the likes of which had never been seen at any studio.

Marcel Delgado repaired the original Kong model and began to build an additional Kong, so that one star player could be on the set while the other was being refurbished from the rigors of production. Delgado had built the first Kong armature himself, owing to the fact that the project did not have full studio approval and resources, but the new armatures were built by RKO's mechanical department, complying with a six-page diagram. Both Kongs were substantially the same except that the new Kong's arms were slightly longer. Because of Delgado's build-up methods and the constant repairs necessary to keep the models ready to face the cameras, Kong's visage varies from shot to shot. Later, a third Kong model was built for the New York scenes. This version was larger, standing 24 inches tall, with significantly longer arms in proportion to the body and a smoother pelt. This Kong also may have been used in the cave and ledge scenes, and in a few shots of the ape's rampage through the village.

Many months of work lay ahead before the cameras would cease turning on Production 601.

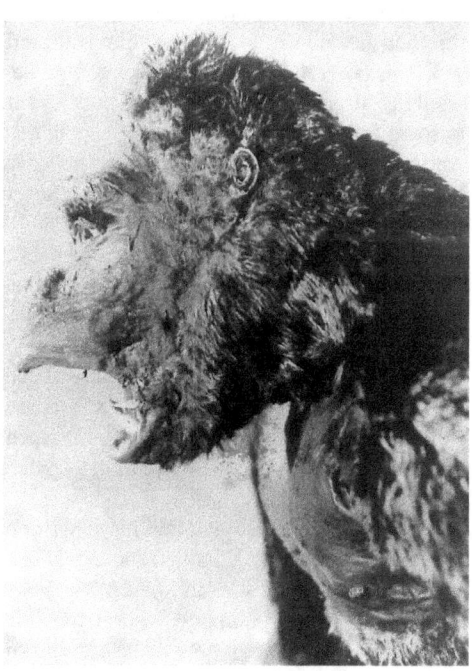

The Kong models suffered constant wear-and-tear.

"We Really Had a Happy Company, There"

> I suppose I shall always be known for pictures of that ilk—of which *King Kong* is, I suppose, with all due respect, the ilkiest. And I do cherish that identification.—Fay Wray, at Dallas' U.S.A. Film Festival; 1990

In an NBC-Radio Network interview, Merian Cooper reconstructed the circumstances that led to his creation of *King Kong*:

"The world is getting smaller every year. I mean, it's becoming too civilized. I can remember when the world was a grand old place—a place full of unexplored lands, choked with adventure. In those days, Schoedsack and I used to run away to the ends of the world, confident of finding real motion-picture material. But now, what's a fellow to do? Where is he to go?

"Persia, where Schoedsack and I made *Grass*; Siam, where we made *Chang*; and all the other colorful spots where we have made films: Borneo, Sumatra and the Archipelago—no longer is there any mystery or hidden adventure in those places. Although there are few spots left to explore, I can't give up the idea of making adventure films. And this very obstacle... has made me dream again. And that dream is: If I had it in my power to plot the greatest adventure of a lifetime, one I could actually participate in, what would it be?

"It would be this: Halfway around the world, somewhere in the Malay waters, there would be an unexplored land known as Skull Island. On this island would dwell a tribe of strange savages but not half so queer as their god whom they worship, a frightful god known to them as King Kong, a towering beast, 50 feet in height, who would have the power to crush a human being in the palm of his hand. To capture that animal and bring him back to Broadway, New York, to my way of thinking, would be a swell adventure. I don't know what the details of the story would be. I know only that in the story I would have a crazy motion-picture producer go in search of this monster. He would take with him a motion-picture company which would include only one girl. This powerful beast, King Kong, who never in all his life had gazed on a beautiful thing, would be strangely attracted to this pretty white girl[1]—attracted to her, perhaps, as he might be to some frail but beautiful flower. In some manner, I could bring this beast back to New York. And then the monster, thinking of this beautiful human toy..."

Although this statement was made after the fact, it and the drawings used to pitch the test film combine to provide a reasonably accurate reconstruction of the concept before an actual shooting script had been prepared. James Creelman contributed many good ideas but proved incapable of delivering a screenplay that suited Cooper or Ernest Schoedsack. They found too many stumbling blocks to the breakneck pace they had envisioned, too much dialogue that seemed ill suited to the characters.

As David O. Selznick's assistant, Cooper was in a position to take his pick from the vast array of writers under contract to RKO-Radio Pictures. This group included Beulah Marie Dix, Robert Benchley, J. Walter Ruben, Ralph Spence, Bernard Schubert, Garrett Fort, Ralph Block and many other dependable wordsmiths. To the surprise of everyone at the studio, Cooper handed the script to Ruth Rose.

Now, Mrs. Schoedsack had never written a screenplay. Her literary experience consisted of articles about the William Beebe expeditions and one romantic short story, "Trade Winds," which had been published in *The Ladies' Home Journal*. Cooper felt that, whatever her lack of studio experience, Ruth knew what it was like to be a member of a dangerous expedition in a tropical jungle infested with wild beasts; she knew the rough-hewn sailors who man the decks of tramp steamers; and she knew what manner of person it takes to make pilgrimages to unexplored lands—how they talk, and how they react to danger: She had been one, after all, and she had married one. Ruth was equally familiar with Broadway and its blustery jargon.

"Put *us* in it," Cooper told her. "Give it the almost Victorian kind of dialogue that it needs to make the fantasy stand up. Establish everything before Kong makes his appearance so that we won't have to explain anything after that. Give it the spirit of a real Cooper-Schoedsack expedition."

The studio executives were opposed to introducing Kong so late in the story. They insisted that Kong should appear at the beginning. Cooper and Schoedsack, however, were adamant in their insistence upon using their own formula in constructing the script. This system had proved highly successful in its first application, *Chang*, and it had worked fine on *Rango* and *The Most Dangerous Game*.

Carl Denham (Robert Armstrong) films Ann Darrow (Fay Wray) in *King Kong*.

Mrs. Schoedsack concentrated at first on conversational sequences, which her husband staged before the official script was completed and mimeographed.

"When I was writing," she told us, "it always had to be with a pencil. Then the poor girls in the typing pool had to struggle with the result. Except for copying business letters, the darned [typewriter] bothers me. And I could never dictate because I was so self-conscious about what [a secretary] might think of my efforts. Silly."

The Ruth Rose script retained intact Cooper's test reel, including the *Creation* scene with the Triceratops. Although it sufficed to satisfy the home office as to what to expect, the shooting script differs considerably from the finished product. The writer stayed on the set all during the months that followed, editing and rewriting day by day. She threw out anything that proved superfluous or impeded the flow of action, and she changed dialogue to conform to the random developments of production and to maintain the celebrated Cooper-Schoedsack pace.

The producers knew they had the writer they needed when they read the opening line: "Hey! Is this the moving-picture ship?" Ruth had thrown out several pages of explanation and in only nine syllables succeeded in getting the story under way. A few more lines inform us that the boss, Carl Denham, is "crazy"; that the S.S. *Venture* carries a crew three times larger than normal; that there is on board "enough ammunition to blow up the harbor"; that Denham has ordered some pineapple-sized gas grenades "strong enough to knock out an elephant"; and that Denham has searched in vain for an actress willing to join up. By the time Denham has told Ann Darrow that she is headed toward "money and adventure and fame on a long sea voyage" and Ann has met the handsome first mate, the story is fundamentally established. More dark hints follow about the destination and the nature of the mysterious Kong, along with the introduction of a beauty-and-beast theme. From here, nothing had to be spelled out.

Denham, who seems cold-blooded at first, emerges by degrees as a heroic protector combining the personalities of Cooper and Schoedsack. Traits of Schoedsack are evident in Driscoll, the hard-nosed, gentle-hearted lug who pretends to be a woman-hater. Capt. Englehorn somewhat resembles the intrepid William Beebe. The lovely Ann Darrow becomes an extension of Ruth Rose Schoedsack—although the screenwriter insisted such an idea never occurred to her.

One crucial bit of story material came from an unexpected source: Esteban Clemente, aka Steve Clemente, a Yaqui Indian who was known in vaudeville as the world's greatest knife-

On board the *Venture* with Frank Reicher (left), Robert Armstrong, Bruce Cabot and Fay Wray

thrower, was at work on *The Most Dangerous Game* as a Mongolian servant. Although he possessed an incredibly malevolent grimace, Clemente was a likable and mild-mannered little man who became a friend of Cooper and the Schoedsacks. One day, he told them of the difficulty he had encountered in hiring a pretty girl to serve as the mock-target for his stage act. After all the talent agencies had refused to help him, Clemente took to walking the streets in search of someone sufficiently comely and courageous to handle the job. Finally, he saw a shabbily dressed but very attractive young woman standing at a lunchroom window, gazing in like a child outside a toy store. Clemente suggested she dine with him. Frightened, but too hungry to refuse, she accepted. After Clemente managed with considerable difficulty to explain why he was interested in her, she accepted the job. It is scarcely a happenstance that this encounter, combined with episodes from Ruth Rose's early career, resembles the opening sequence of *Kong*.

Schoedsack said his wife's script was easy to film:

> The characters are believable—I didn't have to ask them to do anything impossible or ridiculous—and she never bothered me with descriptions of sets, only mentioned the locations where the scenes took place. She probably knew it wouldn't do any good because I always had to figure something out with the location or with the art department—something practical, and something I could use. Nothing annoys me more in a script than long-winded descriptions of settings by writers whose only experience is behind the typewriter and who have no idea of the technical and expense problems involved. Of course, studio techniques are entirely different from the ones we used out in the jungle, making things of what already was there. The secret of our success with animals in these pictures was that we found out first what the animal would do and then incorporated this into the action of the story. This is quite different from trying to force something to happen as dreamed up by some dope behind a typewriter in Hollywood who has had no experience with the actual things he's writing about. That's why Ruth's scripts were so good: She knew all her characters.

King Kong is essentially a fantastic version of the realistic *Chang* in its expansion of genuine adventures into the realm of the impossible. The slow, deliberate buildup was necessary so that the viewer's suspension of disbelief could be maintained to the end. It would have been ruinous to permit the viewer to stop and think during the extravagant scenes following the introduction of the monsters: The audience must be swept along with the action. The success of this formula has been demonstrated by default by most of the fantasy films that have attempted to duplicate the success of *King Kong*, however well- or ill-made they might be in the technical sense. The only significant advancement of this tactic has been to incorporate a brief action-packed segment, then settle down to the brief explanatory scenario before the action resumes—as in the much more recent likes of *Raiders of the Lost Ark*, *Aliens* and *Jurassic Park*.

Ruth Rose created a language for the natives of Skull Island, identified in the film as resembling "the language the Nias Islanders speak." The Production Code Administration, leery that this mumbo-jumbo might contain some indelicate phrases, demanded that an English translation of all native dialogue be submitted for approval. The author complied, although she considered it unlikely that the picture would be seen by the isolated inhabitants of Palau Nias, which lies in the Indian Ocean west of Sumatra. Herewith, we present a translated sample of the Australasian-based language, spoken on screen by Noble Johnson, as the tribal chief:

"Malem ma pakeno! [The woman of gold!] Kong wa bisa! [Kong's gift!] Kow bisa para Kong! [A gift for Kong!] Dana, temp malem na hi? [Strangers sell woman to us?] Sani sita malem ati—kow dia malem ma pakeno. [I will give six women like this for your woman of gold.]"

The Production Code invoked the same rule in later years, when Mrs. Schoedsack created the Arabic-based language of the mythical land of Kor for *She* (1935) and the speech of a fictitious African tribe for *Mighty Joe Young* (1949).

Noble Johnson, one of the natives for whom Ruth Rose created a language for use in *King Kong*.

"Ruth used just the kind of romantic dialogue I wanted," said Cooper. "It was perfect! Monte and Creelman and I wrote some, but Ruth did 90 percent of it." One of Cooper's contributions is the supposedly ancient Arabian proverb that opens the film: "And the Prophet said: And lo! The Beast looked upon the face of Beauty. And it stayed its hand from killing. And from that day it was as one dead." Schoedsack's distinctive touch is evident in the salty dialogue aboard ship and in the jungle.

One of Ruth Rose's greatest improvements was the scrapping of an involved sequence showing how Kong was brought to New York. Edgar Wallace had attempted such a transition, but nowhere near as effectively as Mrs. Schoedsack handled it: She moved the action directly from Skull Island to Broadway with a few lines, spoken by Denham as he surveys the unconscious Kong:

"Send to the ship for anchor chains and tools. Build a raft and float him to the ship. We'll give him more than chains. He's always been king of his world, but we'll teach him fear. Why, the whole *world* will pay to see this! We're millionaires, boys—I'll share it with all of you! In a few months, it'll be up in lights: 'Kong, the Eighth Wonder of the World!'" Dissolve to a shot of a Broadway marquee, with Denham's very words up in lights.

Slickly dialogued love scenes were the order of the day during the early '30s, when writers and directors from the stage exerted a strong influence on the cinema. Ruth Rose chose instead to capture the sort of talk one might expect from a tough seafaring man who has fallen in love for the first time:

"Don't laugh! I'm scared for you!" Jack Driscoll tells Ann Darrow. "I'm... I'm sort of scared *of* you, too. Ann, I... Say, I guess I *love* you!"

"But Jack," Ann replies, "You *hate* women!"

"Yeah, but you aren't women. Ann, I don't suppose... You don't feel anything like that about *me*, do you?"

And here, the lovers embrace. The scene is both amusing and touching. Cabot, who was anything but shy around women, had a great deal of difficulty with this scene, one of the few for which Schoedsack demanded numerous takes.

Cabot, scion of an aristocratic French-Indian family of Carlsbad, New Mexico, was handicapped by a lack of acting experience when he made *Kong*. Prior to that, he had played a few bit parts under his real name, Jacques de Bujac. After attending New Mexico Military Institute, Swanee Military Academy and New Mexico University, he worked his way over much of the world at a variety of unusual occupations: archaeological bone-gatherer on the Southwestern Plains, seaman on a freighter, sparring partner for a boxer, oilfield roughneck, road surveyor, civil engineer, Wall Street broker and nightclub manager. David Selznick met him at a Hollywood party and placed him under contract.

Tenderness amid the turmoil

"I didn't know enough about pictures at that time to know what *Kong* was all about," Cabot said. "I just did what I was told and collected my weekly paycheck." By 1935, the *New York Times* would hail Cabot's highly professional performance in *Show Them No Mercy!* as one of the year's finest: "Bruce Cabot gives a terrifying performance as a surly killer who is transformed by liquor and nerve into an irresponsible madman," wrote critic André Sennwald, citing the "cold brutality and macabre humor" Cabot brought to the role. Cabot proved equally memorable as Magua in *The Last of the Mohicans* and as a lifelike Public Enemy No. 1 in *Let 'Em Have It*.

Bruce Cabot

For 40 years, the six-foot-two actor alternated between heroism and villainy, taking time out for duty in World War II as an Army Intelligence officer in Africa, Sicily and Italy. Cabot's off-screen life was as colorful and exciting as the roles he played. When he died of throat cancer on May 3, 1972, at the age of 68, the obituary notices invariably were headlined with the phrase "*King Kong* hero," despite his having followed this first prominent role with scores of others.

Robert Armstrong had a notable career in the theatre and motion pictures before he portrayed the fast-talking Carl Denham, the role for which he is best remembered. Armstrong dropped out of law school at the University of Washington in Seattle in order to tour with a vaudeville company, later becoming the leading man in New York with Jimmy Gleason's stock company. A hit play, Gleason's *Is Zat So?*, brought Armstrong a movie contract with Pathé in 1926. His first film was *The Main Event*, in which he can be seen as a prizefighter.

"I had been in Hollywood just long enough to establish myself as a silent actor when sound came in," Armstrong told us. "Then, the producers started looking for stage actors and paying them big salaries to come out here. I kept shouting, 'Hey! How about me? I was *raised* on the stage! Listen to me! Me! ME!' But they wouldn't notice, and I soon found myself playing support to the guys who had supported me on the stage a couple of years earlier!" By the early 1930s, Armstrong was getting better roles, such as that of the dynamic fight promoter in Universal's *The Iron Man*. "I was fortunate to get the Denham role," Armstrong said.

A thoroughgoing professional, Armstrong made more than 100 pictures as well as stage and television appearances before a coronary attack forced his retirement in 1952. He played heroes, villains and character roles (such as Tojo in *Blood on the Sun*) with uniformly fine results. One of Armstrong's last television performances was a guest-shot on *The Red Skelton Show*. In the middle of a sketch, apropos of nothing, Skelton ad-libbed a showstopper: "Say, did you ever get that monkey down from that building?"

Armstrong died on April 21, 1973, at the age of 82. Although in his later years he became white-haired, Bob Armstrong retained throughout the robust aspect and commanding geniality of a born sportsman—and his voice remained precisely that of Carl Denham. His closest friends to the last were the Schoedsacks and Fay Wray.

Once during the 1960s, Armstrong was reminiscing about his experiences in silent pictures: "Phyllis Haver was a sweet, lovely girl," he said. "She was almost as nice as Fay—but of course, *nobody* is *that* nice." Anyone who has ever known Fay Wray can only concur. There have been

Fay Wray as Ann Darrow

more gifted actresses, and there have been a few with a more striking physical beauty, but never have the contradictory qualities of sex appeal and virtue been blended more strikingly in one woman. The girl every red-blooded man would like to rescue and protect, she was the perfect choice to play Cooper's Beauty.

The daughter of a rancher, Fay Wray came to California from Alberta, where she was born in 1907. While a student at Hollywood High School, she appeared in a regional pageant, the annual *Pilgrimage Play*. By 1923, at age 16, she was handling bit roles at various studios, moving on to leads in Hal Roach comedies and Universal Westerns. In 1926, Erich von Stroheim selected her to play the lead in his monumental Paramount picture, *The Wedding March*, which led to a long succession of roles opposite the reigning male leads at Paramount. Cooper-Schoedsack Productions, whose partners had been delighted to work with Miss Wray on *The Four Feathers*, brought her to RKO for *The Most Dangerous Game*. She was at the time married to the brilliant but erratic author, John Monk Saunders (of *Wings* and *The Dawn Patrol*), whose career was blighted by drugs and drink and ended in suicide. A second marriage, to writer Robert Riskin, met with tragedy when Riskin was paralyzed by a stroke; Miss Wray gave up her career to look after her husband for several years, returning to the screen only after his death.

Her blue eyes and fair skin made her seem a natural blonde in *Kong*, and that is the way the public still regards her. In her scores of other pictures, she appears with her own brown hair. For years, she was typed as an ingenue in horror pictures, a pattern that actually had taken shape before *King Kong*. She fled to England in the middle 1930s in an attempt to break the mold—only to find herself cast in similar roles. For reasons that defy understanding, this very popular actress was denied top-shelf stardom although she usually was featured opposite the top male stars of the major studios.

A gifted writer and musician, Miss Wray long harbored mixed feelings toward her horror- and-adventure pictures, hoping to return to the higher-minded assignments she had known under von Stroheim and Josef von Sternberg. But it is through the thrillers that she has retained a lasting recognition—some of her pictures, including *Kong* and *Mystery of the Wax Museum*, attaining regard as classics—while many loftier dramas of the Depression years have been forgotten. In 1976, at the Telluride [Colorado] Film Festival, Miss Wray graced ceremonies marking the publication of George Turner's *The Making of King Kong*. As late as the 1990s, she continued to make crowd-pleasing appearances, including a spotlighted surprise guest shot at an Academy Awards ceremony. Fay Wray passed away in 2004.

The doughty Capt. Englehorn was superbly realized in the person of Frank Reicher, a Munich-born writer, director and actor. A wiry little man who kept fit by swimming, Reicher was a leading figure in the theatres of Berlin, London and New York. He made a few films as early as 1915, returned to the stage until the late 1920s, then returned to the movies for keeps. Reicher died at age 89 on January 19, 1965.

Reicher's acting required little direction. Occasionally, Schoedsack would say, "That was a little strong, Frank," or "Let's give it a little more," and Reicher would be perfect in the next take. "He was the best actor we had," said Schoedsack, "and he helped the other actors along. He knew exactly what tempo was right for any scene."

The black actor Noble Mark Johnson (aka Mark Noble) was artificially blackened and covered with tattoos and ceremonial scars for his role as the tribal chief. Missouri-born in 1881 and raised in Colorado Springs, Johnson attended school with Lon Chaney; they renewed their friendship as fellow actors in the formative years of feature filmmaking. Johnson was technically a mulatto, so fair-skinned that he could play a wide variety of ethnicities, including the Cossack of *The Most Dangerous Game*, a Chinese in *The Mysterious Dr. Fu Manchu*, a Nubian in *The Mummy*, a Polynesian in *Moby Dick*, a Persian in *The Thief of Bagdad* and a Cuban zombie in *The Ghost Breakers*. His most oft-repeated casting was as an Indian chief or warrior, which led many viewers to assume Johnson to be a Native American. Johnson had been a founder during the 1920s of a pioneering black-ensemble company, the Lincoln Motion Picture Co., and found his earliest roles in such pictures as *A Western Governor's Humanity* (1915), *The Realization of a Negro's Ambition* (1916) and *A Trooper of Troop K* (1917). He left the Lincoln company for full-time contract work at Universal.

"He was like his name—Noble," Bruce Cabot said of Johnson. An impressive figure, six-foot-two and heavily muscled, Johnson could appear primitively cruel in one film and immensely sympathetic in another. He was a soft-spoken and gentle soul offscreen. Johnson left the movies in the early 1950s—with a fleeting return, via television's *Lost Island of Kioga*, during the 1960s—and invested in Nevada real estate. Johnson died on January 9, 1978, at Yucaipa, California, and was buried at Newhall, California's Eternal Valley Memorial Park Garden of Peace.

Sam Hardy, cast appropriately as a Broadway character, was a stage actor for 23 years, dividing his time between comedies and dramas with the occasional leading role in the silent movies. A big, sociable man, Hardy was a close friend of W.C. Fields and other bigger-than-life show-business personalities. Most of his film roles were more prominent than his brief appearance in *King Kong*.

Steve Clemente is virtually unrecognizable under the witch-doctor makeup in *Kong*. The Indian actor, who most often portrayed the villainous half-breed once considered indispensable to Western adventures—his nearest rivals being the Apache Charles Stevens and the Turkish Frank Lackteen—died in 1950 at age 65.

The plug-ugly crew of the *Venture* was made up of Western heavies and stuntmen. Among the more conspicuous are Dick Curtis, who earned the title of "the meanest man in Hollywood" by menacing innumerable Western heroes from 1918 until his death in 1953; and the husky former boxer John P. "Blackie" Whiteford (1889-1962). The one clean-cut crewman is James Flavin, a young New York actor who also co-starred that year with his future wife, Lucile Browne, in the Universal serial *Phantom of the Air*. Flavin specialized over the long haul in playing tough police detectives. The Chinese Victor Wong, originally scheduled for a bit part, proved so effective a laugh-getter that his role was enlarged during production.

King Kong was not an easy picture for anyone involved, thanks to the many technical problems to be surmounted. But a pleasant camaraderie developed among the players and staff. "We really had a happy company, there," said Schoedsack.

1 And yes, the ethnological attitudes and gender bias implicit in this statement are quaint at best and bigoted at worst—quite at odds with Cooper's obviously greater enlightenment as a citizen-of-the-world globetrotter. The movie itself makes it implicit, however, that Kong has gazed upon some generations of native beauties, and that it is the tribesmen who demand Ann Darrow for their next sacrifice, replacing a native woman, because Miss Darrow's very blondeness calls for an unexpectedly drastic change in tradition. This condition might be suspect in the context of a Hollywood movie dreamed up by an American white man of the economic upper crust, if not for Cooper's distinction of having observed such tribal behaviors at first hand.—M.H.P.

When Inventions Become Necessary

Production of such a picture requires extreme care to create *[the]* illusion of actuality.—*Modern Mechanix & Inventions Magazine,* April 1933

For those who might believe that the school of fatuous blowhard show-biz reportage, from purportedly respectable publications, began with *People Weekly* magazine, a bit of perspective: *Time,* that bastion of cultural and political authority—and ancestor of *People*—assured the nation on March 13, 1933, that "*King Kong*... was not made entirely by enlarging miniatures. Kong is actually 50 feet tall, 36 feet around the chest. His face is six-and-a-half feet wide with 10-inch teeth and ears one foot long. He has a rubber nose, glass eyes as big as tennis balls. His furry outside is made of 30 bearskins. During his tantrums, there were six men in his interior running his 85 motors."

The April 1933 *Modern Mechanix & Inventions* magazine ill-informed its followers that Kong is "a normal-size actor in [an] ape costume." Two pages of drawings show such an imaginary actor scaling a miniature facade built horizontally along a floor; emoting in front of a process screen on which warplanes are projected; and being filmed in composite against a red screen on a "negative insensitive to red light, recording only the ape's actions, taken in blue light, to add to scenes already on the negative." Fay Wray, according to this credulous account, had been photographed separately, her image "cut and placed in the ape's hands, each frame individually photographed to show progress of action, as moving arms, etc."

"This," the magazine concluded with solemn mock authority, "is known as 'animating.'"

And such writing is known as so much banana oil.

A French publication reported that an actor in an ape-skin was reduced by trick photography and superimposed onto drawings of a jungle. Many writers have repeated this howler.

Another oft-repeated story is that Charles Gemora, the Filipino actor who portrayed gorillas in innumerable movies from the 1930 *The Unholy Three* to *Ingagi* to *Murders in the Rue Morgue,* also portrayed Kong. Gemora would have none of this hogwash[1]—but his responsible denials did nothing to stop the baloney merchants. One writer, after allowing that Kong was a stop-action miniature in most scenes, declared that it was Gemora who climbed the Empire State Building in the long shots of that sequence. To compound the confusion, Gemora's wire-service obituary notices stated that his "most famous role was that of King Kong."

Then, the *Chicago Sun-Times* revealed on December 21, 1969, that one Ken Roady "really is King Kong. During his time, Roady made 133 films, but his biggest was as the 50-foot gorilla in the 1933 classic." Roady told the paper's gee-whiz reporter that he "worked on that picture for more than a year. Got paid $150 a week and never could get along with either Fay Wray or Robert Armstrong, who were the stars of the picture. They never realized how important I was to them, I guess." Roady has been identified in other sources by the name Carmen Nigro; his outlandish pretense of "being King Kong" renders him handily the most remarkable member of a crackpot lot whose exponents have elsewhere been caught claiming to be George "Spanky" McFarland of the *Our Gang* comedies and Joe Besser of the Three Stooges—even in years *after* the amply documented deaths of the authentic personages.

Reams of such misinformation have been published. This is presumably the result of the traditional journalistic reluctance to let facts stand in the way of a sensational story. The fact, though self-evident, bears hammering:

> No gigantic motorized robots and no men in ape-suits were used at any time in the making of the film. So there.

No gigantic motorized robots and no men in ape-suits were used at any time in the making of the film. So there.

King Kong is, as Ernest Schoedsack often declared, "the product of *many* contributions." One contribution of inestimable value was that of Sidney Saunders, supervisor of RKO-Radio's paint department, who unveiled an important technical development just as the *Kong* test reel was getting under way. This cellulose-acetate screen, a refinement of the rear-projection process, was destined to become a basic necessity in studio production technique. Rear projection permits actors to perform in front of a translucent screen, onto the back of which is projected a previously filmed scene. The camera records both the new action and the projected background in a single take.

Cameramen for years had been experimenting with this principle but were seldom successful because of the inherent difficulties. Those celebrated German cinematographers, Karl Freund and Günther Rittau, had managed some workable projection effects in *Metropolis* (1926), and Willis O'Brien is said to have used a projected background in one scene of *The Lost World*. A particularly knotty problem lay in the need to synchronize the shutters of the camera and the projector. In projection, an image is flashed onto the screen for one 48th of a second; then, the shutter closes and blots out the light until the next frame moves into the aperture and is projected. The eye, through the phenomenon known as persistence of vision, holds one image long enough for it to blend into the next, so that the black intervals between frames are not perceived. The camera's eye is not deluded, however, and therefore the camera and the projector must operate in unison. Otherwise, the variability of exposure will cause the re-photographed image to flicker.

Conventional projection mechanisms proved too unsteady for process work because the slightest jiggle becomes obvious when a projected scene is juxtaposed with solid foreground objects. Other problems included the so-called *hot-spot*, that noticeably brighter light at the center of a projected image; and *fall-off*, the diminishing illumination at the edges and corners of a frame.

Previous rear-projection screens were made of sandblasted glass. Aside from their being necessarily small, these screens produced a middle-gray image with no sparkling highlights nor rich blacks. The images were dulled further by the need to use filters to control *hot-spot* and *fall-off*. The screens were fragile, un-insurable and costly to replace. Their breakage had caused serious injuries at two studios.

The Saunders screen, however, was flexible, non-breakable and impervious to the heat of the Photoflood lamps. It measured 16 by 20 feet—two feet greater in any direction than any glass process screen. Stretched onto a frame, the Saunders screen resembled a sheet of waterproof canvas. Initial tests showed brilliancy increased by more than 20 percent and *hot-spot* reduced by more than 50 percent. True white highlights and intense blacks were achieved in rear projection for the first time, and the overall tonal range was broadened greatly. The projector was re-engineered for this use, the traditional Maltese Cross projection mechanism being replaced with the pilot-pin movement of a production camera, providing a rock-steady picture.

The first scenes to utilize Saunders' screen are those in *Kong* which show Fay Wray in a tree-top (live foreground) being menaced by the Tyrannosaurus (projected background) and observing the subsequent battle between the reptile and the ape. The animation footage of the beasts was weeks in the making. Miss Wray's scenes, by comparison, could have been filmed in only a few hours—if only all the bugs peculiar to the process had been known in advance.

Shutter synchronization was achieved by use of the then-new Selsyn-interlock motors on both camera and projector. These 220-volt, three-phase motors would turn at exactly the same rate of speed, assuring synchronization of both sets of shutters, pilot pins and pull-down mechanisms.

Considerable difficulty was encountered in matching the intensity and direction of lighting in the separate elements so that they would appear to have been photographed at the same time in a single location. One thorny problem was the necessity of keeping reflected light and foreground spill-light from leaking onto the screen and causing flares and washouts. All lighting had to be controlled with *barn doors* (flat extensions on lighting units, used to direct or narrow the beams) and *gobos* (black flats used to shield certain areas from unwanted light).

Mastering the intricacies of the new process required days of shooting, including one non-stop session of 22 hours that left everybody exhausted. Fay Wray recalled being "sore all over" from crouching in the tree-top for long stretches. The finished shots—which remain in the final cut of *King Kong*—even withstand comparison with process work done years later with vastly improved equipment and know-how. A more striking demonstration of the possibilities of rear projection can scarcely be imagined: The Tyrannosaurus, a refugee from *Creation*, appears large enough to swallow the actress in a gulp. The success of these scenes earned Saunders a special award from the Motion Picture Academy for his part in "the development of and effective use of the translucent cellulose screen in composite photography."[2]

The shooting of these scenes was a memorable occasion for one of the technicians because it was his job to carry Miss Wray to and from the tree-top for each take. The man was selected for the assignment because he knew the locations of various objects that might cause the actress

The very definition of the possibilities of rear projection

to stumble. The crewman told us the chore was "mildly erotic" and said other technicians waited their turns to take his place.

The success of the Saunders Process shots led Cooper to suggest that the principle could be adapted for a corollary effect—the placement of actors into the miniature settings with the prehistoric monsters. The idea was a sound one, although a great deal more complex than it would seem, and O'Brien set himself to the task of developing it as a practical method. Miniature rear projection proved indispensable, a more flexible and satisfying technique than the unwieldy stationary mattes by which actors had been placed into the miniature tableaux of *The Lost World*. O'Brien had had some success with miniature projection on *Creation*, but in much less elaborate setups than he would employ on *Kong*.

The initial problem was to find a suitable material from which to make the transparency screens. The spray-painted cellulose of the big rear-projection screen was too grainy to be photographed at close range as part of the miniature setups. Ground glass, tracing cloth, tracing paper and other materials were tested with similarly lacking results. The tiny screens eventually were made of surgical rubber sheeting—used primarily for surgeons' gloves—stretched onto wooden frames. Not only was the material free of grain, but *hot-spot* and *fall-off* could be controlled by varying the tension of the screen. Of course, the rubber deteriorated rapidly under the heat of the lighting barrage and had to be replaced frequently.

The major problem encountered in miniature projection was the critical matching of scale, textures, lighting and perspective, which could be exaggerated mercilessly when projected onto a movie-theatre screen. These considerations required the most intricate calculations in preparing both the full-scale action and the elements of the miniature.

Among the first scenes using miniature projection are those in which Cabot hides from Kong in a shallow cave. The actor, in an image filmed previously on a matching set of the cave, was rear-projected onto a screen set several inches back from the opening of the miniature cave. The

Above and below: The compositing of the cave sequence

image had to be positioned this way because light used to illuminate the miniature would wash out the rear-projected image if it struck the rubber screen. Each frame of Cabot was projected and re-photographed as a still image with each manual alteration of Kong's position. Glass paintings were used to add surrounding rocks and foliage to the full-scale close views of the cave.

Zöe Porter, Cooper's secretary, one day received a call to report to one of the stages. There, she found Cooper examining a gigantic hand and arm, unfinished and covered roughly with sponge-rubber. Cooper told her to sit in the open palm. When she did so, Mrs. Porter was shocked to find herself being lifted high into the air. Cooper was delighted with this first test of his latest gadget, and for years thereafter Mrs. Porter prized a photograph of the occasion. Marcel Delgado, who later added the intricately detailed skin, nails and hair to the articulated armature, was dissatisfied with the design of the paw because it could not form a cup-like shape in the manner of a true hand. It was nevertheless an impressive prop, with properly jointed digits, and would prove invaluable to many important scenes.

The main function of the big hand was to hold Fay Wray, who wrote of the experience in the *New York Times* of September 21, 1969: "How Fay Met Kong, or the Scream That Shook the World." From her reminiscence:

> ... Then I saw the figure of Kong. He was in a miniature jungle habitat, and was less than two feet tall! It was only the great furry paw, in which I would spend the next 10 months, that was absolutely enormous... The hand and arm in which my close-up scenes were shot was about eight feet in length. Inside the furry arm, there was a steel bar, and the whole contraption (with me in the hand) could be raised or lowered like a crane. The fingers would be pressed around my waist while I was in a standing position. I would then be raised about 10 feet into the air to be in line with an elevated camera. As I kicked and squirmed and struggled in the ape's hand, his fingers would gradually loosen and begin to open. My fear was real as I grabbed onto his wrist, his thumb, wherever I could, to keep from slipping out of that paw! When I could sense that the moment of minimum safety had arrived, I would call imploringly to the director and ask to be lowered to the floor of the stage. Happily, this was never denied for a second too long! I would have a few moments' rest, be re-secured in the paw, and the ordeal would begin all over again... a kind of pleasurable torment!"[3]

By means of projected backgrounds, the hand and Miss Wray appeared to be nearly a thousand feet in the air when Kong examined his captive while perched atop the Empire State Building. In another memorable shot, the arm was combined with the miniature in an over-the-shoulder view as Kong lifted Miss Wray from the jungle floor. The most unusual use of the arm was for a scene devised and personally animated by O'Brien, in which Kong, comfortably seated near the summit of his mountain stronghold, tears away pieces of the actress' dress, gently strokes her body with his fingertips and sniffs the lingering feminine scent. Here, miniature projection was used to make the arm appear to be connected to the miniature Kong. This sequence

Fay Wray in the giant hand

The Making of King Kong

Miniature back projection: Fay Wray, big hand and King Kong

ran into censorship trouble several years later, although it turned out considerably less erotic than O'Brien had envisioned it: Miss Wray had been expected to finish the scene in the near-nude. The actress refused to carry the scene beyond the limits of decency and insisted upon being covered under the scanty garments she was permitted to retain.

Other full-size properties included a foot and lower leg of Kong, to permit close-ups of men being trampled, and the lower body of a Pteranodon that tries to carry Miss Wray away from Kong's lair. The most spectacular prop was the huge head, chest and shoulders, for close-ups of Kong. The construction—coupled with decoy disinformation spread by the studio's publicists—may have given rise to *Time* magazine's flight of fantasy, but its purpose was strictly that of registering an astonishing range of emotion, from Barrymore-manner eyebrow-wagging to rage. Delgado tried to convince Cooper that the full-scale head would not be worth the effort for the limited use it would receive. Forty years later, at a screening at Anaheim's Motion Picture Hall of Fame, Cooper gleefully pointed out to Delgado each scene featuring the big head. Delgado had to admit that the prop was tremendously effective.

Some scenes in which foreground and background action had to be photographed at different times and places were combined through the Dunning Traveling Matte Process, which permitted filming of greater scope than could be achieved with rear projection. This process had been used with great success at several studios during 1930-31: Columbia thus was able to show the explorer Paul L. Hoefler seeming to photograph action he had shot months earlier, in *Africa Speaks*. MGM, in *Anna Christie*, combined New York Harbor location scenes with new sound-stage action involving Greta Garbo and Charles Bickford. The most famous moment in *Trader Horn*, Mutia Omoolu's spearing of a rampant lion, is a Dunning shot, as are numerous scenes of *Tarzan, the Ape Man*. At RKO, Carroll Dunning screened for the brass a film showing

The unexpectedly versatile full-size bust of Kong

how the trick work in *Tarzan* had been pulled off. O'Brien, who had already accomplished four excellent Dunning shots for *Creation*, used the process in *Kong* for scenes such as one where a dinosaur attacks Denham and his men.

The Dunning system was patented in 1927 by a 17-year-old schoolboy, C. Dodge Dunning, son of Carroll Dunning, vice president of the Prizma Color Process Co. It took the elder Dunning two years to convince the U.S. Patent Office that his son's invention would work. The basic idea, which combines new photography with contact printing in a single operation, hinges on the principle that an object of a certain color becomes invisible when viewed through a filter of the same color. The object becomes distinct when viewed through a filter of a contrasting color.

After a negative of the background action has been made, a positive transparency is prepared in which the silver particles that make up the black-and-white image are bleached away and replaced by a yellow-orange dye. This toned print is loaded into a specially designed camera magazine with a reel of raw negative stock, the latter passing through the camera behind and in contact with the orange positive print. If a brightly lighted blue backdrop, of the hue complementary to the orange dye, is photographed by the production camera through the orange print and onto the raw stock, the result is a duplicate black-and-white negative of the scene from the orange positive film, which has been printed onto the raw stock by exposure to the blue backdrop. The illuminated blue backing functions as a printing light.

If actors and/or props are placed between the camera and the backdrop and are lighted through orange filters identical to the dye on the orange print, then these objects are combined on the

The storming of the gate

new negative with the background action. The background does not print through the actors (as a double exposure) because the orange-lighted actors mask out the blue printing light with their own bodies. The raw film records a completed composite negative showing the actors seemingly in the environment previously photographed, the backgrounds being printed around—and, to all appearances, behind—the players. One drawback of the process was that the background animation had to be shot in advance, and the actors had to time their performances to match an image they could not see. To cue the actors, a technician viewed background footage on a Moviola and tapped a bell at the crucial moments.

Some other scenes were achieved with the more complicated Williams Traveling Matte Process, which also utilized two films and a blue backing but permitted the use of *hard light* (meaning

Director of Photography Eddie Linden stands in for Fay Wray in a matte shot. Glass art at right is unfinished in this test.

pure-white light) in foreground action. This feature was particularly useful in filming vast scenes with complex lighting, such as Kong's first appearance in the native village. The inventor, Frank D. Williams, pioneered the principle of the traveling matte, patenting the first such process in 1916. Refinements of the original Williams system enabled the scenes of the Brontosaurus' rampage in London in *The Lost World* and the dazzling flying-carpet scenes in Raoul Walsh's *The Thief of Bagdad* (1924). Williams, a true genius of the cinema, also helped devise the special techniques used by his former assistant, John P. Fulton, on *The Invisible Man* (1933). Williams' improved double-matting system was introduced in 1932, just in time for *King Kong*.

A key member of Vern Walker's camera-effects department was Linwood Dunn, a leading expert in the then-new art of optical printing. Dunn and his assistant, Cecil Love, with engineer Bill Leeds, had developed for RKO an optical printer. The device seems primitive by comparison with those which Dunn would much later equip his independent lab/studio, Film Effects of Hollywood, but at the time it was the most efficient in existence. Dunn and Love later designed the Acme-Dunn Optical Printer, the first special-effects printer to be manufactured for the trade; it earned them a 1944 Academy Award for technical achievement.

Kong's benefit was that this innovation enabled Dunn to convince Willis O'Brien to stop trying to match composite work by trial-and-error in the camera, and to go with a system "where we could see what we were doing and get it right the first time," as Dunn told us.

The ingenuity and hard work of this remarkable technical crew was summed up by critic Relman Morin in the *Los Angeles Record*: "*King Kong* is a supreme product of the coordination of human imagination and human skill."

1 Of course, Gemora *may* have modeled, or provided reference photographs, for the *Kong* artists, given his prominence within the industry during these years and according to his surviving family members. Gemora *did* play a Kong takeoff in a never-completed short subject called "The Lost Island," which is discussed in the chapter on "Preludes, Prologues & Progeny."
2 This award was shared with technicians from Fox Film Corp., and with Fred Jackman of Warner Bros.
3 Miss Wray's article was reprinted as "King Kong and Me" in the *San Francisco Chronicle*.

The Expedition to Skull Island

"So we've come all this way to take a picture of a wall!"
"Not the wall...what's behind the wall."—Exchange between Driscoll and
Denham, as preserved in the *Mystery Magazine* serial

The cost of filming a picture over such a long period of time would have been prohibitive, had it been necessary to keep the cast on salary during the entire 55 weeks. In those pre-Screen Actors Guild days, it was possible to use actors only when needed, re-hiring them later for additional shooting. Schoedsack, a fast director who seldom called for a retake, was able to keep the live action moving at a clip, but the special-effects work was agonizingly slow, requiring beyond normal patience from all concerned.

The actors worked for several weeks at a stretch, then were given time off for as much as two months while the animation work caught up with the live action. During these periods, they graced other films, some of which were released before *Kong* was finished. Bruce Cabot made his official début in *Roadhouse Murder*, filmed during one such hiatus. Fay Wray honed her specialty as the Menaced Innocent in First National's *Dr. X* and *Mystery of the Wax Museum*. Schoedsack took time out to direct sequences expanding Wesley Ruggles' *The Monkey's Paw*[1] from an unintentional featurette to a brisk feature-length running time.

Schoedsack directed most of *Kong*'s live action at the RKO-Pathé Studio, south of Washington Boulevard in Culver City. The studio had been built in 1918 by Thomas H. Ince, after whose death in 1924 the lot was purchased by Pathé Exchange, Inc., and became the site of many serials, features and the early comedies of Hal Roach. Under the aegis of the trademark Pathé Rooster, there appeared Harold Lloyd, William "Bill" Boyd and Will Rogers; Stan Laurel and

Fay Wray made *Mystery of the Wax Museum* with Lionel Atwill during down time on *King Kong*.

The colossal 75-foot wall used in *King Kong* had been built for *The King of Kings* and refinished for *Kong*.

Oliver Hardy, independent of one another in prelude to their celebrated teaming; those famous chapter-play romancers Walter Miller and Allene Ray; and numerous others. Cecil B. De Mille, after his parting with Paramount in 1925, established his own production company on the Pathé lot. There, he produced several features and personally directed four epic works, including his favorite, *The King of Kings*. By 1929, the studio was heavily in debt, and De Mille and Roach arranged production-distribution deals with their wealthy neighbor, Metro-Goldwyn-Mayer.

RKO, which had been operating in cramped quarters at the 13 1/2-acre Radio Studio (built in 1920 by the British firm of Robertson-Cole), bought the Pathé lot in January 1931. The stock-market collapse and the necessary industry-wide conversion to talking-picture technology left RKO in grim financial straits, and there was considerable dissent among the company's directors regarding the wisdom of operating a second studio.

Pathé's 40-acre layout encompassed 11 sound stages, superb property-and-drapery departments, spectacular standing sets, a meandering ravine and a segment of Baldwin Hills. Conspicuous among the sets were those representing the Old Jerusalem, *à la mode* De Mille, that had been built in August 1926 for *The King of Kings*. Some of the big artificial cliffs and boulders from the Place of the Skull had already been used on the jungle set for *The Most Dangerous Game*. A colossal wall about 75 feet high, several tiers of broad steps, a flagstone floor and some massive Romanesque columns remained of the Council House interior, which actually was an outdoor set without a ceiling. In the center of the wall was a rectangular opening 60 feet tall and twenty feet wide, which originally had been hung with massive draperies. This remnant of De Mille's Holy Land became the site of Skull Island's ruined city.

Art director Al Herman had his craftsmen cover the wall with weird carvings and jungle undergrowth. In the opening was placed an immense double door, constructed of vertical planking and equipped with an enormous wooden bolt. A tocsin gong, about 12 feet high, was mounted

The sacrificial altar can be seen through the open gates on the set of *King Kong*.

on top above the opening. The pillars were reduced to ruin and partially buried under vines and moss. Wooden scaffoldings and scaling towers were erected along the wall to suggest that the natives kept the structure in repair to protect themselves from the jungle.

When King Vidor's *Bird of Paradise* expedition returned from the Hawaiian Islands early in 1932, it was decided that the scenes of native dancing were unsuitable and that retakes would be staged by Busby Berkeley with music by Max Steiner and dancing by 35 Hollywood chorines. For this purpose, an authentic-looking Polynesian village was erected at Pathé. These grass houses later were moved to the Council House set to become part of the village of the Skull Islanders. Native canoes and shipboard interiors from *Bird of Paradise* likewise were commandeered for *Kong*.

Three spectacular sequences involving hundreds of tribespeople were filmed at the Council House site: Here we find the first encounter with the natives during the ceremony in which a black girl is supposed to become "the bride of Kong"; the nighttime ritual in which Ann Darrow is bound over for sacrifice; and the long sequence in which the lovers return from the jungle with Kong following to ravage the settlement. The sacrificial altar was built full-scale outside the gate and duplicated in miniature for scenes with Kong.

The night scenes are especially impressive. Sixty-five electricians were employed to handle the 350 lamps required to light the set and the horde of weirdly costumed extras. Schoedsack was ready to begin shooting at nightfall on August 11 when a heavy fog rolled in from the west. Enormous amounts of food and soft drinks were catered in to keep the milling extras from becoming restless while the director and his crew waited and worried. The fog finally lifted at midnight, and shooting commenced. The fire department was on hand, drawn by the villagers' ceremonial torches.

On the outside, looking askance...

The jungle side of the wall was built in miniature, its stone-like surface intricately textured in glue mixed with sand and cornmeal. Through a split-screen effect, the actors were shown standing along the top. To get the necessary elevation, the players were lined up atop Sound Stage 10, near the studio's front gate on Washington Boulevard. The scores of torches soon drew a crowd, whose gawkers had assumed the studio was on fire. One executive, who had approved the purchase of Pathé in the knowledge that it was heavily insured, was reported to have said, "I'll give somebody $10,000 to burn the place down!"

...and on the inside, looking out

The Making of King Kong

The scenes in which Ann becomes "the bride of Kong" are pictorially the film's most exquisite.

The scenes in which Ann becomes "the bride of Kong" are pictorially the film's most exquisite. The lighting effects are dazzling, and the cameras move through the massed players with a virtuosity worthy of D.W. Griffith in his prime. After Ann has been taken outside and bound to the altar, the closing of the gates is shown in a series of monumental, formalized compositions that make her utter isolation seem more terrifying than her plight when in the hands of the savages. The ceremony is accompanied by some of Max Steiner's most impassioned music, its wildness heightened by the pagan cries from the villagers.

The episode where Kong breaks through to commence his rampage is the stuff of an inspired nightmare. The doors were pulled open by four concealed tractors, and Kong was later matted into the opening by the Williams Process. Schoedsack encountered difficulty in getting the extras to react properly to the desperate situation when all they saw beyond the gates was a bright blue backdrop.

Although most of the action in the village was directed by Schoedsack, Cooper staged the scenes in which a native is bitten to death by the great ape, for which he used the life-size bust of Kong. He also directed two scenes in which natives are crushed underfoot. Archie Marshek recalled: "The big foot was lowered by a crane onto the players—who, incidentally, were Ray Turner and Harold Knox. Ray had one of the most expressive faces in the business, with this remarkable ability to make his eyes bulge, and he could portray humor or wonder or terror with the most economi-

Kong is overcome by gas bombs on the beach in this composite scene.

cal of glances. Both actors were terrified. Ray leaped up after the foot had been lifted and took off in a run, covered with mud, yelling: 'I'm *through*, Boss! I just saw Saint Peter a-reachin' for his fountain pen!'"

Both directors worked on the scenes in which Kong is overcome by gas bombs on the beach, but for the most part they worked separately. So divergent were their methods that they found close collaboration in the studio to tax their patience with one another. It was quite a different matter from their expeditions, where nature and circumstances called for teamwork.

"I'd get irritated with Coop because he was so slow," Schoedsack recalled. "He couldn't visualize anything, so he had the artists around to help. He'd do everything over and over to get it just right. I worked fast all the time. He made a big thing out of the scene where Kong was lying on the beach with natives running by. I wanted to just shoot it and get it over with."

Some of the shipboard scenes were made aboard a freighter out of San Pedro. Others were done at the studio using mock-ups of portions of the ship. Several diffused shots of the crew at work as the steamer gets under way are beautifully atmospheric and are matched perfectly with the studio shots. The actors portraying the seamen are genuinely salty types. Schoedsack even enlisted a bearded and bowlegged English tar to cast the lead-line during the fog sequence.

The sequence of Ann's screen test aboard ship was filmed at the studio on a stage equipped with a plain backdrop. The effect of a distant sea horizon was simulated by painting the drop in two tones and having it raised and lowered by stagehands.

During the screen-test sequence, Robert Armstrong was supposed to adjust the lenses of his camera and insert a rectangular filter into the matte box while explaining that he always cranks his own camera because a cameraman he had hired for a jungle film fled when a rhinoceros charged the camera. On each take, the actor was unable to fit the filter into place—much to the amusement of the camera crew. Schoedsack finally cut away from the scene at the crucial moment to a shot of the sailors watching the action. Later, the remainder of Ann's test was filmed,

Fay Wray screams at the top of her lungs!

including the famed scene where the girl, under Denham's direction, covers her eyes and screams at the top of her lungs. This time, only one take was necessary—to Fay Wray's relief.

While the scenes of the shipboard search for the kidnapped girl were being set up, Cabot disappeared. At last, he emerged from a gear locker where he had hidden a bottle of whiskey. When Schoedsack reprimanded him, Cabot tried to kid the director out of his anger by breaking into a comical dance. Schoedsack, normally the least temperamental of his profession, slapped Cabot hard—twice. The chastened and sobered actor, although badly shaken, finished the day's shooting without further incident. Schoedsack still spoke regretfully of the episode, decades after the fact. Cabot not only forgave the outburst, but spoke fondly—long afterward—of "the gumption the ol' boy showed, givin' me what I had comin' to me." It was the only time Schoedsack ever struck one of his players, although he said he was sorely tempted on other occasions when working with such antagonistic boozers as John Barrymore, Alan Mowbray and Louis Calhern. "I nearly came to blows, though, with John Ford," Schoedsack told us, "during the time when we were making *Mighty Joe Young*."

A replica of the *Venture*, 12 feet in length, was used to show the ship in the fog. The imposing miniature duplicated faithfully all external details of the real steamer, the studio shipboard mockups and the personnel on deck. The human figures, carved from wood by John Cerisoli, were superbly detailed, even to the pipes smoked by Denham and Capt. Englehorn. The plates of the ship's hull were constructed from illustration board and painted to resemble metal long exposed to the sea. The thousands of rivets were brass escutcheon pins. The effect of the ship's sitting on the ocean was achieved without actually launching the fragile miniature into the water.

Beach scenes at Skull Island were filmed near San Pedro. The long shot of the initial landing shows the actual ocean in the foreground, the players and the boats on the beach in the middle distance and, via a glass painting, the Great Wall and Skull Mountain in the far distance. The glass art actually stood within a few feet of the camera. Soaring gulls were superimposed to add

The beach scene on Skull Island shows the actual ocean, actors and boats with a glass painting of the Great Wall and Skull Mountain.

The non-floatable model of the *Venture*

depth and movement. The closer views of the landing were photographed from a high angle to eliminate the necessity of a background. For the reverse angles of Denham and his party on the beach after Kong has been subdued, a glass shot was employed to place the *Venture* offshore against a night sky. This shot then was projected in miniature behind the unconscious figure of Kong lying on the beach.

Schoedsack's camera technique in the live-action scenes is far different from the photography of his expeditionary films. Availing himself of the cranes and dollies at the studio, he kept the camera moving most of the time, whether out of doors or on the sound stage. The fluidity of these shots complements the necessary rigidity of the majority of the scenes involving animation.

But even in the Dunning and Williams composite shots, the camera is surprisingly mobile. Careful shooting of separate elements to be combined and perfect timing of the ultimate shot were required for such scenes as the one where the camera follows the players as they approach the fallen Stegosaurus.

A new technique that became standard procedure in rear-projection work was employed to show Robert Armstrong and Bruce Cabot walking past the writhing body of the Stegosaurus. The players walked on a treadmill in front of a screen, on which was projected a scene where the camera moved along the seemingly gigantic carcass. Willis O'Brien had planned scenes for *Creation* using this technique, but he was not able to put the system to use until *Kong* demanded such breakthroughs.

Equally intricate was the planning of full-scale scenes, to be combined with animation via miniature projection. O'Brien was usually on hand to assist in establishing proper lighting and spatial relationships for the ultimate matching. The live portions were photographed well in advance of the animation, preceding the final combination shot by weeks or even months.

The scene in which natives on a scaffolding throw spears at Kong was shot over a period of months. In August, Schoedsack directed the warriors throwing their weapons and being knocked off. Miniatures of the village were constructed later, with the rear-projection screen blended in. Next, Kong was animated and the live action was re-photographed frame by frame with him. Finally, in January of 1933, Cooper directed additional extras in native garb running in front of a blue screen to be matted into the foreground.

1 See "Preludes, Prologues & Progeny."

Pipes, Pliers, Primroses & Other Problems

Hey! Look! Kong is mad!—A Crucial Early Response

The production of *Kong* made unusual demands upon the assigned personnel, who in numerous instances were required to step out of their normal routines and call on talents of which they may have been unaware.

Veteran film editor Archie Marshek showed such gumption in a projection room confrontation[1] with Merian Cooper that he found himself promoted to Cooper's assistant.

The offer came as "quite a shock to a guy expecting to be canned," Marshek told us.

> I guess he liked the way I stood up for myself, as *he* would have done. I said, "Yes," and was put to work on *Kong*.
>
> When I started, they were taking tests on the ape, working on his facial expressions and so on. Coop's pipe was always going out, and he never had any matches. I didn't even smoke, but I soon learned to have a pocket full of kitchen matches on the set because he was constantly saying, "Archie, have you got a match?" Dorothy, his wife [they would marry in 1933], always got a kick out of that.
>
> I spent a lot of time running back and forth between RKO and the Williams lab, where they made most of our composite shots. It was a little pie-shaped building on Santa Monica [Boulevard]... I'd have to see that they got those little bleed lines out and explain what Coop wanted, and they'd have to do it over until it was right. I worked on the stage with O'Brien, ran the dailies with Cooper and O'Brien and worked on the editing, although I didn't actually cut the picture—Ted Cheesman did that.

Marshek found working with Cooper to be a lively chore. He continued in the role of assistant beyond *Kong*, contributing to such films as *The Son of Kong* and *The Last Days of Pompeii*. Eventually, Marshek returned to the Moviola, cutting many films at Paramount.

Walter Daniels, at 27, was assigned to Ernest Schoedsack as production assistant. Like the director, Daniels was at once artistic and rugged, having been both a lithographer and a rancher in Colorado before entering the movies as Will Rogers' propmaster. He also shared Schoedsack's droll sense of humor.

In addition to his work on the set, Daniels functioned as unit business manager and even secured a yacht so that Schoedsack could throw a weekend party for the cast and crew. Daniels became assistant production manager at RKO in 1935 and was appointed studio manager six years later. He continued in the same capacity when the studio was purchased by Desilu Productions. When he died, in 1969, Daniels had spent 46 years at the studio under many changes of ownership.

It was Willis O'Brien who said:

> The miniature technician cannot bring his set to the screen single-handed. It is fundamentally an artist's conception but requires the united efforts of many craftsmen, its success depending entirely upon the combination of artistic, photographic and mechanical effects, each person being a specialist in his field but also having a general knowledge of the whole.
>
> When making *King Kong*, it was necessary to have a large staff of experienced men to carry on the work. A group of men were kept busy building and repairing the animals or executing any mechanical necessity that was

O'Brien and Gibson attended wrestling matches, noting action that might prove applicable to Kong's approach to fighting.

required. Another group built the miniatures, which included a New York Elevated Railway re-created in detail and jungle settings on a tropical island. Mario Larrinaga and Byron Crabbe made the sketches and later painted the backings and glasses for the sets after the miniatures were drawn up and put to work. Besides these men, others were necessary for the actual working of the miniature.[2]

The members of O'Brien's technical staff were men who just happened to be in the right place with the right skills at the right time. The heads of the various departments from which they were recruited resented having to furnish personnel without having authority over their work. Most of the artisans and technos had worked on *Creation*, and by the time *Kong* was put into production this curiously assorted group was able to contribute a variety of skills learned during the prior year.

O'Brien selected as his first assistant a beefy studio grip or handyman, E.B. "Buz" Gibson, who, typical of men of his calling, was able to handle a multitude of jobs. O'Brien and Gibson shared several outside interests, including archery and boxing. While working on the Kong-vs.-Tyrannosaurus match, O'Brien and Gibson attended prizefights and wrestling matches as a matter of routine, noting bits of action that might prove applicable to Kong's semi-human approach to fighting. Animation was something new to Gibson, but with O'Brien's help he learned rapidly. He helped with the animation and supervised the construction of some large properties, such as the massive bust of Kong. Although O'Brien preferred to work solo on animation that was particularly subtle or touchy, Gibson participated in such complicated scenes as the fights between monsters. He also animated several key scenes alone, most notably Kong's climbing of the Empire State Building.

Another husky and affable sort, Fred Reefe, was an expert builder and a master at improvising mechanical gizmos. Reefe was responsible for many of the contrivances used in the full-scale Kong. He frequently helped O'Brien and Gibson in animation when the under-the-table fastening job became difficult and when animals had to be held in leaping positions by concealed devices.

Orville "Goldy" Goldner worked in Don Jahrous' miniatures shop, specializing in creating effects props and in matching textures for scenes involving miniature and full-scale composites. A background in the fine arts and experience in puppetry and puppet animation—including a late-1920s animated-ostrich piece utilizing the voice of Pinto Colvig, Walt Disney's original Goofy—made Goldner a natural for O'Brien's unit. For *Creation* and *Kong*, Goldner built miniature trees and sets, matched foliage with rock textures, animated birds and aircraft, worked with live animals and devised trick riggings.

John Cerisoli, an elderly Italian who spoke little English, was the studio's master sculptor. Working alone in a cramped shop adjoining the sound department, Cerisoli carved the wooden prototypes (and stand-ins) of the animals as well as the dozens of articulated miniatures of the human characters. He also fashioned the skulls of the some of the working animals. The Tyrannosaurus, for example, had a wooden skull covered with thin copper.

"Buz" Gibson animates Kong on the Empire State Building model.

W.G. "Gus" White, a studio grip, became a jack-of-all-trades for the unit. In addition to making props and rigging sets, the stocky Texan became so adept at miniature construction that he continued in this field. One noteworthy achievement was White's building of the ancient city that would be systematically destroyed for Cooper's 1935 production of *The Last Days of Pompeii*.

Carroll "Shep" Shepphird was employed in the art department but had a desire to work in photographic effects. O'Brien gave him the highly technical job of laying out construction plans for the effects sequences, even to the exact placement of characters and the positions of the cameras. Shepphird also determined what lenses would be used, preparing charts showing the sizes of screen images at various distances when photographed with lenses of varying focal lengths. Thirteen lenses were used, ranging from a focal length of 40mm to a moderate telephoto of five inches. One chart was a perspective diagram showing the relative sizes of a man as seen by a 40mm lens at distances from the camera of 10 to 100 feet. Shepphird never returned to the art department; at the time of his retirement, he was head of visual effects at MGM.

Walter Plunkett designed the costumes of the Skull Islanders.

Others worked on *Kong* as a part of their regular jobs. Van Nest Polglase, art director, made preliminary plans for the full-scale sets and assigned the unit art direction to Carroll Clark and Al Herman. Thomas Little, head of the property department, supplied set decorators and propmasters to dress the Clark-Herman sets. Costume designer Walter Plunkett contributed Fay Wray's beauty-and-beast costume and the elaborate attire of the Skull Islanders. Harry Redmond, Jr., was responsible for the fog effects in two sequences. There were others—many others.

The studio's top cameramen were placed off-limits to *Kong*, which would have kept them tied up for many months. RKO's aces—men like Henry Gerard, Lucien Andriot and Edward Cronjager—were needed for the glamorous assignments, the star vehicles with Constance Bennett, Richard Dix, Dolores del Rio and Irene Dunne. Cooper settled for Edwin G. "Eddie" Linden as chief cameraman in charge of all photography, both live-action and miniature. The unbilled backup director of photography was Kenneth Peach, Sr., a veteran effects man, who alternated with Linden in supervising the full-scale and miniature shoots. First assistant camera chief was Bert Willis. Linden's Cooper-Schoedsack credential served him hardly at all in the greater scheme of his career, for he wound up back at the Poverty Row studios. After grinding out scores of low-budgeters for such studios as Regal and Producers Releasing Corp., Linden regained some prestige at Columbia in the last months of his life.

Elsewhere among the lensmen, J.O. Taylor had gained repute as a documentary shooter before becoming a lighting cinematographer. He had followed Pancho Villa throughout the Mexican Revolution, shooting spectacular Real World situations that were used for generations as stock footage. (Villa was so enamored of the star treatment that he agreed to fight his battles only during the daylight hours.) Taylor's ability at capturing massed action is much in evidence in the New York street scenes of *Kong*. Vernon L. "Vern" Walker had assisted Fred Jackman in the camera-effects department at First National before joining RKO as assistant to effects supervisor Lloyd Knechtel. Shortly after *Kong* went into production, Knechtel left the studio and Walker succeeded him. A big, hearty man with a thorough knowledge of trick photography, Walker held the job until his death in 1948.

Vernon L. Walker and Linwood G. Dunn with the new optical printer used in filming much of the effects work in *King Kong*.

Among the assistant/operative cameramen involved with *Kong* was the youthful William Clothier, who became one of the industry's top color cinematographers. Clifford Stine, a member of Linden's team in lighting and testing intricate composite shots, also rose to fame as a director of photography and spent five years as head of the special-effects department at Universal. Linwood Dunn, who had operated a camera on the miniatures in *Creation*, became Vern Walker's assistant in charge of optical photography while *Kong* was in production. William Reinhold, an assistant cameraman, gained prominence in the documentary arena.

G. Felix Schoedsack, the director's brother, not only operated a camera but also helped to launch a trend in still photography: Production stills at that time were made with large-format cameras on sheet film, but the task of shooting the miniatures with such bulky equipment proved difficult. Felix, as the proud owner of a newfangled Leica 35mm camera and all its deadeye-precision accessories, convinced the bosses that the small negative was practical for generating stills for publicity and promotional purposes. This was one of the first times that the 35mm rig, dismissed within the profession as merely a candid-snapshot device, was used for finer purposes.

All the crew members wore rubber-soled shoes because of a studio rule born with the sound-film era. They quickly learned that Cooper's abrupt visits were heralded by the clacking of his hard-heeled English walking shoes—a useful warning when everybody was taking a breather.

"Eventually, we realized that Mr. Cooper walked harder than usual when he came to see us," animator Orville Goldner recalled. "The fact is that he was very much a gentleman and didn't *want* to catch us unawares."

The animation required abnormal skill, patience and attention to subtle details and conditions. Intense incandescent light was both necessary—and unreliable. All lamp-globes were replaced at the beginning of each scene because a burnout would spoil the shoot: The intensity of a replacement lamp would not be the same.

"Experience is the only teacher," O'Brien said. "Each new set is an individual problem and requires separate treatment. There is no set rule or method by which you can classify all miniatures."

It soon became evident that an animation scene, once begun, must be carried through to completion without lengthy interruption. Some of the early scenes were ruined because they were left hanging before completion at the end of one work day and finished the next. When screened, these scenes betrayed sudden startling changes because the live plants used in miniatures tended to grow, die or otherwise become noticeably different. Lamps would not re-light at the same intensity due to variations in voltage or filament deterioration. Real plants had to be watered frequently because of the heat from the lamps. The resulting humidity caused some plants to grow faster than usual. When animation of a scene proceeded without interruption, such growth was normally imperceptible. But any delay in the process would show up jarringly as a jump on the screen.

The thin copper fronds and ferns, made with immense skill and patience for the miniature jungles, might ruffle into different positions if an opened door allowed a draft of air. Personnel were encouraged *not* to leave or enter a stage, or even move about unnecessarily, during the animation process. An in-rush of cool air could cause a large incandescent lamp to explode.

The often-told story of the primrose best illustrates the delicacy of this process. Nobody noticed the blooming of one such plant during the animation of a crucial sequence—until the rushes were projected the next morning. Then, it was found that the scene contained a perfect time-lapse opening of the pure-white flower, which of course appeared gigantic within the miniature context. A re-shoot was unavoidable.

Stuntmen relax on a log in this test. Matte and glass art will be refined before the scene is filmed.

On another occasion, artisans Orville Goldner and Peter Stich were knocked to the floor with a tremendous *bang!* when the hose of an acetylene tank, used to heat painting materials, exploded. The tank toppled and started to burn the wooden floor and a huge black drape that separated this set from the others. Stich and Goldner tried to douse the flames. A studio fireman with the picturesque name of Fat Burns was summoned, but before he could arrive Mario Larrinaga hoisted a huge bottle of drinking water from a nearby cooler and smashed it into the tank, quenching the blaze. Larrinaga was taking no chances that his hours of glass-painting work might be destroyed. The feat was counted remarkable by all concerned, owing to Larrinaga's rather small stature. Stich was sidelined for several days by second-degree burns and a temporary loss of hearing.

Another animator worked on a scene for several hours before he discovered he had left a pair of pliers lying within foreground camera range. The tool's handle appeared as only a long, gray mass. Unable to bear the thought of starting afresh, the artist slowly and carefully moved the pliers out of the scene, frame-by-frame, as he animated the dinosaur featured in this particular action. Anyone who might notice would fancy the object a snake—if, that is, anyone could be diverted from the main action unfolding on screen.

Kong's rabbit-fur pelt, as Delgado had predicted, proved to be a problem. When several of the RKO suits showed up unannounced at a work-in-progress screening, Cooper and Schoedsack felt their hearts sink as they watched Kong's hair ripple with each between-the-frames touch of the animators' fingers. Artful back-lighting only emphasized the unwelcome effect.

Marcel Delgado

But another unheralded response saved the day: "Hey! Look! Kong is mad!" one of the executives cried delightedly as the ape roared his defiance. "Look at him bristle!"

---

1 See "Preludes, Prologues & Progeny," under *The Phantom of Crestwood*.
2 O'Brien's words are drawn from his article, "Miniature Effects Shots," in the May 1933 issue of *International Photographer*.

The Making of King Kong

"It Wasn't Easy, Working for Coop"

Kong himself should have been in the running for the Best Actor Oscar for 1933. And he should have won.—Robert Bloch; conversation with the authors; 1985

"He was a holy terror, and I was scared to death," Zöe Porter told us, recalling the day in October 1931 when she became Merian Cooper's secretary at RKO. Soon, however, Mrs. Porter realized that her employer's gruff manner masked a gallant and sympathetic nature and a consuming loyalty. She continued to work for Cooper until his death more than 40 years later. "He was a real genius," Mrs. Porter told us. "I don't think there's more than one mind like his in any generation."

"It wasn't easy, working for Coop," camera ace Linwood Dunn recalled. "He was such a perfectionist. Sometimes it was very frustrating. He'd look at a scene we'd worked on for a long time and say something like, 'I think it would be better if [Kong] scratched with his *left* hand.'"

One scene that gave Cooper second thoughts was a part of the test film in which the Arsinoitherium chased the sailors onto the log bridge. Cooper ordered the action to be re-filmed using a Styracosaurus, a bulky reptile with an ornate, multi-horned head. Both versions eventually were thrown out because Cooper believed they diverted attention from the main situation. At this point in the yarn, the action is moving so swiftly that a viewer hasn't time to ponder why the men stay on the log instead of retreating into the jungle. The Styracosaurus eventually would have its moment in *The Son of Kong*.

Scenes of the sailors falling into the gorge to be devoured by gigantic creatures proved yet a greater show stopper. The men's fate was so horrifying that it risked distracting the audience from the plight of Fay Wray. The sequence was altered so that the men were seen falling to instant death in a rocky chasm. Jointed dummies six inches tall were dropped into the canyon and photographed with a camera running at eight times normal speed to produce the slow-motion effect necessary to the illusion of bulk. The dummies stubbornly refused to react as real bodies would. Experimentation proved that weights placed in various parts of the figures would cause them to lurch properly on landing. Even without spiders, the scenes generate a shudder. The anguished screams were supplied by sound-effects man Murray Spivack, whose distinctive voice also is heard during the shipwreck sequence of *The Most Dangerous Game*. A gigantic lizard was substituted for the spider that had climbed toward Cabot's hideaway in the first filming. Also jettisoned from the chase were the scenes featuring a Triceratops and the huge snake that menaced Fay Wray during the action at the gorge.

Merian C. Cooper and Fay Wray pose for a publicity shot for *King Kong*.

"It wasn't easy, working for Coop," remembered Linwood Dunn. Cooper (seated left of Fay Wray) poses with partner Schoedsack on the set of *King Kong*.

The first version of Kong's initial appearance—as he arrives at the sacrificial altar—received an initial nixing from both Cooper and Schoedsack. The animation of Kong and the trees as they were pushed aside lacked the smoothness of other key moments. Kong's entrance was filmed again with minor refinements, and again and yet again. By the end of the production schedule, 16 versions had been completed. The one used in the final cut is the *first* version filmed. Despite its shortcomings, it was judged the most effective.

The film's inimitable visual style was attained largely through the imaginative drawings of Mario Larrinaga and Byron Crabbe. Working from O'Brien's action outlines and following his order to strive for the style and mood of Gustave Doré, these men made hundreds of drawings and sketches. Not only were the artists responsible for the design of the film, but they also rendered the glass and background paintings that became integral to the miniature settings. The men who crafted the three-dimensional elements followed closely the Larrinaga-Crabbe art. To assure that the original drawings would be reproduced accurately in the technical art, O'Brien commissioned the design of an ingenious opaque projector so the drawings could be thrown onto the glass as guides to the painting. The projector was duly constructed, but Larrinaga refused to use it—he had no need of such artificial assistance.

O'Brien's emulation of Doré as a basis for cinematographic lighting and atmosphere may have originated with the pioneering cameraman and special-effects expert Louis W. Physioc, who declared in 1930: "If there is one man's work that can be taken as the cinematographer's text, it is that of Doré. His stories are told in our own language of 'black-and-white,' are highly imaginative and should stimulate anybody's ideas."[1]

The scenes in Kong's Skull Mountain were particularly complicated.

The Doré influence is strikingly evident in the island scenes. Aside from the lighting effects, other elements of Doré's illustrations are patent. Most clearly influential are the Doré plates "The First Approach of the Serpent," from Milton's *Paradise Lost*; "Dante in the Gloomy Woods," from Dante's *The Divine Comedy*; "Approach to the Enchanted Palace," from Perrault's *Fairy Tales* and "Manz" from Chateaubriand's *Atala*. The gorge and its log bridge bear no slight resemblance to "The Two Goats," from La Fontaine's *The Fables*, and the lower reaches of the gorge may well have been designed after the Biblical illustration "Daniel in the Lions' Den." The wonderful scene in which Kong surveys his domain from the natural balcony of his mountaintop home is suggestive of "Satan Overlooking Paradise," from *Paradise Lost*, and "The Hermit on the Mountain," from *Atala*.

O'Brien appears to have invented the three-dimensional glass-and-miniature settings he pioneered in *Creation* and brought to public view in *Kong*. This technique was too time-consuming to appeal to the studios, although O'Brien was able to use it to a lesser extent in several later pictures. The animators and inventors Ub Iwerks (on his own, and as a wage slave to Walt Disney) and the Paramount-subsidized Fleischer Bros. achieved similar results, though without the added solid forms, in their celebrated multiplanar cartoons of the later Depression-into-wartime years. Marcel Delgado often bemoaned the fact that most dimensional-animation producers "never take any pains with the sets. They just use a few trees and rocks. In *Kong*, the sets have depth. You can see into them for miles, it seems."

The scenes in Kong's Skull Mountain cavern were particularly complicated, requiring an unusually large number of special processes. The setting itself is a complex amalgam of glass art and miniature construction. The pool from which the snakelike Elasmosaurus emerges is real water, photographed separately and projected in. Another matte was necessary to introduce a pit of bubbling lava into the foreground. Steam, filmed with backlighting against a black-velvet background, was superimposed. Two separately photographed and projected images were necessary to place Fay Wray on a ledge at the left and to show Bruce Cabot hiding among the rocks. Kong, the reptile and the miniatures of the human characters (necessary for certain portions) were animated by O'Brien while assistants manipulated the projected images. The absolute synchronization of all these processes was a formidable undertaking.

Although miniature projection replaced the old stationary-matte process in most instances, a variation of split-screen matting was useful in putting certain live-action elements into such animated scenes as these. The mattes were executed similarly to glass shots, the artist matting out the desired portions of the scene by applying opaque black paint to a sheet of glass mounted in front of the camera. When the first shot was made through the glass, the black area (neither transmitting nor reflecting light) permitted the portions of the negative that recorded the matted area to remain unexposed. The live-action portions were then filmed through a glass containing a counter-matte that covered the exact area that had been exposed on film in the first shot. (Live-action sequences are customarily shot first.) In certain scenes, such as those showing architectural features, it was necessary to use a hard-edged matte. Those using jungle foliage permitted a soft-edged matte that was somewhat easier to control. Any overlapping of the components resulted in white masses or lines at the points of match-up, while any space left between the components resulted in black areas. Avoiding these deficiencies, known as *pluses* and *minuses*, was most important.[2]

Running water was matted into other scenes. The Los Angeles River flows by in the foreground as Kong carries Fay Wray through the jungle after vanquishing the Tyrannosaurus. The waterfall at Skull Mountain was photographed in the Sierra Nevada Mountains; it also can be seen in *The Most Dangerous Game*. This effect of combining "living" water with animated beasts is an O'Brien trademark, first seen in *The Lost World* and repeated in the surviving footage of *Creation*, as well as in *The Son of Kong* and *Mighty Joe Young*.

O'Brien cited *Kong*'s most difficult scenes as those in which the ape fights a Pteranodon that attempts to fly away with Fay Wray. This sequence was in work for seven weeks. Some of the more reactionary critics have accused O'Brien of applying a mouthful of sharp teeth to a creature known to have been toothless in real life, but the teeth these crix *think* they saw in the picture exist only in the still photos, the work of an overzealous retouch artist. O'Brien's truer violation of natural history is that a real Pteranodon could hardly carry off a human being: Although its wingspan ran to nearly 30 feet, the hollow-boned monster was very lightweight. Some paleontologists maintain that Pteranodons could not fly but merely glided down from high crags. *Yeah, right*, as the wise old Oriental saying goes. These eggheads neglect to consider how such a "non-flying" monstrosity could regain its lofty perch.

The clifftop battle

> In the 1975-76 hardcover and paperback editions of *The Making of King Kong*, George Turner wrote: "O'Brien noted that few vertebrates have an alternating arrangement of dermal appendages and thus had the [Stegosaurs'] plates organized in pairs—to the dismay of some scientists and the approval of others." Indeed, this is the appearance on screen and in the familiar production stills. In times more recent, George seized an opportunity to examine a surviving miniature. He was surprised to find that the plates alternate slightly and made known to a friend, Peter Von Sholly, his intention to correct that point in an eventual revised edition. So here it is, corrected. I took a look at some photos that were made when the Stego was being repaired, and the plates do appear to be slightly offset from one another—not paired.
> —Douglas Turner

The Stegosaurus in the middle distance

Be that as it may, O'Brien's winged reptile not only flies, but packs grabbing-and-lifting strength and flaps about as furiously as a captive eagle when grasped by Kong. Keeping the Pteranodon aloft *and* animating the pounding wings made the staging unusually difficult. Further problems lay in the movements of the actors, requiring animated mannequins in certain portions of the frame and projected figures in others.

Paleontology be damned in the crucial light of artistic license. The Elasmosaurus is more slender than those known to science, and its swimming limbs are less prominent; it echoes Harry Hoyt's description, in his *Creation* story, of "a snake with legs." *Kong*'s Stegosaurus combines the well-known *Stegosaurus Ungulatus*, which bore two spectacular rows of bony plates along its back and two pairs of lacerating spikes on its tail, with the less familiar Kentrosaurus, whose tail held numerous paired spikes. The *Kong* Stegosaurus is considerably larger than the known specimens, which are less than 30 feet in length.

The great sauropod, Brontosaurus—or more correctly, *Apatosaurus*—is depicted properly (insofar as was known at the time) as an amphibious creature 70 feet in length. For dramatic purposes, the head is exaggerated and the ferocity of the beast is quite at odds with scientific opinion. Because Stegosauri and sauropods were herbivorous and stupid, the conventional wisdom holds it unlikely that they would attack human interlopers—if indeed there had *been* humans, interlopers or otherwise, in the various ages of dinosaurs—but humankind knows well that such herbivores as elephants, rhinoceroses and hippopotami are ready and willing to attack. The Brontosaurus in *Kong* uses its mouth as a weapon but does not feed upon its victims.

The Brontosaurus moves through the foggy swamp.

Surviving image from the lost spider-pit sequence

Among the *Kong* creatures that did not make the final cut, the Triceratops and its young conform to scientific opinion in most particulars except scale: They are larger than real. Likewise for the Styracosaurus, kin to Triceratops. The Arsinoitherium was not a dinosaur but a gigantic mammal that held forth in Egypt, long after the dinosaurs had gone extinct. The legs of this Oligocene beast resembled those of the elephants; the body was somewhat rhino-like; and the skull sported two massive horns, side-by-side, on the face. Call it entirely probable that the animal was as awesome and belligerent in life as in O'Brien's vision, and call it a pity that this Arsinoitherium became a casualty of the cutting room. The giant spiders and bugs and the octopoid of the gorge were wholly imaginary, although some arachnids and insects of the Carboniferous period *were* abundantly larger than those that exist today. (Some of these pit denizens later made an appearance in 1957's *The Black Scorpion*, a late-in-life reassertion of Willis O'Brien's artistry.) A large reptile shown in the excised version of the gorge sequence appears to be one of the proto-mammalian reptiles found in the Permian deposits of Africa, the dog-like Cynognathus.

The snake that was removed had its living, 60-foot prototype in Egypt during the dawn of the age of mammals. A peculiar reptile that menaces Bruce Cabot during the gorge episode is by and large imaginary, although it exhibits known features of the Desmatosuchus, whose fragmentary remains have been found in the Triassic beds of the Texas Panhandle-Plains. The gigantic vulture, Teratornis, and the birdlike reptiles, Rhamphorynchi, are scientifically correct.

A residue of mystery clings to even such a well-known dinosaur as the *Tyrannosaurus Rex* or "tyrant lizard king." The Tyrannosaurus that battles Kong conforms to known facts of the day. In life, this reptile was about 50 feet in length and packed a greater bulk than other carnosaurs. Its skull was approximately four feet long and armed with curved, dagger-like six-inch teeth. The hind legs were massive and powerful, but the forelimbs were so degenerated as to be almost

The death struggle with the Tyrannosaurus

uselessly limp. These tiny arm-like appendages are the only part of the skeletal structure not completely known; they have provoked tedious combative speculation. Some scientists contend that each *manus* supported only two digits (as in the related Gorgosaurus). Others hold out for three digits (as in the somewhat similar but decidedly more lightweight Allosaurus). O'Brien and Delgado followed the counsel of the helpful paleontologist Barnum Brown, of the American Museum of Natural History, and went with the three-digit theory.

Such are the fauna of Skull Island: a mixing of giants from wildly varying eras of prehistory, reconstructed according to dramatic imperative. As for the star of the show, Kong is purely a product of the imagination, filtered through authentic simian anatomy. Cooper used a gigantic ape as his hero because, as he put it: "Dinosaurs... were all right as menacing influences..., but they were clumsy and inhuman whereas apes are similar to man." Cooper made it clear that he "had no intention of making a 'plausible' picture. In fact, I couldn't imagine anything *more* implausible."

The notion of an ape as big as a dinosaur has since become somewhat less fantastic than it seemed to Cooper: The Leakey African expeditions of times more recent have unearthed the remains of a baboon that dwarfs the largest living gorilla. Even the oversized dinosaurs, so depicted in response to Cooper's oft-repeated demand to "make it *bigger*," have been vindicated by the discoveries of dinosaurs in Baja California much larger than those known in the day of Merian C. Cooper. One of these is a type of Trachodon more than 100 feet in length; the maximum length of this most prolific of dinosaurs had once been established at 40 feet. And *living* prehistoric hangers-on have come to light in the years since *Kong* was conceived: The most spectacular example is the huge Devonian bony fish Coelacanth, captured off Madagascar in 1938. It must be admitted, all the same, that in the case of *King Kong*, truth is *not* stranger than fiction.

"*King Kong* represents the goal of more than 20 years," Willis O'Brien said in 1933. "For that long a time—and that is a long time in motion pictures—I have delved into other bygone periods, studied the life of animals before the ascent of man, preparing myself for the day when someone would dare to reproduce on the screen the giant beasts that once ruled the world. Without knowing it, I was waiting for *King Kong*. That is the picture for which I have studied 20 years. I feel it has been worth the long years of research."

David Selznick recommended that the Motion Picture Academy grant O'Brien a special award for his unique work. O'Brien insisted that the names of eight key associates be included in any such honor. The Academy informed Selznick that a special-effects citation would demean the earnestly artistic nature of that august institution. Honors in this category were not initiated until 1940—and it was not until 1995 that the self-important Academy of Motion Picture Arts & Sciences would accommodate an active governing sector in this specialized, highly influential, field. This status now would enable a field of more than 130 visual-effects specialists to elect three of their number as Governors of the Academy. "By granting branch status to our visual-effects members," declared President Arthur Hiller, "the Academy is acknowledging another important contributor to state-of-the-art filmmaking as it really exists today." (And, if we may display the effrontery to add, as it *really had existed* since the dawn of cinema. There was a time when the very act of filmmaking *was* a special effect.)

There is little doubt that, with Kong himself, O'Brien created a performance that ranks with the finest characterizations of the screen. No other artificially created presence, however skillfully executed or cleverly maneuvered, has struck such a responsive chord with the film-going masses. O'Brien's Mr. Joseph Young of Africa, from 1949's *Mighty Joe Young*, is actually a better-designed and more expressive ape, but Joe is too lovable to achieve the tragic dignity that O'Brien invested in Kong. O'Brien's later monsters, including the title predators of *The Black Scorpion* and *Behemoth, the Sea Monster*, are sufficiently scary-looking but scarcely commune with the audience. Likewise for the cold-blooded monsters of Ray Harryhausen's *The Beast from 20,000 Fathoms* and *The Valley of Gwangi*—although Harryhausen's towering stranger from Venus in *20 Million Miles to Earth* is possessed of a tragic magnificence that calls to mind the impression left by Kong.

The great hero-villains of literature and cinema, however misshapen in body or soul, have in common certain qualities that range beyond the commonplace ability to inspire unease or terror. We are touched by their very *alone*-ness, their frustrated longings, their foredoomed struggles against inexorable Fate. The cruelties of Richard III, Ahab, Heathcliff, Hamlet and Long John Silver make their personal undoings all the more poignant. The Invisible Man and Dr. Jekyll became monsters because they tried rather a bit too hard to benefit humanity. The vampire and the werewolf, for all their repellence, are more pitiable than their most innocent victims, for they are condemned to an unending torment. The Golem, the Monster of Frankenstein and the misshapen Quasimodo, cut off as they are from love or companionship or even understanding, inspire sympathy more so than hatred. Satan, that most pernicious of villains, suffers yet from his ancient fall from celestial grace.

Only the most gifted actors are able to convey such complexities as to provoke the desired emotional response. Such an ability made stars of William S. Hart, Lon Chaney, John Barrymore, Emil Jannings, Conrad Veidt, James Cagney, Bela Lugosi, Edward G. Robinson and Boris Karloff—players whose gifts transcend physical effectiveness. That Willis O'Brien was able to invest a creature made of metal, wood, rubber, glass and fur with a personality sufficient to rival the most memorable performances of the screen, must be considered one of the few *bona fide* miracles of cinematic achievement.

1 Physioc's comments are drawn from his article, "Cinematography as an Art Form," in the 1930 *Cinematographer's Annual, Vol. I.*
2 This is the *positive* condition. The *negative* print would be the opposite.

The King in New York

… onto the talking screen… to stagger the mind of man!—From the Opening Night Program Book

I wish you would look up those two excellent aviators who played pilot and gunman in the airplane. You ought to sign them up at once.—Ernest B. Schoedsack to Merian Cooper; Following a First Screening of *King Kong*

"It isn't *big* enough!" Merian Cooper howled when he screened the first tests showing Kong at large in New York City. Ernest Schoedsack agreed: However awesome the gorilla appeared within his own jungle, he was dwarfed by the towering stone cliffs of the big town.

Although Kong was referred to in the publicity materials as standing 50 feet tall, he was actually represented as much smaller. His proportional size was originally selected to provide an effective dramatic relationship with the human players. That an inordinately huge monster is as impersonally uninteresting as a hurricane has been demonstrated *ad nauseam* by those dreadful Japanese films of the 1950s and onward, featuring an impossibly vast whatzus called Godzilla. It was rightly deemed that Kong must be thought of as a personality capable of pathetic yearnings and righteous indignation, rather than as a natural disaster.

For the jungle scenes, the technos worked on a basic scale of one inch-equals-one foot, making Kong appear to be 18 feet tall. The full-scale head, built to chomp down on a man with scarcely more than head and feet protruding, was scaled as though Kong stood nearer 30 feet tall. For some scenes, Cooper ordered the scale adjusted to suit the dramatic needs of the moment. It was Cooper's concern that the beast must always appear gigantic, but never so huge as to cut off his interest in the humans.

A symbolic exaggeration from the publicity materials

A wooden stand-in Kong and Empire State Building in front of the projected N.Y.

"We realized we'd never get much drama out of a fly crawling up the tallest building in the world," Schoedsack told us. By this time, too much work had been accomplished to permit a new start. After much gnashing of teeth, the producers decided they would film the city scenes in a different scale, making Kong appear 24 feet tall—and hope that the audiences would be too engrossed in the action to notice. The varying immensity of Kong actually works whether or not one consciously notices it, conveying at least subliminally the ape's escalating ferocity as his crisis deepens. (Yet another Kong model, this one 24 inches tall, was constructed for the New York scenes.)

Schoedsack and Eddie Linden went to New York to photograph the night-effect shot of New York Harbor and the Hoboken Docks that opens the film; the early-morning scene of the ship leaving the harbor; views of the Empire State Building; and action involving the Navy aircraft. None of the actors made the trip, all their city scenes being shot in the studio. Kong also did all his N.Y. scenes in California—in sets duplicating the streets in miniature.

The night exterior of the theatre in which Kong makes his Broadway début is a combination of art and a busy street scene. The interiors were filmed in the old Shrine Auditorium in Los Angeles, which Schoedsack rented for a day's use. The principals enacted their scenes on a stage before an audience of dress extras. Kong, photographed separately on a miniature stage, was matted in.

The leading players and the actors appearing as newspapermen are shown in the wings of the stage when Kong leaps from the platform after breaking free. In reality, Kong was lowered in barely perceptible steps of animation. The actors were introduced through miniature projection in this and a subsequent scene where Kong smashes the stage door (made of thin copper for animation

The press corps regards Kong.

The Making of King Kong

Kong at large in New York City

purposes) at the back of the theatre and emerges into the alley as the players in the background race toward a hotel across the street.

The lower level of the hotel was executed in full-scale and miniature. Fay Wray and Bruce Cabot were filmed hurrying into the lobby of the large set just as a real car crashed into the façade near the doors. The driver then leapt out and ran inside while the tuxedoed passenger lay on the sidewalk as though stunned. The actor's next scene shows him writhing and dying between the massive jaws of the full-sized head of Kong. A scene done in miniature animation, intercut, shows Kong approach the building, then grab up the struggling man and bite him. After the close shot, Kong flings the body to the ground, then tears away the hotel's marquee and hurls it onto a crowd of extras. The miniature shots were projected behind the stampeding extras, and the full-scale marquee was dropped onto them after the miniature marquee had been thrown (animated) out of the top of the frame. A masterful touch typical of the Cooper-O'Brien perfectionism is the cloud of dust (superimposed) that bursts forth from the marquee as Kong rips it from the building.

Kong's climbing of the miniature hotel was photographed from various angles, with spotlights from below providing a garish glow. The beams of incandescence were animated so that they would sweep over the ape.

The most nerve-wracking moment of the entire picture finds Kong peering into a high window at a sleeping woman, then smashing a paw through another window to snatch her from the bed. The screaming woman is borne through the window, head down, and held far above the street while Kong regards her. When the monster realizes she is not Ann, he disdainfully opens

A peeping Kong searches for Ann in New York City.

his fingers and the woman falls headlong to her death. Here is the ultimate nightmare, shattering in its more-than-symbolic evocation of nocturnal invasion and brutality.

The face that looks into the window in this and other scenes is one of the miniatures. The full-size head proved too inflexible to convey the impression that Kong was hanging onto the building while moving about. The unbilled actress (Sandra Shaw, a.k.a. Victoria Balfe) who so effectively plays the victim is shown in the grasp of the huge paw, both in the room and as she is held over the process background of the street. An animated figure was used for the more distant views when she is held and then dropped. Delgado's articulated giant hand released the woman convincingly in the close-in shot. The last part of the sequence consists of a dizzying down-shot toward the spotlights at street-level as the woman (now, superimposed) plummets.

A different, abandoned, version had the woman talking on the telephone when the hand reached for her. Also scrapped was a scene where Kong's appearance at a window broke up a poker game.

Kong's recapturing of Fay Wray was photographed in the same technique as the scene with the unfortunate woman. Miss Wray and Cabot are shown in the room as the monstrous face rises into view outside and then registers recognition. The face withdraws, and Kong's full-scale arm crashes in through another window. The arm is withdrawn, and Kong looks in again to see Miss Wray swooning across the bed as Cabot seizes a chair as a weapon. Again Kong thrusts the mighty hand, toppling Cabot and drawing the bed to the window. It lifts Miss Wray carefully and holds her over the background of the street. The miniature Kong ascends, carrying the miniature figure representing Miss Wray.

Plans at first called for Kong to leap from roof to roof, and several buildings were constructed to scale for this depiction. These structures, though not used as intended, are seen in the background when Kong and Miss Wray are atop the hotel. Miss Wray, via miniature projection, takes the place of the animated figure when Kong sets her down for a moment before grabbing her up again and clambering over the side. More of the buildings are shown in a reverse angle when Bob Armstrong and Cabot appear on the roof.

Kong's last stand against the Navy's airborne might

Buz Gibson animated Kong's scaling of the Empire State Building, wiring the model into position with each step along a ladder of dowels. Kong was positioned on the real edifice in two scenes, and on a miniature building in others by means of the blue-backing process.

The four Navy biplanes and their pilots came from Floyd Bennett Field. Schoedsack contributed $100 to the Officers' Mess Fund, and the pilots were detailed on official orders "to cooperate with the producer of *Kong* in the making of certain scenes involving Naval aircraft in flight over New York City." The pilots received $10 each under the table and were so elated that they decided to surprise the director with a show of appreciation. Schoedsack got a surprise, all right: He and Linden were shooting the approach of the aircraft when suddenly they realized the planes were linked together by lines decorated with flags! After the unwanted decorations were removed, the artists captured good ground-and-aerial scenes. The airborne business was shot from a Curtiss-Wright Travel Air camera plane from Roosevelt Field.

The biplanes were basic-training craft, Curtiss 02C-2 and Navy NY specimens. They were photographed flying in formation, peeling off and diving at their imaginary target, then looping and attacking from the other direction. Twenty-eight scenes of the genuine craft were intercut with scenes filmed in miniature and in process. The commander of the formation was killed in a crash only a few weeks after he had led the attack on Kong.

The cityscapes seen behind Kong as he perches on the miniature mooring mast were painted in three planes of depth by the Larrinaga brothers, Mario and Juan, and Byron Crabbe. The illusion is far superior to that achieved in some test shots where a projected photographic background was used. The glass paintings and backing were unusually large in this instance, being about 12 feet wide. This size was necessary for an unusual effect in which Kong is seen through the eyes of the pilots of the attacking aircraft. The camera was made to dive toward the defiant beast via steps of animation down a wooden ramp. These are the most elaborate examples of animating the camera itself, an effect that O'Brien had pioneered tentatively more than a dozen years

The wounded Kong in his last moments

earlier in "The Ghost of Slumber Mountain." The tracking ramp ran about 24 feet, enabling a swooping approach.

The illusion of the aircraft darting around the building was difficult to achieve because of the forced perspective of the set. This effect required model aircraft of various sizes, each scale representing a different distance. The planes ranged in wingspan from four inches to about 15 inches. It was also necessary for Carroll Shepphird to calculate the speed at which the airplanes would appear to be moving at various simulated distances from the camera. The speed was regulated by the distance traversed with each frame exposed—that is, if a four-inch model were moved in steps of one-quarter of an inch, then a 12-inch model would be advanced in three-quarter-inch steps.

The airplanes were suspended on hair-thin piano wire, stretched between pulleys situated beyond camera range. The wires had to be kept taut because piano wire kinks if allowed any slack. The models moved *with* the wires rather than *along* them, the wires being weighted at the forward end and released from the other end in carefully controlled steps. To facilitate accuracy in measuring the increments of movement, a hook at the control end was engaged in the mesh of quarter-inch hardware cloth (the galvanized steel-wire screen used in cages for small animals) with each step forward. This method also had been used for animating birds in the jungle scenes.

While the airplane sequence was being planned, Cooper asked animator Orville Goldner to join him for lunch. While they dined, Cooper asked: "Can you do a peel-off with little airplanes behind the Empire State Building?"

Goldner explained to Cooper the problems of rigging four tiny balsa aircraft and taking them smoothly through the maneuver in quarter-inch steps. Finally, however, Goldner declared he thought he could do it—although secretly he dreaded the idea. After laying out a system and rigging for such a scene, Goldner was relieved to learn that it would not be needed because Schoedsack's New York footage included the peel-off shots.

The scene in which an airplane crashes down the face of the building is a composite. As Gus White dropped the burning model from a scaffolding past a blue backing, the falling craft was combined in the camera with a previously made shot of the building. In this and most of the other

The Making of King Kong

Schoedsack (left) and flight commander at Floyd Bennett Field, planning the attack on the Empire State Building.

such scenes, a miniature building was used, but the genuine structure appears briefly in two scenes as the planes approach.

Fay Wray appears on a ledge of the mooring mast via miniature projection. An animated dummy substitutes for her when Kong holds her in his hand. She is also seen in the full-scale hand against a vertigo-inducing process shot of the city, as seen from what was then its highest elevation.

During his New York trip, Schoedsack secured details and measurements of the pinnacle of the building to guide the art department in constructing an actual-size replica. The large prop was built on a sound stage and, by October 1932, was ready for close-ups of Miss Wray and the scenes in which Armstrong and Cabot hurry to her rescue.

Close-up shots of the pilots and gunners were made at the studio with mock-up aircraft and composite backgrounds. The stalwart flight commander and his handsome chief observer in these scenes are none other than Cooper and Schoedsack, performing under Schoedsack's direction. This unusual bit of casting was the result of Cooper's remark: "We should kill the son-of-a-bitch ourselves."

A gripping version of Kong's fall was filmed in composite, with the body hurtling away from the camera toward the street nearly 1,000 feet below. This scene was spoiled by a phantom-image effect: The building showed dimly through Kong's body. (Phantom-imaging can be seen in such *Kong* knock-offs of the 1950s as *The Amazing Colossal Man* and *Attack of the 50 Ft. Woman*.) It was decided to use a more conventional view in which a loosely jointed dummy would plunge down the profile of the building. Because the scale model of the 102-story building was necessarily small, the problem of camera speed appeared insuperable. Carroll Shepphird's calculations indicated that the degree of slow-motion required to make the fall appear sufficiently ponderous was beyond the capability of the day's high-speed cameras.

A special mounting was built to hold a Bell & Howell camera and a drive motor, which were connected with a rubber hose. The plan was for the rubber hose to shear off in case the camera jammed. The set was flooded with a blinding light, which was necessary to get an exposure at the abnormally high shutter speed. The motor was revved to its maximum rate, exposing the frames of film at more than eight times the normal speed. The camera screamed as though in agony as the technicians wondered whether it might be torn apart under the stress. The dummy toppled from its perch—and the film stuck. The hose failed to shear, and the film accordioned in all the gates. Several of the camera's gates were sprung, and the film was crammed in so tightly that the operators had to cut it out, bit by bit, with a penknife. Several days later, the camera was again ready for operation. After a few tests, the scene was successfully captured.

The script plays the final scene atop the Empire State Building with Denham and a policeman looking down toward the street below. But a savvy last-minute decision moved the scene to ground level: The crushed body of Kong has drawn massed spectators when Armstrong appears and delivers the famous closing speech. The head, arm and upper torso of the fallen giant lie in

Kong's fall was ruined by a phantom-image effect.

the foreground—one of the miniatures—and the crowd is seen beyond in miniature projection. The effect is splendidly tragic. Live action was shot January 20, 1933, with 108 crowd extras.

With the live-action sequences substantially completed, Schoedsack was loaded down with crew members and equipment and dispatched to the Syrian Desert in December 1932 to film backgrounds for a proposed yarn by Philip MacDonald, *Arabia*.[1] The expedition was conceived along the same lines as *Lives of a Bengal Lancer*—that is, location footage to support studio scenes with the star players—and shared a similarly unfortunate fate. Cooper, left to handle post-production on his own, continued to shoot new footage even as editing, sounds effects and scoring were beginning. O'Brien's crew struggled to complete the effects work.

The end of December and the beginning of January saw a flurry of varied shooting, largely on process stages. The life-size head leered, snarled and gnawed as gleefully on Skull Islanders as on New Yorkers. The gigantic foot mashed tribesmen into the mud. Scampering natives, photographed against a blue screen, were added to the foregrounds of scenes in which Kong rampages through the village. The airplane mock-up made a return to the process

The effect of Kong's death is splendidly tragic.

The Making of King Kong

Live action shot using doubles for the stars, blends with miniature glass and live water.

Merian C. Cooper with Kong

stage for additional flying scenes—this time, with mere actors (George Daley and James Barton) doing the flying in lieu of the producer-director team. Doubles for Fay Wray and Bruce Cabot were photographed running through Nicholas Canyon, to be optically combined with miniatures and a real waterfall from the High Sierras. The film inched toward completion.

"It's in 13 reels," Archie Marshek said when he brought Cooper the news that Ted Cheesman had finished editing *Kong*.

"No picture of *mine* is going out in 13 reels!" Cooper exclaimed. "I'll shoot an extra sequence to bring it up to 14 reels."

"We can recut it so the reels aren't so full and make it a 14-reeler," Marshek suggested, but Cooper was adamant.

Now, movie studios are notorious for harboring superstitions. There is no

Notice the miniature billboard for *Denham's Monster* in this production shot.

such thing as a Stage No. 13 or a Dressing Room No. 13. Marshek believed, however, that Cooper wasn't all that superstitious: "He really wanted an excuse to film another sequence he had in mind."

Willis O'Brien's men soon were at work on one of the most elaborate miniature sets of all, a detailed reproduction in three-quarter-inch scale of New York's elevated streetcar tracks. Here, Cooper and O'Brien staged the memorable scenes in which Kong wrecks a train just before his final ascent. A large number of players were used in the 30 additional shots.

The realistic structures bear such signs as "Gibson & Co.," "Delgado & Co.," "Goldner's Chocolates" and the like—creators' signatures on a monumental job of work. Artists created tiny posters advertising *Chang* and *Denham's Monster*, and they built minute lighting fixtures, railings, switch-boxes, mazda and neon signs, autos, fire escapes, traffic signals, trash receptacles and innumerable other details necessary for realism. Live actors seem to flee (via traveling matte) along the streets and watch (via split-screen process) from the windows of adjacent buildings. A man on crutches hobbles out of Kong's path. After the crash, animated figures scramble out of the coach windows and scurry to safety.

The effect of Kong as seen from the engineer's cab of the approaching train was achieved by mounting a camera and a spotlight on a dolly and moving them in stop-motion along the rails toward the monster. These scenes are so smoothly animated that many writers have assumed them to be live-action shots with an ape-suited actor. While this might seem a logical method, in the manner of the much later Japanese monster pictures, it would have required building the set four times as large as the one used in *Kong*. The set was scaled to accommodate an 18-inch gorilla.

J.O. Taylor's camera caught some memorable displays of panic as the extras and stunt artists tumbled about in the full-scale set of the doomed train. A number of minor injuries resulted, but the sequence is superb.

Neither the producers nor their superiors were satisfied with the 14-reel version. It was too long to suit the New York office, as there was at the time a virtual taboo on features running more than 100 minutes. There were too many lapses of pace to suit Cooper, who joined Ted Cheesman

The Styracosaurus didn't make the final cut of *King Kong*.

in the cutting room and, after much sweating and cursing, emerged with a feature of 11 reels. Even the credit titles were shortened considerably before the film was pronounced ready. The final cut consists of 846 scenes, 11 art titles, 23 dissolves and nine in-out fades.

Gone were several of Marcel Delgado's best monsters—the Triceratopses, the Arsinoitherium, the Styracosaurus and what he called "the great crawling things of the pit." Gone was the journey of Ann and Jack down the river, along with Kong's furious descent of Skull Mountain. Gone were numerous bits of business and gags and snips of dialogue—painful but necessary sacrifices.

O'Brien and his crew, as they viewed the final release version, mourned those hundreds of man-hours lost. The cineaste may well shed a tear for the intrinsic value of what was thrown away, just as one must pine for *Creation* and Schoedsack's "natural drama" version of *The Lives of a Bengal Lancer* and the Abyssinian films of 1923 that would have become the first Cooper-Schoedsack epic if not for a gas leak and the bare flame of a watchman's lantern. Here are classic examples of that proverbial spilled milk over which one must not weep.

For Cooper was right, of course. He set his jaw and scissored his own manifested genius with a ruthlessness that can only have given him nightmares. In doing so, he delivered to the public a movie that holds the attention at every turn, each second of its 100 minutes. It is one of the few films that builds its suspense deliberately and then holds it, brooking no useless action, no wasted words, no show-offish side-plotting—a job of work without paunch or padding. Cooper's skill as an editor is no less remarkable than any of his other accomplishments.

Schoedsack did not take part in the editing or post-production work on *Kong*. When he returned from Arabia in February 1933, there was but little time left to make alterations. Archie Marshek arranged for Schoedsack a screening on the morning of February 15. A memo to Cooper summed up Schoedsack's feelings:

> There are a number of minor points which struck me when looking at KONG this morning, such as the shortening of the dissolve at the end of the departure scene, shortening or speeding up the elevated sequence, etc., which Archie tells me have already been taken care of.

The only other suggestions I can make at this late date are a few minor ones, which of course cannot affect the music.

Could we not cut in at least one of the close-up scenes of Kong untying Ann at the altar? I think the quality of these shots is fully as good as the quality of the long shot, in which Ann's removal from the altar is very vague.

I suppose there is nothing to do about Kong's first entrance, or is there?

I definitely do not like the dubbed-in moan or groan from Ann on her close-up on the altar. Did you notice it? She sounds sick, not scared.

Cabot's reaction at the window in the gate when he sees [that] Ann has been carried off, is, and always has been, bad. Couldn't we shorten his close-up when he looks? It would be improved if we could cut away from the close-up to a flash of Kong and back to the opening of the gate—thus omitting Cabot's weak reaction. This would be well worth while if the music permits.

I wish we could eliminate some of Ann's repetitious screaming in the New York chase, but I suppose it is too late.

How about a short burst of gunfire on the first zooms of the plane at Kong? As it is, it looks like they are only playing at first.

I want to congratulate you on the work out of the lab, which is, in my opinion, definitely better than any of the other animation and quality in any of the other jungle scenes. I was most agreeably surprised.

Then, in a joshing reference to his and Cooper's gimmick-casting cameo at the climax, Schoedsack added:

I wish you would look up those two excellent aviators who played pilot and gunman in the airplane. You ought to sign them up at once.

Important changes had taken place at RKO-Radio Pictures: David Selznick, impatient with increasing interference from the New York office, had announced his resignation on Feb. 3 and accepted a position at Metro-Goldwyn-Mayer. Merian Cooper was named as Selznick's successor.

The studio heads never had liked the title of the Cooper-Schoedsack production, *Kong*. They believed it sounded too much like *Chang* or *Rango*—the public might mistake it for another back-to-nature film. Selznick, in one of his last executive acts before leaving RKO, approved the final title for the forthcoming release: *King Kong*.

1 The Arabian film, later scheduled as *The Uncrowned King* and *A Fugitive from Glory*, was intended as a starring picture for John Barrymore. It was never completed—although some of the expeditionary footage eventually turned up in 1943's *Action in Arabia*.

The Finishing Touches

...we wanted a *big* sound.—Murray Spivack

Murray Spivack, RKO's 31-year-old director of sound effects, had prepared on July 19, 1932, a cost estimate for his department's contributions to Production 601, which had just been re-christened *Kong*. With only a hazy idea of how some of the effects could be accomplished—the talking-picture era not yet having called for any work comparable—Spivack studied the script and itemized the unusual sounds he was expected to provide. His notes reveal a great deal about the concept of the film at that stage of production.

All sound effects were added after the filming was completed, including Fay Wray's screams, which were recorded in a single strenuous session and dubbed in as needed.

"*Kong* presented many problems," Spivack told us. "I worked on it for about nine months, and we had to come up with a lot of new ideas. Sound equipment was very limited then, although we no longer had to record music, effects and dialogue at the same time the way we did a couple of years earlier."

In his native New York City, Spivack had been percussionist in a symphony orchestra that specialized in recording music for the silent pictures. The group was made up of first-chair musicians from the best such ensembles in the East, and its conductors included such heavy-duty maestros as Hugo Riesenfeld, Erno Rapée, David Mendoza and Josiah Zuro. Spivack said this all-star orchestra had one flaw: "In the strings, we had 16 concert masters, and this caused us a lot of trouble because they were individuals rather than ensemble players."

Spivack's recognition of the value of teamwork makes his soundtracks distinctive. His work earned for various studios eight Oscars and 14 Academy Award nominations.

Spivack entered the infant sound-film recording field in New York and in 1929 came to Los Angeles as recording technician and assistant musical director for Joe Kennedy's Film Booking Offices (or FBO Pictures), which shortly thereafter evolved into RKO-Radio. The studio used the Richard Dix film *Seven Keys to Baldpate* as a proving ground, for which Spivack created wind-and-thunder noises that were considered sensational at the time.

The creation of a voice for Kong was entirely subject to invention. The sound department had amassed a library of sounds made by real animals, comprising about 500,000 feet of roars, barks, growls, snarls and hisses. Spivack knew that any of these sounds would be too familiar—as well as too brief for a monster of Kong's proportions. Even an elephant's trumpeting cry lasts only eight to 10 seconds, where the finished footage showed Kong in the act of roaring for as long as 30 seconds at a stretch.

"I went to the Selig Zoo and arranged to record some lion and tiger roars at feeding time," Spivack said. "The handlers would make gestures as though they were going to take the food away from them, and we got some pretty wild sounds. Then, I took some of these roars back to the studio and put them together and played them backwards. I slowed them down, sort of like playing a 78-r.p.m. record at 33, until the tone was lowered one octave, and then I re-recorded it. From this, we took the peaks and pieced them together. We had to put several of these together, in turn, to sustain the sound until Kong shut his mouth... Then, we added a sound rail to the end so it would die down naturally instead of coming to an abrupt stop. That's how I conceived the roar of Kong."

There was no precedent to guide the sounds made by Kong when he would try to express his affections for Fay Wray. For these scenes, the voice of Kong became that of Spivack, who uttered low, guttural grunts of varying duration into a megaphone. By slowing the track and re-recording it, he achieved a timbre suitable for a simian seven times taller than a living gorilla.

"I wrote to the curator at the Lincoln Park Zoo in Chicago and asked for advice regarding the voices of dinosaurs," Spivack said. "When the reply came, I had to translate his scientific

Kong's roars lasted as long as 30 seconds at a stretch.

language into English. It seemed to be saying, 'You fool! Those animals didn't have vocal cords, and therefore they didn't have voices!' Well, I couldn't tell that to Mr. Cooper. We couldn't show a 50-foot-long monster and not have it roar—it would be laughed off the screen!"

Dr. J.W. Lytle, curator of vertebrate paleontology at the Los Angeles County Museum, told Spivack that varying degrees of hissing sounds would be appropriate for the dinosaurs. Because the Brontosaurus was amphibious, Spivack added some croaking sounds to the reptilian hisses of the gigantic sauropod.

"For the screeches of the Tyrannosaurus, I made most of the sounds with my mouth and then slowed the track down," Spivack said. "Most of the animal cries were made this way. The Pterodactyl's squawks were those of some bird—I forget which kind—which were slowed way down for depth. Almost all of our animal sounds were slowed down, because we wanted a *big* sound."

The heavy breathing of the monsters was sometimes simulated by a bellows. Compressed air and unusual noises such as a panther's purr were combined in certain instances with the voice of Spivack or of his assistant, Walter G. Elliott. The bellowing of the Triceratops was simulated by

A voice for a voice-less animal—Murray Spivack's unprecedented assignment.

The Making of King Kong

The death-rattle of the Tyrannosaurus was recorded as Elliott, with a mouthful of water, gurgled into a microphone.

grunting and growling through a double-gourd resonator. The death-rattle of the Tyrannosaurus was recorded as Elliott, with a mouthful of water, gurgled into a microphone.

"The sound of Kong beating his breast proved to be one of our most difficult problems," Spivack said. "I simulated that by hitting Elliott on the chest with a tymp-stick [a soft-headed drumstick designed for kettledrums, or tympani] while an assistant held a microphone to Elliott's back. Kong's footsteps were made by walking toilet plungers covered with sponge rubber across gravel and recording the sound with plenty of bass.

"We had trouble with gunshots in those days because the loud noise would sort of paralyze the mike," said Spivack. "A lot of sound men had to simulate them with slap-sticks. I discovered I could record real shots by using a .22 bullet and removing half of the powder. In *Kong*, the rifle shots are real.

"When we were doing the train sequence, I had such a confusion of sounds, the noise was terrific," Spivack continued. "When Cooper saw it, he said, 'Murray, there's a car going by; he should honk his horn.' We only had three tracks at the studio then—one for dialogue, one for music and one for effects—which is pretty primitive when you consider that I had 77 channels in the parade sequence of *Hello, Dolly!* Our equipment was so limited that if we needed additional sounds we had to go through another generation of recording. I told [Cooper] it would lower the quality of the recording. He got mad. I said, 'Be sensible, Merian; you couldn't hear a car horn in all that noise if we *did* it.' He insisted he wanted it. Pretty soon, we were shouting at each other, and right in the worst part of it I started to laugh. He looked surprised and asked, 'What are *you* laughing at?' I told him, 'Do you know that when you get mad your forehead turns a bright red?' He started laughing, then, and finally he said, 'Okay—have it *your* way,' and left."

Working closely with the musical director, Spivack developed an innovation that would render the soundtrack more nearly seamless: the harmonizing of sound effects with music. After the score had been prepared, the sound effects were altered in pitch to conform consonantly to the music. This unprecedented technique rendered bearable the almost uninterrupted cacophony of roars, shrieks, crashes and thunderous orchestrations that are heard during the last two-thirds of the movie.

The head of RKO's music department was an energetic little Austrian whose father and grandfather had been the biggest impresarios in Vienna. Richard Strauss was his godfather, and his youth was spent in the company of Jacques Offenbach, Johann Strauss and Gustav Mahler. A musical career was inevitable for a man with such a heritage and a name like Maximilian Raoul Walter Steiner.

The musical world took note of Max Steiner when, at age 15, he won the Emperor's Gold Medal for completing in one year the four-year course of study at the Imperial Academy of Music. The following year, Steiner was conducting *The Beautiful Greek Girl*, his original operetta, which ran for a year at Vienna's Orpheum Theatre. Several others of his compositions were published, and a symphonic suite was performed by the Vienna Philharmonic. In 1906, at 18, Steiner went to England, where he established himself as a composer, concert pianist and conductor of the 110-member orchestra of the London Opera House.

In 1914, Steiner was declared an enemy alien, subject to deportation. Through the intervention of the Duke of Westminster, Steiner managed to journey to America. He practically starved during his first weeks in New York, but in a surprisingly short time he rose from vaudeville pianist to orchestrator and conductor for William Fox's chain of theatres. During the next 14 years, he orchestrated and conducted for the Ziegfeld Follies and for *George White's Scandals* and shows staged by Victor Herbert, Jerome Kern, George Gershwin, Harry Tierney and Vincent Youmans.

While conducting Jack Donohue's *Sons o' Guns* in Boston, Steiner was approached by William LeBaron, then chief of production at RKO-Radio, who wanted him to join the studio at $450 a week. Steiner arrived at RKO in 1929 and orchestrated Tierney's music for the film version of *Rio Rita* and another musical, *Dixiana*.

Studios at that time were steering away from background music because of recording problems and a prevailing notion that dramatic scoring was a passé hangover from the silent screen. Nevertheless, when the spectacular *Cimarron* was filmed, LeBaron called for an impressive score. W. Franke Harling was supposed to do the music, but he could not accept because of a commitment to Paramount. Steiner, as musical director, was instructed to hire a name-brand composer for the film, which was scheduled to open in four weeks. He approached George Gershwin, Leopold Stokowski and Percy Grainger, all of whom asked for a year's time and from $250,000 to $350,000 to do the job. Steiner composed the music within the stingy time-frame allowed; his score was so highly praised by the critics that he was given a raise of $50 a week.

By 1932, Steiner had developed innovations that gave RKO's soundtracks a distinctive, instantly recognizable presence. He liked to use leitmotifs for the

A piece of music for the "Sacrificial Dance" from *King Kong*

The complete *King Kong* score, which was released by Marco Polo in 1996.

major characters, somewhat in the manner of Wagnerian opera. His most unusual practice was the accenting and enhancing of the images on screen with musical cues, underscoring each bit of action instead of providing merely a prevailing mood. Although there are many who express distaste for this approach—known derisively as *mickey-mousing*, for its resemblance to cartoon-synchronization technique—several important films would doubtless have been far less impressive without the dramatic emphasis provided by Steiner's intricately conceived scores.

RKO President B.B. Kahane had his doubts about *Kong* and was skeptical that the public would accept an animated ape as a serious dramatic presence. Kahane told Steiner: "We've spent so much money in the year and a half we've worked on it, so please don't spend any additional money on music." He instructed Steiner to put together a score from existing tracks. Steiner was disappointed because he saw tremendous musical possibilities in *Kong*. Cooper, realizing that proper scoring would lend a greater semblance of life to the animation, told Steiner to get an original score under way: "Don't worry about the cost because I'll pay for the orchestra or any extra charges." Steiner set to work with enthusiasm and the close collaboration of Cooper and Spivack.

"Maxie, that music isn't right for *Kong*," Cooper complained when he heard part of the proposed score. "It sounds too much like something out of a Broadway stage show." Steiner, appalled, replied that he didn't know what Cooper wanted. "I mean that we can't use that damned stage music for this picture," Cooper said. "This is a *movie*. Now, I don't know anything about music, but I *do* know that we need *movie* music, not *stage* music. That stuff might be all right for those pictures everybody's making where the camera's in an icebox[1] and everybody is standing around in those little sets, but this picture is made out in the open with the camera moving."

It was true that Cooper knew what he wanted, and he spent many hours consulting with the composer during the eight weeks the score was being written. Steiner told us that his approach was to "write what I see on the screen," and he became excited by what he saw in *Kong*. He timed each scene with a stopwatch so that his musical phrases would complement each nuance of action. He worked day and night until he was near collapse. Finally, he conducted a 46-member orchestra[2] for the music track, which was engineered by Spivack. The music added $50,000 to the budget—and a good investment it was, too, for no wedding of music, sound effects and pictures ever produced a more stunning offspring. Cooper arranged for a bonus for Steiner, stating that 25 percent of the film's effectiveness derived from the music.

It is difficult to imagine such an impassioned, often dissonant, hair-raising score coming from the genial composer of *The Beautiful Greek Girl*. Steiner called it one of his few "modernistic" scores and said that it "worried" some of his friends in Vienna and the American Euro-classical realms—but won him new admirers in France and Russia. (*King Kong* was extraordinarily popular in France; a surviving export print has proved to contain small but significant deviations from the well-known U.S. version in sound effects and cutting.)

Steiner's score is built largely upon three motifs. "King Kong" is a descending three-note figure that not only provides a leitmotif for the ape but also would serve in years to come as an inspiration for the defining music of the *Kong*-like *Creature from the Black Lagoon* series, as well as Hammer Films' bombastic re-inventions of the *Dracula* myth. "Jungle Dance" symbolizes the natives of Skull Island. "Stolen Love" is a plaintive melody that suggests the beauty-and-beast longings that motivate Kong. These themes are paraphrased and deployed throughout in numerous variations. Among other compositions are "The Forgotten Island," "A Boat in the Fog" and "Sea at Night," all of which suggest the tone poems of Claude Débussy. "The Sailors," introduced as a march as the men plod through the jungle, is redeveloped as pulsing chase music during several episodes. "Aboriginal Sacrifice Dance," scored for orchestra and male chorus, is played during the first native ceremony. Kong's arrival on Broadway is heralded by "King Kong March," in the style of a theatrical overture.

Music figures through most of the film, the exceptions being the New York and shipboard scenes prior to the arrival at the island, the fight with the Tyrannosaurus (which is so filled with furious sounds as to make music superfluous) and the battle with the airplanes.

Steiner's earnestness of approach is transmitted to the subconsciousness of the viewer, contributing immeasurably to the suspension of disbelief so crucial to a wholly fantastic adventure. The precise conformity of the music to the flow of images results in a unity seldom achieved in the combining of the visual and sonic arts. The growing love between Ann and Jack is emphasized by waltz-like string passages in a lush Romantic style, the mystery of an uncharted sea by softly ominous chords with the disturbing polyrhythms of distant drums, the frantic terror of pursuit by Cyclopean giants by *scherzi* calculated to accelerate the beating of one's heart. Music accompanying the native ceremonies conveys the frenzy of barbaric religious passion.

It is in the delineation of the complex emotional state of Kong himself that the music achieves its greatest expressiveness. Kong's savagery is accented by brassy, dissonant variations on the "King Kong" figure. The "Stolen Love" motif subtly underlines the tragic side of his nature, portraying his loneliness and the painful bewilderment inherent in unrequited love. This theme is developed to its apogee of power and finally resolved in the finale as Kong mutely bids Ann farewell and gives himself up to the sacrifice that was, from the beginning, inevitable. It would be difficult to overestimate Steiner's share in creating a classic tragic figure from what could have been merely a monster, however remarkably depicted in the visual realm.

Four selections were published as sheet music by Sam Fox Music Co.: "The Forgotten Island," "A Boat in the Fog," "Aboriginal Sacrifice Dance" and "King Kong March." A concert suite comprising the main themes was published and recorded much later.

All this music proved extremely durable and was used by Steiner and his successors at RKO—Roy Webb, Nathaniel Shilkret and Constantin Bakaleinikoff—for dozens of subsequent features and innumerable editions of *RKO-Pathé News*. Among the soundtracks containing sizable chunks of the *Kong* music are those of *The Last Days of Pompeii*, *The Last of the Mohicans*, *Muss 'Em Up*, *We're Only Human*, *Back to Bataan* and *Michael Strogoff*. Steiner reprised portions of this material for several of his much later works for Warner Bros. "A Boat in the Fog" builds suspense as admirably for Bette Davis in *A Stolen Life* as it had for the passengers of the S.S. *Venture*. Shortly before his death in 1972, Steiner told us that *King Kong* was among his personal favorites.

Oscar Levant, who was on staff at RKO at the time *King Kong* was produced, said of the score: "Full of weird chords, strident background noises, rumblings and heavings, it was one of the most enthusiastically written scores ever to be composed in Hollywood. Indeed, it was always my feeling that it should have been advertised as a concert of Steiner's music with accompanying pictures on the screen."

By March 1933, *King Kong* was ready to be shown to the exhibitors. Insiders predicted it would be a sensation, and even the diehard dissenters in New York gave in, authorizing the preparation of the biggest promotional campaign in the studio's history. A large, garishly colored pressbook contained a message to exhibitors that is worthy of preservation:

> Into a show-world grown weary of namby-pamby plots stalks the gigantic figure of KONG! The very name conjures up visions of a realm crowded with strange sights! If ever there was a show sired by the spirit of P.T. Barnum, it's this Hippodrome of thrills and daring adventure staged in the arena of Earth's creation. KING KONG comes like a gift from showman's heaven... a picture... big... original... startling... to blast away with its dramatic dynamite the lethargy that now holds show business in its grip! For the first time in months comes a SHOWMAN'S PICTURE...

The national magazine ads, featuring Mario Larrinaga's drawing of the Empire State Building climax, used only one line: "THE PICTURE DESTINED TO STARTLE THE WORLD!"

S.L. "Roxy" Rothafel, impresario of New York's two largest theatres—Radio City Music Hall and the New Roxy—knew an audience-grabber when he saw it. Against the advice of his associates, Rothafel dared to open the film at both houses (total seating: 10,000) on the same day. A large newspaper advertisement heralded the event on opening day, March 2, and included a description of the accompanying stage presentations:

JUNGLE RHYTHMS—brilliant musical production. Entire singing and dancing ensemble of Music Hall and New Roxy—Spectacular dance rhythms by ballet corps and Roxyettes—Soloists—Chorus—Symphony Orchestras—Company of 500—Novel features.

Even with tickets selling at Depression prices, Rothafel's gamble paid off handsomely. Crowds queued up four abreast at both theatres, and in the first four days of its run *King Kong* set an all-time world attendance record for an indoor attraction, bringing in $89,931 in hard-earned coin. To accommodate the crowds, it was necessary to run 10 shows daily. "Ten thousand seats weren't enough," Rothafel reported joyously.

Sid Grauman, the West Coast's answer to Roxy Rothafel, was not to be outdone, although he had to wait until March 24 to stage the official premiere in Hollywood at the Chinese Theatre. A special *King Kong* edition of *The Hollywood Reporter* announced the event with a unique 28-page insert printed in four colors on two kinds of heavy stock, with parchment end sheets and covers stamped from pure sheet copper. The layout was the work of Keye Luke, the Chinese artist-actor better known for his *Charlie Chan* pictures with Warner Oland.

"This is a Grauman opening in the full sense of the word," wrote Louella Parsons in the *Los Angeles Examiner*.

NO MONEY yet
NEW YORK DUG UP
$89,931
IN 4 DAYS
(MARCH-2-3-4-5)
to see
"KING KONG"
AT RADIO CITY
SETTING A NEW ALL-TIME WORLD'S RECORD FOR ATTENDANCE OF ANY INDOOR ATTRACTION
COOPER-SCHOEDSACK PRODUCTION..RKO RADIO PICTURE

First-nighters had plenty at which to gape: In addition to the customary spotlights and celebrity interviews, the life-size head and shoulders of Kong greeted the patrons in the forecourt. On stage, Jimmy Savo emceed a spectacular prologue that included a 50-voice African-styled choral ensemble and a dance troupe of extravagantly costumed black chorines, performing "The Dance of the Sacred Ape" and 16 other numbers. Reviewers on both coasts were generous with praise for the film.

The national release followed on April 10. The resulting flood of box-office returns put paid temporarily to RKO's chronic financial problems, lifting the studio out of debt for the first time.

"We brought that picture in for only $430,000," Cooper revealed later. "That was the actual cost, but those bookkeepers tacked on the cost of *Creation* and a lot of so-called 'overhead.' The 'official' cost was $650,000."

---

1 In many early talkie productions, the camera was confined to a soundproofed, windowed Celotex booth known as an icebox, which kept the motor's whir from registering on the soundtrack—but of course sacrificed motion.
2 Our earliest sources had cited 80 members, and other accounts have ranged as high as 85. The 46-piece orchestra can reliably be called the correct figure, with the census varying on occasion.

An Outbreak of Sequelitis

I'm the worst businessman there ever was—except Schoedsack. He's even worse.—Merian C. Cooper

If we'd had a percentage deal, we wouldn't be such nice people. We'd be rich.—Fay Wray

By the time *King Kong* made its début, David O. Selznick had departed from RKO-Radio Pictures. Merian C. Cooper had reorganized many departments and was busily living up to a vow to have 11 features launched into production by April 15. Early in March, Cooper had announced that one of the pictures already started was *Jamboree*, which would be filmed under strict security. Ernest Schoedsack's Arabian film was delayed for completion in the studio and on desert locations near Yuma. Of the mysterious *Jamboree*, Cooper would reveal only this: "It will be produced on the same elaborate scale that attended the making of *King Kong*." He added that the picture was "well under way," with Schoedsack directing from a script by his wife, Ruth Rose.

"We called it *Jamboree* to keep people from visiting the set," Schoedsack told us. "If they'd known we were making another *Kong* picture, they'd have driven us crazy trying to find out how it was done." The film, of course, was *The Son of Kong*, the inevitable sequel to a hit. Cooper had approached the New York office with the idea and was told to "go ahead with it and make it even bigger." Cooper's enthusiasm was dampened somewhat when he learned the budget would be $250,000.

"It was a case of 'If you can't make it bigger, you'd better make it funnier,'" said Ruth Rose,

invoking the old standby Broadway axiom. To combat budgetary restrictions, Cooper arranged for key personnel to claim royalties in lieu of part of their salaries. Filming was done at the Radio lot, at the nearby Warner Ranch, at sea and on Santa Catalina Island. Most of the production crew of *King Kong* worked on *Son*. Shooting was completed in October.

The Son of Kong has suffered the fate of most all sequels: virtual eclipse in the shadow of a superior predecessor. Certainly, *Son* cannot compete in terms of spectacle or horrific impact, but it is a fascinating creation in its own right and provides intriguing footnotes to the source film. Most importantly, *Son* provided the artists involved with an opportunity to polish and improve their trailblazing techniques. The animation compares favorably with that of *King Kong*, and the composite work—utilizing an improved double-matting process—is considerably slicker.

Also superior are some of the characterizations, especially that of Carl

Helen Mack and Robert Armstrong with *The Son of Kong*

Denham, as played again by Bob Armstrong. The Denham of *King Kong* is a loyal and stalwart friend in need, but also an aggressive opportunist who can tell a hungry waif, "I'm not bothering with you just out of kindness." There is much more to the character than could have been brought forth in a single picture, and Denham's personality receives a fuller exploration in the sequel.

"For me, personally, the role was better than before," Armstrong told us. "It gave me a great deal more character, swell dialogue and love scenes. Denham was a character audiences could identify me with; many actors work all their lives without getting that."

Frank Reicher, Victor Wong, Noble Johnson and Steve Clemente were also enlisted to re-create their roles. The Reicher and Wong roles were expanded considerably. Wong's role, as in *Kong*, was added and beefed up by degrees after completion of the formal shooting script. Johnson and Clemente appear only briefly because some planned action involving the natives was eliminated.

Armstrong's leading lady, Helen Mack, is appealingly strong as a typical Ruth Rose heroine, not unlike Fay Wray's Ann Darrow, although Miss Mack's portrayal looks forward to Terry Moore's role in *Mighty Joe Young* more so than it harks back to Miss Wray's presence in *Kong*. Human villainy, more along stock melodramatic lines, is ably represented by the most cowardly, sniveling blackguard imaginable, as portrayed by John Marston, and by a mutinous crew led by Ed Brady as a surly Marxist agitator.

The title character is a wholly sympathetic monster, despite his awesome potential for destruction. Scaled to appear 12 feet tall, the young Kong has blond hair and a remarkably expressive countenance. As apes will do, he often imitates the actions of his human companions to amusing effect. He is, however, suitably ferocious when the occasion so demands. The hair is virtually free of the unwanted animation riffling that had plagued the handlers of Kong, Sr.

Three juvenile Kongs were constructed over the skeletons of original Kongs. Close-ups were made without the use of a large mechanical head, but the articulated Kong hand, re-designed in some particulars, is shown in two key sequences. Schoedsack would use a similarly designed *human* hand in 1939's *Dr. Cyclops*. The voice of Kong, Jr., was built upon the chattering of baby gorillas, as recorded at the San Diego Municipal Zoo. The roar of the ape as he fights a gigantic bear and a dragon was taken from the battle cries of tigers and elephants—combined, played backwards and slowed to the proper depth of tone.

Except for the Brontosaurus, which surfaces briefly, the monsters are new. *Kong*'s Styracosaurus, which failed to survive Cooper's cutting-room purge, belatedly appears, with smoother animation than that accorded the quadrupeds of the source film.

Three juvenile Kongs were constructed over the skeletons of original Kongs.

The bear, scaled to suggest a height of 15 feet, chases Denham and Miss Mack; tumbles and shakes his head when stunned by a shotgun blast; and engages in a roughhouse battle with the ape. Because bears can be by turns frightening and comical, this beast makes an ideal foil for a fight sequence played as much for laughs as for thrills. A dragon-like reptile, created by Marcel Delgado on O'Brien's orders to "build something nobody has ever seen before," is the ape's opponent elsewhere. This singularly evil-looking monstrosity has large, clear eyes that appear almost luminescent. A sea monster, another Delgado original, is the film's most terrifying denizen—gracing four shots where it rises from the depths to devour the villain. Except for a hair-

The sea monster is the film's most terrifying denizen in *The Son of Kong*.

A dragon-like reptile, created by Marcel Delgado, threatens the Son of Kong.

raising animated close-up, this monster was operated mechanically, exactly as the Brontosaurus was handled in *King Kong*.

Miniature rear-projection work was used extensively to place Armstrong and Miss Mack in scenes with the ape and in a sequence in which players are pursued and cornered by the Styracosaurus. A nine-inch animated figure of Armstrong was used to enable Kong, Jr., to lift Denham to safety from a collapsing cave; for scenes of Denham and the ape scaling Skull Mountain as it sinks into the sea; and for the long shots of Junior holding Denham above the water at the climax.

John Marston is shown in composite with the sea monster as it rises. The snake-necked creature is then shown from a different angle, seizing a miniature dummy and shaking it in a dog-like manner before dragging it under. The earthquake that destroys the island, as accomplished in a combination of miniature and full-scale work, is an exciting spectacle—although the schedule did not permit O'Brien to stage the stampede of dinosaurs envisioned in the script. Some unusual composite work was required by scenes in which the animated figures of Junior and Denham are seen in the same frames with raging ocean waters, landslides and rain.

The Pathé lot was sold shortly after production had started, obliging Schoedsack to find a new jungle for the full-scale shots—hence the location work at Catalina. The Mario Larrinaga-Byron Crabbe glass art and the malevolently detailed miniature jungles are as intricately beautiful as those of the original. The native village is kept in the distance, depicted by glass art. A vast cave-temple containing a gigantic idol is an impressive miniature set.

Max Steiner's fresh score is apparently his first in the style he would use a decade later for *Casablanca*—a style, in fact, that film-music theorists and composers call "the *Casablanca* technique." (Somehow, "the *Son of Kong* technique" doesn't sound quite highfalutin' enough.) Dramatic variations are worked out from the melody of a plaintive song called "Runaway Blues,"

The animated cave bear from *The Son of Kong*
which Helen Mack introduces early along. The paraphrased theme is especially effective in a sequence involving a murder and a fire, and also during the fight with the bear; each instance is a remarkable example of what a skilled composer can develop from simple thematic matter. The lyrics are the work of Edward Eliscu, an author/producer/actor/tunesmith whose more famous songs include "More Than You Know," "Without a Song," "Flying Down to Rio," "Orchids in the Moonlight" and "The Carioca." A three-note theme for Kong, Jr., is used extensively, and key themes from *King Kong* are woven into certain scenes. There are many lighthearted touches, such as a melodic quotation from the traditional Hebrew "Mazeltof" when Junior makes a gesture associated with Old World Jewry.

The Son of Kong is rather slow in getting under way. As in *King Kong*, all story elements are established up front so that there will be no interruption once the action starts. The ship reaches the doomed island at about the halfway mark.

The first half contains an outstanding sequence, staged with consummate skill by Schoedsack.

Original artwork of the Son of Kong and cave bear meeting

The title character is a wholly sympathetic monster, despite his awesome potential for destruction.

It depicts the striking down of the leading lady's drunken father by the villain; the fire that destroys the traveling show tent that the victim and his daughter call home; the freeing of the trained animals therein by the girl; and her desperate attempts to rescue the dying man. The camera moves alongside Helen Mack through the blazing rooms and, kicking obstructions from her path, she drags the unconscious man out into the open and then hurries back to retrieve her dress and wardrobe trunk, seconds before the canvas shack collapses. Steiner's emotion-charged music; Miss Mack's intense performance; and Schoedsack's attention to detail and adroit use of the camera to confront the viewer with the danger—all add up to a richly moving and suspenseful episode. This action was filmed quickly and without complications on the Warner Ranch grounds.

Equally remarkable is an unusually long scene in which the camera follows the players and their lifeboat through a narrow channel between towering (miniature) cliffs. Flawlessly executed in composite using a method devised by Schoedsack, the vista betrays no sign of fakery. The effect is repeated with the addition of storm effects as the boat is shown retreating through the same passage, now buffeted by the sea as boulders come tumbling.

The Making of King Kong

Willis O'Brien was said to have been unhappy with the tongue-in-cheek approach to *The Son of Kong*.

O'Brien provided a number of those delightful *lagniappes* that distinguish his work from that of any other player in the field. Water ripples about the quicksand in which the ape is caught. A bubbling spring and a running stream punctuate the Styracosaurus' moment in the limelight. Animated birds soar across the foreground in some shots and flit among distant branches in others.

More than 150 off-stage workers were required for the production. The location shots of the five principals, at sea and on Catalina, required the services of the director, three assistants, eight grips and property men, two laborers, seven sound recordists, eight electricians, two wardrobe women, one script clerk, three cameramen, a makeup artist, a hairdresser, a doctor, two carpenters, two horticulturists and 20 sailors. Schoedsack recalled: "I've got to *tell* you, I developed a real longing for those days when Coop and I worked all by ourselves, way off in the wilds."

The Son of Kong was profitable in the United States, but it was in the foreign market that it really paid off. It fared especially well in the Orient and in Malaysia, being one of the few Hollywood-made films depicting that part of the world that looked sufficiently authentic to be accepted there.

O'Brien, beset with private-life disappointments during production, was said to have been unhappy with the tongue-in-cheek approach to *The Son of Kong*. He proved reluctant to discuss the film in later years.

Remember 'Cavalcade'—?

> So great is its impact that I venture to predict it [*King Kong*, that is] will not be forgotten even in 1960—destined to become a living legend, part and parcel of American folklore.—Lloyd Arthur Ashbuck; 1933

King Kong's most celebrated set, the Great Wall, saw further use in several other films before it went out in—literally—a blaze of glory. Pathé was sold in April 1933 to a syndicate that rented the facilities to independent producers. Through the use of Pathé's first-rate sets, stages, properties and equipment, such small companies as Sol Lesser's Principal Productions, Nat Levine's Mascot Pictures, Edward Small's Reliance Pictures and George R. Batcheller's Invincible-Chesterfield Corp. managed to achieve a major-league look in their films.

Lesser's serial, *The Return of Chandu*, starring Bela Lugosi, was filmed at Pathé during the summer of 1944 and made splendid use of what remained of Skull Island, now represented as the fabled Island of Lemuria. Each of its 12 episodes opened with the tolling of the very gong that Noble Johnson had tolled to summon Kong. Much action was shot around the wall and in the village.

Merian C. Cooper returned in 1935 to borrow the wall for his spectacular independent production for RKO, *She*, wherein the refurbished set can be seen as the entrance to a palace carved from a Siberian mountainside.

David O. Selznick leased Pathé in 1936 as the home of Selznick-International Pictures and during the next dozen years produced his most famous films there. The Great Wall expired in the Grand Manner on December 10, 1938, when special-effects expert Lee Zavitz staged the burning of Atlanta for *Gone with the Wind*. Suitably camouflaged to resemble background buildings,

The Great Wall from *King Kong* was destroyed in the burning of Atlanta scene in *Gone With the Wind*.

the wall was laced with pipes, through which a mixture of 20 percent rock gas and 80 percent distillate was fed to atomizers. The fuel flow was controlled electronically from a pumping station that permitted the atomizers to be activated, or otherwise, in an instant. Another control fed alternating flows of oil and water, so that the fire could be started and extinguished on cue. The system used more than 1,000 gallons of fuel per minute, sending tongues of flame 200 feet into the air. Within about six minutes, the wall crumbled into ashes. As in 1932, Washington Boulevard and the Baldwin Hills were crowded with spectators. Among the guests inside the walls was the British actress Vivien Leigh, and it is said that Selznick decided that night upon casting Miss Leigh as *GWTW*'s Scarlett O'Hara.

The mock-ups of the S.S. *Venture* made countless cinematic journeys after the Skull Island expeditions. The day and night shots of the ocean from *The Son of Kong* were likewise subjected to much use to provide process plates for many a romantic movie voyage. One beautiful glass-miniature animation scene from *Son*, showing birds flying among the distinctive trees of Skull Island, provided an appropriately fantastic process background for a sequence of Orson Welles' *Citizen Kane* (1941).

King Kong did its bit for the solvency of RKO again in 1938, when it was reissued to heavy grosses, capitalizing on the industry's desire to test an international censors' ban on horrific pictures. The fans were shocked to find that the Hays Office had ordered drastic cuts of scenes deemed too strong for the stricter U.S. censorship code enacted four years earlier. Even so, Kong seemed a robust leading man at a time when the leading box-office stars were Deanna Durbin, Sonja Henie, Shirley Temple and Gene Autry.

One of the scenes in New York, which was deemed too violent.

Only about three minutes were removed, totaling 29 scenes. Three scenes showed men being bitten to death by the brontosaurus, which was permitted to claim only three victims instead of five. Three additional cuts did away with the sequence where Kong tears away Fay Wray's dress. Eight sacrifices involved shots in the native village—the ones Ernest B. Schoedsack had disliked—showing natives being bitten to death and crushed underfoot, along with a view of Kong smashing a scaffolding laden with spearmen. Three showed Kong biting a New Yorker to death. A dozen made up the sequence in which Kong drops a woman from the hotel building, although portions of this action were retained in the reissue trailer.

Another reissue, in 1942, was a great financial success. Entirely new posters and a more modern-style trailer heralded the release, and Willis O'Brien's name was added to the advertising materials—although his middle initial was mis-given as *J*. The 1942 prints appear to have been made from a release copy rather than from the original negative, and the entire Empire State Building sequence is

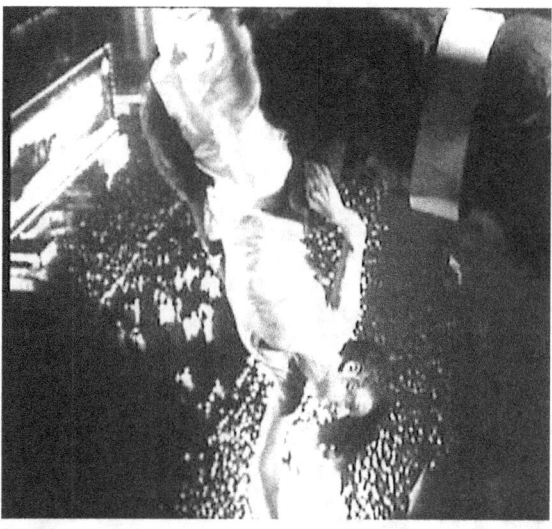

This scene of a woman dropped by King Kong was also censored.

printed out-of-frame. The same held true with RKO's reissue prints of 1952 and 1956. New posters were prepared for these versions, and *Kong* was offered on a double bill with, in each instance, a Val Lewton thriller: *The Leopard Man* in 1952 and *I Walked with a Zombie* in 1956.

After the demise of RKO as a producing company, *King Kong* became a television favorite—its broadcast popularity exceeded only by that of *The Wizard of Oz*, which has the Technicolor advantage.

In 1956, censorship having relaxed somewhat, RKO announced that it would restore the scenes removed in 1938. A search of the studio vaults failed to unearth the missing footage, however, and it was believed lost forever. It was not until 1971 that any missing portions were restored under the interim ownership of Janus Films. The footage was found in an attic in Philadelphia, and all but the first three shots grace the Janus prints. The original main and end titles remained missing, however, until the 1980s. It was then, under the more lasting proprietorship of Turner Entertainment—Ted Turner, not George Turner—that a full-scale restoration was mounted with George Turner among the consultants, going back to fine-grain positive footage from 1933 (the camera negative having long since vanished) for a *Kong* that, today, looks immeasurably more vivid than any of its big-screen reissues or TV-syndicate prints over the long haul. Turner Entertainment also delivered a digitally colorized video edition of *King Kong* during this period of reclamation and restoration; this novelty represented no threat to the genuine article.

In each incarnation, *Kong* has proved a success, brought in a great deal of money, and cinched its status as a classic. Most of the critics loved the film in 1933, but *Kong* was hardly a *prestige* film. But the beauty of the beast has become evident to film historians.

Does anybody out there remember *Cavalcade*? Probably vaguely if at all, although Frank Lloyd's epic filming of a Noël Coward play won the Academy Award for Best Picture of

Schoedsack directed *Dr. Cyclops* with Albert Dekker in 1940.

Merian C. Cooper and John Ford were the producers of *Rio Grande* (1950).

1933—the year for which *King Kong* garnered nary an Oscar nomination in any category. Twenty years later, however, *King Kong* was cited when Charles Brackett presented a special Oscar to Merian Cooper for "his many innovations and contributions to the art of motion pictures," and again some months later when Jesse Lasky presented Cooper with a special award from the Hollywood Chamber of Commerce.

After the release of *The Son of Kong*, Cooper conceived a second sequel, flashing back to the misadventures of the Denham expedition in bringing Kong to New York, with the ape escaping ashore somewhere in the Malay Archipelago. Schoedsack talked him out of it. Much later, when Cooper was in charge of production for the Cinerama organization, it was rumored that *King Kong* would be remade in that tri-camera process under its original title, *The Eighth Wonder*. Cooper, however, withdrew from the company, and no such venture was initiated.

Although it is the most popular of the films made by the Cooper-Schoedsack team, *King Kong* is but one of many highlights in long and exciting careers. There followed many more films, flying adventures in another global war, travels to distant lands and enough excitement for hundreds of ordinary lifetimes. The Cooper-Schoedsack partnership had technically disbanded by the middle 1930s, then rallied over a decade later for an almost-reunion (with Schoedsack

One of the last photographs of Willis O'Brien, taken as he worked at his drawing table at Film Effects of Hollywood on *It's a Mad, Mad, Mad, Mad World.*

as a hired-gun director) on *Mighty Joe Young* and, finally, a collaboration in the newfangled Cinerama superscreen process.

But the artists remained pals to the last. Their teaming really ended on the morning of April 21, 1973, with the death of Merian Coldwell Cooper at age 78, only a few hours after the passing of his old friend, Robert Armstrong.

Ruth Rose Schoedsack and Ernest Beaumont Schoedsack lived out their lives in Santa Monica, California. Ruth died on June 8, 1978—Monte's birthday. A year later, Schoedsack told us he was "still in shock" from the loss. He died in December 1979.

Willis O'Brien, though dogged throughout by personal and financial problems, continued to contribute his unique skills to the movie industry at whatever opportunity. There were many disappointments and unrealized projects. OBie was animating the complex miniatures of *It's a Mad, Mad, Mad, Mad World* for Linwood Dunn when felled by a heart attack at age 76 on November 8, 1962.

For all who helped bring Cooper's wildest dream to the screen, *King Kong* was a unique experience—as expressed most eloquently in the words of Carroll Shepphird: "I've always been glad I was allowed to be a part of that wonderful picture."

Preludes, Prologues & Progeny: Kong and Crucial Kin

I did like it [the movie]. All I said was, "It's no *King Kong.*"—Tobey Maguire to Charlize Theron, after their characters have viewed the 1939 *Wuthering Heights* in *The Cider House Rules* (1999)

No *Kong* is an island, of course, Skull Island notwithstanding. And no picture so wondrous as *King Kong* can exist in a cultural vacuum. Herewith, we present a detailed inventory of those pictures without which *Kong* might never have come into being—and of the more significant sequels, descendants and follow-throughs (false starts and finished results alike) that owe their souls to the still-reigning popular favorite. All are steeped to one degree or another in a heady brew of Adventure, Romance and Terror, which happened to be George Turner's favorite combination of storytelling values.

THE GHOST OF SLUMBER MOUNTAIN (1919)
(World Cinema Distributing Corp.)

Here we find the distillation and decisive advancement of techniques that Willis O'Brien had brought nearer a polished form during 1915-1917 via such rough-hewn yockers as "The Dinosaur and the Missing Link," "Prehistoric Poultry" and "R.F.D. 10,000 B.C."—all distributed via the Edison company.

"The Dinosaur and the Missing Link" originated as a $5,000 free-agent production underwritten by Herman Wobber. It is of singular interest in the present context for its ape-man character, Wild Willie. These prototypes for bigger things—"fascinating finger-painting from a soon-to-be master artist," as the historian and restorationist Scott MacQueen has characterized them—are slapdash comedies, unsophisticated in every way save their conception. "The Ghost of Slumber Mountain" marks a vast leap forward.

As "Ghost" opens, a chap known as Uncle Jack is regaling his nephews with a story that dissolves promptly and presumably into a flashback: At a haunted cabin in a forest, Jack finds a strange optical instrument. The ghost of a hermit appears and instructs Jack to gaze through the device. To his amazement, Jack sees a Brontosaurus grazing in the valley. A gigantic flightless bird, a Diatryma, enters the scene and devours a snake. Two Triceratopses engage in furious combat. The victor is attacked in turn by an Allosaurus. As the flesh-eater triumphs, the ghost vanishes. The Allosaurus rushes toward Jack. Jack fires on the beast and runs. Just as the monster is about to chow down on him, Jack wakes from a dream.

When his nephews realize that Uncle Jack has been telling a whopper, they pummel him heartily.

Legend has it that Willis O'Brien played Uncle Jack—and there *is* a physical resemblance—but O'Brien declined to affirm or deny this, saying only that he had forgotten the names of the players. The ghost is shown in a suitably wraith-like double exposure. "The Ghost of Slumber Mountain" marks a ferocious surge in the art of dimensional animation, easily surpassing prior work by O'Brien or anyone else. It clearly is the legitimate forebear of *The Lost World* and *King Kong*. The animation of the creatures is excellent, but O'Brien's use of the camera is generally unimaginative by comparison with his later efforts. Composition and editing are unremarkable, lighting is of the natural variety and O'Brien shows a reluctance to draw near his subjects. The gulf between "Ghost" and *The Lost World* is in these respects very wide.

CREDITS: Presented by: Paul H. Cromelin; Producer: Herbert M. Dawley; Director: Willis H. O'Brien; Technical Supervisor: Dr. Barnum Brown; Length: 520 Feet; Released: 1919

THE LOST WORLD (1925)
(First National Pictures)

George E. Turner scooped the massed community of film scholarship in 1968, when he unearthed long-buried coverage from the *New York Times*: "DINOSAURS CAVORT IN FILM FOR DOYLE," with the sub-heading "Spiritist Mystifies World-Famed Magicians with Pictures of Prehistoric Beasts." The credulous report concerned the evening of June 2, 1922—to wit, a gathering of the American Society of Magicians at New York's Hotel McAlpin. Harry Houdini, who was as celebrated a debunker of mysticism as he was a master illusionist and escape artist, had brought as a guest his friend Sir Arthur Conan Doyle, an unabashed believer in spiritualism. Doyle had at first declined the invitation, for magicians tended to ridicule his beliefs, but at the last minute he accepted and attended in the company of Adolph S. Ochs, publisher of the *Times*, and other special guests. Doyle had a presentation in store.

Their first sight of a monster pterodactyl.

The Lost World

After the master magicians had displayed their latest tricks, Doyle addressed the assemblage: "If I brought here in real existence what I show in these pictures, it would be a great catastrophe. These pictures are not occult. This is psychic because everything that emanates from the human spirit or human brain is psychic. It is not supernatural. It is the effect of the joining on the one hand of imagination and on the other hand of some power of materialization. The imagination, I may say, comes from me. The materializing power comes from elsewhere." That said, the creator of both Sherlock Holmes and popular literature's greatest scientific explorer, Prof. George Challenger, announced he would brook no interrogation and ordered the lights cut.

What was seen that night moved the *Times* reporter to exult: "[Doyle's] monsters of the ancient world, or the new world which he has discovered in the ether, were extraordinarily lifelike. If fakes, they were masterpieces."

Doyle, of course, soon thereafter spilled the beans in a public statement addressed to Houdini, explaining that a moving picture was being made of the Doyle novel *The Lost World*: "The dinosaurs... have been constructed by pure cinema, but of the highest kind."

The resulting near-ancestor of *King Kong* turned out spectacularly well, easily surpassing most other such films—especially the various attempts at explicit remakes. In other respects, *The Lost World* is far less effective than *King Kong*, which has the advantages of a strong central character capable of evoking both sympathy and terror, a stronger love story amid the desperate adventure, vastly stronger dramatic emphasis and—most crucially—the breakneck pace that defined the Cooper-Schoedsack style. *The Lost World*, even in the shortened cuts that followed the 10-reel 1925 release, rambles annoyingly and too often introduces its dinosaurs in a painfully matter-of-fact way as they trudge and amble through the jungle.

The settings are much more striking than those of "The Ghost of Slumber Mountain," pointing the way to the magnificent green hells of *Creation*, *King Kong* and *The Son of Kong*.

The animation—when projected at the proper silent speed—is superb. Dramatic lighting, which had proved lacking in the earlier O'Briens, adds tremendously to the presence of the monsters, particularly in fire-illumined night scenes that anticipate the emphasis upon composition and chiaroscuro that OBie would bring to subsequent works.

Drastic cutting over the years, for second-run neighborhood theatres and abbreviated reissue programs and special rental purposes, would gradually reduce *The Lost World* to a five-reel shadow of itself—less, in some versions. A significant rebuilding and expansion was completed in 1992, for a Lumivision laserdisc edition under supervision of the master film restorationist Scott MacQueen. Then, MacQueen and an *ad hoc* committee called Friends of the Challenger Expedition tackled yet a fuller reconstruction during the middle 1990s. This venture was occasioned by the discovery of a reel of animation tests, along with lost-and-found primary-source footage from a long-neglected storage depot in the Czech Republic. The well-past-due shipment of this original-release material back to America required the additional bureaucratic amenity of a hazardous-waste permit, owing to the chemical instability of the nitrocellulose film stock. Clean-up and image transfer proceeded agreeably enough, but the actual rebuilding at George Eastman House in Rochester, New York, proved a heartbreaker: Footage was indiscriminately re-inserted without regard for MacQueen's painstaking narrative reconstruction. Technicians went berserk with the color-tinting process, rendering garish even the more subdued scenes. One carelessly inauthentic addition—a close-up insert of an IBM Selectric typescript, purporting to represent a page from an early-day typewriter—bespoke a general impatience with a project that deserved better than such institutional hackwork. MacQueen's Lumivision edition remains the most satisfying and accessible reconstruction, but a 1968 five-reel edition, un-tinted, from Blackhawk Films is also a beauty-and-a-half.

CREDITS: By Arrangement with: Watterson R. Rothacker; Supervisor: Earl Hudson; Director of Dramatic Narrative: Harry O. Hoyt; Research and Technical Director: Willis H. O'Brien; Scenario and Editorial Director: Marion Fairfax; Based on: Sir Arthur Conan Doyle's 1912 Novel, *The Lost World: Being an Account of the Recent Amazing Adventures of Professor George E. Challenger, Lord George Roxton, Professor Summerlee, and Mr. E.D. Malone of the Daily Gazette*; Photographed by: Arthur Edeson; Chief Technician: Fred W. Jackman; Settings and Architecture: Milton Menasco; Contributing Animator: Joseph L. Roop; Film Editor: George McGuire; Technical Staff: Marcel Delgado, Homer Scott, J. Deverraux Jennings and Vernon L. Walker; Additional Direction: William Dowling; Length: 10 Reels; Released: June 22, 1925

CAST: Bessie Love (Paula White); Lloyd Hughes (Edward J. Malone); Lewis Stone (Sir John Roxton); Wallace Beery (Prof. Challenger); Arthur Hoyt (Prof. Summerlee); Margaret McWade (Mrs. Challenger); Finch Smiles (Austin); Jules Cowles (Zambo); Bull Montana (Ape Man); George Bunny (Colin McArdle); Charles Wellesley (Maj. Hibbard); Alma Bennett (Gladys Hungerford); Virginia Browne Faire (Half-Caste Girl); Nelson MacDowell (Lawyer)

GRASS: A NATION'S BATTLE FOR LIFE (1925)
a.k.a.: GRASS: THE EPIC OF A LOST TRIBE
a.k.a.: GRASS
(Paramount/Famous Players/The Lasky Corp.)

Marguerite Harrison, an American writer, sets forth from Turkey into the heart of Asia in search of a forgotten tribe. After considerable difficulty, she finds the ancient Baba Ahmedi tribe of the Bakhtiari on the shores of the Persian Gulf, where the nomads tend great herds of sheep

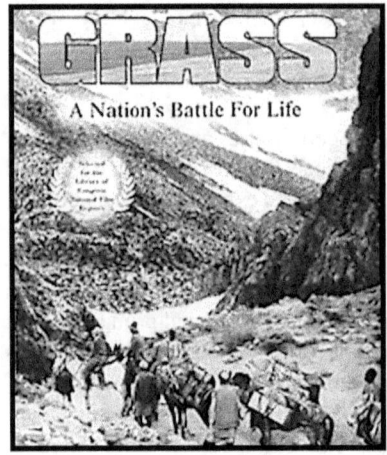

and goats. This is their home in winter, but in the spring all vegetation is killed by the intense heat, and the tribe must migrate to the mountain valleys at the edge of the Central Persian Plateau. Mrs. Harrison accompanies them on this dangerous journey across the awesome Zardeh Kuh Range, a journey no white person has accomplished. Forty-six days later, the migration ends as the tribe successfully brings its herds to the grasslands necessary for survival.

Funds were not forthcoming for a proposed companion shoot, which would have concentrated on a specific Bakhtiari family, or for a return trip to shoot the re-migration in the fall. Merian Cooper and Ernest Schoedsack were forced to use their film as it stood. A brief shot of the filmmakers was staged near Paramount's Astoria Studios. They were far from satisfied with the finished work and always spoke of *Grass* as "a great lost opportunity," as Schoedsack put it, adding: "not enough time or money—it was thin and overstuffed with nonessentials to bring it up to a commercial length."

Reviews were enthusiastically positive, but many critics held the view that was later parodied in *King Kong*: "I go out and sweat blood to make a swell picture, and the critics say, 'If it only had love interest, it would gross twice as much."

Quinn Martin of the *New York World* wrote: "With a leading man of the Valentino sort and a leading woman such as Leatrice Joy or even Gloria Swanson,... [the picture] might have been woven into a film drama so tremendous in its sweep that all other screen plays of the type known as a 'big' would have fallen into utter insignificance beside it."

In 1970, when college-campus protests were all the rage, Schoedsack looked back on *Grass*: "In 1926, [*Grass*] was shown to the students of Princeton. Back in those dim, dark days, the boys didn't know about outboard shirt-tails and long hair, but they had heard about sex, and sex was what they wanted in their movies and sex was what this one didn't have for them. And they were misled by the title, and this made them very cross. So they protested. No, those simple, primitive fellows didn't occupy any buildings or break any windows or set fire to anything. They simply voted *Grass* the worst picture of the year, and I was inclined to agree with them, but for somewhat different reasons.

"*Grass* was not a box-office success," Schoedsack continued. "It did pay off that big $10,000 investment, not a great deal more, but there were other dividends that those jolly fellows didn't know about. One of those was a firm and enduring collaboration and friendship between Cooper and myself. Another was the memory of a very pleasant trip. It might even be called high adventure." Fifty years later, when a remake was in production by other hands entirely, Cooper, Schoedsack and Mrs. Harrison were still fondly remembered among the nomadic locals.

Whatever its imperfections, *Grass* remains the cornerstone of an important school of picture-making and the foundation of Cooper-Schoedsack Productions. It led to many helpful developments, including the immediate support of the pioneering film tycoon Jesse L. Lasky.

CREDITS: Producers: Marguerite E. Harrison, Merian C. Cooper and Ernest B. Schoedsack; Musical Score: Dr. Hugo Riesenfeld and Dr. Edward Kilenyi; Preview Length: 10 Reels; General Release Length: Seven Reels; Released: March 30, 1925

CAST: Marguerite E. Harrison (Herself); Amir Jang (Tribal Chief); Lufta (Son of Chief); Merian C. Cooper and Ernest B. Schoedsack (Themselves)

CHANG (1927)
(Paramount Publix Corp.)

The influence of *Chang* on the later Cooper-Schoedsack films—especially *Kong*—can hardly be overstated. *Chang* provided *Kong* with its very model of construction, right down to the mysterious force that is introduced and identified only after a suspenseful buildup. Tigers, leopards and snakes serve as secondary menaces, precisely like the dinosaurs of Skull Island. Audiences were requested not to reveal the meaning of the word *Chang*, and the advertising and publicity kept the faith with this veil of hyperbolic secrecy. The mystery surrounding Kong, though admirably sustained in the movie itself, was diluted because the gigantic ape was exploited heavily in the advertising materials.

Equally significant is the impact of *Chang* upon W.S. Van Dyke's *Trader Horn* and *Tarzan the Ape Man*, which preceded *King Kong* as jungle spectacles. Van Dyke conferred with Schoedsack before embarking to Africa to film *Trader Horn*. The elephant stampede of the *Tarzan* picture, although filmed in California with a tame herd and a great deal of process photography, very closely resembles the climax of *Chang*.

The story concerns a jungle family whose home in Northern Siam (Thailand) is under siege by big cats. The father rallies his neighbors to hunt down the region's tigers and leopards, using deadfalls, decoys and camouflaged pits. The beasts' great cunning enables many of them to elude capture, but eventually the jungle is cleared of predatory cats and peace reigns—temporarily.

Then, the crucial rice crop is trampled by a *chang*, the most feared beast of all. A *chang* is trapped in a pit and is revealed to be a baby elephant. The animal is tied to a pole supporting a house. Soon, the mother elephant arrives and frees her young by demolishing the hut.

The farmer and his family flee to the next village with word that the Great Herd is approaching. This is a band of some 300 wild elephants, unseen in the area for 50 years. The rampage destroys the village. The villagers round up most of the elephants and train the captured animals to become allies against the jungle.

Stock footage from *Chang* can be seen in numerous jungle films. Most notably, the Great Herd would stampede again in two Paramount pictures, *The Last Outpost* (1935) and *The Jungle Princess* (1937). An early-1950s attempt to transform *Chang* into a color version of itself—utilizing hand-painted frame enlargements, re-photographed much in the manner of cartoon production—was abandoned on account of its labor-intensive costliness.

During the mid-1950s, Cooper, with backing from C.V. Whitney, attempted to do remakes of *Grass* and *Chang*. Explained Schoedsack: "Coop wanted to do a new version of *Grass*, and I tried to talk him out of it. In this business, you must never look back. Things had changed over there since we were there. He sent a crew over there anyway, a bunch of those union guys. They drove around in cars awhile, took some shots of the mountains and spent about $300,000 of Whitney's money. *Chang* was even more hopeless than the *Grass* remake, and they gave it up. It just wasn't there anymore."

CREDITS: Producers: Merian C. Cooper and Ernest B. Schoedsack; Music: Hugo Riesenfeld; Titles Written by: Capt. Achmed Abdullah; Interpreter: Kru Muang; Chief Trapper: Tahn; Length: Eight Reels; Released: April 29, 1927

CAST: Kru (Man); Chantui (Woman); Nah (Boy); Ladah (Girl); Mike (Himself); Bimbo (Himself)

GOW, THE HEAD HUNTER (1928)
(Capt. Edward A. Salisbury)

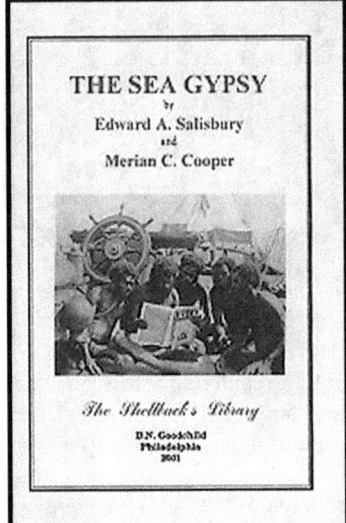

The Sea Gypsy was written by Cooper and Capt. Edward A. Salisbury and describes their adventures.

Although Merian Cooper and Ernest Schoedsack are formally credited here as photographers, they denied their participation. The film is a generally plotless collage of travelogue footage from the expeditions of the grandstanding Capt. Edward Salibury, whose ship, the *Wisdom II*, voyaged the South Pacific during 1920-23 taking pictures, collecting artifacts and seeking adventure. Cooper and Schoedsack were along for the final leg of the journey.

This adventure, such as it is, begins in Fiji, home to a somewhat civilized people who only three generations past had lived as cannibals. The patchwork trek moves on to the Western Solomons, the New Hebrides and the Eastern Solomons. The payoff comes late in the game, with a war party dispatched to bring home freshly harvested skulls from the latest conquest.

Salisbury's apparent generosity with screen credit was no generosity at all, but rather opportunism: By 1929, *Grass* and *Chang* had earned for Cooper-Schoedsack Productions an identity more bankable than Salisbury's. The attempt to capitalize on the Cooper-Schoedsack reputation was all the more flagrant due to the fact that "A Napoleon of the Solomons," the account of Salisbury's dealings with the tribal chieftain Gow—ghostwritten by Cooper—had appeared in *Asia* magazine in September 1922, the very month that had found Cooper leaving San Francisco to join the expedition in Singapore while Schoedsack was at the massacre in Smyrna.

A 1934 revamp brought about a superficially talkie-fied version called *Gow* (a.k.a. *Gow the Killer* and, later, *Cannibal Island*). Cooper and Schoedsack go unacknowledged in the 1934 cut.

CREDITS: Photography Officially Attributed to: Merian C. Cooper and Ernest B. Schoedsack; Length: Seven Reels; Released: October 20, 1928

CAST: Capt. Edward A. Salisbury (Himself)

THE LOST EMPIRE (1929)
(Capt. Edward A. Salisbury/Frederick J. Burghard)

While Capt. Salisbury waited impatiently on board the ship, Cooper and Schoedsack were entertained by the Prince Regent of Abyssinia, whom they photographed on the march with his massive armies. To this footage, Salisbury added footage from Sumatra, the Andaman Islands and Ceylon, along with Arabian footage by Schoedsack, to make a documentary feature. Cooper is credited as editor, writer and titler, but he—like Schoedsack—was involved only in producing the raw footage. Salisbury originally cobbled the film together in 1924 under the title *In Quest of the Golden Prince*, then rechristened it *The Lost Empire* for a New York showing in June of 1929.

In 1934, the Abyssinian footage was re-edited into a feature called *The Golden King*, and advertised—misleadingly—as a Cooper-Schoedsack production.

CREDITS: Presented by: Capt. Edward A. Salisbury; Narrative Titles and Editing Attributed to: Merian C. Cooper; Photographed in Part by: Ernest B. Schoedsack and Merian C. Cooper.

THE FOUR FEATHERS (1929)
(Paramount Famous Lasky Corp.)

Young Lt. Harry Faversham (Richard Arlen), scion of a family of soldiers in the service of the British Empire, is possessed of a morbid fear that he will besmirch the family name through cowardice. When he learns that his regiment is being sent to Africa to put down a revolt of Dervish fanatics, Faversham resigns his commission. Each of three comrades—Capt. Trench (William Powell) and Lts. Castleton (Theodore von Eltz) and Durrance (Clive Brook)—gives to Faversham a white feather, the symbol of cowardice. A fourth feather is bestowed by Feversham's fiancée (Fay Wray). The disgrace precipitates

The Four Feathers

the death of Harry's father (George Fawcett). When the warriors fall into the hands of the enemy, a disguised Faversham comes charging to the rescue in a series of breathtaking escapades—and returns the feathers.

No camera tricks or optical lab effects were used to combine the African footage with that filmed at the studio and in the California desert. The result was so nearly perfect that some critics took the producers to task for using such a small amount of authentic footage—of which there is plenty, of course.

When Paramount added 800 feet of unused footage to *Grass* to get length, both Cooper and Schoedsack were disappointed. After completing their edit of *Chang*, they sidestepped the risk of unwanted padding by destroying the unused footage. David O. Selznick thwarted the partners on *The Four Feathers* by ordering additional studio scenes, quite after Schoedsack's cut. Cooper and Schoedsack decided that they should personally edit all future productions.

Remakes of *The Four Feathers* include Zoltan Korda's 1939 version and Don Sharp's television feature of 1977.

CREDITS: Producers, Cinematographers and Directors: Merian C. Cooper and Ernest B. Schoedsack; Associate Producer: David O. Selznick; Additional Direction: Lothar Mendes; Additional Photography: Robert Kurrle; Based on the Novel by: A.E.W. Mason; Screenplay: Howard Estabrook; Adaptation: Hope Loring; Film Editor: Ernest B. Schoedsack; Title Cards: Julian Johnson and John Farrow; Music: William Frederick Peters; Assistant Directors: Ivan Thomas, Doran Cox and Walter Daniels; Sound: Roy Pomeroy; Length: Eight Reels; Released: June 12, 1929

CAST: Richard Arlen (Lt. Harry Faversham); Fay Wray (Ethne Eustace); Clive Brook (Lt. Durrance); Capt. Trench (William Powell); Lt. Castleton (Theodore von Eltz); Slaver (Noah Beery); Ahmed (Noble Johnson); Zack Williams (Idris); Harold Hightower (Ali); Philippe de Lacy (Harry at Age 10); Edward J. Radcliffe (Col. Eustace); George Fawcett (Col. Faversham); Augustin Symonds (Col. Sutch)

CREATION (1929-32)
(RKO-Radio Pictures, Inc.; Unfinished)

In the summer of 1929, from his office at Tec-Art Studios on Melrose Avenue, Harry O. Hoyt announced that he was writing a dinosaur picture called *Creation*. Early in 1930, Hoyt submitted his story treatment to RKO-Radio Pictures. From his Project Prospectus:

> Purposely, no attempt is made to paint the picture in pastels. The very size of the animals and the vast cataclysm of nature which we depict call for the brightest of colors [figurative speaking, that is] and the broadest of brushes. This is offered as an attempt at entertainment on a colossal scale...
>
> It is planned to utilize the services of [Willis O'Brien and Marcel Delgado], who have constructed and animated these animals in [*The Lost World*]. Recently developed trick devices made these scenes with the animals very real... This picture cannot be compared with any other picture being produced today. It is neither drama nor comedy, and yet it contains both of these elements. It is adventure-melodrama of a highly imaginative kind. Only through the medium of the motion picture is it possible to attempt verisimilitude. The stage cannot attempt it—the novel must leave much to the reader's imagination. On the screen, we have the perfect illusion—these terrible monsters breathing, fighting and bleeding in mortal combat among themselves and with the people.

A good man with words was Hoyt, whose enthusiasm—along with a screening of *The Lost World*—convinced William LeBaron, RKO's vice president for production, that *Creation* could be the kind of spectacle he needed to follow up on his Western epic, *Cimarron* (1931). LeBaron assigned *Creation* the then-grandiose budget of $1,201,813.53. This was about five times the cost of a typical top-of-the-line production and would have made *Creation* the studio's most costly project until *Gunga Din* (1939).

O'Brien supervised superb production illustrations and continuity sketches (ancestors of storyboarding) by Mario Larrinaga, Byron Crabbe and Ernest Smythe. Beulah Marie Dix fashioned a screenplay from Hoyt's story. Delgado began building animation models: two Brontosauri; at least two adult and two baby Triceratopses; two Tyrannosauri; two Stegosauri, a Pteranodon and another wingéd reptile; a Styracosaurus; numerous birds; and that great Egyptian horned mammal, the Arsinoithereum. Mechanical expert Charles Christadoro built a full-scale baby Triceratops about the size of a Shetland pony, equipped with walking and breathing devices, and the full-size head of an adult Triceratops.

Hoyt explained that the animals were based on "sketches drawn by the celebrated artist, Charles R. Knight... They are variously from 15 to 36 inches in length and are built of imported German dental rubber over a brass framework which is cast in molds. This framework is hinged with universal friction joints so they are able to move their legs, necks, hands, etc. In what is termed the 'close-up' animals, there is a bladder which is pumped up and the air released to give the appearance of breathing. They also have glass eyes, which are movable in their sockets, and their mouths open and close and have teeth. The background animals have no [breathing apparatus], their eyes are painted and the only movement is [in] their legs and necks."

The story combines elements of *The Lost World* and J.M. Barrie's *The Admirable Crichton*. A tornado and an earthquake devastate the coast of Chile. An Army submarine rescues the passengers of an American yacht just as the vessel is destroyed by a waterspout. A promontory rises from the sea, and the sub is sucked into the cavity. The vessel surfaces in a lost world inside a volcano, where all the crewmen are killed by prehistoric monsters, including a rhinoceros-like Arsinoitherium and Pterodactyls. Love blossoms between Elaine, daughter of the yachtsman, and Steve, a penniless young intellectual who serves as tutor to Elaine's kid brother. Steve becomes the leader of the survivors. Ned Hallett, Elaine's rejected fiancé, angrily stalks and kills a baby Triceratops, only to be done away with by the mother. Eventually, the others are rescued by Chilean airplanes.

Original art from *Creation*

Karl Brown, the great cinematographer, director, writer and special-effects artist, was hired as director of photography and visual F/X. Assisted by cameramen Linwood G. Dunn and Harold Wellman and artist-technician Orville Goldner, Brown photographed miniature sequences of the destruction of a coastal village, the rising of the island and the wrecking of the yacht, and the submarine scenes.

"Most of this work was done entirely underwater," Brown revealed, many years after the fact. "For the storm at sea, I poured in carbon tetrachloride, which created [turbulence]. We had to show a mountain rising from the sea, along with lava, steam and explosions. The mountain was built in sections, and the steam was canned milk.

"When a twister was supposed to come along..., we used a canoe paddle to create a vortex in the water and poured in negrosin, a black powdered dye soluble only in alcohol, down the funnel. We couldn't make it come forward to the camera, so we moved the camera up to it and got the same [effect]."

Goldner told us that the first two tanks had cracked under internal pressure, so a third version was developed with thicker, more heavily braced glass—which "caused the cinematographer to complain about distortion." Goldner added: "The first takes of the headland rising from the water lacked the desired ponderousness, even with heavy over-cranking [slow motion], so they thickened the water with clear gelatin."

Brown filmed O'Brien's animated beasts, as well, compositing some of them with an in-camera traveling matte system known as the Dunning Process, which is somewhat similar to the blue-screen technique of times more recent. One sequence showed the goring and trampling of several seamen by the Arsinoitherium, which also dislodged a log bridge, hurtling others into a gorge.

Another sequence filmed by Brown involved a mother Triceratops and her two youngsters. The passage also utilized several trained animals: Snooky, a famous chimpanzee who starred in two-reel novelties at Universal; one of big-cat handler Olga Celeste's jaguars; a kinkajou; and a stork. In this footage, one of the little Triceratopses strays, watches a jaguar kill a stork, encounters a gigantic kinkajou and finally is shot by Hallett. The mother races to the scene, pursues Hallett, pins him with an uprooted tree, then finally gores him and tosses the body away.

The angry mother Triceratops charges the killer of her offspring in *Creation*.

Both Snooky and the jaguar ran amok and had the personnel ready to panic. O'Brien declared: "No more live animals!"—and with good reason. The big cat, when uncaged, was supposed to run into a clearing, pounce upon a chicken concealed in the foliage, then run out of camera range into another cage. A man was stationed overhead to close the gate once the cat was safely inside. Now, jaguars are as a class unpredictable, and this one had its own agenda: The beast seized the bird, but instead of devouring it on the spot, he carried it to the other side, intent on jumping atop the cage to finish his meal. The crewman, terribly vulnerable as he crouched on the cage, stood his ground while the jaguar stared and snarled. At last, the jaguar brushed past the man and jumped over the top of the cage with the sole objective of finding a quiet place to chow down. He then cleared the low wire barrier that separated the set from the camera and crew. Miss Celeste told everybody to keep still, but some members of the crew scattered. One electrician, who had shown fear from the start of the shoot, scrambled up a ladder. The jaguar, still intent on devouring his catch, finally crouched beside the barrier. Miss Celeste grabbed the cat by the wonderfully loose skin over the shoulders and rump and heaved him into the cage.

Elsewhere, a technician had rigged a branch that Snooky was supposed to drop onto the little dinosaur. In this precarious tree-fork perch, Snooky decided to start a playful wrestling match with the techno. On the first take, Snooky failed to pull the branch free. The crewman climbed back into the tree and re-loosened the branch. A second take also failed. The disheveled man climbed back into the tree, this time wiring the branch so loosely that it would come off at the least tug.

But this time, Snooky gave the branch a hard yank. It came away so easily that the temperamental ape was thrown off balance and nearly fell from the tree. Snooky was infuriated, and there is nothing cute about an angry chimp: Even a youngster is as strong as a man and can deliver a vicious bite. Snooky swung from vine to vine, screeching and snarling. Finally, he hit the floor running, wrecking props and equipment right and left. Encountering a tub of plaster of Paris, used for mending sets, Snooky thrust his face into the powder and emerged with a mouthful. The trainer was horror-stricken: If Snooky should swallow the plaster, it would prove fatal. The entire crew began chasing the ape about the stage, up and down ladders and through the trees to keep him too distracted to swallow. In due time, he was cornered and captured and forced to spit out the plaster. Snooky was undaunted, unharmed and unapologetic.

"O'Brien was left-handed and worked quickly," said Brown. "It was a hell of a thing to watch him work with those little animals. The little [Triceratops] was only about five inches long."

Creation would have been the first talking picture of its kind. Hoyt was cannily aware of this distinction and declared: "Melodrama is always heightened by sound. It is the thing which we hear, not what we see, in the still of the night, that chills us. Now that we can hear the roar of these beasts in battle in addition to seeing them, we can attain perfect realism." Set to appear in the picture were Joel McCrea as Steve, Ralf Harolde as Hallett and comedian Benny Rubin as Benny, a valet. An impressive musical score was being written by a young symphonist, Eddison von Ottenfeld.

But Hoyt never got to hear his beasts roar. Production was halted when David O. Selznick replaced LeBaron at RKO, and Hoyt was laid off before any sounds could be recorded. The only cast member to perform on camera was Ralf Harolde. Hoyt's frustrations, after three years' work, were only compounded when he tried to retrieve the rights to his script and the studio refused. Von Ottenfeld salvaged the music by rearranging it for the concert hall: His *Dinosaur Suite* was performed at the Hollywood Bowl.

At Merian C. Cooper's insistence, O'Brien and his crew were kept on payroll. Cooper realized that O'Brien's methods would enable the production of a picture Cooper had dreamed for years—the project that would become *King Kong*. Cooper had O'Brien make "two scenes of men fighting a dinosaur" and had him slow down the motions of the creature. These Dunning Process shots were, according to the collaborative *Kong* scenarist Edgar Wallace, most impressive. This footage also is missing.

Cooper secured permission from New York to spend $10,000 on a one-reel test for his personal epic, then called *The Beast*, about a gigantic ape at large on a dinosaur-infested island. Certain scenes from *Creation*, involving the Triceratops and Ralf Harolde, were utilized in the test reel and then retained in a rough cut of *Kong*. They were eliminated in the final editing and presumably ended up in the silver retrieval bin.

Some viewers of *Kong* have wondered why the sailors do not retreat from the log bridge when they see Kong on the other side of the gorge. This is because they originally had been chased onto the log by the Arsinoitherium in scenes picked up from *Creation*. Later, the scene was remade with the Styracosaurus pursuing the men. Both versions were dropped from the final cut and have long since been lost.

Only scraps of *Creation* are known to exist today. These include the Triceratops sequence, with footage of the chimp; scenes with the jaguar and the kinkajou; the baby dinosaur's stroll through the jungle; the killing of the baby; and some shots from the chase. These scenes are excellent, and the composites with Ralf Harolde and the little dinosaur are actually finer than any of the compositing in *Kong*. All the storm scenes and undersea effects may reasonably be presumed lost. Some of *Creation*'s dinosaurs and several full-scale and miniature settings were utilized in *King Kong*, and the Styracosaurus finally had its moment of glory in *The Son of Kong*. A second winged reptile, a Diamorphodon, was later stripped; its wing armature was used on several creatures in such films as *Witches' Brew* (1979), *Caveman* (1981) and *Q* (a.k.a. *The Wingéd Serpent*; 1982). Most of the models have survived into the present day in private collections.

RANGO (1931)
(Paramount Publix Corp.)

"Just a little picture—a trifle, really," Ernest B. Schoedsack told us of *Rango*. And yet in its day, *Rango* prompted Paramount honcho Jesse L. Lasky—in a rare personal involvement with the publicity mechanism—to hail the picture as "the greatest entertainment in the history of the screen" and moved the *New York World* to declare it "the best animal picture of them all."

A little boy of the civilized West is shown firing at a cardboard tiger with a pop-gun. His uncle, an explorer, watches and then tells the story of a real tiger. (The prologue was innovative at the time and set a standard for expeditionary films yet to come.)

Sumatra, Indonesia, is home to both tigers and orangutans. Here, a hunter named Ali and his son, Bin, reside in an upper jungle and lay traps to protect the villagers farther down their mountain. Bin makes a pet of Rango, a baby orang, who is later freed by his own father, Tua. Grim jungle dangers are contrasted with comedy involving apes and monkeys. Eventually, Bin is pursued by a tiger. Rango diverts the beast's attention and is killed. Bin frees his tethered water buffalo, which kills the tiger. Ali and Bin embrace as Tua watches from the trees, inconsolable in his grief.

Schoedsack deftly humanizes the apes, with touches both humorous and pathetic by turns. For years afterwards, he was accused of sacrificing Rango for the climactic scene. In fact, he left the young ape alive and well in the northwestern wilds of Sumatra. The charging tiger was filmed from the comparative safety of a pit, in the front of which was installed an 18-by-14-inch slab of inch-thick plate glass. Ruth Rose held Rango atop her head, so that he appeared to be standing in front of the camera. When the tiger stepped onto the trail, Schoedsack leapt from the pit and gave forth with a slobbery Bronx Cheer—his foolproof means of infuriating a big cat. The beast charged, of course, and leaped—apparently onto the ape, which was safely behind the glass. Later on, Schoedsack filmed a scene of a tiger pouncing on an ape-skin dummy and shredding it. This harrowingly realistic bit of mayhem, conceived and staged in the jungle without any studio work, is typical of Schoedsack's ingenuity.

After the tiger has received its comeuppance, an overburdened tree limb snaps, dumping a gallery of chattering monkeys onto the carcass of their enemy. This savvy bit has the look of an accident, but it actually was staged. The idea came from a genuine happenstance Schoedsack had witnessed in a Jewish settlement in Russia: A group of men sat in a tree, watching troops march past, when suddenly the limb broke and they were spilled into the street. The *modus operandi* of Cooper-Schoedsack demanded that most story elements derive from the realm of personal experience; in turn, the Sumatran expedition yielded a great deal of story material that would be used in *King Kong*.

Rango was a watershed picture in its day, spurring such popular interest in the Cooper-Schoedsack pictures that Paramount reissued *The Four Feathers* at about the same time. The *New York Sun* held that *Rango* must be "the most fascinating study of jungle life ever offered for popular entertainment." The *New York Times*, usually a grump when it came to dissecting the movies, allowed as how *Rango* "tells a human story in terms so strong and so simple it seems this tale must have its page in the Bible."

"Its theme, the struggle of man and his brother ape against the manifold terrors of the jungle, is so close to nature, so free from guile in the telling," added the *Times*, "that by watching it the spectator may not notice the guiding intelligence behind the film and the care with which the story has been molded from the materials of nature."

CREDITS: Presented by: Adolph Zukor & Jesse L. Lasky; Producer, Director, Author and Editor: Ernest B. Schoedsack; Assistant to Producer: Ruth Rose; Cameraman: Alfred Williams; Sound: Roy Pomeroy; Associate Editor: Julian Johnson; Music: W. Franke Harling; Running Time: 76 Minutes; Released: March 7, 1931
CAST: Claude King (Uncle); Douglas Scott (Nephew); Ali (Hunter); Bin (Hunter's Son); Tua (Ape); Rango (Son of Tua).

THE MOST DANGEROUS GAME (1932)
(RKO-Radio Pictures, Inc.)

For this first in a series of Cooper-Schoedsack mystery-adventure films at RKO, the partners chose Richard Connell's influentially popular short story about a Russian general named Zaroff, late of the Czar's Army, who lives for the hunt. Brute animals no longer offer the challenge he requires, and so he *creates* a game worthy of his mettle. Retiring to a small island in the Caribbean with a trusted Cossack servant, Zaroff stocks his preserve with human beings, the survivors of arranged shipwrecks. When famed hunter Sanger Rainsford is cast ashore, the madman conceives his greatest stalk. But Rainsford wins the match, kills Zaroff in a duel of swords—and succeeds him as keeper of the island and all its treacheries.

This masterful yarn has all the elements of a first-rate movie thriller, save one: There is no love interest. To compensate for the loss of the purely masculine vantage and the sacrifice of the caustic finale, Cooper and Schoedsack ordered Zaroff made even more horrid: "He cannot love until he has known the thrill of the hunt with a human being as his prey," explained Cooper. "Such an atavistic creature is the man who by his savage interests dominates the most dangerous game." As for planting a woman amid such lupine intrigues, Cooper had no qualms: "Woman has retained, fortunately, the fighting, dominant blood of the savage... I always thought that the 'most dangerous' game would be one in which a woman was involved."

Cooper was delighted with the elaborate jungle set because it dovetailed with his plans for *King Kong*. Whenever possible, Cooper commandeered the *Game* set for *Kong* preparations, provoking tensions between the partners. In the final resolve, and professional antagonisms aside, the use of the setting in both films creates a palpable kinship and underscores the constancy of purpose that united Cooper and Schoedsack over the long stretch.

Joel McCrea, at 26, was assigned the Rainsford role. Fay Wray, of *The Four Feathers*, proved an ideal leading lady. Noble Johnson, also of *The Four Feathers*, and professional knife marksman Steve Clemente weighed in as subordinate menaces. Robert Armstrong began here his long association with Cooper and Schoedsack, playing

Joel McCrea and Fay Wray in *The Most Dangerous Game*

a tragicomic role. Leslie Banks, cast as Zaroff, was an English stage star who had never before graced the screen; he easily steals the show from all others concerned.

Photographically, *The Most Dangerous Game* is a *tour de force*, with particularly striking visuals in the chase. There is even a scene of birds rising from the foliage, animated by the *Kong* crew's Orville Goldner.

"I knew the picture was going to be a classic as soon as I'd seen the dailies," recalled editor Archie Marshek. Schoedsack, a lifelong music lover, said he made a conscious effort to compose the film as though it were a symphony. He succeeded admirably. One critic called it "60 of the most exciting minutes of your life."

RKO delivered a formal remake, *A Game of Death*, in 1945, with Edgar Barrier as a conveniently Germanized huntsman. Like *Kong* itself, *The Most Dangerous Game* has since inspired any number of takeoffs, knock-offs and outright rip-offs that detract none at all from the superior original.

During 1994-95, the easygoing and amenable George E. Turner found himself maneuvered into narrating a commentary track for a Roan Group laserdisc edition of *The Most Dangerous Game*. Ill-at-ease with the hasty preparations for his part of the presentation, George delivered an improvised play by play that he was assured would be edited to suit him—but no such thing. George regarded the *ad libitum* finished product as an embarrassment, but it makes for fascinating listening today as a document of our principal author's devotion to the populist art of film appreciation.

CREDITS: Executive Producer: David O. Selznick; Associate Producer: Merian C. Cooper; Directors: Ernest B. Schoedsack and Irving Pichel; Screenplay: James Ashmore Creelman; Based on Richard Connell's *Golden Book Magazine* Story of October 1930; Photographed by: Henry Gerrard; Camera Operator: Russell Metty; Assistant Cameraman: Willard Barth; Art Director: Carroll Clark; Film Editor: Archie S. Marshek; Music: Max Steiner; Sound: Clem Portman; Stills: Gaston Longet; Running Time: 63 Minutes; Released: September 16, 1932

CAST: Leslie Banks (Zaroff); Joel McCrea (Bob Rainsford); Fay Wray (Eve Trowbridge); Robert Armstrong (Martin Trowbridge); Noble Johnson (Ivan); Steve Clemente (Tartar); William Davidson (Captain); Dutch Hendrian (Servant); Hale Hamilton (Woodman); James Flavin (First Mate)

THE PHANTOM OF CRESTWOOD (1932)
(RKO-Radio Pictures, Inc.)

Much as the Mark Frost-David Lynch production of *Twin Peaks* would originate on television in 1990 as an eerie, serialized whodunit and then detour onto the big screen with a 1992 feature film, so *The Phantom of Crestwood* came into being as a radio serial, only to conclude as a movie. Broadcast over the NBC Radio Network, this tale of a slain high-society prostitute became a national obsession over the course of six weeks, concluding with the nagging question, "Who killed Jenny Wren?" The only way to learn the identity of the Phantom would be to see the film from NBC's sister company, RKO-Radio Pictures.

Producer Merian C. Cooper's other big release of 1932 was, of course, *The Most Dangerous Game*, directed by Ernest B. Schoedsack. The adventurous filmmakers also were at work on *Kong* all during this period. Cooper's hands-on attention to *Crestwood* yielded a terrific anecdote from the cutting room:

Film editor Archie F. Marshek was assigned to cut both *Game* and *Crestwood*. Cooper instructed Marshek to eliminate a patch of dialogue that he felt slowed the action of *Crestwood*. Cooper and director J. Walter Ruben screened the sequence.

Karen Morley and Anita Louise in *The Phantom of Crestwood*

Ruben objected: "Hey! There's a page-and-a-half of dialogue missing!"

Cooper turned to Marshek: "Archie, what happened to all that dialogue?"

"Why, you said to cut it out." Wrong answer.

"Don't tell me that, you son-of-a-bitch!" exploded Cooper, to which Marshek replied: "You can go s—t in your hat!"

Marshek, recounting the episode for us in 1968, said he stormed out of the screening room and went to his office, telling coworkers, "I guess I've just been fired." Abruptly, however, Cooper phoned, asking Marshek to restore the footage. Two weeks later, Cooper invited Marshek to become his assistant on *Kong*.

The Phantom of Crestwood opens with a radio announcer welcoming the audience to the movie. The listeners' patience is gratefully acknowledged, and the film proceeds to retrace the scam that will land Jenny Wren (Karen Morley) in deadly peril. Ricardo Cortez plays a suave crook who finds himself obliged to solve the case before the police can arrive and pin the murder on him. A mansion full of hypocritical big-shot suspects keeps the suspense cranked until the final moments.

Crestwood's radio-serial prelude had proved sufficiently successful that *King Kong* was given a similar treatment, though without the cliffhanger ending. A self-contained, half-hour dramatization of *Kong* aired on February 10, 1933, over NBC-Radio, coinciding with the start of a novelized *Kong* serial in *Mystery* magazine. *Kong*'s big-screen premiere in New York had already taken place when NBC-Radio began broadcasting a more generously detailed six-part *Kong* adaptation on March 18, 1933. The serialization continued on March 25, the day after the Los Angeles theatrical premiere at Grauman's Chinese Theatre, and progressed on April 1, April 8 and April 15, concluding on April 22. The radio cast included Robert Armstrong and Fay Wray. Recordings of NBC's *King Kong* are not known to exist—not to say that the programs are *known not* to exist.

> Those who knew my father, George Turner, were always amazed at his memory. On the way to a screening of *The Phantom of Crestwood* during the early 1990s, he told me: "I haven't seen the movie since it first came out [at which time, George would have been seven years old], but…" Then, he proceeded to synopsize the plot and describe artistic details. Suffice that he remembered more then about *The Phantom of Crestwood* than I do now.

CREDITS: Executive Producer: David O. Selznick; Associate Producer: Merian C. Cooper; Director: J. Walter Ruben; Screenplay: Bartlett McCormick; Story: Bartlett McCormick and J. Walter Ruben; Photographed by: Henry Gerrard; Art Director: Carroll Clark; Assistant Director: James Hartnett; Film Editor: Archie F. Marshek; Musical Director: Max Steiner; Recording Engineer: D.A. Cutler; Running Time: 77 Minutes; Released: October 14, 1932

CAST: Ricardo Cortez (Gary Curtis, a.k.a. Farnsbarns); Karen Morley (Jenny Wren); Anita Louise (Esther Wren); Pauline Frederick (Faith Andes); H.B. Warner (Priam Andes); Mary Duncan (Dorothy Mears); Sam Hardy (Pete Harris); Tom Douglas (Tom Herrick); Richard "Skeets" Gallagher (Eddie Mack); Ivan Simpson (Henry T. Herrick, alias Vayne); Aileen Pringle (Mrs. Walcott); George E. Stone (the Cat); Robert McWade (Sen. Herbert Walcott); Hilda Vaughn (Carter); Gavin Gordon (William Jones); Matty Kemp (Frank Andes); Clarence Wilson (Apartment House Manager); Eddie Sturgis (Bright Eyes); Robert Elliott (Tall Man)

THE MONKEY'S PAW (1933)
(RKO-Radio Pictures, Inc.)

Thirty-year-old David Oliver Selznick was still orienting himself as new executive producer at RKO in 1932 when he purchased the film rights to a popular story, "The Monkey's Paw," and its stage-play adaptation. Selznick had fond hopes for the property: His father, Lewis J. Selznick, had released a successful English-made version 10 years prior, and Universal had announced its intentions of a remake just before RKO acted on the option.

RKO released its version on Friday, January 13, 1933—a fitting date, for the picture seemed jinxed from the outset. It was slaughtered by the trade press: An industry paper declared: "Worst RKO to Date." Mainstream critics ignored it, exhibitors shunned it and it went virtually unseen.

Like many another commercial failure, *The Monkey's Paw* was a fascinating film—*was* being the operative word, for the point is impossible to prove today. Much of the negative has vanished from the studio vaults, and no full print is known to exist. It wants consideration in the present context because of the presence of Merian C. Cooper, Ernest B. Schoedsack and other talents, especially in the realm of figure animation, involved with the making of *King Kong*.

That lead director Wesley Ruggles, who produced and directed RKO's biggest and most prestigious picture of the time, *Cimarron* (1931), was assigned to a picture budgeted at only $153,574.46 (vs. RKO's top-of-the-line starting rate of $200,000), is more explicable than it would seem. Ruggles' stock had fallen since William LeBaron vacated the chief-of-production post. Selznick, a former Paramount executive who had replaced LeBaron at RKO, did not share LeBaron's enthusiasm for Ruggles' work. Ruggles quickly arranged to follow LeBaron to Paramount, using *The Monkey's Paw* to complete a contract.

Shooting began on Friday, August 12, 1932, with an upheaval in casting that forced a re-start on—of course!—the 13th. Technical failures compromised the shooting all along, and Ruggles infuriated his bosses by enlisting the services of a mean-tempered Javanese ape that was just right for the cruel story but alarmingly difficult to handle. Linwood Dunn, RKO's chief of optical effects, composited the malicious grimaces of the creature onto various backgrounds with unnerving results.

The title prop, a mummified paw that bears a relentless curse, was constructed on a flexible armature by Marcel Delgado, a mainstay of Willis O'Brien's *Kong* team. *King Kong* was deeply into production by this time. The paw was given the illusion of life by Orville Goldner, using stop-motion animation. Goldner revealed that the task was "comparatively simple because the paw was animated on a fixed axis and didn't shift its weight as [*Kong*'s] dinosaurs did."

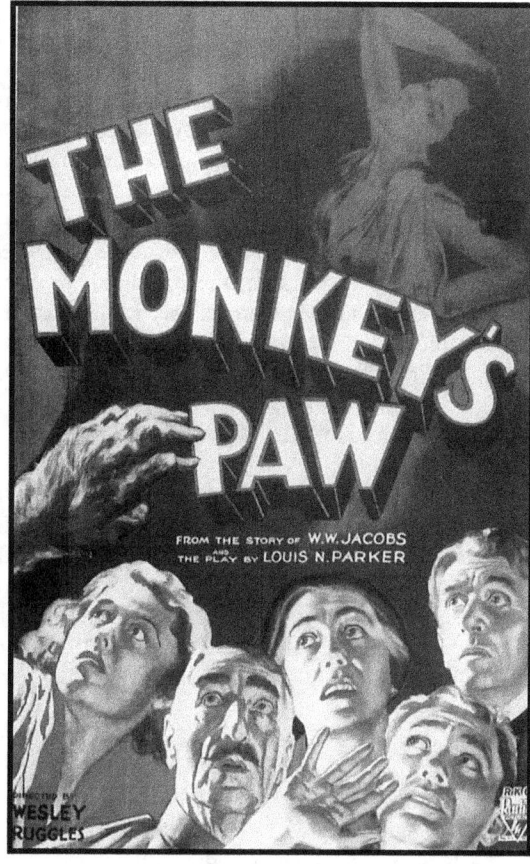

The tale hangs on a British military man, Sgt.-Maj. Morris (C. Aubrey Smith, Old Hollywood's perfect guardian of the Crown's better interests), who visits his elderly friends, Mr. and Mrs. White (Ivan Simpson and Louise Carter). The Whites' son, Herbert (Bramwell Fletcher), works as a flywheel operator at a power station. Morris shows them the paw but insists they must not touch it, for the thing is deadly. He explains that whoever possesses the paw is granted three wishes. Touching an empty sleeve to signify a missing arm, Morris says *his* three were granted—to his regret. Tragedy now descends on the White household, following in the wake of an idle wish for money. In the movie version—though not in the source-story—the ghastly experiences prove to have been a dream.

The first, supposedly finished, version clocked in at just over half an hour—overlong for a short subject, and way too short for a feature film. Producer Merian C. Cooper, Selznick's executive assistant, commissioned an expansion that would add a measure of back-story and military spectacle to an otherwise stagebound film. Ernest B. Schoedsack was precisely the right man to direct these additions, inasmuch as the prologue was set in India and Schoedsack had recently spent several months in that country shooting location scenes for Paramount's *Lives of a Bengal Lancer*. Schoedsack, who ordinarily preferred the rigors of expeditionary filming, spoke fondly of his duties on *The Monkey's Paw*. Later, he directed additional sound-stage sequences, some of them utilizing a revolutionary new process screen developed by Sidney Saunders; the Oscar-winning Saunders System also figured in *Kong*'s centerpiece battle between the ape and the Tyrannosaurus. Max Steiner's score was strong on atmosphere and foreboding mood, augmented by the work of an East Indian orchestra. The final production tab on *Paw* came in only $5,010.36 over budget.

Such painstaking work deserved a kinder fate, but the press preview was a disaster, and the trade papers' condemnation was almost categorical. The just-a-dream ending is unfortunate, but explicable in light of the story's unbearable concentration of anguish. Today, the film would find a readier acceptance in a marketplace better attuned to doom-laden, even grisly, subject matter. But in 1933, *The Monkey's Paw* was a maverick that could not be merchandised. The studio wrote the film off as an embarrassment and was only too willing to let it sink into an obscurity from which it has never emerged.

CREDITS: Producer: Merian C. Cooper; Director: Wesley Ruggles; Director of Additional Scenes: Ernest B. Schoedsack; Associate Producer: Pandro S. Berman; Screenplay: Graham John; Stage Play: Louis N. Parker; Original Story: W.W. Jacobs; Photographed by Leo Tover; Additional Photography: Jack MacKenzie, Edward Cronjager, J.O. Taylor and Harold Wellman; Art Director: Carroll Clark; Unit Art Director: Syd Ullman; Musical Director: Max Steiner; Assistant Director: Doran Cox; Set Decorations: Thomas Little and G. Rossi; Photographic Effects: Lloyd Knechtel, Vernon L. Walker and Linwood G. Dunn; Effects Technicians: Harry Redmond, Jr., Marcel Delgado and Orville Goldner; Film Editor: Charles L. Kimball; Sound Engineer: Hugh McDowell, Jr.; Music and Effects Recording: Murray Spivack; Unit Manager: Fred Fleck; Second Assistant Directors: Fred Spencer and Hal Walker; Makeup: Sam Kaufman, Paul Stanhope, Mae Mark and J. Baker; Hairdresser: Alma Hendrickson; Gaffer: J. Almond; Stills: Ollie Sigurdsen; Titles: Consolidated Film Industries; Sound System: RCA Photophone; Running Time: 58 Minutes; Released: January 13, 1933

CAST: Ivan Simpson (Mr. White); Louise Carter (Mrs. White); C. Aubrey Smith (Sgt.-Maj. Morris); Bramwell Fletcher (Herbert); Betty Lawford (Rose); Winter Hall (Mr. Hartigan); Herbert Bunston (Sampson); Nena Quartero (Nura); LeRoy Mason (Afghan); Nick Shaid (Hindu Fakir); Col. Gordon McKee (Police Sergeant); Scott McKee (Electrician); J.M. Kerrigan (Cpl. O'Leary); Leo Britt (Lance Corporal); Lal Chand Mehra (Hindu Lover); Nigel DeBrulier (Hindu Fakir in Prologue); Harry Strang, Angus Darrock and Harold Hughes (Sergeants); George Edwards (Juggler); Gordon Jones (Soldier); James Bell (Flautist); Sidney Bracy (Pensioner); Aggie Steele (Barmaid); Harry Allen (Commissioner); Will Stanton (Bookmaker); Ed Miller (Mule Driver); John George (Hindu); Joey Ray (Merchant); C. Monsoor (Orchestra Leader)

KING KONG (1933)
(RKO-Radio Pictures, Inc.)

The story, it should go without saying, has been amply told in the preceding pages. We offer herewith the following cast-and-credits roster, compiled over the span of two and maybe even three lifetimes, as exhaustive if not definitive—never can tell when some new scrap of revelation will come to light:

CREDITS: Executive Producer: David O. Selznick; Producers and Directors: Merian C. Cooper and Ernest B. Schoedsack; Screenplay: James A. Creelman and Ruth Rose; Idea Conceived by: Merian C. Cooper and Edgar Wallace; Contributing Writer: Leon Gordon; Chief Technician: Willis H. O'Brien; Technical Staff: E.B. "Buz" Gibson, Marcel Delgado, Fred Reese, Orville Goldner and Carroll Shepphird; Art

Technicians: Mario Larrinaga and Byron L. Crabbe; Director of Photography: Eddie Linden; Second Director of Photography: Kenneth Peach, Sr.; First Assistant Director of Photography: Bert Willis; Assistant Directors of Photography: Vernon Walker and J.O. Taylor; Musical Score: Max Steiner; Sound Effects: Murray Spivack; Settings: Carroll Clark and Al Herman; Sound Recordist, RCA Photophone System: E.A. Wolcott; Film Editor: Ted Cheesman; Production Assistants: Archie F. Marshek and Walter Daniels; Scenario Associate: Horace McCoy; Operative Cameramen: Edward "Eddie" Henderson, Felix Schoedsack and Lee Davis; Assistant Cameramen: Bert Willis, William Reinhold, William Clothier and Clifford Stine; Optical Photography: Linwood G. Dunn, Cecil Love and William Ulm; Production Process: Sidney Saunders; Dunning Process Supervision: Carroll H. Dunning and C. Dodge Dunning; Williams Matte Supervision: Frank Williams; Special Effects: Harry Redmond, Jr.; Sculptor: John Cerisoli; Construction Technician: W.G. White; Technical Artists: Juan Larrinaga, Zachary Hoag and Victor Delgado; Associate, Sound Effects: Walter G. Elliott; Makeup Supervision: Mel Berns; Set Decor: Thomas Little; Supervising Art Director: Van Nest Polglase; Costumes: Walter Plunkett; Costume Supplier: Western Costumes, Inc.; Assistant to Merian Cooper: Zöe Porter; Painting Technician: Peter Stich; Camera Aircraft Pilots: Duke Krantz and George Weiss; Technical Advisors: Dr. J.W. Lytle, Dr. O.A. Patterson and Dr. Harry C. Raven; Art Titles: Pacific Title Co.; Running Time: 100 Minutes, Reported as 110 Minutes in Preview Form; Released: Following New York Premiere on March 7, 1933, and Los Angeles Premiere on March 24, 1933

CAST: Fay Wray (Ann Darrow); Robert Armstrong (Carl Denham); Bruce Cabot (Jack Driscoll); Frank Reicher (Capt. Englehorn); Sam Hardy (Charles Weston); Noble Johnson (Native Chief); Steve Clemento (Witch King); James Flavin (Second Mate); Victor Wong (Charley); Paul Porcasi (Socrates); Russ Powell (Dock Watchman); Ethan Laidlaw, Blackie Whiteford, Dick Curtis, Charles Sullivan, Harry Tenbrook, Gil Perkins, Bud Mason, Harry Cornbleth, Frank Gerrity, Harry Walker, Jack Saunders, Edward Clark, Skeets Noyes, Walter Taylor, Larry Fisher, Roy Brent, Bill Dagwell, Hugh Starkey, Bill Fisher, Shorty English, Tex Duffy, Jimmy Dime, Leo Beard, Joe Dill, Jack Silver, Bert O'Malley, Jack Perry, Richie McCarew, Walter Klimpton, Art Flavin, Harry Claremont, T.C. Jacks, Ralph Bard, Bill Van Vleck, Beauregard Bonifacio, Charles Sewell, John Collins, Van Alder, George Magrill, Charles Hall, Kid Wagner, Sailor Vincent, Sam Levine, Jockey Haefeli, Duke Green, Jack Gallagher, H.R. Warwick, John Northpole, Walter Kirby, Earl "Hap" Hogan, Fred Berhle, Al McDonald, James Casey, and Tex Higginson [Also Seen as Taxi Driver] (Crewmen); Jim Thorpe, John Crawford, Nim Nixon, Edward Patrick, T.J. Rankin and Gus Robinson (Native Dancers); Everett Brown (Native in Ape Costume); John Wade, Milton Shockley, John Brakins, Sam Marlowe, Ivory Williams, Tobias Tally, Al Knight, Charles Washington, William Duran, Henry Martin, Floyd Shackleford, Johnnie Bland, Jack Best, George Washington, Cliff Ingram, Roy Thompskin, Earl Turman, Blue Washington, Odel Conley, Onest Conley and John Davis (Warriors); Madame Sul-Te-Wan (Handmaiden); Etta MacDaniel (Native Woman); Wade Walker, William Dunn, Ed Allen, A.J. Prather, Walter Knox, Ray Turner, Jack West, Tony Shelly, Nathan Perry, Alice Nichols, Kathryn Curry, Nathan Curry, Annie L. Johnson, Evelyn Garrison, Etta Mae Allen, Rose Dandridge, Etta Mae Henry, Joe Flourney, Almeta Muse, Fanny Donahue, Lawrence Green, William Solder, Katherine Sparks and Harold Knox (Natives); Hannah Washington, James Adamson, Bernice Dandridge, Rena Marlowe, Malcon Potts, Mahlon Potts and Harold Garrison (Native Children); Irene Henry (Baby); Bill Nye and George MacQuarrie (Police Captains); Frank Fanning, Monte Vandegrift, Frank Meredith and Tim Lonergan [Also Seen as Usher] (Police Officers); Allen Pomeroy (Motorcycle Policeman); Ivan Thomas (Conductor); Joe Marba (Motorman); George Daly (Machine Gunner); Lew Harvey and Pat Harmon (Gunmen); Eddie Sturgis, King Mojave, Harry Eaton, Mae Marrin and Larry McGrath (Ballyhooers); Jean Fenwick, Hazel Howell, Betty Gale, Bill Williams and LeRoy Mason (New Yorkers/Theatre Patrons); June Gittelson (Fat Woman); Oliver Eckhardt (Husband); Vera

Lewis (Dowager); Eddie Boland, Lynton Brent and Paddy O'Flynn (Reporters/Cameramen); Frank Mills, Frank O'Connor, Russ Saunders, Harry Bowen, Eddie Hart, Peter Duray, Wesley Hopper, Roy Stewart, Charles O'Malley, Jack Smith, Ed Stevens, Ed Reed, Ed Rochelle, Jack Chapin, Harry Mount, Ralph Easton, Frank Cullen, Frank Angel, Walt Ackerman and Arnold Gray (Reporters); James Harrison and Lee Phelps (Cameramen); Jack Pratt (Radio Announcer); Dorothy Gulliver and Carlotta Monti (Young Women); Veronica "Rocky" Balfe [a.k.a. Sandra Shaw] (Hotel Victim); Barney Capehart, Bob Galloway, Eric Wood, Dusty Mitchell and Russ Rogers (Navy Pilots); Reginald Barlow (Engineer); Merian C. Cooper (Flight Commander); Ernest B. Schoedsack (Chief Observer); and Walter Downing, John L. Johnson, Harry Duvall, Gertrude Sutton, Helen Worthington, Jean Doran, Florence Dudley, Betty Burns, Tom O'Grady, Harry Strang, Lillian Young; *Note*: Syd Saylor Mistakenly Listed as Reporter in Some Sources

DOUBLES & STUNT PLAYERS: *For Miss Wray*: Aline Goodwin, Pauline Wagner, Lee Kinney, Lillian Jones, Marcella Allen and Cherie May; *for Bruce Cabot*: Al McDonald and Gil Perkins; *for James Flavin*: Bud Mason; *for Robert Armstrong*: Charles Sullivan, Bob McKee, Mike Lally and Bob Williams; and Mike Graves, Duke Green, James Casey, Dorothy Curtis, Frank Cullen, Joe Dill, Charles Watt, Harry Wagner, Mike Lally, James Casey, Tex Higginson, Sam Cummings, Edith Haskins, Billy Jones, Chic Collins, Johnny St. Claire, Jack Holbrook, Betty Collins, Loretta Rush, Bobby Rose, Frances Mills, Harvey Perry

KING KLUNK (1933)
(Universal Pictures Corp./Walter Lantz)

This unusual, and unusually prompt, parody deserves special mention: Walter Lantz's cartoon "King Klunk" condenses the theme into one reel as an adventure in the *Pooch the Pup* series, with forgotten 'toon hero Pooch assuming the Carl Denham role, even to the extent of attending to his own camera. The Tyrannosaurus fight and the grand finale are the highlights of the short subject, which boasts striking character designs, a grisly ending for the ape and a whiplash job of directing by Lantz and William Nolan. Lantz would take a hand in later years in a chain of futile attempts to get *The Lost Atlantis* (see pages 221-222) into production.

CREDITS: Producer: Walter Lantz; Directors: Walter Lantz and William Nolan; Running Time: 7 Minutes; Released: Spring-Summer 1933

BLIND ADVENTURE (1933)
(RKO-Radio Pictures, Inc.)

Virtually forgotten in the greater scheme of the Cooper-Schoedsack partnership, this robust filming of an original scenario by Ruth Rose was assembled from start to finish during the summer of 1933—in the midst of the March-to-August production of *The Son of Kong*.

Robert Armstrong stars as a wealthy American at large in London. He encounters an apparent murder case, complete with vanishing corpse, and meets a young Canadian woman with the alluring name of Rose Thorne (played by *The Son of Kong*'s Helen Mack). The adventure develops promptly into an espionage chase, with Miss Mack in peril and Armstrong using his wits to maneuver traitors John Miljan and Ralph Bellamy into a stand-off.

Director Ernest Schoedsack packs the brisk running time with the suspenseful pacing and sense of jubilant adventure, however desperate the circumstances, that characterize the unit's work across-the-board. Ruth Rose's screenplay is characteristically marvelous in its compact efficiency, with particularly strong characterization in Miss Mack's role and a dashingly impulsive daredevil part that fits Armstrong like the proverbial glove. Henry Gerrard's cameras capture a splendidly fog-bound illusion of London.

CREDITS: Executive Producer: Merian C. Cooper; Associate Producer: David Lewis; Director: Ernest B. Schoedsack; Assistant Director: Ivan Thomas; Story and Screenplay: Ruth Rose; Additional Dialogue: Robert Benchley; Photographed by: Henry Gerrard; Camera Operator: Robert De Grasse; Assistant Cameraman: George Diskant; Settings: Van Nest Polglase and Al Herman; Editor: Ted Cheesman; Assistant Editor: Fred McGuire; Propmaster: William Carr; Music: Max Steiner; Sound: Hal Bumbaugh; Assistant Recording Engineers: Jean Speak and L.C. Carroll; Chief Electrician: Guy Gilman; Chief Grip: Tom Clement; Stills: Ollie Sigurdson; Running Time: 65 Minutes; Released: August 18, 1933

Robert Armstrong and Helen Mack in *Blind Adventure*

CAST: Robert Armstrong (Richard Bruce); Helen Mack (Rose Thorne); Roland Young (Burglar); Ralph Bellamy (Jim Steele); John Miljan (Regan); Laura Hope Crews (Lady Rockingham); Beryl Mercer (Elsie); Forrester Harvey (Proprietor); Henry Stephenson (Maj. Thorne); Tyrell Davis (Gerald Fairfax); Desmond Roberts (Harvey); Charles Irwin (Bill); Fred Sullivan (General); George K. Arthur (Drunkard); Ivan Simpson (Butler); Phyllis Barry (Gwen); John Warburton (Reggie); Marjorie Gateson (Mrs. Thorne)

THE SON OF KONG (1933)
(RKO-Radio Pictures, Inc.)

Carl Denham (Robert Armstrong) is a broken but defiant man as this hasty sequel reintroduces him, hiding out from the press and the ambulance-chasers. The disaster of Kong's escape notwithstanding, Denham cannot resist reminding himself of his Grand Adventure: He has decorated his lodging-house room with a lurid poster advertising Kong's début. With help from his shipboard pals and a friendly writ-server (Frank O'Connor), Denham escapes and puts back out to sea. There follows an encounter with a pretty tent-show entertainer, Helene (Helen Mack), in the Malayan port of Dakang. An act of treachery and murder puts Denham back on the trail to Skull Island. As though he wouldn't have returned, one way or another. Helene, who has fallen for Denham, stows away.

Cast ashore on Kong's island following a mutiny, the Denham party and Helene encounter the expected tribesmen and dinosaurs, a less predictable gigantic bear, and a yet less expected smaller version of King Kong, who routs the bear. The ape befriends the castaways, killing a dragon-like reptile and finally sacrificing himself in the act of saving Denham from a flood. The explorers' chance discovery of a fabulous treasure will make them wealthy, if only they can get back to civilization. An approaching ship assures them of rescue, and Helene sweet-talks Denham into marriage.

Desultory in every way save for the welcome return of our old friends Carl Denham, Charley the cook (Victor Wong), Capt. Englehorn (Frank Reicher), the Chief (Noble Johnson) and the Witch King (Steve Clemente), *The Son of Kong* nonetheless plays out pretty much as a sequel should: The special effects are generously deployed but never overkilled. The junior version of Kong is possessed of enough ferocity to render his forcibly cute looks almost beside the point. And the subordinate creatures are magnificently imagined—especially a reptilian whatzus, unknown to natural history, that menaces Robert Armstrong and Helen Mack within a cave. John Marston makes much of a run-of-the-mill villain role and is granted a most satisfying death scene in the jaws of a sea serpent.

The story bears a general resemblance to Tiffany Studios' *The Enchanted Island* (1927), but *The Son of Kong* can scarcely be considered an outright reworking of that picture.

CREDITS: Executive Producer: Merian C. Cooper; Associate Producer: Archie F. Marshek; Director: Ernest B. Schoedsack; Story and Screenplay: Ruth Rose; Photographed by: Eddie Linden, Vernon L. Walker and J.O. Taylor; Music: Max Steiner; Settings: Van Nest Polglase and Al Herman; Assistant Directors: Ivan Thomas and William Cody; Assistant Director, Additional Scenes: Walter Daniels; Sound Effects: Murray Spivack; Recorded by: Earl A. Wolcott and Hal Bumbaugh, RCA Photophone System; Editor: Ted Cheesman; Assistant Editor: Henry Berman; Chief Technician: Willis H. O'Brien; Technical Staff: E.B. Gibson, Marcel Delgado, Carroll Shepphird, Fred Reefe and W.G. White; Art Technicians: Mario Larrinaga and Byron L. Crabbe; Special Effects: Harry Redmond, Jr.; Associate, Sound Effects: Walter G. Elliott; Cameramen: Bert Willis, Linwood Dunn, Clifford Stine, Eddie Pyle, Edward Henderson and Felix Schoedsack; Assistant Cameramen: William Reinhold, Clarence Slifer and James Daly; Set Decor: Thomas Little; Gaffer: S.H. Barton; Grip: Tom Clement; Assistant Grip: Pete Bernard; Propmaster: Gene Rossi; Props: Ken Koontz and Bill Carr; Sound Recordists: Jim Speak and Bill Turner; Stills: Gaston Longet; Hairdresser: Mary Raffa; Script Supervisor: Betty Miserae; Costumers: Walter Plunkett; Wardrobe on Set: Maxine Lockwood and Homer Watson; Makeup: Mel Burns; Additional Makeup: Al Senator; Gaffer: George Marqunie; Williams Process Supervision: Frank Williams; Dunning Process Supervision: Carroll Dunning and C. Dodge Dunning; Production Manager: C.J. White; Running Time: 71 Minutes; Released: December 22, 1933

CAST: Robert Armstrong (Carl Denham); Helen Mack (Helene Peterson); Frank Reicher (Capt. Englehorn); John Marston (Helstrom); Victor Wong (Charley); Ed Brady (Red); Lee Kohlmar (Mickey); Clarence Wilson (Peterson); Katherine Ward (Mrs. Hudson); Gertrude Short (Lady Reporter); Gertrude Sutton (Servant); James B. Leong (Trader); Noble Johnson (Chief); Steve Clemente (Witch King); Frank O'Connor (Writ Server); Constantine Romanoff (Bill); Harry Tenbrook (Tommy); Leo "Dutch" Hendrian (Dutch); Ken Kuntz, Gene Rossi, Homer Watson, Tex Higginson, J. Goff, Jack Richardson, Frank Hendrian, Frank Mills, F. Garrety and Harry Cronbleth (Sailors); Claude Payton (Sailor and Shoelace Peddler); Ed Rochelle (Newshawker); Sam Levine (Fruit Peddler); Jimmy Leong (Bartender); Nathan Curry (Native); Cy Clegg (Sailor and Stunt Artist); Jack Holbrook (Stunt Artist); Lawrence Green (Double for Noble Johnson)

THE LOST ISLAND (1934)
(Christie Studios; Unfinished)

"The Lost Island" was begun early in 1934 as one of the first live-action short subjects to be made in the new Technicolor three-color process. It intended itself as an imaginative musical-comedy variation on the *Kong* theme, mounted with considerable scope. The "human" "actors" were marionettes designed and constructed by Blanding Sloan, Wah Ming Chang, Charles Cristadoro and Mickey O'Rourke. Wah Chang became better known many years later for his extraordinary animation effects for the George Pal productions of *The Wonderful World of the Brothers Grimm*, *The Seven Faces of Dr. Lao* and *The Time Machine*.

Characters in *The Lost Island* included exaggerated representations of Mae West and the Marx Bros. Kong, this time, actually *was* Charles Gemora in one of his famous ape suits. (Newfound information from Gemora's surviving kin suggests that the Filipino ape-impersonator may have modeled, or provided photographic models, for *Kong*'s designers. Gemora's prominence at the time would lend credibility to the idea.) Other monsters were played by ingeniously costumed actors. *King Kong*'s Orville Goldner was production manager. Eddie Ward composed the original music. The director was LeRoy Prinz, Paramount's ace choreographer-director. Ray Rennahan was cameraman.

The Lost Island was abandoned when finances ran out. The Technicolor photography, which was much more costly than the single-film systems that became the norm, had rendered the project impossibly expensive for Al Christie's small organization.

The three-color Technicolor process made its live-action debut later that year in "La Cucaracha," a two-reel short produced by Pioneer Pictures for RKO. The short won awards and high praise for all involved—including Pioneer's production chief, Merian C. Cooper.

SHE (1935)
(RKO-Radio Pictures, Inc.)

"My empire is of the imagination," declares the cruel monarch known as She-Who-Must-Be-Obeyed in Merian C. Cooper's production of *She*. So was Cooper's empire one of the imagination. That mutual truth was uppermost in the filmmaker's mind when he decided he must make a fittingly imaginative epic follow-through to *King Kong* from Henry Rider Haggard's popular and enduring novel.

The tale hangs on Ayesha, a beautiful, 2,000-year-old queen whose seemingly eternal life stems from a mystical flame deep in the African jungle. She fancies a modern-day explorer, Leo Vincey, to be the reincarnation of her lover of antiquity, but he insists he loves Ustane, a native girl. Ayesha steps into the flame, trying to induce him to do likewise—but this time, she shrivels to a mummified state.

At least three silent-screen versions had been made: These include an Edison version of 1908; a Fox Film Corp. version of 1917, starring Valeska Suratt; and an Anglo-German production of 1925, the year of Haggard's death. Universal had bought the rights in 1932 as a proposed vehicle for Boris Karloff and Tala Birell; John L. Balderston's never-produced script is a grim horror story, very much in keeping with his work on *Dracula*, *Frankenstein*, *The Mummy* and *Bride of Frankenstein*. Cooper, who in 1933 succeeded David O. Selznick as vice president for production at the financially beleaguered RKO-Radio Pictures, bought the property from Carl Laemmle's similarly troubled Universal and tried to borrow *Frankenstein*'s James Whale to direct.

Cooper suffered a near-fatal heart attack in September 1933 and quit RKO the following May. Meanwhile, he and his wealthy friends, John and Cornelius Whitney, had bought into the Technicolor Corp., which was trying to launch a new three-color process. The

Whitneys and Cooper also formed Pioneer Pictures expressly to produce features in Technicolor. Cooper, to wrap up his RKO contract, struck a deal to deliver two big titles, *She* and *The Last Days of Pompeii*—intending to make these in Technicolor. RKO granted a budget of $2 million for both productions, with about $100,000 allowed for Technicolor. This was a gigantic budget: RKO's top-shelf productions typically cost about $200,000.

Cooper wanted his pal Ernest B. Schoedsack to direct both titles, and he asked Schoedsack's wife, Ruth Rose, to write the screenplays. She agreed to both, but insisted it would be impossible to film *She* effectively, despite Cooper's enthusiasm and reassurances; he was even planning a sequel, based on Haggard's own *Ayesha*. Schoedsack nixed his own involvement with *She*, on the same grounds as Ruth, but signed on to direct *Pompeii*.

At length, Cooper settled for the actor and aspiring director Irving Pichel, who had served as dialogue director on *The Most Dangerous Game* and had solo-helmed a fine mystery, *Before Dawn*, in 1933. Pichel had gone begging for director assignments since then; the unexpected breakthrough on *She* opened up a distinguished new career. While Pichel would concentrate on the dramatic thrust, Cooper hired the architectural designer Lansing C. Holden as co-director in charge of visual aspects.

Cooper proved unable to convince MGM to loan out Greta Garbo for the title role. Likewise with Marlene Dietrich at Paramount, which also refused to lend Joel McCrea and his wife, Frances Dee, for the youthful leads. Paramount did offer Randolph Scott, who at the time was a second-string leading man and Western star. Cooper accepted Scott and gave the ingenue role to RKO's Helen Mack and the key character-man part to a new arrival from England, Nigel Bruce. The title role went to a striking beauty named Helen Gahagan, who had signed with RKO in 1932 but had yet to make a movie. The wife of the established star Melvyn Douglas, Miss Gahagan was possessed of a regal height and an assured presence honed on the New York stage and as an operatic soprano. *She* proved to be the only movie for Miss Gahagan, who makes a lovely and forbidding tyrant but lacks the crucial sensuality and seems incapable of communing with the camera. Nine years later, Miss Gahagan became a member of Congress but retired from politics in 1950 after losing to Richard M. Nixon in a bitterly contested Senate race.

Abandoning horror for exotic mystery, Cooper relocated the setting to Arctic Asia, within an anomalous volcanic temperate zone. The script conferences veered beyond even the imagination of Haggard. Cooper asked Miss Rose: "Is there anything else we can put in there to make it more exciting?"

"It already has everything but a saber-toothed tiger," she replied.

"Great!" shouted Cooper. "Why didn't *I* think of that? A saber-toothed tiger! Write it in!"

Unable to convince the boss that she had spoken facetiously, Miss Rose let it go with a *dead* saber-tooth, frozen in a glacier. Cooper played along, but he insisted upon making the creature as big as an elephant. (Cooper's commonest complaint, on any project, was this: "It's not *big* enough.") As the distinguishing *big*-ness of *She* escalated, Cooper received a daunting report, just on the cusp of production: His budget had been cut in half, and he would have to stretch $1 million over both *She* and *Pompeii*. So much for Technicolor, although the process remained in place on Pioneer's short subject "La Cucaracha," and on Pioneer's breakthrough feature, *Becky Sharp*, which was destined for an RKO release. Just as *Becky* was wrapping on March 12, 1935, principal photography was begun on *She*—in black-and-white.

The Cooper version begins with an expedition to rediscover the flame of eternal life. The chief explorer is Leo Vincey (Randolph Scott), whose ancestor had found the miraculous fire some 500 years ago. The perils mount with an avalanche, a cannibal siege and the discovery of She, herself, who fancies Leo the reincarnation of his ancestor, her lover of centuries past. The treacheries gather from here with an appropriate fidelity to Haggard, climaxing with the shriveling of the queen as she attempts to demonstrate the power of the flame. The settings are uniformly stunning, and the Great Wall from *King Kong* serves as the entrance to the hidden empire of She. The dissolution of the queen is accomplished smoothly for welcome horrific impact, thanks to a series of progressive makeup effects that are revealed gradually in optical dissolves.

Max Steiner delivered the exuberant musical score under daunting pressures of deadline. The score is itself a daunting work, to be surpassed in magnitude only by Steiner's music for *Gone with the Wind* (1939).

Randolph Scott's inexperience matches that of Miss Gahagan. More on the mark are Helen Mack, Nigel Bruce and, as a high priest pursuing a hidden agenda, Gustav von Seyffertitz. The customers, who had flipped over *King Kong*'s robust rambunctiousness, found *She* too much of the art-film variety. Box-office returns failed to cover the cost, but *She* has gained many champions in times more recent.

Remakes and takeoffs of times more recent include the Seven Arts/Hammer Films *She* of 1965, starring Ursula Andress; a 1968 sort-of sequel, bearing the grammatically problematical title *The Vengeance of She* and starring Olinka Berova; and an Italian-made cheesecake-slapstick *She*, from 1984, in which the voluptuous Sandahl Bergman replenishes her youth with a hot-springs dunking—the better to cater to the oglers in the audience. This last-mentioned owes more to Robert E. Howard's *Conan* yarns, and even to the Three Stooges, than to Rider Haggard.

CREDITS: Producer: Merian C. Cooper; Associate Producer: Shirley C. Burden; Directors: Irving Pichel and Lansing C. Holden; Adaptation, Continuity and Dialogue: Ruth Rose; Based on: H. Rider Haggard's 1886 Novel, *She, a History of Adventure*; Additional Dialogue: Dudley Nichols; Music: Max Steiner; Photographed by: J. Roy Hunt; Photographic Effects: Vernon L. Walker; Art Director: Van Nest Polglase; Associate: Al Herman; Costumes: Aline Bernstein and Harold Miles; Sound Recordist, RCA Photophone System: John L. Cass; Editor: Ted Cheesman; Dance Director: Benjamin Zemach; Set Decor: Thomas Little; Optical Effects: Linwood G. Dunn; Makeup: Carl Axcelle; Matte painter: Mario Larrinaga; First Assistant Director: Harry D'Arcy; Second Assistant Director: Charles Kerr; Camera Operator: Eddie Pyle; Assistant Cameramen: James Daly and Charles Burke; Matter Photography: Guy Newhard; Orchestrations: Bernhard Kaun, Maurice de Packh and Edward Powell; Music Recorded by: P.J. Faulkner, Jr.; Sound Effects: Walter G. Elliott; Assistant Sound Recordist: Ralph Spotts; Assistant Film Editor: Roland Gross; Production Illustrators: Lansing Holden, R. Doulton Stott, Harold Miles, George Russell, Mario Larrinaga, Vsevelod Ulianoff, Stanley Johnson, Charles Ohmann, Dan Sayre Groesback and Dennis Holden; Mosaic Throne Designed by: Alex Hall; Gaffer: Leo Green; Head Grip: Marvin Woods; Propmaster: Charles Sayres; Wardrobe: Eleanor Fieldhouse and Sandy; Hairdresser: Hollis Barnes; Script Continuity: Gloria Truebe; Assistant to Mr. Cooper: Zoe Porter; Nurse: Esther Coleman; Research: Elizabeth McGaffy; Technical Advisor: Dr. Luido Gorgastin; Running Time: 96 Minutes, Cut from 101 Minutes at Preview; Released: July 12, 1935

CAST: Helen Gahagan (Ayesha); Randolph Scott (Leo Vincey); Helen Mack (Tanya Dugmore); Nigel Bruce (Holly); Gustav von Seyffertitz (Billali); Samuel S. Hinds (John Vincey); Noble Johnson (Cannibal Chief); Lumsden Hare (Dugmore); Jim Thorpe (Captain of the Guard); Julius Adler (High Priest); Arnold Grey and Bill Wolfe (Priests); Ray Corrigan and Jerry Frank (Guards)

THE LAST DAYS OF POMPEII (1935)
(RKO-Radio Pictures, Inc.)

Suggesting Cecil B. De Mille more so than its own Cooper-Schoedsack-Rose coalition, *The Last Days of Pompeii* is primarily a religious parable jazzed up with adventurous spectacle. Ruth Rose's screenplay makes annoyingly much of the guilt-ridden relationship of Preston Foster's blood-sport profiteer to his adopted son—Foster had been a poor but honest blacksmith until he lost his wife and their child in an accident—and it rather disingenuously presents Jesus Christ as a mystery man until the closing moments of heavenly reconciliation.

Martyrdom runs rampant on both godly and earthly planes. The adopted boy, Flavius (David Holt), is the offspring of a gladiator whom Marcus (Foster) has dispatched in the arena. Flavius suffers obviously fatal injuries during a horse-thieving raid staged by Marcus on orders from

Pontius Pilate (Basil Rathbone); the boy is healed by a stranger known only as "the Lord." Later yet, Marcus looks the other way when the stranger is crucified. Finally, Flavius (now played by John Wood) becomes an outlawed liberator of the oppressed; he is captured and sentenced to fight to the death within Marcus' own arena. Mount Vesuvius gets in the final word—a finely wrought eruption, of course—and Marcus dies while rescuing Flavius and a band of fugitive slaves. Marcus receives a hearty and forgiving welcome into the celestial realm.

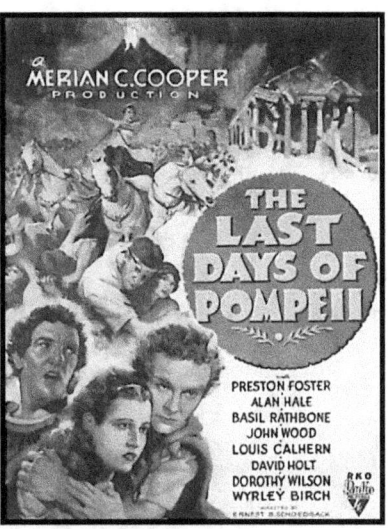

The screen story bears but the most passing resemblance to Sir Edward Bulwer-Lytton's often-filmed novel, being more bravura pageantry than genuine epic. Ruth Rose told us that she never quite managed to wade through the dense verbosity of the novel. Even so, Basil Rathbone makes a splendidly treacherous Pilate. Preston Foster is more of an acquired taste, looking altogether too dumpy to be any kind of unbeatable gladiator. Director Ernest B. Schoedsack grumbled for years after the fact about "the ordeal of trying to build a picture around Preston Foster and his fat arse." Foster nonetheless handles the emoting with genuine feeling in the best Wallace Beery sentimental tough-guy manner. The larger point of *Pompeii*, however, is Willis H. O'Brien's disaster footage, which is skillfully integrated with the right intimate moments of terror and poignance. The recycling of music from *King Kong* at once distinguishes and lessens the picture, which thus announces itself as an echo of greatness.

CREDITS: A Merian C. Cooper Production; Production Associate: John Speaks; Director: Ernest B. Schoedsack; Screenplay: Ruth Rose; Original Story: James Ashmore Creelman and Melville Baker; Inspired by: Sir Edward Bulwer-Lytton's 1834 Novel, *The Last Days of Pompeii*; Collaborator on Adaptation: Boris Ingster; Contributors to Treatment: G.B. Stern and Jerry Hutchison; Photographed by: J. Roy Hunt; Chief Technician: Willis H. O'Brien; Assistant Director: Ivan Thomas; Special Effects: Harry Redmond; Photographic Effects: Vernon Walker; Photographic Technician: Eddie Linden; Art Director: Van Nest Polglase; Associate Art Director: Al Herman; Art Technician: Byron Crabbe; Editor: Archie F. Marshek; Set Dresser: Thomas Little; Artist: Aloys Bohnen; Costumer: Aline Bernstein; Musical Score: Roy Webb; Supervisor of Dance Numbers: Russell Lewis; Sound Recordist: Clem Portman; Sound Effects: Walter Elliott; Music Recording: P.J. Faulkner, Jr.; Researcher: Elizabeth McGaffey; Running Time: 96 Minutes; Released: October 18, 1935

CAST: Preston Foster (Marcus); Alan Hale (Burbix); Basil Rathbone (Pontius Pilate); John Wood (Flavius); Louis Calhern (Prefect); David Holt (Flavius as a Boy); Dorothy Wilson (Clodia); Wyrley Birch (Leaster); Gloria Shea (Julia); Frank Conroy (Gaius); William V. Mong (Cleon); Murray Kinnell (Peasant); Henry Kolker (Warder); Edward Van Sloan (Calvus); Zeffie Tilbury (Wise Woman); John Davidson (Slave); Ward Bond (Gladiator).

WAR EAGLES (1938-39)
(Metro-Goldwyn-Mayer Corp.; Unfinished)

Merian Cooper and Willis O'Brien planned *War Eagles* as a Technicolor epic for MGM. O'Brien was ready for a fresh breakthrough, having spent a frustrating three years of setbacks and

Production drawing for *War Eagles*

disappointments—and of sheer joblessness on the very turf that he had been among the first to stake out. OBie had many ideas for imaginative films and wasted no time in trying to bring them into development, but the corporate backing eluded him. In fairness to the studios, of course, it bears mentioning that O'Brien's plans would have been outlandishly expensive to realize.

Cooper, who had become a producer at MGM, came to the rescue with an idea that could only be developed with O'Brien's collaboration: *War Eagles* was envisioned as a heroic fantasy about dinosaurs and a lost society of Vikings who ride gigantic eagles within an unexplored "blind spot" near the North Pole. Eventually, these bird-straddling warriors would engage enemy dirigibles in a battle over New York City.

O'Brien worked on pre-production during 1938-39. Marcel Delgado built several movable figures, including flying and walking models of the birds on an inch-equals-foot scale, and several Allosauri. Illustrator Duncan Gleason made numerous drawings and paintings. Howard Richmond's set designs were developed into large-scale miniature settings.

Some color footage was made with the birds and men fighting the dinosaurs. Surviving frames, now in a private collection, are stunning. Five bird armatures—two flying and three sitting—also survive in a private collection.

On September 1, 1939, World War II began and the Axis powers united amid the Sino-Japanese War. Merian C. Cooper, who had been a flying ace during World War I, left MGM to fight the Japanese.

War Eagles was shelved. The new global war had rendered the theme of dirigible combat obsolete.

THE LOST ATLANTIS (1938-40)
(Harry O. Hoyt/Columbia Pictures/Lantz & Nassour; Unfinished)

At around the same time as *War Eagles*, Harry O. Hoyt had grown impatient with nearly a decade of nursing his bitterness over the collapse of *Creation* at RKO-Radio. Hoyt's career had suffered from his three-year absence from the screen at the crucial beginning of the talking-picture era, and he settled for sub-par employment with Monogram Pictures and other Poverty Row studios. Meanwhile, Hoyt committed self-plagiarism with a scenario called *The Lost Atlantis*—in which another submarine would be drawn into another lost world. Once more, the villain would kill a baby dinosaur, only to be pursued and slain by the mother.

After several years of trying to find a backer, Hoyt came close in 1938 after joining with Fred Jackman, the technical effects director of *The Lost World*, and former Monogram president Trem Carr, who had become a producer at Universal. Columbia Pictures honcho Harry Cohn was impressed with the pitch and advanced the partners $20,000 to make a two-reel (about 20 minutes' running time) test. Cohn promised the go-ahead for a high-budget feature—*if* the results impressed him favorably; otherwise, Columbia would use the footage in a serial.

A premature advertising announcement

The animation test was produced during several months at Jackman's new effects studio in Burbank. Marcel Delgado, on a visit there, reported observing a room staffed by women, working on dinosaur models. Delgado recalled the miniatures as looking "cuter than they should have been" and said the creatures lacked the reptilian ferocity and leathery skins that he considered essential. Columbia generated some lovely advance advertising, including a press flier showing a Ceratosaurus emerging from ancient ruins and a mother-and-baby pair of Monoclonii. But Cohn changed his mind, and the film wound up stuck on high-center.

Then, Walter Lantz—the cartoon maestro at Universal Pictures—and independent producer Edward Nassour decided to have a go at it. Lantz built a set six feet square in his studio. "The footage... thus far is notable for its smoothness," wrote Douglas W. Churchill in the *New York Times* on November 17, 1940, adding: "According to current plans, [Lantz] will use the test footage in one of his cartoon shorts to find out what the public thinks of it." But plans changed abruptly, influenced by the labor-intensive and extravagant process itself. In 1973, Lantz told George Turner: "Utilizing a method of model animation invented by Nassour, we made one reel," including a fight between dinosaurs. Lantz said the models were small, the human figures standing only two inches high, and the project was abandoned "because it proved too expensive and time-consuming." (Nassour would later use this process in 1956's *The Beast of Hollow Mountain*, from an O'Brien story that resembles *Gwangi* more so than "The Ghost of Slumber Mountain.") None of this Lantz-Nassour *Atlantis* footage has been found.

Or has it?

In fact, we have grown to suspect that some of the Lantz-Nassour footage *may have* reached the screen. In 1951, Robert L. Lippert produced *The Lost Continent*, an almost-good yarn about scientists and soldiers at large on an uncharted island. They are pursued by an angry Brontosaurus and observe a battle between Triceratopses, and one of the party is gored by a Triceratops—all incidents that the Hoyt scenario had depicted. The only special-effects credits are assigned to Augie Lohman, a specialist in mechanicals, and Ray Mercer, who handled the titles and optical printing. Lohman told George Turner that the creatures were not of his making, and that he didn't know who built or animated them. This animation is smooth, but the creatures *are* rather "cute" and lacking in intimidating presence (consistent, perhaps, with Delgado's description) and are seen mostly in long shots—a give away that the models were very small. Are these the dinosaurs from *The Lost Atlantis*? Your guess is as good as ours, but we suspect they are.

GWANGI (1941-42)
(Colonial Pictures/RKO-Radio Pictures, Inc.; Unfinished)

Willis O'Brien struggled through two more years of frustration following the *War Eagles* debacle. Then, he entered into a partnership with John Speaks, who had worked on *The Last Days of Pompeii*. Speaks' production company, Colonial Pictures Corp., was headquartered at RKO in Culver City. O'Brien and Speaks developed a project called *Bamboula*. In May of 1941, RKO agreed to "employ Colonial... to assist... in the production of one picture," to be produced by Speaks and O'Brien. When the working title was challenged in light of a 1924 stage musical called *Bamboula*, the project was rechristened *Gwangi*. RKO President George Schaefer approved a hefty top-of-the-line budget of $552,000, and extensive preparations were undertaken at RKO-Pathé.

The intention was to combine the exciting action of a Western adventure with a dinosaur fantasy—a unique idea, at the time. There was some topicality in that *Gwangi* was suggested by news reports that a species of tiny horse lived in certain remote parts of the Grand Canyon. There also was an Indian legend that gigantic monsters lived on an unreachable plateau of that same mighty gorge. The horse story proved to be a shaggy-dog story, of course, and the plateau, when reached, yielded no such wonders. The story was altered, and the Grand Canyon became the mythical Pinnacle Rocks.

O'Brien's story finally made its way, most often piecemeal (with and without authorization) into the likes of Ed Nassour's *The Beast of Hollow Mountain* (1956), the 1960 near-miss *Dinosaurus!*—and of course Ray Harryhausen's legitimate reworking of 1969, *The Valley of Gwangi*. Some of the ideas also were slotted into O'Brien's own collaborative *Mighty Joe Young*. The original concerns J.T., a young woman who owns a Wild West hippodrome, and Tuck, her rival and lover, along with an eccentric professor, a mysterious Indian and a corps of adventurous frontiersmen. They follow a trail of miniature horses into a forbidden valley, where they are menaced by Gwangi, a 35-foot Allosaurus, and a Triceratops and a Pteranodon. They capture Gwangi and haul the creature to a settlement, introducing the dinosaur as a circus attraction. Caged lions escape and attack Gwangi, who kills the big cats and then sets out to destroy the village. Finally, Tuck commandeers a truck and forces the beast over a cliff to its death.

O'Brien worked with Cecil B. De Mille's production illustrator, Dan Sayre Groesback, in storyboarding the screenplay, whose writers included the novelist Harold Lamb and Emily Barre, Jerry Cady and William Hamilton. With *King Kong*'s art director, Al Herman, O'Brien planned the sets, which were built as miniature mock-ups. Harry Cunningham, a remarkable technician and inventor, constructed four miniature projectors and tooled the steel-jointed dural skeletons of several prehistoric monsters including a Pteranodon, a Triceratops and the title beast. Marcel Delgado performed his usual superlative job of creating the details of the scaly beasts. Technicolor technician George Cave was consulted regarding the problems of making so complex a film in three-strip color.

Duncan Gleason made large key illustrations of action highlights. Jack Shaw produced several large oil paintings. Juan Larrigana, Mario's older brother, prepared a half-dozen massive glass paintings to be combined with live action. Irving Reis, a noted stage director (not to be confused with the like-named special-effects cinematographer), was assigned to

This image would be modified as a key sequence in *Mighty Joe Young* (see p. 225).

direct the first unit commencing November 19 and due for completion by January 10. This shoot would comprise most of the live-action interiors and exteriors. Attached for leading roles were Anne Shirley and James Craig, the romantic team of William Dieterle's *All That Money Can Buy*; comedy star Edgar Kennedy, who at the time was holding forth in his own series of RKO two-reelers; and George Cleveland.

O'Brien was set to direct the second unit, utilizing doubles and stunt riders, on a 17-day schedule beginning October 15. This segment was to include work at Pathé, the RKO Ranch at Encino, Goebel's Lion Farm, the Petrified Forest and the Painted Desert in Arizona, and Vasquez Rocks northwest of Los Angeles. Vasquez Rocks is a dazzling spread of towering hogback formations of yellowish sandstone. As a movie location used hundreds of times, it has stood in for the Carpathian Alps (*Dracula*) and the mountains of Tibet (*Werewolf of London*), as well as Afghanistan, the Khyber Pass and many regions of the untamed Western frontier. Vernon Walker, chief of RKO's camera-effects department, was in charge of second-unit photography, including scenes to be used as process projection backgrounds.

Gwangi was afflicted by circumstances similar to those that had aborted *Creation*—but this time there was no happy ending, no new *King Kong* to prevent *Gwangi*'s hard work from having been in vain. *Gwangi* was replaced on the schedule by a lackluster remake of *Little Orphan Annie*, of all things! The scrapping followed organizational changes within the studio, with some of the new officials challenging the validity of the dinosaur epic. The death blow was administered by the insipid findings of a private-sector bureaucratic coalition called the Institute of Audience Opinion, a division of the Gallup Poll, which RKO had enlisted to assess *potential* popular reactions to various works in progress. Gallup reported that nobody knew how to pronounce *Gwangi* and that the majority of citizens thus polled said they would not enjoy a picture about dinosaurs. Moreover, none of the respondents felt that Technicolor would make such a film more palatable. This, of course, is the same Gallup Poll that had foreseen Alf M. Landon defeating Franklin Delano Roosevelt in 1936.

On the morning of January 29, 1942, John Speaks was informed that the studio would not pick up its option to continue production of *Gwangi*. Costs had already mounted to $50,442.95, plus music department expenses. Speaks tried for another four months to rescue the project. He was unable to convince RKO that it was a bad idea to throw away such an investment, and he maintained that a finished *Gwangi* could turn a hefty profit. Speaks then tried to purchase the screenplay and the cumulative body of work thus far, intending to sell a co-production package to some other studio. On April 30, he wrote this memorandum to Joe Nolan, vice president in charge of commitments: "[I]n December, we were ready to start second-unit shooting. Technical preparation was and is 100 percent. The script is excellent... My fear is that the present studio executives were not really familiar with the setup. The entire art and technical preparations, blueprints, layouts, *etc.*, are set up on Stage No. 5 at Pathé. Seeing the layout is the only way anyone can really understand the excellent possibilities of the picture."

Despite a prevailing belief that no actual filming had been accomplished, there is evidence that certain scenes *were* shot. Marcel Delgado told us: "OBie made a sequence with the Allosaurus." The daily report sheets show such charges as $5,935,45 for art, $680.68 for process photography, $2,501.46 for animation, $39.50 for stills and $1,879.18 for cameramen, plus charges for transportation, raw stock and lab work for backgrounds and optical printing. Work reported as done included miniature sequences and chase scenes, mattes and animation, Paul Sawtell had begun composing a musical score during November. On December 1, with a 38-piece orchestra, he recorded some 12 minutes of dramatic cues, including main and end titles and some Native American-style music. The next day, Sawtell supervised the recording of seven cowboy ballads by a Western quartet.

In March 1943, Sid Rogell, an executive producer at RKO, attempted to reinstate *Gwangi*. He hired Ruth Rose Schoedsack, scenarist of *King Kong*, to evaluate the script and make revisions, shorten the opening sequences and make the characters more intriguing. The studio brass nixed the idea.

The screenplay and surviving photos of O'Brien's continuity drawings were purchased a generation later by Charles H. Schneer and Ray Harryhausen. With a considerably changed story line (but a fundamental fidelity to the original relationships among characters), the picture was filmed in Spain in color and released in 1969 by Warner Bros.-Seven Arts as *The Valley of Gwangi*. This version boasts superb animation by Harryhausen—almost overcoming an ill-conceived fire-scene finale that caused audiences of the day to holler "Fake!" at the screen—but it was widely panned by the critics on grounds of its old-fashioned melodramatic essence. Good as Harryhausen's creature effects are, this come-lately *Gwangi* could only have fared better with O'Brien's miniatures.

Some of O'Brien's miniature sets and other artifacts were rediscovered during the 1980s in a loft at what is now Culver City Studios—tiny monuments to a monumentally lost cause.

A GAME OF DEATH (1945)
(RKO-Radio Pictures, Inc.)

Though a formal remake of *The Most Dangerous Game* (1932), *A Game of Death* is but a desultory B-unit production from RKO. It is unrelated to the Cooper-Schoedsack interests except as an echo of the grand source film. Noble Johnson, however, graces both ensemble casts.

That said, *A Game of Death* remains a worthwhile rediscovery, with an able show of strapped heroism from John Loder, a winning lady-in-distress portrayal from Audrey Long and a Grand Manner job of overreaching villainy from Edgar Barrier. Barrier's character was strategically Germanized to supply a suggestion of Nazi influence (and to sidestep any perceptions of Russian-bashing) during those climactic days of the World War II: The film was in production during February-March 1945, but found its way into release only after the war's formal culmination.

The visceral horrors of the original could scarcely be duplicated this time out, given the dampening influence from 1934 onward of the Legion of Decency. Director Robert Wise, an alumnus of the Val Lewton unit at RKO-Radio, compensates with a strong sense of breakneck pacing. *A Game of Death* runs nine minutes longer than *The Most Dangerous Game*.

CREDITS: Producer: Herman Schlom; Director: Robert Wise; Assistant Director: Doran Cox; Dialogue Director: Anthony Jowitt; Screenplay: Norman Houston; Based on: Richard Connell's Story, "The Most Dangerous Game," from the 1930 *Golden Book* Magazine; Photographed by: J. Roy Hunt; Optical Effects: Vernon L. Walker and Linwood Dunn; Art Directors: Albert S. d'Agostino and Lucius Croxton; Editor: J.R. Whittredge; Décor: Darrell Silvera and James Altweis; Gowns: Renie; Musical Director: Constantin Bakaleinikoff; Musical Score: Paul Sawtell; Sound: Phillip Mitchell; Re-Recording: James S. Stewart; Running Time: 72 Minutes; Released: Following New York Opening during the Week of November 23, 1945

CAST: John Loder (Don Rainsford); Audrey Long (Ellen Trowbridge); Edgar Barrier (Eric Kreiger); Russell Wade (Robert Trowbridge); Russell Hicks (Whitney); Jason Robards (Captain); Gene Stutenroth (Pleshke); Noble Johnson (Carib); Robert Clarke (Helmsman); Edmund Glover (Quartermaster); Bruce Edwards (Collins); Jimmy Jordan (Steward); Vic Romito (Mongol); Jimmy Dime (Bulgar).

MIGHTY JOE YOUNG (1949)
(Arko, Inc./RKO-Radio Pictures, Inc.)

Ernest B. Schoedsack had lapsed to far lesser responsibilities after *The Last Days of Pompeii*, slumming briefly at Larry Darmour's Columbia-affiliated low-budget-thriller studio—where he helmed *Trouble in Morocco* and *Outlaws of the Orient*, both in 1937—before finding a brief resurgence in 1940 at Paramount with the bombastic *Dr. Cyclops*, a Big Science retelling of a centerpiece episode from *The Odyssey*. Schoedsack's professional association with Merian C. Cooper had come to an end as Cooper developed broader industrial ambitions; Schoedsack's contributions to the Allied effort in World War II, with his near-blinding as a consequence, also had sidelined his involvement in movie-making. The director's refusal to indulge in the manipulative gamesmanship of corporate Hollywood also helped to preserve his status as an outsider. But Schoedsack came impressively back to directing nine years later as a hired gun for John Ford and Cooper on *Mighty Joe Young*, with a screenplay by Mrs. Schoedsack, Ruth Rose, from Cooper's original story.

Participating animator Ray Harryhausen has attributed much of *Joe*'s story to Willis H. O'Brien: "Film scripts are seldom the product of just the writer," Harryhausen told us in 2000.

"I know from experience. I witnessed at first hand how many of O'Brien's drawings and ideas were incorporated... He wasn't just a technical creator on the project. He was always present at the Cooper/Schoedsack/Rose story conferences. O'Brien's new drawings were many times incorporated into the story line, with the credit going to the writer. And of course, the trick-roping scene in *Mighty Joe* was taken from the script of *Gwangi*."

Mighty Joe Young, with its tale of a huge but more nearly docile jungle ape brought to civilization with heartbreaking results, is actually *King Kong*, writ small—smaller, even, than *The Son of Kong*. Not even the technical advances of the animation process can elevate *Joe* to the grandeur of the source film. But as a *Kong* family reunion, and as a breakthrough assignment for the young Ray Harryhausen, *Mighty Joe Young* is a marvel and a delight.

Schoedsack found the project less than delightful, however: "Mr. John Ford was a mean old bastard," the director grumped during one of our meetings during the late 1960s. "Thought he knew all there was to know about directing—which, of course, one might suspect he *did*, what with his own track record—and threw his weight around at every opportunity. Thought he could barge in and tell me everything I was doing wrong. Him being the boss, and all that."

Ford's well-known harsh obstinacy posed somewhat more a hassle for Schoedsack than had Cooper's periodic appropriations of *The Most Dangerous Game*'s jungle set, back in 1932. And where Schoedsack could confront Cooper on equal footing during the span of their man-to-man partnership, Schoedsack served *Joe Young* as a work-for-hire artist with no such recourse.

Schoedsack did, however, have the advantage of Cooper's pride in having enlisted him to direct: "I damn near quit over our tug-of-war scene between Joe and all those strongmen," said Schoedsack, referring to a comical set-piece that is one of the film's sharper crowd-pleasers. "Mr. John Ford barges in, hollering about how we're doing it all wrong, that we need to shoot it *this* way, the way he'd do it if *he* were directing, instead of the way *I've* got it blocked out and set up, and just disrupts the shoot all to hell.

"So I storm out, telling Ford to knock himself out—I quit—go to hell—like that—and next thing you know, Coop's in there, trying to smooth things over and reminding Ford that he's not the director-of-record, y'know, so lay off. My authority was somewhat better established after that, but I'd pretty well lost my appetite for directing after *Joe Young*." Schoedsack returned to the arena only hesitantly thereafter, helming a prologue for the spectacular superscreen gimmick-process film *This Is Cinerama* (1952)—once again in cahoots with Cooper.

Mighty Joe Young introduces its main attraction as an infant gorilla of commonplace size, adopted as a pet named Joe by Jill Young (Lora Lee Michel), an explorer's daughter in Africa. Jill grows to lovely young womanhood (played now by Terry Moore), and Joe grows to an unnatural enormity. When show-biz impresario Max O'Hara (Robert Armstrong, essentially parodying *Kong*'s Carl Denham) arrives with a troupe of cowboys to capture lions for a nightclub attraction, the safari meets Joe in a hostile encounter. Joe is about to do away with Max when Jill intervenes. Sensing a spectacular ticket-selling prospect, Max manipulates Jill into bringing Joe to America. Gregg Johnson (Ben Johnson), a rodeo champ with the O'Hara party, becomes somewhat friendlier with Jill and gains Joe's trust.

The grim lessons of Kong's New York tragedy are replayed on a tinier scale when Joe, as the piéce de resistance at Max's Golden Safari nitery in Hollywood, reacts violently to a prank from a drunken patron and winds up demolishing the showplace. (Cooper, in a nostalgic nod to the bygone days of a more thoroughly collaborative partnership with Schoedsack, directed the scenes of destruction at the nightclub.) Condemned to death, Joe is freed in a ruse by Max, Jill and Gregg. Just before they can reach the safety of an outbound ship, the fugitives spot a burning orphanage and stop to render aid. Joe rescues one remaining child but injures himself. Declared a hero, Joe is granted safe passage back to Africa—along with Jill and Gregg.

Ruth Rose was about as fond of leading lady Terry Moore as Schoedsack was of John Ford. "One should *never* mention Terry Moore's name in the same breath as Fay Wray!" Mrs. Schoedsack told us. "She was all sweetness and light on the screen, but she possessed *nothing*

The tug-of-war deteriorates into a slugfest in *Mighty Joe Young*.

of Fay's class or delicacy." Of course, the part of Jill requires little delicacy or elegance under fire, being for all practical purposes a tomboy who bosses the mighty ape around like some mountainous playmate. The film's element of menace is directed entirely *at* Joe, whose closest approximation of ferocity lies in his strength and entirely justified indignation—unlike Kong, who invited sympathy in spite of his being the most dangerous wild creature at large on an island (Skull Island *or* Manhattan) laden with perils.

Schoedsack said Ben Johnson "made working on *Joe Young* something more of a delight—he would have fit right in with the original *Kong* company."

Johnson, the Oklahoma-born son of a world-champion steer-roper, broke into pictures as a horse-wrangler in the 1940s, then "doubled for [John] Wayne, [Gary] Cooper and others for five or six years," as he told us in 1969. "Then, Mr. [John] Ford put me under a seven-year contract as an actor. My first [starring] picture was *Mighty Joe Young*. If it hadn't been for Mr. Ford, Mr. Cooper and Mr. Schoedsack, I wouldn't have a dime now. They made me save my money and invest it."

Johnson said he took a tremendous interest in the special-effects work: "I worked on *Mighty Joe Young* about six months, but it took them over a year to finish it because of all the animation and special effects. I watched Willis O'Brien a lot, at the shop, and was with him at his office a lot. He was great—I think the best man they ever had in that field. I had to be there to consult with him on a lot of the technical stuff, like what a horse can do and how to ride and rope. For an action animation scene, like if you ride a horse and rope a calf, it takes 14 shots for each movement. It takes 14 shots when you twirl the rope, 14 shots to throw the rope, 14 shots for the rope to reach the critter and 14 shots for the critter to get roped."

Joe's production company, Arko, Inc., was organized expressly for the picture's sake by RKO-Radio and Argosy Pictures, an outfit owned by John Ford and Merian Cooper. The reunion-like

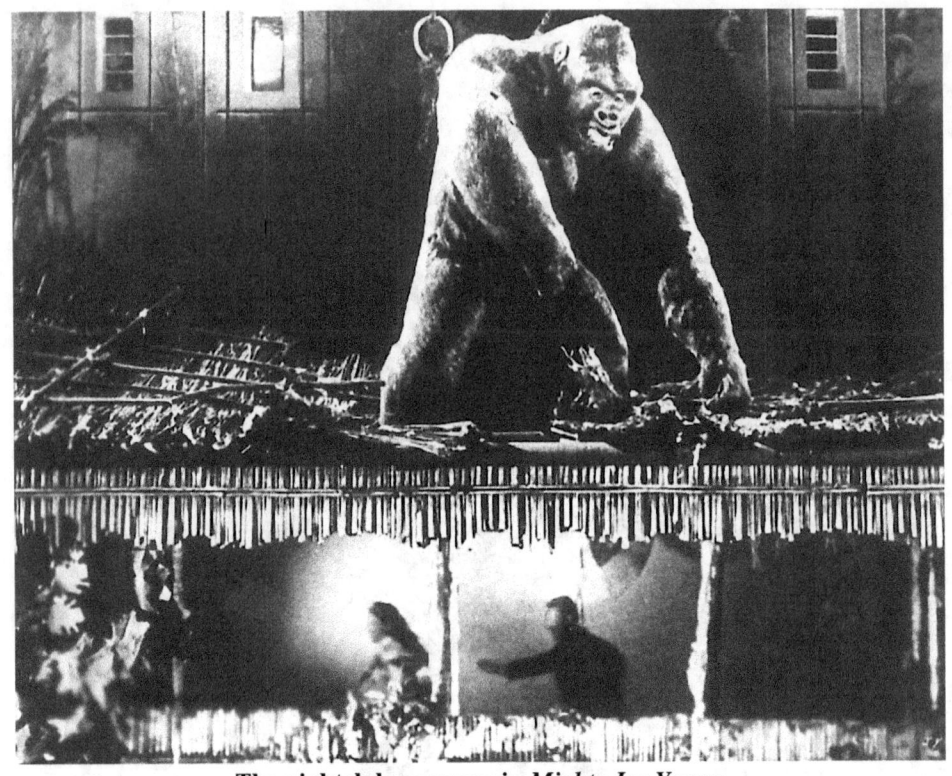

The nightclub rampage in *Mighty Joe Young*

aspect ran deep: In addition to Armstrong and the key behind-the-scenes creators of *Kong*, there were actors James Flavin, Milton Shockley and Harry Strang; editor Ted Cheesman; animation technician Marcel Delgado; and cameraman Bert Willis.

The scene with "all those strongmen," which brought to a head the antagonisms between Schoedsack and Ford, was an elaborate display of celebrity-gimmick casting: Ten professional boxers and exhibition wrestlers, including former heavyweight champ Primo Carnera and grappler Charles Post, a.k.a. Man Mountain Dean, were pitted against the gorilla in a monumental game of tug-of-war. Here is one of the film's most striking effects, introducing each of the human dynamos as a marvel of intimidating strength and caricatured savagery—and then having Joe playfully show them up as though they were so many schoolchildren. Ruth Rose recalled that Carnera wallowed wholeheartedly in the charade, picturing himself so genuinely in combat with an imaginary gorilla that, at the end of the shoot, "Primo was shivering like a baby."

John Ford, according to Schoedsack, had wanted to present the guest antagonists as "just an impersonal mass of muscle," where Schoedsack insisted on introducing each man as a ferocious individual in his own right. Schoedsack's storytelling instincts prevailed, and the film is all the richer for that.

This feature-film début for animator Ray Harryhausen found the 27-year-old artisan working more closely with O'Brien than had been planned, asserting a self-taught mastery of the medium with real confidence. "OBie had nothing to prove, no tendency to lord it over the new kid on the block," Harryhausen told us, "and he listened to my ideas as though I were more of a colleague than I actually could have been at the time. OBie was the master, and I the student, but his attitude was one of acceptance, of enthusiasm to teach and to learn in the process." This last big-picture assignment for O'Brien—short of his farewell on *It's a Mad, Mad, Mad, Mad World*, that is—marked the beginning of a distinguished major-league career for Harryhausen.

O'Brien told Schoedsack that Harryhausen impressed him "right off the bat" by coming well prepared to *Joe Young*: "He had read up on gorillas, and he had made careful notes from his own viewings of my earlier pictures, so he actually brought ideas for refinements that were inspiring to me." Once a decisive look had been established for Joe—who started out as a more natural-looking gorilla, but was modified to sport a set of childlike, larger-than-normal eyes—several models were built, ranging in height from five to 18 inches. The fur came from unborn lambs, providing a denser surface that would not ripple as noticeably as King Kong's rabbit-pelt covering. Miniature human figures, lions, horses and vehicles completed the array of animation properties.

The final tab on *Mighty Joe Young* came to $1.8 million, but the box-office returns were disappointing. O'Brien received the Oscar for Best Special Effects.

An unattributed knock-off of *Joe Young* surfaced in 1982 as *E.T., the Extraterrestrial*, from Steven Spielberg. A formal remake, from 1998, of *Mighty Joe Young* is chiefly of interest in the immediate context for its handful of homages to the source film: Ray Harryhausen and Terry Moore have a shared cameo appearance. Bill Paxton lobbied for and won the leading heroic role on the strength of a lifelong idolization of Ben Johnson. Johnson and Paxton had worked together on two pictures, the crime melodrama *Back to Back* in 1989 and the Southern-fried soap-opera *The Evening Star* (Johnson's final picture) in 1996.

CREDITS: Presented by: John Ford and Merian C. Cooper; Director: Ernest B. Schoedsack; Screenplay: Ruth Rose; Story: Merian C. Cooper; Technical Creator: Willis H. O'Brien; Photographed by: J. Roy Hunt; Optical Effects: Linwood Dunn; Operative Cameraman: Emmett Bergholz; Gaffer: Frank Uecker; Stills: Alex Kahle; Photographic Effects: Howard Stine and Bert Willis; Art Director: James Basevi; Assistant Art Director: Howard Richmond; Film Editor: Ted Cheesman; Set Dressing: George Altwies; Customer: Adele Balkan; Musical Director: Constantin Bakaleinokoff; Musical Score: Roy Webb; Song: "Beautiful Dreamer," by Stephen Foster; Sound: John L. Cass and Clem Portman; Sound Editor: Walter Elliott; Makeup: Gordon Bau and Harry Ray; Hair Stylists: Hazel Rogers and Fae Smith; First Technician: Ray Harryhausen; Second Technician: Peter Peterson; Technical Staff: George Lofgren, Marcel Delgado and Fitch Fulton; Unit Production Manager: Lloyd Richards; Production Effects: Jack Lannon; Script Supervisor: Dorothy Cormack; Grip: Louis Anderson; Running Time: 94 Minutes; Released: July 30, 1949

CAST: Terry Moore (Jill Young); Ben Johnson (Gregg Johnson); Robert Armstrong (Max O'Hara); Mr. Joseph Young of Africa (Himself); Frank McHugh (Windy); Douglas Fowley (Jones); Denis Green (Crawford); Paul Guilfoyle (Smith); Nestor Paiva (Brown); Regis Toomey (Young); Lora Lee Michel (Jill at Age 7); James Flavin (Schultz); Madame Sul-Te-Wan (Kifa); Cliff Clark (McManus); Primo Carnera, Charles "Man Mountain Dean" Post, the Super Swedish Angel, Ivan Batchelor, Ivan Rasputin, Sammy Stein, Sammy Menacker, Wee Willie Davis, Henry Kulky and Karl Davis (Strongmen); Joel Fluellen and Mansfield Collins (Tall Natives); Kermit Maynard (Red); Fred Kennedy, Frank McGrath, Dick Farnsworth and Bryan Hightower (Cowboys); Robert Johnson (Ali); Milton Shockley (Native); Edward Short (Ahmed); Mary Field (Secretary); Ray Walker and William Newell (Agents); Byron Foulger (Jones); Eugene Borden (Costume Designer); Max Willenz (Caricaturist); Chester Clute (Doctor); Janet Warren (Receptionist); Kay Christopher, Ellen Corby, Ann Archer and Luella Bickmore (Nurses); Hal Melone (Bank Messenger); David McKim (Soda Jerk); Cerrita Camargo and Leonard Bluett (Dancers); Lee Tung Foo, Jack Gargan, Joe Gray and Dick Ryan (Waiters); Pat Barton (Cigarette Girl); John Gallaudet, Michael Brandon, Al Murphy, Joe Devlin and Joey Ray (Reporters); Bill Wallace (Player); Billy Wayne (Stage Manager); Charles Lane and James Burke (Producers); Irene Ryan (Southerner); Juan Varro (Gigolo)

THE SONG OF KONG (1971)
a.k.a.: KONG MANIA: A STUDY IN PLANNED INSANITY
(Fort Decibel Audio Studio, Santa Monica)

The start of the 1970s found Ernest B. Schoedsack long since retired from the picture-making business, which he considered incidental to his career, at any rate. He had grown increasingly impatient with a barrage of questions, whether fannish or scholarly, about *King Kong*. Nearly blind but as creative and intellectually adventurous as ever, Schoedsack immersed himself in music appreciation and sound-recording technology. In Fort Decibel, his backyard recording studio, he worked at refining existing music, dictating audio letters and occasionally recording his poetry (such as "The Tale of the *Wisdom II*," a humorous account of the 1923 shipwreck) and songs. Schoedsack's hobby was typical of the artist—the last in a lifetime of pioneering ventures, approached almost offhandedly but foreshadowing the industry-standard devices of sampling and Audio Collage, as refined several years later in (unrelated) commercial projects by such artists as David Byrne, Van Dyke Parks, Frank Zappa and George Clinton.

For "The Song of Kong," Schoedsack combined audio from *King Kong*, as recorded from a television broadcast by a friend, with his own vocal performance. He distributed the finished result among his circle of friends. Fay Wray was somewhat offended by a stanza in the first version, so Schoedsack altered the lines and recorded a new version. The following is a transcript of (with all deference to Miss Wray) that second presentation:

SCHOEDSACK: We have had in the past *King Kong* and *The Son of Kong*.
   Now we present *The Song of Kong*.
   A Cooper-Schoedsack Production.
   Inspired by Merian C. Cooper; written, produced and directed by Ernest B. Schoedsack.

(Music from *King Kong*.)

(Noble Johnson is heard chanting, in character as the tribal chief.)

ROBERT ARMSTRONG AS CARL DENHAM: Have you ever heard of—Kong—Kong—Kong—Kong—Kong—Kong—Kong—Kong—Kong—Kong—Kong—Kong...

(Voice fades as music swells.)

SCHOEDSACK: That monotonous refrain
   Hammers through my weary brain
   'Til I think I'll go insane—or I've gone.
   Ev'ry Sunday, come what may,

Some damned nut will surely say,
"Did you watch TV today? It was on."

(Fay Wray screams.)

SCHOEDSACK: Well, in case you didn't know,
Kong was made at RKO
Nearly 40 years ago—in '33.
It's a big, horrendous show,
And although the cost was low,
It has made a lot of dough—not for me.

(Fay Wray moans.)

SCHOEDSACK: This tall, dark and handsome lover—
See his picture on the cover—
Towered 50 feet above her—pretty Fay.
Beauty and the Beast's theme,
His the roar and hers the scream—
All from Merian Cooper's dream—so they say.

(Kong roars. Music swells. Fay Wray's screaming continues.)

Judging from *The Song of Kong*'s verses, Schoedsack probably would have appreciated *Queen Kong*.

SCHOEDSACK: All that lamentable noise
Disturbs an adult's poise
'Tis belovéd by little boys—of all ages.
Fay's terrifying screams
Give them pleasure, so it seems,
In the form of awful dreams—of Kong's rages.

(Fay Wray screams. Kong grunts. Sirens wail. Screaming continues.)

SCHOEDSACK: Will this racket ever stop?
Will I have to call a cop?
No! There's always a new crop—of devout.
I can't hear Max Steiner's score
In this terrible uproar
I can't take it any more—let me out!

(Sound effects: Footsteps; door slams.)

ARMSTRONG AS DENHAM: Have you ever heard of—Kong?

FRANK REICHER AS CAPT. ENGLEHORN: Why, yes.

CREDITS: Writer, Producer, Sound Engineer and Narrator: Ernest B. Schoedsack; Privately Distributed during 1971 *et seq.*

KING KONG (2005)
(Big Primate Pictures, New Zealand/Universal Pictures)

Pre-production drawing for Peter Jackson's King Kong

Academy Award–winning director Peter Jackson, after working his cinematic magic on Tolkien's *Lord of the Rings* saga, turns his attention to a childhood favorite—*King Kong*. The story remains true to Cooper and Schoedsack's vision while bringing state-of-the-art CGI animation to the beauty and the beast tale.

Credits: Director/Writer (Screenplay)/Producer: Peter Jackson; Producers: Fran Walsh, Jan Blenkin, Carolynne Cunningham; Writers: Merian C. Cooper (Story), Edgar Wallace (Story), Fran Walsh (Screenplay), Phillippa Boyens (Screenplay); Cinematography: Andrew Lesnie; Music: Howard Shore; Editor: Jamie Selkirk; Production Design: Grant Major

Cast: Naomi Watts (Ann Darrow); Jack Black (Carl Denham); Adrien Brody (Jack Driscoll); Andy Serkis (King Kong/Lumpy the Cook); Jamie Bell (Jimmy); Kyle Chandler (Bruce Baxter); Lobo Chan (Choy); Thomas Kretschmann (Captain Englehorn)

In a press interview Jackson remarked: "There is a generation of kids today that don't watch black and white films anymore, our generation does do that. I was fine. I love old films and I saw them all the way through my childhood and wasn't concerned at all. But your average teenage kid today just isn't interested in black and white films anymore. They won't watch them. Therefore,

the time has passed that *King Kong*, that lovable story, is really not being seen by the young kids so I just thought it's a very good time to do a remake of *Kong* that can preserve everything that I loved about the original. I don't want to change what I loved about it. I don't want to reinvent it because it doesn't need reinventing. It's not going to be different. It'll be everything that I love about the original. It is a wonderful story. I just thought it's a good time to give kids a realistic looking Kong because that's what they're going to respond to.

"I owe *King Kong* a huge debt personally because it really did get me wanting to be a filmmaker. I truly don't think I would have been a filmmaker if I hadn't been exposed to that movie on TV in New Zealand when I was about nine years old. It just got me so excited about fantasy and the escapism of film. I was swept away and transported to another world when I saw that film. It was a love affair that began at that point with me for fantastic cinema and storytelling."

King Kong's Ann Darrow: Left 1933's Fay Wray, Right 2005's Naomi Watts

In a *Newsweek* (12/6/04) interview when discussing the potential success of *King Kong* as compared to *Lord of the Rings* Jackson told reporter Jeff Giles, "To live the rest of your life trying to top *Lord of the Rings* would be a foolish and unsatisfying thing to do. So you set your sights on making a thoroughly entertaining movie so that people are not disappointed. It is highly unlikely *King Kong* will ever make more money than *Lord of the Rings*." The cheerfully optimistic writer Phillippa Boyens contradicted Jackson, "For the record, *Kong* is going to kick *Lord of the Rings*' ass! It will!"

The *LOTR* creative team of Jackson, Walsh and Boyens in 2003 were offered a 20 million dollar advance by Universal to write, direct and producer the *King Kong* remake. Fan sites are already in full gossip mode as they eagerly count down the days until the December 2005 release.

Jack Driscoll: Top 2005's Adrian Brody; Bottom 1933's Bruce Cabot

Carl Denham: Top 2005's Jack Black; Bottom 1933's Robert Armstrong

The Making of King Kong

"The Ancient Great Plains": George E. Turner's Dinosaur Comics

The comic strips that follow, amplified with anecdotal annotations, are excerpted from George Turner's earliest professional newspaper work of the post-WWII years. The fascination with prehistoric life—and dinosaurs in particular—is the very point of these cartoons, which reappear here for the first time since their original publication in the *Sunday News-Globe* of Amarillo, Texas. The guest-shot appearance of King Kong should come as no surprise.

Though he remained keen on finding a new venue for *The Ancient Great Plains*, George was also beset with doubts about trotting out what he considered his "juvenilia" for a new readership. Of course, George was all of 26 when he crafted the strip—an alumnus of the demanding tutelage of J. Allen St. John, Harold R. Foster and Ben Carlton Mead—and as savvy an amateur paleontologist as he was a working artist.

My restorations necessarily bypass the re-drawing that George had contemplated. Nor is there any point in bringing the information up to date. *The Ancient Great Plains* resurfaces here precisely as created during 1951-52, and as such it needs no superficial "refinements." George's technique improved—so what else is new?—as he cranked out assignment after assignment, and all that has proved necessary is the occasional retouch, working as I am from yellowed newspaper clippings.

—M.H.P.

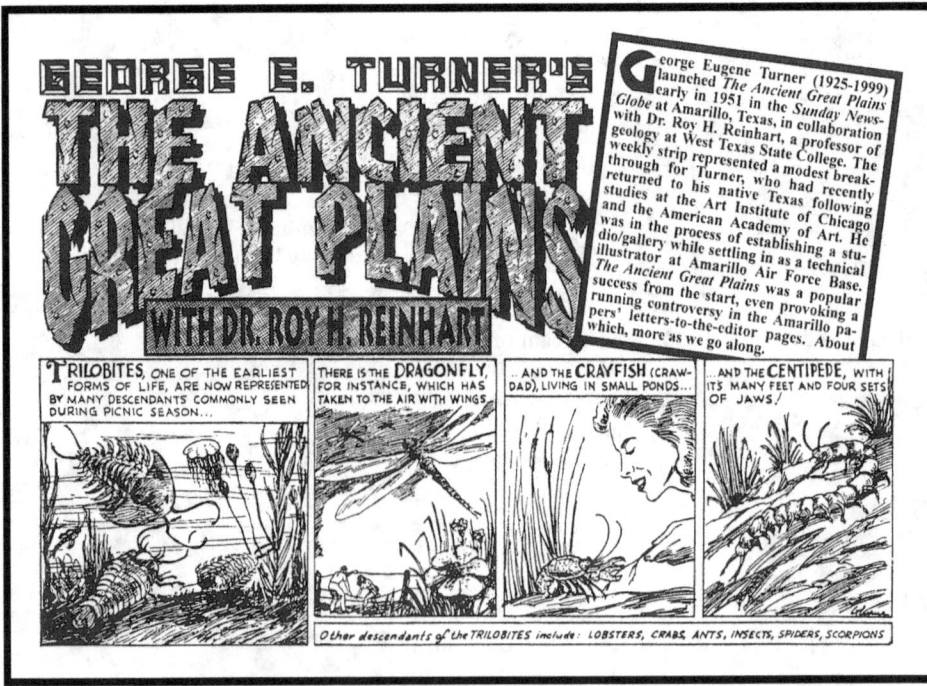

234   *Spawn of Skull Island*

George based the "teaser" at left, announcing the approach of the Turner & Reinhart feature, on a scene from *The Lost World*, the 1925 motion picture that had paved the way for *King Kong* (1933). *Kong*, in its turn, had set George as a child on a pastime-as-career path from which he never wavered. (The mighty Kong himself puts in a guest appearance in *The Ancient Great Plains*.)

George was, of course, also springing from Vince Hamlin's long-running comic strip, *Alley Oop* — which was a daily attraction in the Amarillo papers — and from Charles R. Knight's celebrated paintings, as well as the palaeontological research of Dr. Roy Chapman Andrews and the very prehistory of the Northwest Texas region where Amarillo is situated.

"Dr. Reinhart emphasizes that these strips are being done to increase popular geological interest," declared an announcement in *The Prairie*, the campus newspaper at West Texas State. *The Prairie* also noted that *Great Plains*' principal characters would include "cheesecake-type girls" — presumably in keeping with the professor's aim to foster popular interest.

It was during this period that George perpetrated one of the finer pranks in the history of self-serious acadaemia: One day while visiting the West Texas State campus' Panhandle-Plains Historical Museum — where Dr. Reinhart served as curator — George and fellow illustrator Gene A. Clardy were heading for the main galleries when it occurred to George that they had neglected to sign the guest register. Duly returning to the entrance, where a uniformed guard sat absorbed in a magazine, they approached the massive leatherbound tome. Giving in to a momentary inspiration, George signed a letter-perfect forgery of a famous signature: **Norman Rockwell.**

Turner and Clardy went on about their tour. "We were puttering about the cowboy exhibits," George

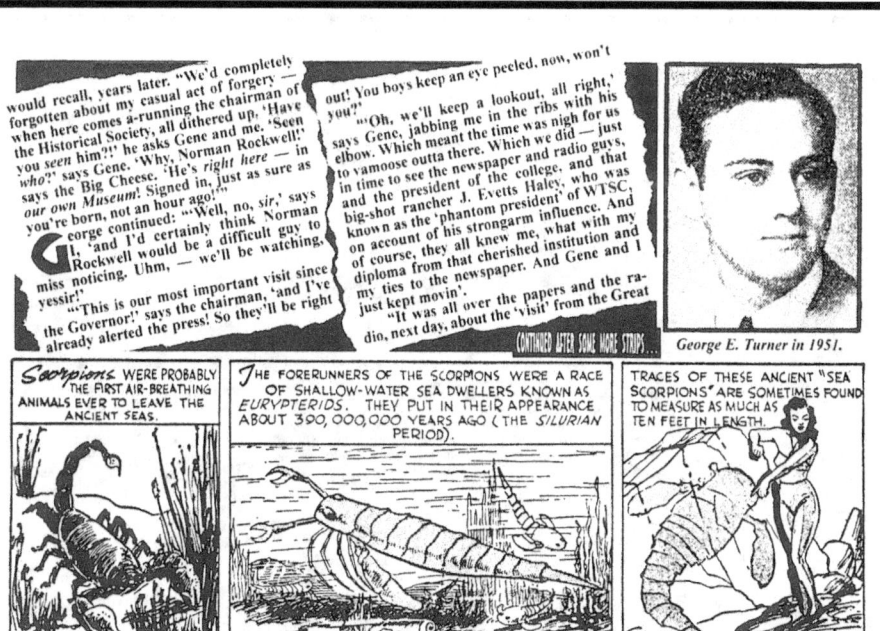

would recall, years later. "We'd completely forgotten about my casual act of forgery — when here comes a-running the chairman of the Historical Society, all dithered up. 'Have you *seen* him?!' he asks Gene and me. 'Seen *who*?' says Gene. 'Why, Norman Rockwell!' says the Big Cheese. 'He's *right here* — in our own Museum! Signed in, just as sure as you're born, not an hour ago!'"

George continued: "'Well, no, sir,' says I, 'and I'd certainly think Norman Rockwell would be a difficult guy to miss noticing. Uhm, — we'll be watching, yessir!'

"'This is our most important visit since the Governor!' says the chairman, 'and I've already alerted the press! So they'll be right

out! You boys keep an eye peeled, now, won't you?'

"'Oh, we'll keep a lookout, all right,' says Gene, jabbing me in the ribs with his elbow. Which meant the time was nigh for us to vamoose outta there. Which we did — just in time to see the newspaper and radio guys, and the president of the college, and that big-shot rancher J. Evetts Haley, who was known as the 'phantom president' of WTSC, on account of his strongarm influence. And of course, they all knew me, what with my diploma from that cherished institution and my ties to the newspaper. And Gene and I just kept movin'.

"It was all over the papers and the radio, next day, about the 'visit' from the Great

CONTINUED AFTER SOME MORE STRIPS...

George E. Turner in 1951.

The Making of King Kong

Man. Somebody had finally thought to place a call to Norman Rockwell's studio — and determined right off that he was nowhere within shouting distance of the Texas Plains, except by telephone. It was a great story, of the 'non-story' variety. Gene's and my role in it would have made it an even keener non-story, but we kept mum. I mean, for *years* we kept mum."

George and Dr. Reinhart had a localized hit on their hands from the beginning of *The Ancient Great Plains*, but the Amarillo Globe-News Co. neglected to seize upon any potential for syndication, not even bothering to share the feature with a sister newspaper in nearby Lubbock. A vigorous letters-to-the-editor response found readers likening George's artwork to the Chas. Knight paintings in Chicago's Field Museum — George was too modest to agree — and inquiring: "Could you give it more space ...?"

One reader, however, promptly launched an impassioned crackpot tirade that threatened to become a series in its own right: "None can with impunity question Dr. Roy H. Reinhart's statistics or factual data," wrote Benjamin Max Franklin, "but his conclusions that the animals roamed these plains and the fish swam

these seas are based on rate-of-erosion, rate and method of strata-forming, and rate of evolution, the true factors of which he has not the slightest glimmering."

Quoth Mr. Franklin further: "The facts are: (1) None of these animals lived here, they were merely buried here. (2) The guiding factors by which the date or time or age are determined are not yet known. Dr. Reinhart's million [years] could be a thousand or a billion," continued the indignant Mr. Franklin. "Hope you cither change these comic strips or else refuse to present them as factual or near factual."

Dr. Reinhart promptly replied: "[I]t appears that the people who study the sciences of geology, palaeontology and archaeology are all out of step with Mr. Franklin ... I humbly admit I have much to learn ... I should certainly like to have Mr. Franklin publish his ideas on the source of the animals found in the [Texas] Panhandle ... If I may use a present-day analogy of Mr. Franklin's theme, 'The people and animals now in Amarillo do not live there; they will merely be buried there.'"

And as to determination of time, Reinhart cited the standard of carbon dating, as subsidized by the federal government since 1940: "When I say a million, I am quoting the physicists; they mean aproximately a million, not a thousand nor a billion."

Undaunted, Mr. Franklin cut loose with a *long* reply, prefaced with these words: "Frankly, the astronomers, geologists, archaeologists, anthropologists, and palaeontologists are out of step."

Here, Franklin asserted a case for a non-rotating Earth, whose spinning would have finally begun "in historic times." He insisted that "the plants and animals that adapted to [this] drastically warmer climate followed [an] ancient sea until it dried up and they were destroyed by the heat." And the scarcity of signs of early humankind (!) was ascribed to indications "only that

CONTINUED

[man] was able to escape the floods or that he ... lived in an area that was not subject to the most violent floods."

Dr. Reinhart published no reply to this posting. Indeed, the professor was getting ready to leave the Great Plains to join the faculty of Miami University at Oxford, Ohio. George Turner carried on ably as a solo with *The Ancient Great Plains*, keeping the feature rooted in science but becoming ever more adventurous with its presentation. In 1952, *Amateur Art & Camera Magazine* devoted an elaborate feature article to the strip, describing George's savvy use of photographs as models for illustration and hailing his ambitious expansion from newspaper cartooning into books and magazines. *The Ancient Great Plains* had run its course during 1952, but it transformed itself immediately into *The Palo Duro Story*. In this more expansive comics feature, George would relate the story of the Spanish invasion of the Southwestern Plains.

Which is, of course, the proverbial story for another day. George Turner was gradually insinuating himself into the

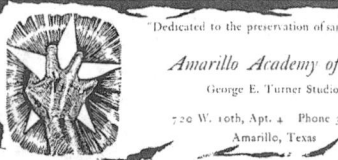

Amarillo papers' newsroom, where he felt more "at home" than he had among the U.S. Air Force bureaucrats or within West Texas' small but stuffy Art Snob community. *The Ancient Great Plains* had made George a phenomenally popular writer-illustrator, even without the prestige of syndication, and the *Globe-News* would provide a nurturing climate for a goodly number of years to follow.

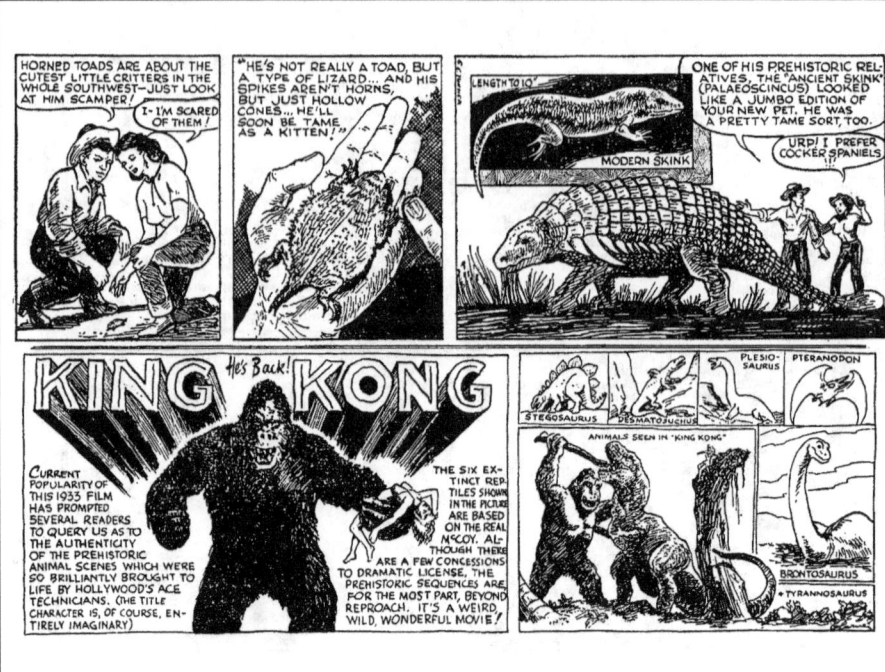

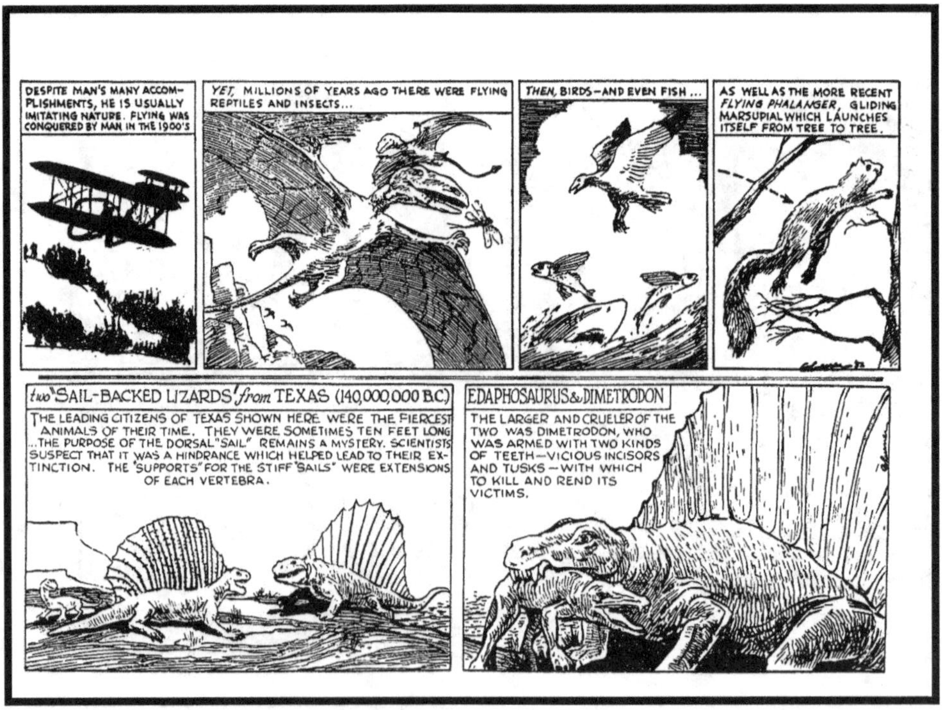

The Lost "She" Comic Strip

The following restoration comes from yellowed and glue-saturated proof sheets that George Turner had kept on file since his childhood. The *She* comic-strip adaptation was commissioned as a promotional device for Merian Cooper's 1935 opus, and was offered free-of-charge to newspapers to run in briefly serialized form around the time of the film's release. Little seen even in its day, the strip is herewith dragged back into the light for the first time. The writer-artist credits seem unlikely to reveal themselves at this late stage; the illustrations betray the influence of Harold R. Foster (best remembered for the early *Tarzan* strip and, later, for *Prince Valiant*) and Alex Raymond (of *Secret Agent X-9*, *Flash Gordon*, *Jungle Jim* and, later, *Rip Kirby*).
—M.H.P.

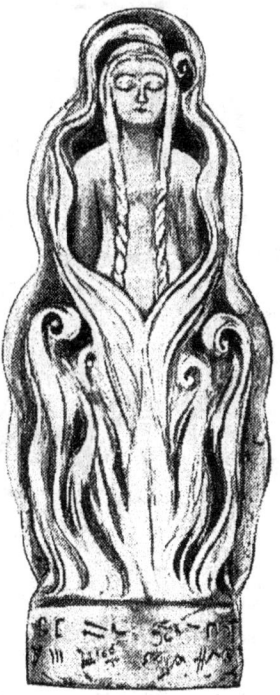

Merian C. Cooper, the guiding intellect behind the 1933 *King Kong*, turned to H. Rider Haggard's epic fantasy *She* for the inspiration of a 1935 film of the same title. Where the screen adaptation served Haggard admirably well, the picture also yielded such promotional detritus as a comic-strip adaptation that might more properly be called *Classics Eviscerated*. This odd condensation was designed to be run in newspapers, in six daily installments, at the time of the film's release — following the storyline smartly enough in its way, but rather foolishly giving away the ending. A restoration follows here — presented intact for the first time since 1935, with the original rambling captions.

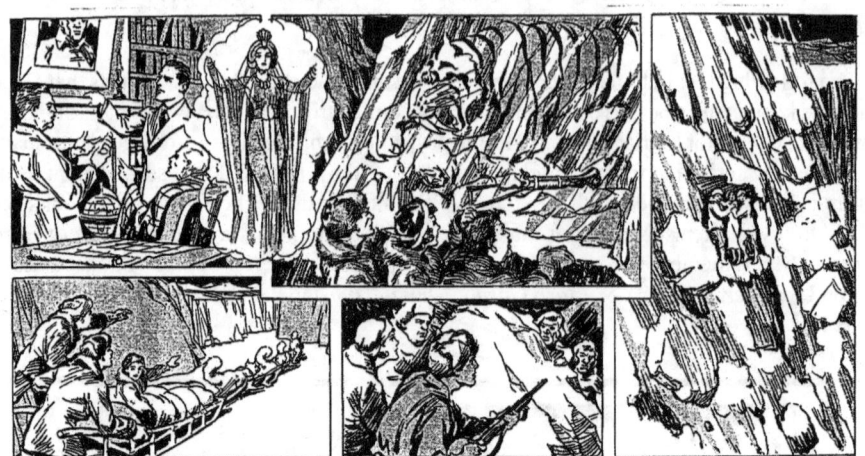

John Vincey, an English scientist who is dying of radium poisoning, sends for his nephew, Leo Vincey, to tell him to seek the mysterious realm of "SHE," where burns the Flame of Life that makes it possible to triumph over death. The secret has been handed down by an ancestor who perished in a previous attempt to solve it and is known only to Vincey and his associate, Archibald Holly. Accordingly, Leo and Holly set out for the secret land, and after many days of arduous travel over the wastes of Muscovy, the amazed party stumble upon the members of the ancient Vincey expedition – frozen in ice and kept intact for 500 years after they were killed by a sabre-toothed tiger. Immediately after the discovery, a landslide destroys the entire party except for the two men and Tanya, daughter of their guide. The disaster reveals a passage through the glacial barrier into a hollow mountain, where they are seized by savage Amahagger cannibals.

The savage Amahagger Cannibals choose Holly as a likely victim for their quaint "hot potting" ceremony, which consists of placing a red-hot metal pot over the victim's head prior to making a meal of him. Leo attempts to save Holly and protect Tanya from the savages single-handedly, but this unequal battle proves too much for him. Already wounded, he is about to be killed when the three are rescued by an old man, Billali, prime minister to "SHE," and attended by soldiers. Billali announces to the exhausted trio that they are to be taken to She-Who-Must-Be-Obeyed, ruler of Kor. They set out for the distant palace of "SHE," with the wounded Leo carried on a litter. Soldiers and the now-captive cannibals follow in the rear. The party travel the mountain cliffs until they reach a clearing disclosing a most incredible valley of radiant beauty, In the center lies the palace of "SHE," carved out of a gigantic piece of living rock.

The party go straight to the great gates of the stone palace of Kor which, when opened for them, reveals a gigantic inner chamber to the throne room. A slave strikes a huge metal ring suspended from the ceiling, which is the signal that announces their arrival. These tremendous inner doors open, and the adventurers face an impressive series of stairs at the apex of which sits a woman of breathtaking fascination. In is "SHE," the mysterious and deathless ruler of Kor. "SHE" addresses Holly and Tanya, but it is soon apparent that her main interest rests upon the silent form of Leo, who lies wounded on the litter. "SHE" commands that Leo be brought near her, and addresses him as *John Vincey*. It is now evident that "SHE" is the *same* woman who loved the original John Vincey, 500 years before. Soon, her strange ministrations revive Leo, and "SHE" speaks to him of her great love – a passion that has waited for centuries.

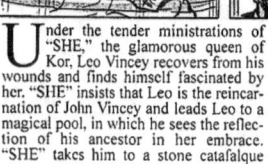

Under the tender ministrations of "SHE," the glamorous queen of Kor, Leo Vincey recovers from his wounds and finds himself fascinated by her. "SHE" insists that Leo is the reincarnation of John Vincey and leads Leo to a magical pool, in which he sees the reflection of his ancestor in her embrace. "SHE" takes him to a stone catafalque upon which lies a body, identical in appearance to Leo. This body is that of John Vincey, his ancestor, who died 500 years before. "SHE" now declares that *he* has come back to her and proceeds to pour a secret liquid over the body, whereupon it vanishes into a vapor. "SHE," meanwhile, is so angered at the savage Amahaggers who attacked Leo that she orders them cast into the Pit of Torture. Leo discloses his real mission to her kingdom and shows her the emblem of the flame given to him by his uncle in England. "SHE," now even more confident that Leo is her long-awaited lover, tries to persuade him to remain with her, offering him eternal life and promising safe conduct out of Kor for his friends.

The Making of King Kong

Billali, prime minister to "SHE," now sees in Leo Vincey a rival and a menace to his power over the Kingdom of Kor. He informs "SHE" that Tanya is in love with Leo and thus represents a threat to the plans of "SHE." Thereupon, the two conceive the diabolical plot of substituting Tanya for the slave girl who is to be sacrificed at the yearly Festival of the Flame in the great Hall of Kings. During this thrilling ceremony, and just as Tanya is about to be slain by a priest and thrown into the Pit of Fire, Leo recognizes the bound and veiled victim. He rushes to the pit and saves her. A terrific battle takes place, pitting Leo and Holly against priests and palace guards. A mad chase follows through an underground passage, to a precipice that is bridged by a huge overhanging rock balanced perilously. Leo, Holly and Tanya leap across safely, but the great weight of their pursuers overbalances the rock and they fall into the bottomless abyss to their deaths.

After their escape from "SHE's" warriors, Leo Vincey, his sweetheart Tanya, and their fellow adventurer Holly continue on into the rock passage and unknowingly enter the secret Cavern of the Flame, where they come face-to-face with "SHE" and Billali. And there in the center of the cavern is the Flame of Life, which flares up six times every hour. "SHE" taunts Tanya, ordering that Leo is to bathe in the flame and live forever while Tanya must grow old and die. Leo declares that he prefers mortal existence with Tanya over loveless eternal life with "SHE." "SHE" attempts to tempt Leo by offering to demonstrate the life-giving properties of the flame. So saying, "SHE" walks into the Pit and calls upon the Flame to continue to preserve her life, youth and beauty. What happens at this climactic moment is the most amazing incident of the story and provides a solution for the dilemma of Leo, his sweetheart and their staunch companion in adventure.

Afterword by Sam Calvin

Age has not withered nor custom staled his infinite ferocity. His appeal seems timeless, so much so that the early prediction of his impact persisting "even in 1960" now amuses us with its quaintness. The jagged charcoal grandeur of King Kong awakens in us a sense of wonder, an awe that is oddly bracing and enticing. The shores of Skull Island may be frightening and dangerous, but we'll take our chances. "It's too late—they've seen us!" We don't want to live anywhere else.

To be sure, before Kong others had whetted our taste for the Promised Land. There was the poetry of a Karloff, the suavity of a Lugosi, the pathos of a Chaney. But for many of us the love affair started with Kong. After all, we were the sons of *Famous Monsters* whose daydreams and nightmares were fueled by that freshly minted miracle, television. During the 1950s, Kong's exploits proved to be a top attraction on the tube, and his success helped to usher in the days of *Shock Theatre*.

As a Monster Kid recently asked, why did the natives build a massive wall to hold Kong in, only to add a massive door to let Kong out? Here's an answer: The door was built for our benefit, and Kong forced it open to help us come home. First Kong freed his Gothic fathers, and we embraced them with the same love that we first gave to the smitten beast. Then Kong's children arose from their primordial slumber, summoned by his mighty roar. While they always stood in their father's shadow, the best of them could also take us where we yearned to be. Kong, his fathers, and his children taught us to love the fantastic. These ancients kept us young. Their strides took root in our souls.

As they say, the perfect is the enemy of the good. Marcel Delgado's gritty giants have been stripped of flesh and tendon pixel by pixel, replaced by sleek and soulless images glowing on a bitmapped screen. The exquisite, hand-wrought glass vistas of Byron Crabbe and Mario Larrinaga have been Photoshopped out of existence. The rough-hewn spirit of life that Willis O'Brien breathed into a small jointed figure has been tamed—nay, emasculated—by the all-too-smooth movements of calibrated wireframes. But Kong endures. Rubber and plastic linked to wood and metal, fashioned by a master artist, brought to savage life by the patience, skill and love of a genius, the Eighth Wonder of the World is better known today than the other Seven. This Giant and God of the world he knew, whose brush with Beauty made him "as one dead," will outlive us all.

(From 1971 to 1974, Sam Calvin, with Ernest Farino, published the magazine *FXRH*, dedicated to the coverage of Special Visual Effects Created by Ray Harryhausen. Calvin and Farino continue to work together on various projects. The curtain first rose on "The Sam & Ernie Show," as the animator Jim Danforth has described the colleagues' work, during a university campus screening of *King Kong*.)

Spawn of Skull Island

Index

A-P-E 37, 63-64
Abbott, Bud 52
Abdullah, Achmed 79
Abominable Snowman of the Himalayas, The 56
Acquanetta 49-50
Action in Arabia 171
Adams, Don 17
Admirable Crichton, The 94, 200
Adventure to the Center of the Earth 45
Africa Screams 52
Africa Speaks 134
Alien (and sequels) 10, 123
All That Money Can Buy 21, 223
Allen, David 64
Allen, Irwin 58
Alley Oop 35, 36-37
"Along the Moonbeam Trail" 88
Altered States 57
Amazing Colossal Man, The (and sequel) 55, 166
Amazon Women on the Moon 66
American Society of Composers, Authors & Publishers 17
Among the Living 47
Andress, Ursula 218
Andriot, Lucien 149
Angkor, or Forbidden Adventure (in *Angkor*) 42
Animal World, The 55, 62
Ankrum, Morris 55
Anna Christie 134
Ape, The (1909; see: *The Human Ape; or, Darwin's Triumph*)
Ape, The (1940) 46
Ape Man, The 49
Ape Woman, The 59
Arabia 167
Arlen, Richard 80, 107
Armstrong, Robert 25, 26, 41, 108, 110-111, 125-126, 143-144, 145, 163, 181, 205, 207, 213-214, 226, 230-231, 233
Arness, James 53
Arnold, Jack 57
Arthur, Jean 79
"Arthur Jermyn" 43

Ashbuck, Lloyd Arthur 187
Astaire, Fred 21
At the Earth's Core 63
Attack of the 50 Ft. Woman 166
Atwill, Lionel 44, 138
Auer, Mischa 43
Austin, Charlotte 58
Autry, Gene 188
Ayesha 217
Ayres, Agnes 38
Baby... Secret of the Lost Legend 65
Bach, Barbara 64
Back to Back 229
Back to Bataan 178
Bacon, Lloyd 42
"Bad, Bad Leroy Brown" 102
Bakaleinikoff, Constantin 178
Balfe, Victoria (see: Shaw, Sandra)
Balaoo, the Demon Baboon 38, 40
Balderston, John L. 215
Bambi 68
Bamboula (see *Gwangi*)
Banks, Leslie 108-109, 205
Barnum, P.T. 17, 22
Barre, Emily 222
Barrie, J.M. (James) 94
Barrier, Edgar 224-225
Barry, Philip 19
Barrymore, John 134, 144, 159
Bat Whispers, The 93
Batman (comics character) 47
Baylor, Jan 56
Beast from 20,000 Fathoms, The 9, 37, 53, 58, 59, 159
Beast of Borneo 44
Beast of Hollow Mountain 52, 55-56, 221, 222
Beautiful Greek Girl, The 175, 177
Beebe, Dr. William 28, 76-77, 121
Beery, Noah 38, 80
Beery, Wallace 39, 77, 91, 92, 93, 219
Before Dawn 100, 217
Behemoth, the Sea Monster 10, 58, 59, 159
Bela Lugosi Meets a Brooklyn Gorilla 53

Bellamy, Ralph 213
Belmore, Lionel 42
Ben Burbidge's African Gorilla Hunt (see: *Gorilla Hunt, The*)
Benchley, Robert 120
Bendix, William 51
Bennett, Constance 149
Bennison, Andrew 40
Beranger, André 42
Bergman, Sandahl 218
Berkeley, Busby 140
Berman, Pandro S. 25
Berova, Olinka 218
Besser, Joe 52, 128
Best, Willie 43
Bickford, Charles 134
Bird of Paradise 140
Birell, Tala 215
Birth of a Nation, The 33
Bitzer, G.W. "Billy" 38, 96
Black, Jack 232-233
Black Scorpion, The 10, 56-57, 157, 159
Black Zoo 59
Blakeley, Colin 61
Blind Adventure 212-213
Bloch, Robert 152
Block, Ralph 120
Blood on the Sun 125
"Blues Passover" 10
Boleslawski, Norma 115
Boone, Pat 58
Boone, Richard 64
Boyd, William "Bill" 138
Boyens, Phillippa 232-233
Brackett, Charles 189-190
Bradbury, Ray 8-9
Brady, Ed 181
Brennan, Kevin 65
Brennan, Ryan 33, 35, 55-56, 64, 65
Bride and the Beast, The 58
Bride of Frankenstein 215
Bride of the Gorilla 53
Bridges, Beau 52
Bridges, Jeff 63
Brigati, Steve 42
Broadcast Music, Inc. 17
Broderick, Matthew 67
Brook, Clive 80, 107
Brooks, Albert 67
Brosnan, John (as Knight,

Harry Adam) 67
Brown, Dr. Barnum 87
Brown, Karl 25, 96, 201-203
Browne, Lucile 127
Browning, Tod 114
Brownlow, Kevin 75
Bruce, Nigel 217-218
Brute Force 38, 40, 44, 92
Budd, Ruth 38
Buildings
Chrysler Building 24, 65
Empire State Building 17, 20, 24, 27, 31, 65, 161, 166, 178, 189
New York Life Building 24
World Trade Center 64
Bulwer-Lytton, Sir Edward 219
Burbidge, Ben (see: *Gorilla Hunt, The*)
Burden, W. Douglas 23, 24, 82
Burns, Fat 151
Burr, Raymond 53, 55
Burroughs, Edgar Rice 63
Burton, Robert 57
Byrne, David 230
Cabot, Bruce 9, 25, 26, 110, 112-113, 124-125, 131-132, 138, 144, 145, 154, 157, 162-163, 168, 233
Cady, Jerry 222
Cagney, James 159
Caine, Michael 68
Calhern, Louis 144
Cameron, James 33
Cannibal Island (see: *Gow, the Head Hunter*)
Captive Wild Woman (and sequels) 49-50
Jungle Captive 50
Jungle Woman 50
Carnera, Primo 228
Carnosaur (and sequels) 36, 67
Carpenter, Edward Childs 41
Carr, Trem 221
Carradine, John 49, 50, 55, 57
Carter, Louise 209
Casablanca 183
Cat and the Canary, The 41, 43
Cat People 21
Cavalcade 187, 189
Cave, George 222
Caveman 64, 203

Celeste, Olga 108, 201-202
Cerisoli, John 30, 144, 148
Chaney, Lon 40, 159
Chaney, Lon, Jr. 44
Chang 18, 23, 77-81, 82, 115, 120, 121-122, 171, 196-199
Chang, Wah Ming 214
Chaplin, Charles 17, 40
Charlie Chan (series) 179
Chayefsky, Paddy 57
Cheesman, Ted 146, 169, 228
Christadoro, Charles 200
Christie, Al 215
Churchill, Douglas W. 221
Cider House Rules, The 67-68, 192
Cimarron 93, 96, 175, 200, 208
"Cinematography as an Art Form" 159
Cinerama 190, 226 (*This Is Cinerama*)
Citizen Kane 21, 188
Clark, Carroll 107, 149
Clemente, Steve (Esteban) 18, 29, 113, 121-122, 127, 181, 205
Clemento, Steve (see: Clemente, Steve)
Cleveland, George 223
Clinton, George 230
Clockwork Orange, A 60
Clothier, William 150
Cohen, Herman 59, 62
Cohen, Larry 64-65
Cohn, Harry 221
Colvig, Pinto 148
Conan (series) 218
Congolaise 52
Connell, Richard 107, 108, 205
Cooper, Gary 227
Cooper, Mrs. Gary (see: Shaw, Sandra)
Cooper, Merian C. 8, 17, 18, 21, 22, 25, 26, 29, 31, 33, 69-75, 76-81, 82-85, 86, 97-100, 102, 107, 109-114, 119, 120-124, 134, 143, 145, 146, 151, 152-153, 158, 160, 165-166, 168-171, 174-177, 180, 190, 191 (death of), 198, 203, 205-207, 209, 215, 217, 219-220, 225-229
Cooper-Schoedsack Productions 69-75, 76-81, 126, 170, 190, 194, 195-198, 204, 205,

212, 218, 230
Corman, Roger 36, 67
Corrigan, Ray "Crash" 46, 51, 52
Cortez, Ricardo 207
Costello, Lou 52
Crabbe, Byron 27, 30, 94-95, 96, 107, 147, 153, 164, 183, 200
Crabbe, Larry "Buster" 50, 113
Craig, James 223
Crater Lake Monster, The 64
Crawford, Joan 62
Crazy Knights 50
Creation 21, 25, 26, 94, 95-99, 101, 102, 105-106, 114, 121, 130, 135, 148, 150, 154, 170, 195, 200-203, 221, 223
Creature (see: *Titan Find*)
Creelman, James Ashmore 25, 26, 76, 102, 107, 108, 111, 120
Creeping Flesh, The 62
Crichton, Michael 67
Cristadoro, Charles 214
Croce, Jim 102
Cromelin, Paul W. 89
Cromwell, John 107
Cronjager, Edward 149
"Cucaracha, La" 215, 217
Cunningham, Harry 222
"Curious Pets of Our Ancestors" 87
Curtain at Eight 44
Curtis, Dick 127
Cusack, John 65
Cushing, Peter 56, 62
Cyclops, The 55
Dahmer, Jeffrey 36
Danforth, Jim 60
Dangling Death 10
Daniels, Walter 146
Dark Carnival 9
Darmour, Larry 225
Darrow, Clarence 42-43
Darwin's Triumph (see: *The Human Ape; or, Darwin's Triumph*)
Davis, Bette 178
Dawley, Herbert M. 39, 88, 89, 91
Dawn Patrol, The 126
Day, Alice 41
De Bujac, Jacques (see: Cabot, Bruce)
Dead Men Don't Wear Plaid

10, 65
Death Watch (see: *Before Dawn*)
Dee, Frances 217
DeLaurentiis, Dino 22, 63, 66
Delgado, Marcel 25, 26, 30, 68, 89-93, 95-100, 105, 116, 117, 134, 151, 154, 163, 170, 182-183, 200, 209, 220, 221-222, 224, 228
De Mille, Cecil B. 21, 94, 139, 218, 222
Denning, Richard 52, 57
Dern, Laura 67
Devil Commands, The 49
De Witt, Louis 56
Del Rio, Dolores 149
Dieterle, William 223
Dietrich, Marlene 217
Dillon, John Webb 38
Dinosaur 68
"Dinosaur and the Missing Link, The" 87, 192
Dinosaur Island 66
Dinosaurus! 58-59, 222
Disney, Walt 46
Divine Comedy, The 103, 154
Dix, Beulah Marie 94-95, 120, 200
Dix, Richard 149, 172
Dixiana 175
Dr. Cyclops 182, 190, 225
Dr. Demento Show, The 35
Dr. Jekyll & Mr. Hyde 53, 108
Dr. Renault's Secret 48-49
Dr. X 138
Dmytryk, Edward 49-50
Donohue, Jack 175
Doré, Gustave 30, 102, 153-154
Douglas, Melvyn 217
Dowling, William 91
Doyle, Sir Arthur Conan 25, 61, 89, 91, 193-194
Dracula (1931) 215, 223
Dracula (Hammer series) 56
Dragon Lizards of Komodo, The 23, 82
du Chiallu, Paul 24
Dunn, Linwood 32, 137, 150, 152, 191, 208
Dunne, Irene 149
Dunning, C. Dodge and Carroll; and Dunning Process 92, 99, 101, 134-136, 145, 201, 203
Dupont, E.A. 53, 57
Durante, Jimmy 52

Durbin, Deanna 188
E.T., the Extraterrestrial *229*
Earles, Harry 40
Edeson, Arthur 91
Eisley, Anthony 61
Eliscu, Edward 184
Elliott, Laura 53
Elliott, Walter G. 173
Eltz, Theodore von 80
Enchanted Island, The *214*
Escape of the Ape, The *38*
Evening Star, The *229*
Explorations and Adventures in Equatorial Africa *24*
Fahrenheit 451 9
Falwell, Jerry 35
Fantasia 46-47
Fauntleroy, Maj. Cedric E. 70
Fields, W.C. 47, 127
Fisher, G. Clyde 89
Flaherty, Robert 74
Flavin, James 127, 228
Fleischer Bros. 40, 154
Fletcher, Bramwell 209
Flintstones, The 35, 67
Flintstones in Viva Rock Vegas, The 67
Florey, Robert 43
"Flying Elephants" 40, 44
Food of the Gods, The *93*
Forbidden Fruit 42
Ford, John 144, 226-228
Forgotten Horrors (series) 42, 43, 44, 45, 46, 48, 49
Fort, Garrett 120
Fossey, Dian 66
Foster, Preston 218-219
Four Feathers, The 23, 80-81, 85, 115, 204, 205
Frankenstein (concept) 60, 64
Frankenstein (1931) 215
Frankenstein (Hammer series) 56, 62
Frankenstein and the Monster from Hell 62
Frankenstein Conquers the World 60
Franklin, Richard 66
Franz, Arthur 57
Fraser, Brendan 67
Fraser, Richard 51
Freund, Karl 129
Friday the 13th *36*
Friends of the Challenger Expedition 195
Frisco, Joe 42
From Hell It Came 59

Frost, Mark 206
Fuller Brush Co. 46
Fuller Brush Man, The 46
Fulton, John P. 137
Gahagan, Helen 217-218
Galataea 33
Game of Death, A 206, 224-225
Garbo, Greta 134, 217
Gemora, Charles 32, 40, 128, 137, 214-215
George White's Scandals 175
Gerard, Henry 115, 149
Gershwin, George 175
"Gertie the Dinosaur" 38
Ghost Jesters, The 45
"Ghost of Slumber Mountain, The" 25, 39, 88-89, 165, 192-193, 195, 221
Giant Behemoth, The (see: *Behemoth, the Sea Monster*)
Giant Claw, The 56, 59
Giant Gila Monster 58
Gibson, E.B. "Buz" 30, 109, 147-148, 164
Gigantis, the Fire Monster 45
Gilbert, Billy 50
Gilette, William 76
Girardot, Annie 59
Gleason, Duncan 220, 223
Gleason, Jimmy 125
Go and Get It 38-39
Godzilla (series) 54, 59, 65-66 (parody), 67 (1998),
Gojira (see: *Godzilla*)
Golden King, The (see: *Lost Empire, The*)
Goldner, Dr. Orville 13, 14, 31, 148, 150-151, 165, 201, 206, 209, 215
Goldthwait, Bobcat 65-66
Goodman, John 35, 67
Goofy (see: Colvig, Pinto)
Gone with the Wind 21, 187-188, 217
Gordon, Bert I. 55
Gorgo 59
Gorilla, The (1927) 41
Gorilla, The (1930) 42
Gorilla, The (1939)
The Gorilla, A Mystery in Three Acts 41
Gorilla at Large 55
"Gorilla Boss of Gotham City, The" (see: *Batman*)
Gorilla Hunt, The 40
Gorillas in the Mist 66

The Making of King Kong   247

Got Milk? campaign 35
Gough, Michael 59, 62
Gow (see: *Gow, the Head Hunter*)
Gow, the Head Hunter 74, 198-198
Gow the Killer (see: *Gow, the Head Hunter*)
Grainger, Percy 175
Grand Hotel 46
Grant, Cary 107
Grass 18, 23, 74-75, 76, 81, 120, 195-197
Grass: A Nation's Battle for Life (see: *Grass*)
Grass: The Epic of a Lost Tribe (see: *Grass*)
Great Rupert, The 52
Grey, Virginia 52
Gribbon, Henry 42
Griffith, D.W. 16, 33, 38, 40, 44-45, 88, 91, 92, 96, 142
Groesback, Dan Sayre 222
Gunga Din 200
Gwangi 59, 60, 221-224
Haggard, H. Rider 215, 217
Hale, Alan 41
Half Human 55
Hairy Ape, The 50-51
Hamilton, Linda 66
Hamilton, William 222
Hamlin, Vincent T. 35, 36-37
Hardy, Oliver 40, 138-139
Hardy, Phil 38
Hardy, Sam 127
Harling, W. Franke 175
Harlow, Jean 110
Harolde, Ralf 96, 97, 203
Harrison, Marguerite 74-75, 78, 195-196
Harryhausen, Ray 8-9, 36, 37, 53, 55, 60, 61, 66, 159, 222, 224, 225-229
Hart, William S. 159
Hathaway, Henry 107
Haver, Phyllis 125
Hays Office 188
Hedison, David (Al) 58
Heisler, Stuart 47
Hello, Dolly! 174
Hell's Angels 93
Henie, Sonja 188
Herbert, Victor 175
Herman, Al 139, 149, 222
Herrmann, Bernard 58
"His Prehistoric Past" 40
Hitchcock, Alfred 66

Hoefler, Paul L. 134
Holden, Lansing C. 217
Holland, Savage Steve 65
Holmes, Phillips 107
Horripilante Bestia Humana, La 60
Horror Express (see: *Panico en el Transiberiano*)
Houdini, Harry 193-194
House of Mystery, The 44
"How Fay Met Kong, or the Scream That Shook the World" 133
Howard, Robert E. 218
Howard, Samuel "Shemp" 50, 52
Hoyt, Harry O. 25, 40, 91, 92, 94-95, 156, 200, 203, 221
Hudson, Earl 91, 92
Hughes, Howard 93
Hughes, Lloyd 91
Humes, Fred 39
The Human Ape; or, Darwin's Triumph 38
Human Apes from the Orient 38
Human Monsters 13
I Walked with a Zombie 189
In Prehistoric Days (see: *Brute Force*)
In Quest of the Golden Prince (see: *Lost Empire, The*)
In the Prehistoric Planet 45
"In the Villain's Power" 87
Ince, Thomas 138
Informer, The 21
Ingagi 32, 42, 43, 46
Institutions and Organizations
  Actors Equity 76
  American Geographical Society 72
  American Museum of Natural History 87, 89, 90, 98
  Boone & Crockett Club 23
  Explorer's Club 81
  Field Museum of Natural History 90
  Fort Worth (Texas) Zoological Gardens 24
  Gallup Poll and Institute of Audience Opinion 223
  George Eastman House 195
  Hollywood Chamber of Commerce 190
  Ku Klux Klan 42
  Legion of Decency 225
  Lincoln Park Zoo (Chicago) 172
  Los Angeles Film Club 75
  Motion Picture Hall of Fame (Anaheim) 134
  National Geographic Society 81
  New York Geological Society 75
  New York Zoological Society 23, 76
  Otis Art Institute 89
  San Diego Municipal Zoo 182
  Screen Actors Guild 138
  Selig Zoo 172
  Society of American Magicians 91
  Smith College 42
  U.S.A. Film Festival (Dallas) 120
Invasion of the Animal People (see: *Rym-dinvasion I Lappland*)
Invisible Man, The 137
Iron Man, The 125
Is Zat So? 125
Island of the Dinosaurs 45
Island of the Lost 60
It's a Mad, Mad, Mad, Mad World 191, 229
It's about Time 58
It's Alive! 60-61
Iwerks, Ub 154
Jack-the-Ripper 66
Jackman, Fred W. 89, 221
Jackson, Peter 22, 232-233
Jahrous, Don 148
Jamboree (see: *Son of Kong, The*)
Jannings, Emil 159
Jassett, Victorin 38
Joe, the Educated Orangoutang 38
Joe, the Educated Orangoutang, Undressing 38
Johnson, Ben 226-229
Johnson, Noble Mark 80, 127, 181, 187, 205, 213, 224, 230
Johran, Dorothy 110
Journey to the Center of the Earth (1909) 58
Journey to the Center of the Earth (1959) 58
Journey to the Center of the Earth (1977) (see: *Where Time Began*)

Journey to the Center of Time 45, 60
Jujin Yokiotato (see: *Half Human*)
Jungle Jim (series) 45, 53
Jungle Manhunt 45, 53
  Killer Ape 53
  Mark of the Gorilla 53
Jungle Princess, The 197
Jurassic Park (and sequels) 35, 36, 66-67, 123
Kahane, B.B. 31, *69*, *175*
Karloff, Boris 46, 61, 159, 215
Katt, William 65
Katzman, Sam 45, 56, 59
Keaton, Buster 39
Kellard, Ralph 38
Kelly, Arthur D. 71
Kelsey, Fred 41
Kennedy, Edgar 223
Kennedy, Joe 172
Kern, Jerome 175
Kerwin, Brian 66
Kilenyi, Dr. Edward 76
Killer Shrews, The 58
King Dinosaur 45, 55
"King Klunk" 212
King Kong
  Academy Awards snub 159, 189
  Aspect and appearance 97
  Autobiographical aspects 23
  Beginnings of 23-24, 81-85, 120
  Budget 107, 179
  Cast and credits 210-212
  Censored footage 188-189
  Drawings in production 117
  Excerpted 68
  Interpretations
    Erotic 19
    Freudian 12-13, 18
    Political 19
  False news reports 21, 128
  50th anniversary 8
  Foreshadowings 42
  Frankenstein vs. King Kong (unrealized concept) 10, 60, 93 (pre-*Kong*)
  French edition 11
  Imitations 37, 59
  Initial release 17
  Mad Monster Party? 61
  Making of King Kong, The 10, 12, 14, 32, 37, 156
  Models 119
  Musical motifs 177
  Music used in other films 178, 184 (in *The Son of Kong*), 219 (in *The Last Days of Pompeii*)
  Opening engagements 178-179
  Pop-cultural references 17, 102
  Pterodactyl scene, 61
  Radio versions 207
  Reissues 188-189
  Remakes 22, 63, 66, 190, 232-233
  Scenario in progress 100-101, 102
  Set construction 139-141
  Size variations 161
  Spider sequence 9, 11-12, 56, 152-53, 157, 170
  Success, commercial 69, 178-179, 188-189
  Success, critical 179, 187
  Test reel 117-119, 121, 129
  Title, challenge to 107
  Titles, working 33, 94, 99, 101, 107, 109, 171 (final christening as *King Kong*), 203
  Tribute to 67
  Variations upon 55, 64-65
  Voice of 172-174
"King Kong and Me" (see: "How Fay Met Kong, or the Scream That Shook the World")
King Kong Escapes 37, 60
King Kong Lives! 37, 66
King Kong vs. Godzilla 37, 60
King of Kings, The 21, 139
King of Kong Island 37, 64
Kingsley, Harold 107
Kingu Kongu No Gyakushu (see: *King Kong Escapes*)
Kingu Kongu Tai Gojira (see: *King Kong vs. Godzilla*)
Knechtel, Lloyd 149
Knight, Charles R. 90, 200
Knight, Harry Adam (see Brosnan, John)
Knowles, Patric 47
Knox, Harold
Komodo Island 23, 24, 82
Konga 59
Korda, Zoltan 199
Kotsonaros, George 40
Kubrick, Stanley 60
Kyser, Kay 13
Lackteen, Frank 127
Ladd, Diane 67
Laemmle, Carl 215
Lamb, Harold 222
Land before Time, The (and sequels) 35
Land That Time Forgot, The (and sequels) 63
Land Unknown, The 57
Landis, Carole 44
Landis, John 66
Landon, Alf M. 224
Lange, Jessica 63
Lantz, Walter 212, 221-222
Larrinaga, Mario 12, 30, 94, 96, 107, 110, 147, 151, 153, 164 (and Juan Larrinaga), 178, 183, 200, 222 (and Juan Larrinaga)
Lasky, Jesse L. 75, 76, 79, 85, 190, 196
Last Days of Pompeii, The 146, 148, 178, 216-217, 218-219, 222
Last Dinosaur, The 64
Last of the Mohicans, The 125, 178
Last Outpost, The 197
Laurel, Stan 40, 138-139
Lauren, Rod 59
LeBaron, William 96, 97, 175, 200, 203
Lee, Christopher 61, 62
Lee, Lila 42
Leeds, Bill 137
Leigh, Vivien 188
Leopard Lady, a Play in Five Acts, The 41
Leopard Lady, The 41
Leopard Man, The 21, 189
Leroux, Gaston 38, 40
Lesser, Sol 187
Let 'Em Have It 125
Lewis, Jerry 53
Lewton, Val 21, 189, 225
Linden, Edwin G. "Eddie" 109, 149-150, 161
Link 66
Little Orphan Annie 223
Little, Thomas 149
Little Women 21
Lives of a Bengal Lancer, The 23, 85, 107, 167, 170
Lloyd, Frank 189
Lloyd, Harold 108, 138
Loch Ness Monster 61, 66
Loder, John 224

Logan, Jacqueline 41
Lohman, Augie 222
London, Julie 51
Long, Audrey 224
Lorraine of the Lions 39
Lost Atlantis, The 53, 212, 221-222
Lost Continent, The 53, 222
Lost Empire, The 74, 198
"Lost Island, The" 32, 137, 214-215
Lost Patrol, The 21
Lost Volcano 45
"Lost Whirl, The" 40
Lost World, The 25, 36, 38, 39, 40, 51, 53, 58 (1960 remake), 66 (1992-93 versions), 89-93, 94-95, 102, 129, 137, 193-195, 200, 221
Lourié, Eugene 37, 58, 59
Love, Bessie 91-92
Love, Cecil 137
Love from Hollywood 92
Love Life of a Gorilla 42
Lovecraft, H.P. 43
Luez, Laurette 53
Lugosi, Bela 43, 44, 49, 50, 53, 159, 187
Luke, Keye 179
Lynch, David 67, 206
Lyon, Henry 56
Lytle, Dr. J.W. 173
McAdams, Annabelle (see: Weenick, Annabelle)
McCay, Winsor 38, 86
McClure, Doug 63
McCoy, Horace 112
McCrea, Joel 108, 113-114, 203, 205, 217
MacDonald, Philip 167
McFarland, George "Spanky" 128
MacLane, Barton 52
McLendon, Gordon 58
MacQueen, Scott 192, 195
Mack, Helen 181, 184-185, 213-214, 217-218
Macy's 39
Mad Monster Party? 61
Mahler, Gustav 175
Mahoney, Jock 57
Main Event, The 125
Malden, Karl 55
Man Mountain Dean (see: Post, Charles)
Man with Two Brains, The 65
Manson, Charles 36

March, Fredric 107
Marshek, Archie 33, 114, 142, 146, 168-169, 206
Marston, John 181-182
Martel, Gregg 58-59
Martin, Dean 53
Martin, Quinn 196
Martin, Steve 17, 65
Marx Bros. 44, 214
Mason, A.E.W. 79
Mason, James 58
Massacre in Dinosaur Valley 65
Mature, Victor 44
May, Virginia 39
Mayer, Louis B. 33
Medina, Patricia 55
Méliès, Georges 16, 86
Mendes, Lothar 81
Mendoza, David 172
Menneskeaben: Darwins Triumf (see: *The Human Ape; or, Darwin's Triumph*)
Mercer, Ray 222
Metropolis 129
Michael Strogoff 178
Michel, Laura Lee 226
"Mickey and His Goat" 87
Mighty Gorga, The 61, 62
Mighty Joe Young 9, 21, 36 (and remake), 37, 50, 53, 67 (and remake), 123, 144, 159, 181, 191, 222, 225-229 (and remake)
Miljan, John 213
Miller, Patsy Ruth 39
Miller, Walter 139
Millhauser, Bertram 94-95, 96
Mister Washington Goes to Town 45
Mitchell, Gen. Billy 70
Mitchell, Cameron 55
Mitchell, Duke 53
Mitchell, Rogn 17
Monkey's Paw, The 138, 208-210
Monster and the Girl, The 47
Monster from Green Hell 56
Monster from the Moon (see *Robot Monster*)
Monster on the Campus 57
Monster Walks, The 43, 44
"Monsters of the Past" 39, 42
Montana, Bull 38, 91
Moore, Coleen 93
Moore, Demi 65
Moore, Terry 181, 226

Moranis, Rick 67
Moreland, Mantan 45, 47, 48
Moriarty, Michael 65
Morin, Relman 137
Morley, Karen 207
Morrow, Jeff 56
Most Dangerous Game, The 21, 26, 102, 107-108, 110, 112-116, 121-122, 126, 139, 152, 155, 205-206, 217, 224-225, 226
Motion Picture Academy Awards (see: Oscars)
Mowbray, Alan 144
Mummy, The 8, 215
Murder, My Sweet 49
Murders in the Rue Morgue 43, 55
Murnau, F.W. 79
Murphy, Bridey 58
Murphy, Eddie 17
Murray, Charlie 41
Muss 'Em Up 178
Muybridge, Eadward 105
My Dog Buddy 58
My Science Project 65
Mystery of Life: A Drama of Life as Told by Clarence Darrow 42-43
Mystery of the Wax Museum 8, 126, 138
NBC-Radio Network 120, 206-207
Nabonga Gorilla 51
Naish, J. Carroll 48-49
Nanook of the North 74
"Napoleon of the Solomons, A" 198
Nassour, Edward 52, 55 (and William Nassour), 221-222
Neanderthal Man, The 53-54, 57
Neufeld, Sigmund "Sig" 51
Never Give a Sucker an Even Break 47, 49
Newfield, Sam 51
Newhart, Bob 17, 82
Night of the Bloody Apes (see: *Horripilante Bestia Humana, La*)
Nightmare on Elm Street, A 36
Nigro, Carmen (see: Roady, Ken)
"Nippy's Nightmare" 87
Nison, Allan 53
Nixon, Richard M. 217
Noble, Mark (see: Johnson,

Noble Mark)
Nolan, Joseph 102, 224
Nolan, William 212
O'Brien, Willis H. 8-10, 17-18, 21, 24-26, 28, 30-33, 39-40, 42, 53, 55-58, 60-61, 86-100, 102-105, 108, 119, 129, 131, 133-135, 137, 145-148, 150, 153-157, 159, 162, 165, 167, 169, 182, 186, 191 (death of), 192, 195, 200-203, 219-220, 222-224-229
Ochs, Adolph S. 193
O'Connor, Frank 213
Odyssey, The 225
Offenbach, Jacques 175
Oland, Warner 179
Old Testament 103, 154
O'Malley, Pat 38
On Moonshine Mountain 92
O'Neill, Eugene 50
One Crazy Summer 65-66
One Million A.C./D.C. 45
One Million B.C. *40, 44-45, 53, 57*
One Million Years B.C. 60
"Original Movie, The" 39
O'Rourke, Mickey 214
Oscars (Motion Picture Academy Awards) 63, 79, 126, 137, 159 (refusal to honor *King Kong*), 172, 189, 229
Ottenfeld, Eddison von 203
Outlaws of the Orient 225
Pace, Terry 9
Page, Genevieve 61
Pal, George 52 (*Puppetoons* series), 214
Palance, Jack 66
Panico en el Transiberiano 62
Paraceleus 8
Paradise Lost 103, 154
Parks, Van Dyke 230
Parshley, Prof. H.M.
Parsons, Louella 179
Pathé Review (see: "Monsters of the Past")
Paxton, Bill 67, 229
Peach, Kenneth, Sr. 149
People That Time Forgot, The 63
Perils of the Jungle, The 51
Person, Charles W.
Peters, William Frederick 81
Petrillo, Sammy 53
Phantom of Crestwood, The 206-208

Phantom of the Air 127
Phantom of the Opera, The 38
Phantom of the Rue Morgue 55
Physioc, Louis W. 153, 159
Pichel, Irving 108, 217
Pidgeon, Walter 42
Pink, Sidney 59
Planet of the Apes 57
Planet of Dinosaurs 45
Plunkett, Walter 149
Poe, Edgar Allan 43
Polglase, Van Nest 149
Pomeroy, Roy 81
Ponti, Carlo 59
Port Sinister 53
Porter, Edwin S. 16, 86
Porter, Zöe 133, 152
Post, Charles 228
"Prehistoric Poultry" 87, 192
Prehistoric Women 53
Primitive Man, The (see: *Brute Force*)
Private Life of Sherlock Holmes, The 61
Professor Creeps, The 48
Psycho (and sequels) 66
Publications and newsgathering agencies
  Amarillo (Texas) *Daily News & Globe-Times* 14, 15
  Asia magazine 198
  Associated Press, the 14
  Boulder (Colorado) *Daily Camera* 11
  Chicago (University of) *Manual of Style* 14
  Chicago Sun-Times 128
  Cinematographer's Annual 159
  Golden Book Magazine 107
  Hollywood Reporter, The 76, 179
  Illustrated World 88, 91
  Los Angeles Record 137
  Los Angeles Times 16
  Modern Mechanix & Inventions magazine 128
  Mystery magazine 138, 207
  National Geographic, The 82
  New York Times 83, 84, 125, 133, 193-194, 204, 221
  New York World 196, 204
  People Weekly magazine 128
  San Francisco Chronicle 137
  San Francisco Daily World 86
  Time magazine 17, 128, 134

  Variety 33, 43, 52
  Publishers
    Luminary Press 14
    Barnes, A.S. & Co. 13, 21
    Tantivy Press, the 13, 21
Q (or *Q: The Wingéd Serpent*) 64-65, 203
Queen Kong 37
"R.F.D. 10,000 B.C." 87, 192
Rabin, Jack 56
Raiders of the Lost Ark 123
Rains, Claude 58
Ramper der Tiermensch 41
Rango 18, 23, 81, 83-85, 93, 115, 121, 171, 204-205
Rapeé, Erno 172
Rathbone, Basil 219
Ray, Allene 139
Ray, Arthur 48
Ray, Fred Olen 66
Redmond, Harry, Jr. 107, 149
Reere, Fred 148
Reicher, Frank 126-127, 181, 213, 231
Reichman, Max 41
Reiner, Carl 65
Reinhold, William 150
Reis, Irving 223
Reisenfeld, Dr. Hugo 76, 172
Rennie, Michael 58
Reptilicus 59
Return of Chandu, The 187
Return of the Ape Man 50
Rhys-Davies, John 66
Rio Grande 190
Rio Rita 175
Ripley's Believe It or Not! 66
Riskin, Robert 126
Rite of Spring 47
Rittau, Günther 129
Ritz Bros. 44
Roadhouse Murder 138
Roady, Ken 32, 128
Roberts, Lynne 48, 53
Roberts, Stephen 107
Robinson, Edward G. 159
Robot Monster 45, 54
Rock, Chris 17
Rogell, Sid 224
Rogers, Ginger 21, 110
Rogers, Will 138, 146
Romero, Cesar 53
Roop, Joseph L. 40
Roosevelt, Franklin Delano 224
Rose, Edward E. 28, 76
Rose, Ruth (Mrs. Ernest B.

Schoedsack) 17, 18, 26, 28-30, 31, 33, 76-81, 120-124, 180-181, 191 (death of), 212-213, 217, 218, 224, 226, 228
Rosenbloom, Slapsie Maxie 50
Rosson, Richard 40
Rothacker, Watterson R. 87, 89, 92
Rothfael, S.L. "Roxy" 178
Roupé, Joseph L. (see: Roop, Joseph L.)
Ruben, J. Walter 120, 206-207
Rubin, Benny 203
Rudolph, the Red-Nosed Reindeer 61
Ruggles, Wesley 93, 138, 208
"Runaway Blues" 184
Rymdinvasion I Lappland 57
St. John, Jill 58
Salisbury, Capt. Edward A. 73, 197-198
Salk, Dr. Jonas 46
"Sam Loyd's Famous Puzzles—the Puzzling Billboard" 87
Santell, Alfred 41
Sarg, Tony 39
Saunders, John Monk 126
Saunders, Mrs. John Monk (see: Wray, Fay)
Saunders, Sidney and Saunders Process Screen 128-131, 209
Sawtell, Paul 224
Schaefer, George 222
Schneer, Charles H. 224
Schoedsack, Ernest Beaumont (See also: Rose, Ruth) 8, 14, 17-19, 21-22, 26, 69-81, 83-85, 93-94, 107-108, 111, 113-115, 120-121, 127-128, 143-144, 146, 151, 153, 160-161, 166, 170-171, 180-181, 183, 185-186, 191 (death of), 196-197, 204-206, 209, 213, 217-218, 225-229, 230-231
Schoedsack, G. Felix 85, 150
Schreiner, Dave 13
Schubert, Bernard 120

Schwarzenegger, Arnold 35
Scopes, John 42
Scott, Randolph 217-218
Scout, The 67
Scream in the Night, A 38
Selassie, Haile (Prince Regent Ras Tafari) 73, 198
Selznick, David O. 25, 33, 69, 81, 85, 97-98, 102, 119-120, 124, 159, 171, 180, 187, 199, 203, 208-209, 215
Selznick, Lewis J. 208
Selznick, Myron 85
Sennett, Mack 22, 6
Seven Faces of Dr. Lao, The 214
Seven Keys to Baldpate 172
Seventh Voyage of Sinbad, The 9
Seyffertitz, Gustav von 40
Sharp, Don 199
Shaw, Jack 223
Shaw, Sandra 31, 163
Shayne, Robert 53-54, 57
SHAZAM! 10
She (1935 and earlier filmings) 123, 187, 215-218
She (1965) 218
She (1984) 218
She-Creature 58
She Demons 45
Shepperd, John 48
Shepphird, Carroll "Shep" 31, 105, 148, 165, 166, 191
Sherlock Holmes 61, 76, 194
Shilkret, Nathaniel 178
Ships, Expeditionary
  Arcturus 19, 28, 72, 75, 76-77
  Wisdom II 22, 73, 230
Shirley, Anne 223
Shockley, Milton 228
Show Them No Mercy! 125
Sills, Milton 93
Simpson, Ivan 209
Sinatra, Frank 59
Skelton, Red 46, 125
Skinner, Otis 76
Sloan, Blanding 214
Smigly-Ridz, Gen. Edward 71
Smith, C. Aubrey 209
Smoky Canyon 45
Smythe, Ernest 95, 200
Son of Ingagi 46
Son of Kong, The 21, 36, 37, 146, 180-186, 188, 190, 213-214, 226

Son of Sam 36
Song of Kong, The 230-231
Sons o' Guns 175
Sopkiw, Michael 65
Sound of Horror 60
Southern-Fried Homicide 10
Spaceship Sappy 45
Speaks, John 222, 224
Spence, Ralph 41, 42, 120
Spielberg, Steven 35, 67
Spivack, Murray 152, 172-174, 176
"Springtime in the Rockies" (song) 46
Springtime in the Rockies (film) 46
Stallone, Sylvester 35
Stamp, Terence 66
Star Trek 10
Stark Mad 42
Starr, Ringo 64
Steiner, Max 32-33, 115, 140, 142, 175-178, 183, 217
Stephens, Robert 61
Stevens, Charles 127
Stich, Peter 151
Stine, Clifford 150
Stokowsky, Leopold 175
Stolen Life, A 178
Stone Age Cartoons (series) 40, 45-46
  "Foul Ball Player, The" 46
  "Fulla Bluff Man, The" 46
  "Granite Hotel" 45-46
  "Pedagogical Institution (College to You)" 46
  "Springtime in the Rockage" 46
  "Ugly Dino, The" 46
  "'Way Back When a Nag Was Only a Horse" 45
  "'Way Back When a Nightclub Was a Stick" 46
  "'Way Back When a Razzberry Was a Fruit" 46
  "'Way Back When the Triangle Had Its Points" 45
  "'Way Back When Women Had Their Weigh" 46
Stone, Lewis 91
Strang, Harry 228
Strange Case of Captain Ramper, The (see: *Ramper der Tiermensch*)
Strange Case of Dr. Rx, The 47
Stravinsky, Igor 47

Streep, Meryl 35
Stroheim, Erich von 17, 33, 126
Studios and Distributors
　American-International Pictures 58
　Argosy Pictures 227
　Arko, Inc. 227
　British Broadcasting Corp. (BBC) 68
　Colonial Pictures Corp. 222
　Columbia Pictures 221, 225
　Culver City Studios 224
　Desilu Productions 146
　Disney Productions *et Al.* 65, 68, 148, 154
　Edison 87, 215
　Film Booking Offices (FBO Pictures) 172
　Film Effects of Hollywood 10
　First National 41, 89, 93 (Warners takeover), 149
　Fort Decibel Audio 230
　Fox 95, 137, 215
　Hammer Films 56, 218
　Invincible-Chesterfield Pictures (George R. Batcheller) 187
　Lincoln & Parker 88
　Lippert, Robert 53, 222
　MGM 85, 139, 148, 171, 217, 219
　Mannikin Films 87
　Mascot Pictures (Nat Levine) 187
　Monogram Pictures 221
　Pathé 138-141
　Paramount 76, 79 (Magnascope process), 81 (Magnascope), 84, 85, 107, 139, 154, 196-198, 204, 217
　Pioneer Pictures 215-216
　Principal Productions (Sol Lesser) 187
　Prizma Color Process Co. 135
　Producers Releasing Corp. 149
　RKO-Radio and RKO-Pathé 13, 21, 22, 23, 25, 33, 53, 69, 94, 96, 102-103, 107, 108-119, 128-129, 137, 138-141, 146, 149, 151, 152, 169, 171, 172 (evolved from FBO Pictures), 175, 178, 182 (sale of Pathé lot), 187, 206, 208, 215-216, 222, 223, 224, 225, 227
　Rankin-Bass 61
　Regal 149
　Reliance Pictures (Edward Small) 187
　Roach, Hal 40, 44, 60, 65, 126, 138, 139
　Rothacker 87, 102
　Selznick-International Pictures 187
　Sennett 69
　Tec-Art 200
　Tiffany Studios 214
　Toho 54
　UFA 42
　U.S. Patent Office 135
　Universal 42, 49, 95, 126, 127, 215, 221
　Warners 93, 96, 102, 224
　World Cinema Distributing Co. 89
Strauss, Johann 175
Strauss, Richard 175
Sunrise 79
Superman (serial) 45
Superman (animated cartoons) 47-48
　"Arctic Giant, The" 47-48
　"Terror on the Midway" 47-48
Suratt, Valeska 215
Swanson, Russell 22
Tarzan (franchise and series) 38, 50, 197
Tarzan's Desert Mystery 45
Taylor, J.O. 149, 169
Technicolor 214-215, 219, 222
Teenage Caveman 45, 57
Temple, Shirley 188
Terror, The 27
Terror Vision 45
Terry, Paul and *Terrytoons* series 46
Theatres
　Criterion Theatre (New York) 76, 81
　Grauman's Chinese Theatre (Los Angeles) 8, 179, 207
　Imperial Theatre (San Francisco) 87
　New Roxy Theatre (New York) 178
　State Theatre (Amarillo, Texas) 54
　Strand (New York) 88, 178
Theron, Charlize 67
They Shoot Horses, Don't They? 112
Thief of Bagdad, The 137
Three Ages 39
3-D Process
　Robot Monster 54
　Phantom of the Rue Morgue 55
　Gorilla at Large 55
　A-P-E 64
Three Stooges, The 44, 52, 128, 218
Things Men Die For 83
Things To Come 10
Thurman, Bill 61
Tierney, Harry 175
Time Machine, The 214
Time Travelers, The 60
Titan Find 10
Titanic 33
Tognazzi, Ugo 59
Trader Horn 93, 197
Trog 62
Trouble in Morocco 225
Turner, Douglas 11, 12, 156
Turner, George E. 9, 10-15, 16, 35, 37, 54, 61, 63, 65, 156, 189, 192, 193, 206, 221-222
Turner, Ray 142-143
Turner, Ted 11, 189
Twenty Million Miles to Earth 159
Twin Peaks 206
Two Lost Worlds 45, 53
"2,000 B.C." 46
Unholy Three, The 32, 40
Unknown Island 51-52
Untamed Women 45
"Up Jurassic Park" 35
Valley of Gwangi, The 61, 159, 222, 224
Valley of the Dragons 45
Vampire Men of the Prehistoric Planet 45
Van Dyke, W.S. 93, 197
Van Horn, Emil 47, 49
Vaughn, Robert 57
Veidt, Conrad 159
Vengeance of She, The (1968) 218
Verne, Jules 58, 64
Viaje al Centro de la Tierra (see: *Where Time Began*)
Video Hound's Golden Movie Retriever 37
Video and home-entertainment

sources
  Blackhawk Films 195
  Lumivision 195
  Rhino Home Video 54
  Roan Group 206
Vidor, King 140
Villa, Pancho 70, 149
Von Sholly, Peter 156
Voyage to the Bottom of the Sea 58
Walker, Vernon L. "Vern" 137, 149-150
Walking with Dinosaurs 68
Wallace, Edgar 26, 76, 99-101, 102, 124, 203
War
  Græco-Turkish War 22
  Russo-Polish War 22
  World War I 22, 69-72
  World War II 54, 220, 225
War Eagles 219-221, 222
War of the Colossal Beast 55
War of the Gargantuas 60
War of the Primal Tribes (see: *Brute Force*)
War, the West and the Wilderness, The 75
Ward, Eddie 214
Warren, James 53
Watts, Naomi 232-233
Wayne, John 227
Weaver, Sigourney 66
Webb, Roy 178
Wedding March, The 33
Weenick, Annabelle 61
Wegener, Paul 41
Weiss, Louis 51
Weissmuller, Johnny 53
Welch, Raquel 60
Welles, Orson 188
Wells, H.G. 10, 93
We're Only Human 178
Werewolf of London 223
West, Mae 214
West, Roland 93
Whale, James 114, 215
When Dinosaurs Ruled the Earth 60
Where Time Began 64
"White Ape, The" (see: "Arthur Jermyn")
White Gorilla, The 51
White Pongo 51
White, W.G. "Gus" 148, 165
Whiteford, John P. "Blackie" 127
Whitmore, James 64
Whitney, C.V. 197
Whitney, John 216
Wild at Heart 67
Wilder, Billy 61
Williams, Frank D. and Williams Process 92, 136-137, 142, 145
Williams, Robin 17
Williams, Spencer, Jr. 46
Williams, Zack 46
Willis, Bert 149, 228
Wimpy, Rex 85
Wings 126
Winters, Jonathan 17
Wise, Robert 225
Witches' Brew 203
Wizard, The 38, 40
Wizard of Oz, The 67, 189
Wobber, Herman 192
Wonderful World of the Brothers Grimm, The 214
Wong, Victor 127, 181, 213
Wood, Edward D., Jr. 58
Wooster Booster firefighting equipment 59
Wray, Fay 8, 18, 20, 25, 26, 29, 31, 32, 81, 108-110, 120, 125-126, 130, 133-134, 144, 152, 154-155, 162-163, 166, 168, 180, 205, 207, 226, 230-231, 233
Wrixon, Maris 51
Wuthering Heights 192
Wynorsky, Jim 66
You'll Find Out 13
Youmans, Vincent 175
Young, Sean 65
Youngman, Gordon "Tubby" 107
Zamba 52
Zappa, Frank 230
Zavitz, Lee 187
Zucco, George 47, 48-49
Zukor, Adolph 81
Zuro, Josiah 172

King Kong cast and crew members from the original Program book

*Coming late 2005 from
Midnight Marquee Press, Inc.*

A new graphic novel

**The Amazingly True Adventures
of Merian C. Cooper &
Ernest B. Schoedsack:
The Creators of King Kong**

www.midmar.com

*"Midnight Marquee Press has given us a series of first-rate books
on subjects that matter to film buffs and historians alike,
even though they've been neglected
by mainstream publishers. I salute them and
wish them continued success."—Leonard Maltin*

*Write for a free catalog
Midnight Marquee Press, Inc.
9721 Britinay Lane
Baltimore, MD 21234
410-665-1198
9:00 a.m. till 6:00 p.m. EST*

*or e-mail
www.MMarquee@aol.com*

Visit our website at www.midmar.com

www.ingramcontent.com/pod-product-compliance
Lightning Source LLC
Chambersburg PA
CBHW071308110526
44591CB00010B/823